Field Rhetoric

FIELD RHETORIC

Ethnography, Ecology,
and Engagement in the
Places of Persuasion

Edited by
Candice Rai and Caroline Gottschalk Druschke

The University of Alabama Press   Tuscaloosa

The University of Alabama Press
Tuscaloosa, Alabama 35487-0380
uapress.ua.edu

Inquiries about reproducing material from this work should be
addressed to the University of Alabama Press.

Typeface: Scala Pro

Cover image: Caroline Gottschalk Druschke
Cover design: Michele Myatt Quinn

Cataloging-in-Publication data is available from the Library of
Congress.
ISBN: 978-0-8173-1995-3
E-ISBN: 978-0-8173-9199-7

Contents

Field Inventions

Illustrations

Figures

Tables

Acknowledgments

We would, first, like to thank the people who enliven the pages of this text and who generously offered themselves and their time for us to learn from and with. We thank, too, the talented authors of this collection for bringing those stories to life and for their energy, patience, good cheer, and wonderful scholarship. We are so grateful for their contributions and wisdom.

We must, too, acknowledge Ralph Cintron, a pioneer of ethnographic work in rhetorical, writing, and anthropological studies, whose scholarship, teaching, and ways of engaging the world have inspired many rhetorically inclined folks, including us. Ralph, we should say, was also our teacher and mentor—there when our own early scholarly research trajectories were just forming, providing a bulk of the fertile soil from which our various projects have grown.

We would also like to thank Daniel Waterman and the entire team at the University of Alabama Press for their support and patience. We deeply appreciate, too, the anonymous reviewers at the press for their time, energy, and careful reading.

Finally, we are both grateful for our shared friendship. Moving along in life as colleagues and friends, now for over fourteen years, we've experienced together many of the joys and hardships that people face, and are thankful for the companionship. We would like to acknowledge our dear travelers and fellow rhetoricians from Chicago: Ralph Cintron, Ann Merle Feldman, Megan Marie Bolinder, Margaret Gonzalez, Lindsay Marshall, Bridget Sullivan Montgomery, Matthew Pavesich, Nadya Pittendrigh, and Stephanie Reich. And, at last, we are grateful for our families: Drew, Hannah, Bear, Bode, Joel, Sanchaman, Junot, the mamas and the papas, the brothers and the sisters. Thank you for loving us and much love to you.

On Being There

An Introduction to Studying Rhetoric in the Field

Candice Rai and Caroline Gottschalk Druschke

The study of rhetoric is both enriched and perplexed by being present, *being there*, in the places where rhetoric does its work. As forms of inquiry predicated on being there, field methodologies—including ethnography, participant observation, oral history, interview, case study, and survey—offer particularly powerful tools for studying the textures of places and politics that shape rhetoric and within which rhetoric emerges, circulates, enacts, and dissipates. Rhetorically inflected fieldwork offers important insights for understanding (and, indeed, tools for participating in): the situated power and force of language; the symbolic means through which people produce meaning, generate social energy, and coordinate action in everyday life; and the connections between language and ontology, rhetoric and materiality, and words and things as they manifest in various places and times. This collection builds on a resurgent return to the field in rhetorical study to reach dual aims: to articulate ways that field methodologies might contribute to understandings of rhetoric and the practices of rhetorical criticism, and to explore how rhetoric and its study might contribute and speak back to interdisciplinary field-based research, more broadly.

We argue that immersing oneself in the dynamic, living, breathing ecologies that give rise to rhetoric and its work enhances the capacity to understand and observe rhetoric as a three-dimensional, situated force. As such, fieldwork is well suited for capturing, comprehending, and sometimes intervening within everyday rhetorical performance and production; for cataloguing and representing myriad vernacular and situated experiences, cultures, practices, embodiments, meaning-making systems, and texts; for grappling with what ethical and meaningful collaboration with human and other-than-human actors might entail; and for building interdisciplinary rhetorical theory and practice capable of responding to the contradictory, complex, shifting, and recalcitrant conditions of our world's salient exigencies. Further, we suggest that these concerns with rhetorical performance and production, vernacular and situated meaning making, ethical collaboration, and complex exigencies, among other things, what we might broadly lump under the heading of rhetorical sensibilities, offer important extensions of existing field methodologies and field-based rhetorical work.

In this collection, we build on conceptions of rhetoric as ecological,[1] emplaced,[2] material,[3] and new material.[4] We understand rhetoric as multidimensional, existing as and tethered to the many forces and tools, histories and consequences, ideas and discourses, things and processes, desires and hopes, public memories and cultural narratives, people and other beings, symbols and materialities, ways of knowing and relating, and all manner else, that constitute and enable the powers of persuasion in any particular place. Beyond this sense of rhetoric as a complex constellation of persuasive forces in the world, we see rhetoric as a capacity of sorts to both perceive and act within this constellation: a form of responsivity and response. Such a capacity might be individual, collective, and even ecological to include human designs and more-than-human things that assemble in this way or that to incline particular lines of sight or action. In this sense, rhetoric becomes a tool—not simply of persuasion, connection, and collective action, but also of perception and orientation within these constellations. And in this perspective, the places of persuasion become not only heuristics for locating and enacting the available means of persuasion, but also the tangible places in which rhetoric as capacity and constellation reveals itself.

In light of its complexity, the study of rhetoric pulls researchers and practitioners in two directions. One direction demands an investigation of the particularities of place and time—the forces, actions, practicalities, and exigencies that make up the dynamic textures of place. In trying to capture rich accounts of rhetoric's emplaced power, one examines the cultural, economic, historical, and material odds and ends that enliven and animate rhetoric here but not there, now but not then, for us but not them. Without such context, one denies rhetoric of its situated resonances, the centerpiece of its secret powers, and is left looking at a deflation of sorts that cannot satisfactorily answer how rhetoric really works. The other direction seeks to transcend the singularities of place, urging one to form abstract takeaways, concepts, theories, axioms, guidelines, pedagogies, and critical readings of rhetoric that sit above the dynamism and idiosyncrasies of everyday life such that rhetorical knowledge might be imagined as transportable, as useful elsewhere, anywhere, for someone, anyone, else.

These opposing pulls of particularity and abstraction bring us face-to-face with an ancient rhetorical crisis: how might we begin our inquiries when every/thing—hyperlocal words, actions, desires, bodies, soils, interactions—is said to be rhetorical, but everything rhetorical is only fully intelligible by looking beyond itself to connections to things ambient, idiosyncratic, and out there in the particularities of biosocial environments? How do we study forces that act, seduce, and guide without intention yet nevertheless shape the terrain of persuasion? Or arguments that move us profoundly without adhering to logic or rationality or even full cognition? Given this tension between, on the one hand, the particularities of place that threaten to be too sprawling to anchor a discipline and, on the other, the abstract rules, concepts, and theories of persuasion that threaten to eviscerate rhetoric of the contexts upon which deep rhetorical knowledge and production depend, what is it that we study when we say we are studying rhetoric? While these tensions between particularity and abstraction exist in all disciplines, there is something fundamental about their endemic and enduring presence in rhetorical study.

Field methodologies are especially promising for navigating these pulls between particularity and abstraction and for infusing fieldwork with the weight of these tensions. Fieldwork allows researchers to study both rhetoric's emplacement and fieldwork's complexity by offering access to and insight into a wider range of texts, perspectives, and experiences than we might otherwise discover. This might include the narratives and arguments offered through interviews and observations; the extra-textual aspects of persuasion and rhetorical performance that require our sensory facilities to perceive, like the sour stench of an alleyway, the sweat on a clam digger's brow, and the bodily warmth of a quick embrace; or the situated rhetorical forces that can only be observed through inhabitation, such as how place, power, materiality, embodiments, texts, and rhetoric intermesh and matter in particular situations.

The authors gathered in this collection—scholars tethered to English and communication, but also to agronomy, biology, ecology, education, natural resources science, and political science—fuse rhetorical sensibilities with field methodologies to illuminate diverse disciplinary (and extra-disciplinary) perspectives on the power of rhetoric in everyday life. Our authors illustrate the values and challenges of conducting research that emerges from being there within case studies that range from contests within urban gentrifying spaces to water quality closures in Maine mudflats and from the effects of digital tools on field research to the human-scale effects of meritocracy within Kosovo's fragile democratic state. In other words, being there to study and experience the ways rhetoric co-constitutes everyday life can offer researchers opportunities to illuminate, reflect on, invent, and potentially intervene in rhetoric's emplacement through a variety of texts, perspectives, and experiences; sensory facilities; and situated rhetorical forces.

Being There with Rhetoric

We recognize that the notion of being there is itself a commonplace, both revered and vexed, within scholarship on field research; it is used to emphasize the immersive nature of qualitative research and the necessity of a researcher's embodied presence, rhetorician or not, to gather data within a field site. Harry Wolcott states simply enough that one underlying aspect of all fieldwork is that it requires "being there,"[5] while Clifford Geertz features being there as essential to one of the core practices of fieldwork: the production of thick descriptions that richly narrate the dynamics of everyday life within a field site.[6] But many scholars both inside and outside the discipline of rhetoric challenge the value of being there for reasons including: researchers' inability to shed the disciplinary, ideological, and identity-based lenses that shape their perceptions; being there as a researcher does not equate to knowing what it means to be "authentically" there (though authenticity is a fraught commonplace in and of itself); and thick descriptions are always already rhetorical, heuristical inventions that can only capture partialities of actual field sites, calling into question the entire enterprise of qualitative research.[7]

These are substantive and significant criticisms that rhetorical perspectives seem uniquely positioned to grapple with. Rhetoric can offer fieldworkers a keen attunement, for instance, to the notion that ethnographic and field-based accounts of the world are implicitly representational, both analogic and heuristical, and tend to offer situated, multiple truths that circulate within a place. Accordingly, the authors in this volume trouble the notion of the transparent value of field events, using them instead as lenses onto the *topoi*, or commonplaces, of field sites; as ways to understand the roles that rhetoric plays in constituting a shared life; and as indicative of the many things that become entangled in human communication, be these material, political, interpersonal, ideological, cultural, economic, or the like. Instead of searching for access to a singular and stable truth offered, legitimized, and anchored by fieldwork, our authors ask what phrases, ideas, forces, practices, and desires have purchase in their field sites, questioning how language, symbols, and other forms of communication interact with, create, and emerge from both local ecologies and global discourses/policies. Among other things, our authors rely on their diverse rhetorical sensibilities to turn their critical gazes, as Ralph Cintron suggests, to the "failed expectation" that language will represent, exactly, the thing—or place, or event—in itself.[8]

Within the emerging subdiscipline of rhetorical field research, being there offers a point of entry for this type of critique. And being there is fundamentally defined both through the presence of the rhetorician's body within a field site (ranging from an interview room to a community meeting and from a public bus trip to a riverbank) and through the practices of inhabitation, observation, participation, and interaction that enable researchers to gather data and/or effect change within the places of persuasion. Without ignoring its fraught complexity as a potentially exploitative methodology,[9] extending the ethnographic concept of being there to rhetorical studies means asking what one might discover about or do with rhetoric by virtue of being there in the field, itself another vexed concept.

The definition of the "field" we are advancing carries both literal and metaphorical connotations, constituting as much the literal places we inhabit and observe as researchers as the representations of those places for persuasive purposes and audiences beyond. Put another way, field sites are simultaneously locations for inquiry; socially inflected ecologies from which rhetoric emerges, circulates, and performs its work; places (as well as metaphors/synecdoche/heuristics for places) in which rhetoric comes to life, entangled with meaning and forces; amalgamations of people, things, materialities, exigencies, public memories, collective dreams, myths, events, macrolevel influences and microlevel energetics that manifest as singularities in place and time; and representations of the places of persuasion that engage in the earnest (if also impossible) labors of bearing witness to the complexities of a place. Traditions of field research provide the means for immersive engagement with and within the complex, nascent, and various manifestations of rhetoric in everyday life, as well as the narrative-driven or performance-oriented genre conventions that facilitate rich, robust representations of worlds far too complex to capture otherwise.

Rhetorical fieldworkers have studied everything from the material, performative, gendered, racialized, and embodied aspects of rhetoric[10] to the networked,[11] environmental,[12] everyday,[13] spatial,[14] vernacular,[15] and publicly consequential qualities of persuasion,[16] among many other inquiries. All of those studies emerged from the practice of being there: not to testify to the singular, observed truth of a site, but to examine, engage with, and sometimes intervene in what Kenneth Burke refers to as "the flurries and flare-ups of the Human Barnyard."[17] Ultimately, this collection seeks to join and enrich emerging and ongoing conversations, some new and some ancient, about the opportunities that field methods afford: for enriching and expanding our approaches to theorizing, studying, and practicing rhetoric in situ; for highlighting the unique limitations, challenges, consequences, and ethical concerns of rhetorically oriented field research; and for exploring ways that rhetoric's study and practice might assist us in solving urgent collective challenges.

The Roots of Rhetorical Fieldwork

While rhetorical study has long insisted on the situatedness of rhetoric, a renewed interest in field methods affords opportunities to expand access to objects of study and their complex interrelations—such as informal texts and accounts, marginal and vernacular perspectives, more-than-human agencies, performance, events, embodiments, affect, materiality—and to craft more richly contextualized, deeply grounded accounts of rhetoric in everyday life that are made possible through ongoing proximity to and immersion in the field. Such interest in fieldwork and such inclinations to expand our objects of study is by no means new to rhetorical study but the recent resurgence of both does reveal in our contemporary moment some need—be this in our theories, practices, objects, methods, and/or inquiries—for more directly engaging (whether to better understand, represent, or intervene within) the complexities of place in our world.

Of course, Dwight Conquergood noted long ago the "thriving alliance between ethnography and rhetoric" as evidence of the "yoking" of "emblematic terms from both disciplines . . . such as 'rhetorical culture' and 'cultural rhetoric.'"[18] That yoking can be seen in the ongoing interdisciplinary and international "Rhetoric Culture" project, which ethnographically explores, as key participants Ivo Strecker and Stephen Tyler put it, the "rhetoricality of culture" and the "creative role of rhetoric in the emergence of culture."[19] The Rhetoric Culture project—which includes Ralph Cintron, Michael Carrithers, Ivo Strecker, Stephen Tyler, Robert Hariman, and others—examines the related questions of what ethnographically inflected rhetoric and rhetorically inflected ethnography might look like, answering with a series of capacious and theory-laden accounts of the political textures of everyday life.[20]

The emergence of studies that engage in what has become known as rhetorical ethnography has taken this accounting of the "rhetoricality" of everyday life into a deep focus on the vernacular aspects of rhetoric,[21] while many of the same scholars honed in, too, on the spatial aspects of rhetoric and rhetoric's ability to enact, emplace, inform, and be informed by the places that had otherwise seemed to fade into the background.[22] Related qualitative work in material rhetoric foregrounded public sites[23] and bodies,[24] in part through a close attention to rhetoric's ancient texts and their emphasis on embodiment, performance, and affect.

The movement to the field represented in this volume, then, emerges, in part, from this shift toward studying local, ordinary, vernacular, deeply situational, and spatial manifestations of rhetoric (and writing) that emerge within everyday life. This interest in the everyday manifests as a sensitivity to the diverse and myriad perspectives, practices, and publics that co-constitute collective life in the world, often under the radar of, or rarified within, public archives and discourse. Fieldwork is recuperative in some ways, but also inventional: attending to and theorizing from the spaces where rhetoric works as facilitating something like the negotiation of life in common. These inventional capacities also allow, in some cases, for the forms of intervention that rhetorical fieldwork can take.

These multidimensional foci on the everyday, the spatial, and the vernacular link to materialist perspectives, which might be broadly defined through interests in the persuasive qualities of bodies, objects, and spatiality and with the interconnections between rhetoric and materiality. This literature is rich and varied, but broadly speaking over the past three decades or so the material turn might be defined by some of the following inclinations that provide the theoretical oomph that has inspired many rhetorical field research projects, both within this collection and more broadly:

1) the proclivity to critique conceptions of rhetoric and persuasion focused strictly on rhetoric's symbolicity in favor of perceiving rhetoric as emplaced, and to study the enmeshments of rhetoric and materiality, words and things, subjects and objects;[25]

2) the acknowledgement of and attunement to non-discursive, non-strategic, extra-linguistic, and material aspects of persuasion, such as affective forces and bodily knowledges;[26]

3) a disposition towards studying rhetoric's consequences, effects, and circulations, as opposed to or in tension with its symbolic content/meaning or with concerns of strict intentionality;[27] and

4) an orientation towards ecological, networked, and ambient perspectives, which rework the rhetorical situation by pointing to its dynamic capacities and expanding the horizon of things that interconnect with and mutually constitute it.[28]

This final broad move toward viewing rhetoric ecologically and ambiently is one that also conceives rhetoric ontologically, and, thus, calls for theorizing the dazzlingly complex and multilayered enmeshments, amalgamations, assemblages, networks, and ecologies that emerge as co-constitutive and deeply emplaced formations of being composed of symbols, language, materialities, bodies, peoples, actors, spaces, things, lines of sight, processes, dispositions, practices, ideologies, ways of knowing, and so on. Albeit to varying degrees, ecological orientations expand the boundaries of rhetoric beyond discursive formations and human agencies to also include consideration of the persuasive agency and influence of relationships among objects, things, spaces, genres, institutions, animals, bodies, affect, and matter. While the connections between words and things, bodies and places, humans and other-than-humans, have been part and parcel of rhetoric since its inception, we argue that rhetorical field methods provide the means and tools for deepening our understanding of these connections in various places and times, such that, following Thomas Rickert, rhetoric itself becomes a modality for attunement.[29] In the chapters that follow, readers will find contributors playing in and through these various material theoretical trajectories.

In addition to such material inclinations, the sometimes-explicit and sometimes-implicit subtext of this collection invokes rhetoric's enduring concerns with praxis, civic action, and social justice, and to action-oriented and activist research practices that attempt to engage communities ethically and to intervene in the world and its pressing exigencies.[30] This work reminds us that rhetorical field studies owe a sometimes-overlooked debt to collaborative and action-oriented projects in subdisciplines of writing studies, such as community-based writing, community literacies, service learning, participatory action research, and professional writing.[31] Broadly speaking, that body of research urges rhetoricians: to engage with communities, publics, and workplaces; to develop partnerships that allow the deep study of the elements of the rhetorical situation relevant to crafting and circulating texts and rhetoric, as Karen Barad puts it, "from the inside"[32]; to understand rhetoric's various and uneven consequences; and to find ethical and situationally appropriate modes of response and intervention. This link to writing studies encourages researchers not only to look beyond the university's walls for objects of critique and analysis but also to develop reciprocal relationships with others and to attend to the production and circulation, not just analysis, of salient arguments. Field-based projects might take cues from community-based writing research that emerges in multiple forms: whether highly institutionalized[33] or deterritorialized[34] or positioning students and scholars as writing about, for, or with communities.[35]

Related studies in participatory action research and professional writing have also provided useful models for field rhetoric by traveling into the community-based and professional sites where writing and rhetoric do their work to offer models, methodologies, and ethical orientations.[36] Despite, or maybe because of, their differences, this collective body of knowledge sets the stage for field rhetoricians in multiple ways: focusing the discipline's attention on nonacademic spaces in which rhetorical practices occur; training a critical eye on the intricacies of power that play out through the policing and privileging of certain types of literacy; and pushing researchers not only to pay attention to the world "out there," but also to physically inhabit it, collaborate with the bodies and materials within it, and even work to change it. This work adopts a critical stance while opening the possibility that the rhetorician might, in fact, intervene in what she studies and become, in Ellen Cushman's words, "an agent of social change."[37] Community-based writing and its related fields first begged the question that the "proper" place of the rhetorician, in both critical and constructive modes, might be "out there" rather than "in here."

This intervention emerges, in part, from the call for critical, activist, and action-oriented practices that not only study the rhetorics of places and people, but also seek to actively *do* rhetoric with others to collectively solve what Horst Rittel and Melvin Webber long ago referred to as wicked problems with multiple public stakeholders and no clear solutions.[38] Within the emerging subdiscipline of rhetorical field methods, one strand of this work traces its roots to Raymie McKerrow's critical rhetoric tradition; these include, among others, Aaron Hess's argument for using critical-rhetorical ethnography to enact "advocacy through direct participation" and Phaedra Pezzullo's work to understand rhetorical performance as advocacy, as well as related research.[39] Paired critical and constructive approaches have emerged, too, in the subdiscipline of rhetoric of science, focused largely on medicine[40] and the environment.[41] This aim of discovering the usefulness of rhetoric for addressing complex, shared problems taps into the long-standing role of rhetoric as a means of addressing public questions in the face of competing, myriad, diverse perspectives and uncertain paths. We hope, too, this tendency offers a path for navigating the complex ethical issues this move necessarily entails.

In sum, rhetorical field research draws on various work associated with the material turn, which theorizes and offers concepts to explain the richness and situatedness of rhetoric and the possibilities for engagement and action. This theoretical inclination includes emergent interest in new materialist and ecological perspectives that offer important reminders to rhetorical fieldworkers to look beyond the human body, both materially and in its symbols, to understand the fullest and most inventive capacities of rhetoric. We value the work of new materialisms to attend to a wider field of agential relations, among humans and other-than-humans alike, and we see those new materialist perspectives as especially potent when paired with community-based and activist perspectives that focus a researcher's vision on hierarchy, power, ethics, and fraught possibilities for action. While these community-based, material, and new material inclinations represent distinct, if overlapping, tendencies and subfields, they share commonalities that give rise to immersive, embodied fieldwork: the call to study rhetorical objects that cannot be solely located in textual artifacts or symbols but that require being there; the call for observing persuasive forces that only a body among other bodies and things in a particular place and time has access to (affective frames, the sensual, the performative, the vernacular, the experiential, the ambient, and so forth); and the need to be present over time to perceive and capture rhetoric's workings within ecologies, networks, and assemblages. Collectively, *Field Rhetoric: Ethnography, Ecology, and Engagement in the Places of Persuasion* emerges from these broadly material, deeply situated, and ecological orientations and is poised to contribute to these conversations not only through theoretical insights, but also via a series of cases and robust methodologies that capture the workings and life of rhetoric in an array of places.

The Lay of the Land

The authors of this collection are linked in their common work to both theorize and enact rhetorical field practices and to consider how the study of rhetoric within its everyday situations and ecologies might serve as a means to better understand and even sometimes intervene within the work of rhetoric in the world. While each chapter works to apprehend some of the subtlety and power of rhetorical fieldwork for both theory-building and praxis, we highlight what we see as some of their most productive and innovative contributions by grouping chapters into the following three sections: (1) Field Methodologies, (2) Field Ontologies, and (3) Field Inventions.

Section 1: Field Methodologies

The chapters gathered in Field Methodologies articulate and experiment with new methods and analytics for field research through extended engagements with farmers, unwed mothers, and community activists in rural, urban, and remembered spaces. Building from interviews, stakeholder meetings, and participant observation, these chapters work to explain the processes of rhetorical fieldwork and theorize from particular cases to introduce agonistic methodology, semantic network analysis, field-based historiography, and rhetorical cartographies as additions to a robust methodological toolkit that enables researchers to explore the complexities and consequences of rhetoric *in situ.*

Caroline Gottschalk Druschke's chapter, "Agonistic Methodology: A Rhetorical Case Study in Agricultural Stewardship," takes up the recent call in rhetoric of science for a turn toward practical engagement and intervention, which she argues demands a methodology that illuminates the ways competing rhetorics are called on, created, and enacted in everyday life. Gottschalk Druschke employs *agôn* as both subject matter and methodology in her research with farmers working to improve water quality in an

Iowa watershed. Identifying material-symbolic points of tension in subjects' descriptions of their beliefs and practices, Gottschalk Druschke attends to the friction that emerges when universal commonplaces like "feeding the world" and "cheap food," as Anna Lowenhaupt Tsing puts it, "enter the fray."[42] Gottschalk Druschke argues that rhetorical fieldwork is an agonistic encounter: forcing the lived experience of discontinuity and irresolvable contradiction, expanding disciplinary understandings of rhetoric, and generating significant insights for intervention.

Heather Brook Adams's chapter, "Historiographic Remembering and Emotional Encounters: Possibilities for Field-Based Rhetorical Research," melds rhetorical analysis, historiography, memory and affect scholarship, and fieldwork to recover US histories of unwed pregnancies and maternity homes, introducing what she calls field-based historiography: a methodology extending beyond the archive to explore pasts that may exist in few places but memory (both intimately private and public). Adams discusses her conversations with participants and investigates how open secrets, communal silences, emotional intensities, and circulating rhetorics of embodied shame contribute to ecologies of rhetorical practices that shape gender, power, and agency.

Carl Herndl, Sarah Beth Hopton, Lauren Cutlip, Rick Cruse, Elena Polush, and Mack Shelley, in "'What's a Farm?': The Languages of Space and Place," explore Bruno Latour's call for a materialist project of bringing people and things together to "compose" a better world by adopting a rhetorical approach to analyzing the transcripts of three rapid technology assessment workshops (one with scientists and engineers, two with farmers) coordinated by one of the authors.[43] Using traditional qualitative coding and thematic analysis with semi-automated semantic network analysis (SNA), they identify major conflicts between the vernacular of farmers and the dominant technical discourse of scientists in destabilizing ways. The authors consider how SNA can "map" the rhetorical practices of two or more groups, illuminating rhetorical places where they overlap as potential sites for intervening in the ongoing activity of emerging publics of scientists and citizens.

In "Rhetorical Cartographies: (Counter)Mapping Urban Spaces," Samantha Senda-Cook, Michael Middleton, and Danielle Endres examine what they call rhetorical cartographies, a method for describing how communities construct their identities in part through the embodied, lived "mappings" of spaces they inhabit and (re)create through everyday practices.

Embodied rhetorical practices (re)make spaces in ways that put spaces and their identities in co-constitutive relationships. The authors apply rhetorical cartographies to contemporary urban and professional spaces to discover how people from different socioeconomic groups map their lived experience. In doing so, they evoke Michel de Certeau's theorization that pedestrians walking the streets discover a radically different place than those viewing it from atop high rises.[44] By tracing several rhetorical urban cartographies, the authors illustrate how this concept explains the embodied activities of urban (sub)cultures and highlight the constitutive rhetorical relationships among identity, embodiment, and space.

Section 2: Field Ontologies

This section explores cases, from war-torn Kosovo to coastal Maine to decaying post-industrial landscapes in the Midwest, that illuminate the idea that rhetoric is of and about the conditions of being. This shift to rhetoric as ontological marks rhetoric as both a modality for attunement, as it is mobilized in Section 1, and an artifact of the dynamic entanglements of place. The authors in this section offer varied examples of deep attunement to sense and affect from the mundane to the sublime—including things like glances, wind, ambient noise, melancholy—while rooting their analyses and interpretations just as deeply into material, ecological, political, and economic worlds.

Ralph Cintron's ethnographic research in "A Bus Trip Named Desire" renders visibile the internal life of rural young men and women who were his accidental companions on a bus trip from Kosovo's capital, Pristina, to North Mitrovica, one of the most explosive political flashpoints on the planet. These stories of individual and national desire amid economic and political turmoil and transition allow Cintron to explore the nation's self-created image of itself as a "managerial modernity"; the need for a vast informal economy from which corruption becomes a critical lifeline for individuals and international elites themselves; the public attempt to replace corruption by international organizations' labor with transparency and meritocracy; and, given all of this, the slide of the ideal of democracy as transparent and just toward oligarchic rule.

In "Belonging to the World: Rhetorical Fieldwork as Mundane Aesthetic," Bridie McGreavy, Emma Fox, Jane Disney, Chris Petersen, and Laura Lindenfeld consider rhetoric and conservation action planning in a three-year ethnography with a diverse group of municipalities, fisheries groups, businesses, nonprofits, and individuals working together along the Maine coast. Their research explores the mundane quality of conservation action planning and the ways that specific objects, as processes, create capacities for rhetoric, where mundane refers to the everydayness and materiality that, together, create what becomes possible. Rhetoric occurs within the daily routines that may appear banal and dull: identifying sources of bacterial pollution, fixing leaky septics, restoring eel grass, and building websites. The mundane quality of conservation action planning emphasizes the vibrant material assemblages—of clams, mud, bacteria, septic systems, humans, technologies, and more—that create rhetorical capacities and help shape planning.

In "Rhetorical Life among the Ruins," John Ackerman's fieldwork in post-industrial, Midwestern neighborhoods considers how everyday physical attributes and material infrastructures engender the commonplaces of invention. If, as he contends, *topoi* are material as well as symbolic emplacements, then the material and economic straits of local communities may constitute the very resources for survival, progress, and political movement in otherwise bleak urban landscapes. Building from Yael Navaro-Yashin, Ackerman considers the catalytic rhetorical capacity of "ruination" as an anthropological, affective occurrence and as a popular urban design principle that shrewdly capitalizes on what comes before and, therefore, what has been rendered available in the rhetorical sense.[45] Here, ruination moves beyond post-industrial narratives of deficit and decay toward accounts of the productive collective capacities of urban spaces that constitute the precondition for resilience and renewal.

Section 3: Field Inventions

While innovation and critical reflection play an important role in the chapters throughout the volume, the contributions to Field Inventions foreground the role and experience of the researcher in especially substantive and consequential ways, exploring the field researcher's dynamic emplacement and the inventional possibilities of the relationships observed and formed through fieldwork. Contributions in this section also place strong emphasis on understanding, marshaling, and pushing against ways that our theoretical concepts and disciplinary inclinations shape the terrain of invention that researchers draw on to understand, capture, and represent the workings of rhetoric in the everyday. Workplaces, advocacy organizations, urban squares, and online spaces are offered in these chapters as the places of persuasion, from which the authors offer new vocabularies, theoretical connections, and reflexive approaches.

In "Fieldwork and the Identification and Assembling of Agencies," Jeffrey T. Grabill, Kendall Leon, and Stacey Pigg's scholarship explores why rhetorical theories and methodologies have long struggled with locating the practicalities of rhetoric as a social practice. They contend that rhetoric's theoretical and methodological vocabulary often stabilizes or isolates rhetors or their performances, creating a distinction, and often a binary, between materials and discourse. Drawing from their collective rhetorical field research on a community arts project and a public environmental controversy, the authors adapt both conceptual and practical apparatuses: studying the work, mechanisms, devices, and actors that do rhetoric, while moving beyond a materials/discourse binary to reconsider what they refer to as the sociomaterials of rhetoric. Through fieldwork, the authors consider new ways to think about who/what does rhetoric and how we understand its impacts, while constructing practical methods for doing rhetoric in the world and conceiving of rhetorical theory as always endeavoring to be useful as a resource for others.

erin daina mcclellan, in "Rhetoric(s) of Urban Public Life," articulates and mobilizes the concept of lived rhetorics—defined as "rhetorics that are always in some phase of formation, part of larger discourses, and related to particular bodies"—to examine our shared and emplaced co-creation of the world. Drawing on qualitative interpretive methods and rhetorical analysis, mcclellan articulates a practice of rhetorical field methodology as critical invention. In the chapter, mcclellan draws on observation and interviews in a public square in Portland, Oregon, to consider critical invention as a process with consequences for both research subject and researcher.

Aaron Hess's scholarship in "Rhetoric, Ethnography, and the Machine: Technological Reflexivity and the Participatory Critic" examines the nexus of the participatory rhetorical critic and digital communication technology. Arguing that rhetorical fieldwork requires reflexive attention to how technology affects the production, transmission, and reception of rhetoric, Hess offers an accounting of how rhetorical critics/ethnographers might consider technological reflexivity by combining embodied rhetorical approaches with theorizing about the digital rhetorical self. Hess draws from various rhetorical fieldwork experiences, including massive mediated protests, public commemoration ceremonies, and smaller moments of vernacular advoca-cy. At times, technology becomes a source of data collection or expression; at others, it affects the nature of advocacy on the street or changes how we produce our own scholarship. Ultimately, Hess proposes interrogations regarding how rhetoricians might reflect upon the nature of fieldwork and technology.

Drawing Constellations

Taken together, this volume offers a collection of related but varying visions, methods, and theoretical underpinnings for rhetorical fieldwork, pointing to the value of engaging in and with the places of persuasion for under-standing utterances in context, understanding objects of study in situ, and offering opportunities for engagement and intervention. While we have gathered here some of the key voices in this emerging subdiscipline, our work is not exhaustive or even entirely representative, and we hope it will serve as a springboard to future discussions, including an exploration of the ethics of rhetorical engagement in the field. We are heartened to see an increased interest in the study and practice of rhetorical field methods, and we look forward to what this work will continue to tell us about rhetoric and about the fields we engage. We hope this volume serves as a flexible road-map for those interested in engaging in the field, and as a touchstone to prompt important conversations about method, practice, intervention, and ethics and about the role of rhetoric in our complex constellations.

Notes

1. Marilyn M. Cooper, "The Ecology of Writing," *College English* 48, no. 4 (1986): 364–75; Jenny Edbauer, "Unframing Models of Public Distribution: From Rhetorical Situations to Rhetorical Ecologies," *Rhetoric Society Quarterly* 35, no. 4 (2005): 5–24; Thomas Rickert, *Ambient Rhetoric: The Attunements of Rhetorical Being* (Pittsburgh, PA: University of Pittsburgh Press, 2013); Nathan Stormer and Bridie McGreavy, "Thinking Ecologically About Rhetoric's Ontology: Capacity, Vulnerability, Resil-ience," *Philosophy and Rhetoric* 50, no. 1 (2017): 1–25.

2. John M. Ackerman, "The Space for Rhetoric in Everyday Life," in *Towards a Rhetoric of Everyday Life: New Directions in Research on Writing, Text, and Discourse*, ed. Martin Nystrand and John Duffy (Madison: University of Wisconsin Press, 2003), 84–117; Danielle Endres, and Samantha Senda-Cook, "Location Matters: The Rhetoric of Place in Protest," *Quarterly Journal of Speech* 97, no. 3 (2011): 257–82;

Caroline Gottschalk Druschke, "Watershed as Common-Place: Communicating for Conservation at the Watershed Scale," *Environmental Communication: A Journal of Nature and Culture* 7, no. 1 (2013): 80–96; Candice Rai, *Democracy's Lot: Rhetoric, Publics, and the Places of Persuasion* (Tuscaloosa: University of Alabama Press, 2016).

3. Carole Blair, Marsha S. Jeppeson, and Enrico Pucci, "Public Memorializing in Postmodernity: The Vietnam Veterans Memorial as Prototype," *Quarterly Journal of Speech* 77, no. 3 (1991): 263–88; Ralph Cintron, *Angel's Town: Chero Ways, Gang Life, and Rhetorics of the Everyday* (Boston: Beacon Press, 1997); Jack Selzer and Sharon Crowley, eds., *Rhetorical Bodies* (Madison: University of Wisconsin Press, 1999); Debra Hawhee, *Bodily Arts: Rhetoric and Athletics in Ancient Greece* (Austin: University of Texas Press, 2004); Barbara A. Biesecker and John L. Lucaites, eds. *Rhetoric, Materiality, and Politics* (New York: Peter Lang, 2009).

4. Rickert, *Ambient Rhetoric*; S. Scott Graham, *The Politics of Pain Medicine: A Rhetorical-Ontological Inquiry* (Chicago: University of Chicago Press, 2015); Jodie Nicotra, "Assemblage Rhetorics: Creating New Frameworks for Rhetorical Action," in *Rhetoric, Through Everyday Things*, ed. Scott Barnett and Casey Boyle (Tuscaloosa: University of Alabama Press, 2016), 185–96; Scot Barnett and Casey Boyle, eds., *Rhetoric, Through Everyday Things* (Tuscaloosa: University of Alabama Press, 2016).

5. Harry F. Wolcott, *The Art of Fieldwork* (Walnut Creek, CA: AltaMira Press, 2005), 58.

6. Clifford Geertz, *The Interpretation of Cultures* (New York: Basic Books, 1973).

7. James Clifford, "Introduction: Partial Truths," in *Writing Culture: The Poetics and Politics of Ethnography*, ed. John Clifford and George E. Marcus (Berkeley: University of California Press, 1986), 1–26; Cintron, *Angel's Town*; Katrina Pritchard, "From 'Being There' to 'Being . . . Where?': Relocating Ethnography," *Qualitative Research in Organizations and Management* 6, no. 3 (2011): 230–45.

8. Cintron, *Angel's Town*, 232.

9. Judith Stacey, "Can There be a Feminist Ethnography?" *Women's Studies International Forum* 11, no. 1 (1998): 21–27.

10. Phaedra C. Pezzullo, *Toxic Tourism: Rhetorics of Travel, Pollution, and Environmental Justice* (Tuscaloosa: University of Alabama Press, 2007); Jennifer Trainor, *Rethinking Racism: Emotion, Persuasion, and Literacy Education in an All-White High School* (Carbondale: Southern Illinois University Press, 2008).

11. Jeffrey T. Grabill, "On Being Useful: Rhetoric and the Work of Engagement," in *The Public Work of Rhetoric: Citizen-Scholars and Civic Engagement*, ed. John M. Ackerman and David J. Coogan (Columbia: University of South Carolina Press, 2010), 193–210.

12. Danielle Endres, Leah Sprain, and Tarla Rai Peterson, "The Imperative of Praxis-Based Environmental Communication Research: Suggestions from the Step It Up 2007 National Research Project," *Environmental Communication: A Journal of*

Nature and Culture 2, no. 2 (2008): 237–45; Carl G. Herndl et al., "Talking Sustainability: Identification and Division in an Iowa Community," *Journal of Sustainable Agriculture* 35, no. 4 (2011): 436–61; Gottschalk Druschke, "Watershed as Common-Place."

13. Cintron, *Angel's Town.*

14. David Fleming, *City of Rhetoric: Revitalizing the Public Sphere in Metropolitan America* (Albany: State University of New York Press, 2008).

15. Gerard A. Hauser, *Vernacular Voices: The Rhetoric of Publics and Public Spheres* (Columbia: University of South Carolina Press, 1999); Gerard A. Hauser, "Attending the Vernacular: A Plea for an Ethnographical Rhetoric," in *Rhetorical Emergence of Culture*, ed. Christian Meyer and Felix Girke, 157–72 (New York: Berghahn Books, 2011); Julie A. Lindquist, *A Place to Stand: Politics and Persuasion in a Working-Class Bar* (Oxford: Oxford University Press, 2002); Karen Tracy, *Challenges of Ordinary Democracy: A Case Study in Deliberation and Dissent* (University Park: Penn State University Press, 2010).

16. Aaron Hess, "Critical-Rhetorical Ethnography: Rethinking the Place and Process of Rhetoric," *Communication Studies* 62, no. 2 (2011):127–52; Rai, *Democracy's Lot.*

17. Kenneth Burke, *The Rhetoric of Motives* (Berkeley: University of California Press, 1969), 23.

18. Dwight Conquergood, "Ethnography, Rhetoric, and Performance," *Quarterly Journal of Speech* 78 (1992): 80–123.

19. Ivo Strecker and Stephen Tyler, eds., *Culture & Rhetoric* (New York: Berghahn Books, 2009), 2–3.

20. Ralph Cintron, "'Gates Locked' and the Violence of Fixation," in *Towards a Rhetoric of Everyday Life: New Directions in Research on Writing, Text, and Discourse,* ed. Martin Nystrand and John Duffy, 5–37 (Madison: University of Wisconsin Press, 2003); Cintron, *Angel's Town*; Michael Carrithers, "Why Anthropologists Should Study Rhetoric," *The Journal of the Royal Anthropological Institute* 11, no. 3 (2005): 577–83; Strecker and Tyler, *Culture and Rhetoric*; Robert Hariman and Ralph Cintron, eds., *Culture, Catastrophe, and Rhetoric: The Texture of Political Action* (New York: Berghahn Books, 2015).

21. Tracy, *Challenges of Ordinary Democracy*; Cintron, *Angel's Town*; Hauser, *Vernacular Voices*; Hauser, *Attending the Vernacular*; Lindquist, *A Place to Stand*; Candice Rai, "Positive Loitering and Public Goods: The Ambivalence of Civic Participation and Community Policing in the Neoliberal City," *Ethnography* 12, no. 1 (2011): 65–88; John M. Ackerman and David J. Coogan, eds., *The Public Work of Rhetoric: Citizen-Scholars and Civic Engagement* (Columbia: University of South Carolina Press, 2010).

22. Ackerman, "The Space for Rhetoric"; Nedra Reynolds, *Geographies of Writing: Inhabiting Places and Encountering Difference* (Carbondale: Southern Illinois University Press, 2007); Fleming, *City of Rhetoric*; Gottschalk Druschke, "Watershed

as Common-Place"; Greg Dickinson, *Suburban Dreams: Imagining and Building the Good Life* (Tuscaloosa: University of Alabama Press, 2015).

23. Rai, *Democracy's Lot*.

24. Hawhee, *Bodily Arts*; Debra Hawhee, *Moving Bodies: Kenneth Burke at the Edges of Language* (Columbia: University of South Carolina Press, 2009); Jennifer LeMesurier, "Somatic Metaphors: Embodied Recognition of Rhetorical Opportunities," *Rhetoric Review* 33, no. 4 (2014): 362–80.

25. Barbara A. Biesecker and John L. Lucaites, "Introduction," in *Rhetoric, Materiality, and Politics*, edited by Barbara A. Biesecker and John L. Lucaites, 1–16 (New York: Peter Lang, 2009); Celeste Condit, *The Meanings of the Gene: Public Debates About Heredity* (Madison: University of Wisconsin Press, 1999); Celeste Condit, "Race and Genetics from a Modal Materialist Perspective," *Quarterly Journal of Speech* 94, no. 4 (2008): 383–406; Michael C. McGee, "A Materialist's Conception of Rhetoric," in *Rhetoric, Materiality, and Politics* (New York: Peter Lang, 2009), 17–42; Sara L. McKinnon et al., eds., *Text + Field: Innovations in Rhetorical Method* (University Park: The Pennsylvania State University Press, 2016).

26. Hawhee, *Bodily Arts*; Sara Ahmed, *The Cultural Politics of Emotion* (New York: Routledge, 2004); Jenny Edbauer Rice, "The New 'New': Making a Case for Critical Affect Studies," *Quarterly Journal of Speech* 94, no. 2 (2008): 200–12; Trainor, *Rethinking Racism*; LeMesurier, "Somatic Metaphors."

27. McGee, "The 'Ideograph'"; Kristie S. Fleckenstein et al., "The Importance of Harmony: An Ecological Metaphor for Writing Research," *College, Composition, and Communication* 60, no. 2 (2008): 388–419; Rebecca Dingo, *Networking Arguments: Rhetoric, Transnational Feminism, and Public Policy Writing* (Pittsburgh, PA: University of Pittsburgh Press, 2012).

28. Edbauer, "Rhetorical Ecologies"; Bruno Latour, *Reassembling the Social: An Introduction to Actor-Network Theory* (Oxford: Oxford University Press, 2005); Clay Spinuzzi, *Network: Theorizing Knowledge Work in Telecommunications* (New York: Cambridge University Press, 2008); Andrew Mara and Byron Hawk, "Posthuman Rhetorics and Technical Communication," *Technical Communication Quarterly* 19, no. 1 (2009): 1–10; Jane Bennett, *Vibrant Matter: A Political Ecology of Things* (Durham, NC: Duke University Press, 2009); Diane Davis, *Inessential Solidarity: Rhetoric and Foreigner Relations* (Pittsburgh, PA: University of Pittsburgh, 2010); Grabill, "On Being Useful"; Rickert, *Ambient Rhetoric*; Read, Sarah, and Swarts, "Visualizing and Tracing: Research Methodologies for the Study of Networked, Sociotechnical Activity, Otherwise Known as Knowledge Work," *Technical Communication Quarterly* 24, no. 1 (2015): 14–44.

29. Rickert, *Ambient Rhetoric*.

30. In this collection, see Gottschalk Druschke; Herndl et al.; McGreavy, Fox, Disney, Petersen, and Lindenfeld; Grabill, Leon, and Pigg.

31. See, for example, Stephen G. Brown and Sidney I. Dobrin, *Ethnography*

Unbound: From Theory Shock to Critical Praxis (Albany: State University of New York Press, 2004).

32. Karen Barad, "Nature's Queer Performativity," *Qui Parle: Critical Humanities and Social Sciences* 19, no. 2 (2011): 121–58.

33. Ann M. Feldman, *Making Writing Matter: Composition in the Engaged University* (Albany: State University of New York Press, 2008).

34. Paula Mathieu, *Tactics of Hope: The Public Turn in English Composition* (Portsmouth, NH: Boynton/Cook, 2005).

35. Thomas Deans, *Writing Partnerships: Service-Learning in Composition* (Urbana, IL: National Council of Teachers of English, 2000).

36. Greg Wilson and Carl G. Herndl, "Boundary Objects as Rhetorical Exigence: Knowledge Mapping and Interdisciplinary Cooperation at the Los Alamos National Laboratory," *Journal of Business and Technical Communication* 21, no. 2 (2007): 129–54; W. Michele Simmons and Jeffrey T. Grabill, "Toward a Civic Rhetoric for Technologically and Scientifically Complex Places: Invention, Performance, and Participation," *College Composition and Communication* 58, no. 3 (2007): 419–48; Stuart Blythe, Jeffrey T. Grabill, and Kirk Riley, "Action Research and Wicked Environmental Problems: Exploring Appropriate Roles for Researchers in Professional Communication," *Journal of Business and Technical Communication* 22, no. 3 (2008): 272–98.

37. Ellen Cushman, "The Rhetorician as an Agent of Social Change," *College Composition and Communication* 47, no. 1 (1996): 7–28.

38. Horst W. Rittel and Melvin M. Webber, "Dilemmas in a General Theory of Planning," *Policy Sciences* 4, no. 2 (1973): 155–69.

39. Raymie E. McKerrow, "Critical Rhetoric in a Postmodern World," *Quarterly Journal of Speech* 77, no. 1 (1991): 75–78; Hess, "Critical-Rhetorical Ethnography," 128; Pezzullo, *Toxic Tourism*; Michael K. Middleton, Samantha Senda-Cook, and Danielle Endres, "Articulating Rhetorical Field Methods: Challenges and Tensions," *Western Journal of Communication* 75, no. 4 (2011): 386–406; Michael Middleton, Aaron Hess, Danielle Endres, and Samantha Senda-Cook, *Participatory Critical Rhetoric: Theoretical and Methodological Foundations for Studying Rhetoric In Situ* (Lanham, MD: Lexington Books, 2015).

40. Christa B. Teston and S. Scott Graham, "Stasis Theory and Meaningful Public Participation in Pharmaceutical Policy-Making," *Present Tense: A Journal of Rhetoric in Society* 2, no. 2 (2012), http://www.presenttensejournal.org/volume-2/stasis-theory-and-meaningful-public-participation-in-pharmaceutical-policy-making/; Christa B. Teston et al., "Public Voices in Pharmaceutical Deliberations: Negotiating 'Clinical Benefit,' in the FDA's Avastin Hearing," *Journal of Medical Humanities* 35, no. 2 (2014): 149–70; Blythe et al., "Action Research"; Herndl et al., "Talking Sustainability"; Carl G. Herndl and Lauren L. Cutlip, "'How Can We Act?' A Praxiographical Program for the Rhetoric of Technology, Science, and Medicine," *Poroi* 9 (2013); Caroline Gottschalk Druschke, "With Whom Do We Speak?

Building Transdisciplinary Collaborations in Rhetoric of Science," POROI 10, no. 1 (2014), doi: 10.13008/2151-2957.1175; Bridie McGreavy, "Resilience as Discourse," *Environmental Communication* 10, no. 1 (2016): 104–21; Caroline Gottschalk Druschke and Bridie McGreavy, "Why Rhetoric Matters for Ecology," *Frontiers in Ecology and the Environment* 14, no. 1 (2016): 46–52.

42. Anna Lowenhaupt Tsing, *Friction: An Ethnography of Global Connection* (Princeton, NJ: Princeton University Press, 2011), 270.

43. Bruno Latour, "How to Talk About the Body? The Normative Dimension of Science Studies," *Body & Society* 10, no. 2–3 (2004): 205–29; Latour, *Reassembling the Social*; Bruno Latour, "Coming Out as a Philosopher," *Social Studies of Science* 40, no. 4 (2010): 599–608.

44. Michel de Certeau, *The Practice of Everyday Life*, trans. Steven Rendall (Berkeley: University of California Press, 1984).

45. Yael Navaro-Yashin, "Make-Believe Papers, Legal Forms and the Counterfeit Affective Interactions Between Documents and People in Britain and Cyprus," *Anthropological Theory* 7, no. 1 (2007): 79–98.

1

Agonistic Methodology

A Rhetorical Case Study in Agricultural Stewardship

CAROLINE GOTTSCHALK DRUSCHKE

Rhetoric of science scholars have increasingly called for a turn toward practical engagement.[1] This so-called applied rhetoric of science would connect critical theorizing with creative intervention by, as Carl Herndl and Lauren Cutlip describe, "mov[ing] us from a focus on saying and representing to a concern for doing and intervening."[2] In this vision, which I share, the embedded rhetorician would find ways to do and intervene in scientific research and practice in theoretically informed and consequential ways. But this shift toward consequential intervention demands a methodology that illuminates how competing rhetorics are called on, created, and enacted in everyday life.

To address that demand, I employ the ancient Greek notion of *agôn*, or productive struggle, as both subject matter and methodology. Focusing on the rhetoric, science, and practice of agricultural conservation, I build on three years of fieldwork with farmers, agricultural landowners, and conservation staff in an eastern Iowa watershed to identify material and symbolic points of tension in subjects' descriptions of their beliefs and practices. Attending to rhetorical commonplaces within agricultural discourses like "stewardship," "feeding the world," and "cheap food," I mark the friction that emerges when universalizing rhetorics of stewardship, independence, and heroism, in Anna Tsing's phrase, "enter the fray."[3] In so doing, I argue that rhetorical fieldwork is itself an agonistic encounter: bursting with the sorts of discomforts and tensions that make researchers sensitive to those that emerge in the lives and words of their research subjects. The agonistic encounter of rhetorical fieldwork shines a light on the lived experience of discontinuity and potentially irresolvable contradiction, expanding disciplinary understandings of rhetoric and generating significant insights for intervention. Agonistic methodology illuminates targets for critique, attunement, identification, and intervention.

Discomfort as Methodology

This chapter emerges from three years of living in and studying my field site: a smallish, predominantly agricultural watershed in eastern Iowa.[4] After spending several years in the area as a college student, I returned as a graduate student intern with the Iowa Department of Agriculture and Land Stewardship (IDALS). There, I worked with the Clear Creek Watershed Enhancement Project, an organization composed of municipal government representatives, farmers and agricultural landowners, state and federal conservation outreach staff, and environmental consultants. Through research, education, and advocacy, the group works to improve water quality in Clear Creek, a twenty-five-mile-long stream in eastern Iowa that drains a sixty-four thousand–acre watershed and flows into the Iowa River and the Mississippi River beyond.

In Clear Creek, I engaged in participant observation at the county conservation office, board meetings, field days, and farmers markets; conducted semistructured interviews with eighteen agricultural landowners and conservation staff; and distributed a survey on conservation attitudes and practices to about one thousand agricultural landowners and operators in the watershed. Broadly, I took a rhetorical-ecological systems perspective that tethered global and local rhetorics and policies of agriculture to related socioeconomic and biophysical systems to better understand the connections and feedbacks between the changing landscape and the changing discourses of agriculture. My central questions included: How do farmers and agricultural landowners come to identify with the watershed?[5] How do gender and land tenure impact conservation knowledge, attitudes, and communication?[6] What forms do global commonplaces of agricultural stewardship take in everyday discourse, and what impacts do they have? And what consequences can this critical work have for intervention and action in environmental problems with no easy solutions?

The ideas and experiences of *agôn*, tension, and discomfort were central to my time in Clear Creek, some of the most productive and most uncomfortable years of my life. My work with the Iowa Department of Agriculture and Land Stewardship began as an internship in the Landscape, Ecological and Anthropogenic Processes (LEAP) National Science Foundation IGERT training program at University of Illinois at Chicago. Because I had deep experience in the realm of small-scale, hyper-local, sustainable agriculture and advocacy prior to LEAP, I assumed my required internship would follow suit. But the LEAP director pushed me to do something that would be, in her words, "uncomfortable." That meant fulfilling an internship with a large state agency that worked primarily with large-scale corn and soy growers. While I was familiar with the rhetorics, material conditions, and practices of sustainable agriculture and local food in the Midwest, industrial agriculture was a foreign world I knew only enough about to abstractly disdain. I hesitantly joined the project only after realizing that I would not be able to engage with the rhetorics of small-scale growers until I understood, intimately and materially, what (and whom) they were arguing against.

But to engage with a group that I then thought of as the enemy challenged me to embrace cognitive dissonance as I had never experienced. If, as Debra Hawhee suggests, "the word *agôn* suggests movement through struggle, a productive training practice wherein subjective production takes place through the encounter itself,"[7] then my "movement through struggle" did not so much produce subjectivity as spark a sort of attunement to vital materialism,[8] a materialism that includes people and socioeconomic structures as well as soil, microbes, rocks, seeds, and hydrologic processes. In other words, my experiences in Clear Creek, and the productive movement through struggle they demanded, brought me to some cascading realizations. Namely, I discovered

- Exploring the fluidity and power of language in environmental issues suggests an important role for rhetoricians and rhetoric in holding together, framing, and mediating within that system;
- Examining the interconnections between organic and inorganic things is key to more fully understanding rhetorical critique and intervention; and
- Attending and attuning to the insights of agonistic struggles offers points of tension and possibility that provide an orientation for rhetoric scholars interested in understanding and intervening in complex, politically charged, public issues.

Crucially, these rhetorical conclusions emerged only from long-term immersion in my field site, and their discovery demanded an agonistic methodology oriented toward rhetoric, tension, and the lived ecologies of which humans are but one small part.

Attunement through Discomfort

But what does this immersion look like? What forms does it take? How can agonistic struggle lead to this sort of attunement with bodies, policies, arguments, and soil, among other things? And how can deep, extended engagement in and with the field engender deep discomfort and insight for intervention? I address those questions, first, with a brief, but hopefully illuminative, example in the constellation that was my time in Clear Creek.

On an early September evening in 2008, having just abandoned my life in Chicago to relocate to Iowa City, Iowa, I took a seat at one of about twenty tables at the Annual Meeting of the Johnson County Iowa Farm Bureau. Despite my best efforts to cloak my presence by dressing cautiously in jeans and a black sweater, the disguise didn't work. From the moment I walked into the South Slope Cooperative Community Building, I felt like all eyes were on me. It wasn't just what I was wearing: I couldn't yet embody Iowan-ness in the way I felt I needed to, and wanted to, for this crowd; my *ethos* was all wrong. My height (a bit too tall at 5'8"), my gender (female), my hair (both too blonde to go unnoticed and not Scandinavian-blonde enough to fit in; thick, long, messy, sans hairspray), and, most of all, the fact that I hadn't attended this Annual Meeting numerous times all conspired against me.

I tried to lose myself in my placemat, on which was printed a facts-and-fallacies-style primer about American farming. Before I had time to consider the Farm Bureau's answer to question number five ["Due to the push in ethanol, there isn't enough corn to go around. False."], the sixty-year-old gentleman next to me spoke up, shattering my solitude: "Who are YOU?" The question was delivered in a tone that implied not a friendly query, but a deep question of belonging: an accusation of trespass. I stammered something between uncomfortable laughs: "Well, I'm here with Laura . . . She's over there [gesturing desperately toward a group of about ten people across the room] . . . We buy produce from local farmers and give it to low-income families in Johnson County." "Okay," he replied, followed by a pause. And then, he delivered the second half of the one-two punch: "So why are you here?"

It turns out that my dinner companion, Clint, was actually a friendly enough guy, and by the time we parted that evening after the Pledge of Allegiance, singing the National Anthem, dinner (green bean casserole, hash brown casserole, pork tenderloin, lemonade, cheesecake), a slideshow (images of a recent visit by Russian farmers ["I don't know where they got those people!" Clint laughed], of the Johnson County Future Farmers' second-place finish in the Farm Bowl at the Iowa State Fair, and of last year's Annual Meeting), an introduction to the elected officials in attendance ("I'm a *FIFTH* generation farmer from such-and-such county and I sure do hope you'll vote for me!"), a "brief" speech from Johnson County's Iowa Farm Bureau representative ("Brief, my ass!" again, Clint), the actual agenda items, a keynote address from the Executive Director of the Iowa Biodiesel Board (fighting what he called the media "propaganda," the "15 million dollar smear campaign" against the biodiesel industry), and the door prize raffle, we exchanged a warm handshake, and Clint made me promise I'd see him again at the next Annual Meeting, which meant that I was now expected to attend.

So concluded my first contact with the Johnson County Farm Bureau (a group whose slogan is "People. Progress. Pride.") and one of the most uncomfortable evenings of my life. That's not to say that the members of the Johnson County Farm Bureau are an unwelcoming crowd, simply that they are a group with good reason to be suspicious of outsiders and a group with which I was (and mostly still am) entirely unfamiliar. In Johnson County, in particular, the Farm Bureau is charged with protecting the interests of the county farmers in the face of increasing development (as Clint explained of developers and eager suburban and exurban homebuyers: "They're ruining a lot of good farmland") and from the left-leaning and largely urban-centric demands of the University of Iowa population in Iowa City (of which I had long been a member).

The president-elect of the all-male board of directors repeatedly stressed that the Farm Bureau sees itself as a "grassroots" organization and that this connection to their grassroots constituents is key to the Farm Bureau's continued power as an advocate for American farmers. During the "Issues" section of the meeting, then, the board invited Farm Bureau members to set the agenda for the County Bureau. Members raised concerns over the County Agricultural Land Use Ordinance and its effect on sustainable agriculture events, over the possibility of growing hemp as a cash crop, over the county's $20 million conservation bond issue, over property taxes and real estate taxes, over the need for infrastructure improvements postflooding. In short, questions of policy, politics, land use, governance, government, gender, economics, organic and inorganic things coalesced.

What began to sink in as I sat through the meeting, looking at and listening to the mostly cowboy boot and starched-shirt-clad middle-aged men (what one farmer friend refers to as "the polyester crowd"), is that at stake in the Farm Bureau Annual Meeting was a public, civic argument about the future of food, of land use, and, ultimately, of something like an equitable political life. The Johnson County Farm Bureau, and the wider agricultural community it represented, was an assemblage of publics that coalesced around arguments related to agriculture, conservation, production, and stewardship. At stake in the meeting were competing rhetorics that shaped and were shaped by federal subsidies, media messages, agricultural markets, political views, religious backgrounds, gender assumptions, and land use policies, not to mention eroding topsoil, flooding, and Roundup Ready seed. Arguments for increased production, debt, synthetic fertilizer, federal subsidies, biofuels crashed into and layered onto arguments for diversified production, agritourism, sustainable food systems. And all of that was haunted by the specters of increased seasonal flooding, fluctuating corn prices, drought, an exodus of young farmers to urban areas, impaired waterways, Gulf of Mexico hypoxia. At the center was anxiety: anxiety about, as many farmer friends put it, "doing the right thing," about protecting farmland and farmers (in financial, spiritual, ideological ways), about protecting masculinity, farm life, topsoil, family inheritances, labor, God. But how would you know that without sitting there with Clint, listening, sweating, worrying, stammering, deciding whether to set aside fifteen years of vegetarianism to take a bite of that Iowa grown pork chop?

These are connections I would never have seen or felt or begun to understand without placing myself physically, awkwardly, painfully into the situation: opening myself to criticism, and surprising kindness, to understand what impacts the practices and rhetorics of urban sprawl, biodiesel, nationhood, and drought had on the everyday perspectives, discourses, and actions of a group of farmers, and, in turn, to understand the feedbacks of those perspectives, discourses, and actions on interrelated material and ideological landscapes.[9]

Rhetoric ↔ Ethnography: A Primer

To hone in on those tensions, my primary approach involved what Ralph Cintron frequently refers to as "the sort of ethnography that rhetorical people do." As Paul Willis and Mats Trondman describe, ethnography is "a family of methods involving direct and sustained social contact with agents, and of richly writing up the encounter, respecting, recording, representing at least partly *in its own terms*, the irreducibility of human experience . . . the disciplined and deliberate witness-cum-recording of human events."[10]

Rhetoricians can take lessons from ethnographers like Johan Pottier, who uses ethnography to provide access to the tools and evidence to critique "expert" policies and their failures to solve lived problems, and Anna Tsing, who mobilizes friction as both heuristic and methodology.[11] Through a method she refers to as "patchwork ethnographic fieldwork," moving from place to place and scene to scene, Tsing focuses on universals like "rights" and "justice," using friction as a heuristic for understanding how universals "enter the fray," to see how "heterogenous and unequal encounters can lead to new arrangements of culture and power."[12] Tsing attempts to highlight how global policies and local responses shape each other, and argues for the need to situate oneself in a given place to better understand how global policies and practices are resisted or adapted in local settings.[13] If agonistic tension conjures a sense of movement through struggle, friction becomes a lens for theorizing that movement, and rhetorical ethnography offers a methodology for witnessing and participating in the struggle.

Building from this important orientation toward participation, friction, and critique, "the sort of ethnography that rhetorical people do," as Cintron puts it, involves disciplined and deliberate attention to the shaping power of language, energies, symbols, objects, discourses, and bodies. Rhetoricians inclined toward ethnographic methodologies embed themselves in real-time unfolding situations: recording what they see and participate in; working to unpack and theorize from the phrases, ideas, ecologies, desires, assemblages, and commonplaces that have purchase in place; and attending to the lives of humans and other-than-humans. Through field methods, ethnographers embed themselves within what Michael Carrithers refers to as "the micropolitics of everyday life" and, at least for my own work, we do and intervene, as Herndl and Cutlip describe, based on those findings.[14] For me, that intervention is rooted in sites of contestation and struggle: actual places and lived arguments where I observe and engage with people and things that clash and contest. And this orientation toward intervention is a distinct ethical stance. Simply, ethnography emerges as the best tool I have found to perform this sort of deep analysis—sensitive to global structures, local experiences, and vibrant matter—and to engage in action and intervention.

Here I employ agonistic methodology, based in rhetorical ethnographic methods, to attend to the *topoi* or commonplaces of agriculture in eastern Iowa—chief among them "stewardship," "cheap food," and "feeding the world"—as they emerge first in printed text and then, significantly, in the words and lives of Clear Creek's farmers and agricultural landowners. As I have suggested elsewhere, fusing the work of Cintron with Crowley and Hawhee, I use *topos* "to mark a word, phrase, or statement that circulates through communal beliefs, evoking the places—both material and symbolic—where persuasive arguments occur" and to highlight both inventive and persuasive aspects of the term.[15] In Clear Creek, these *topoi* emerge as points of contestation: where universal rhetorics conflict with on-the-ground practices; where farmers display particular points of anxiety and contradiction in their attempts to feed their own families, preserve their farmland, protect their water bodies, and feed the world; and where these conflicts lead to emergent beliefs, practices, and arrangements of power. Crucially, the impact and possibility of agonistic terms and points of friction become visible only from immersion in the ongoing unfolding of the agonistic encounter.

Stewardship as Polysemy

Stewardship—the responsible care or management of a person, place, or thing—has been a central organizing *topos* of agriculture in spirit if not always in name, emerging in both the Old and New Testament, as well as in tribal and First Nations' guiding ethics. Because of my embedded experience with farmers across the spectrum of sustainable to industrial growers, I began to notice that "stewardship" functioned like a "God-term" or trump argument, mobilized by a variety of actors to argue for a variety of ends.[16]

A Google search of "agriculture" and "stewardship" in 2017 nets some 23.7 million results, ranging from the Iowa Department of Agriculture and Land Stewardship to the Pan-Africa Biotechnology Stewardship Conference and initiatives like DuPont chemical company's "Excellence Through Stewardship" campaign. Even a cursory review informs the reader that the term stewardship is mobilized in myriad ways for various arguments. Political, religious, and business leaders engage the stewardship *topos* to justify spending, drive economic growth, safeguard national security, enlist religious followers, justify theories of evolution, promote nationalism, advocate for the global commons, support agrarianism, and sell insecticide, among other things. Agrarian Wendell Berry argues for an ecological rather than economic philosophy by insisting, "Wherever we live, we live in nature and by using nature, and this use everywhere implies the requirement of good stewardship," while chemical company DuPont can boost its economic bottom line by selling a broad-spectrum insecticide called "Steward," a product that Berry would certainly oppose.[17] Meanwhile, in the land use and conservation literature, Richard Worrell and Michael Appleby argue, "It is far from clear what the term stewardship actually describes, and how it differs from established terms. . . . It is not apparent what the element of responsibility means, to whom or what is a 'steward' responsible . . . , and how this responsibility is manifested in practice."[18] In a seemingly infinite array of contexts, stewardship's meaning is an open, shifting target.

From spending to growth, religion to science, nationalism to globalism, and agrarianism to chemistry, stewardship means different things both to the speakers who mobilize the term and to the audiences they wish to move and persuade. And these differences have more to do with what Leah Ceccarelli refers to as a cognitive than an attitudinal gap; they are about varying interpretations of the term stewardship (what each speaker and audience member takes the term to mean) rather than judgment of its worth (because all of these rhetors and likely their audience members perceive stewardship favorably).[19] In fact, it is the term's global acceptance that makes it so persuasive: it can be successfully deployed in a wide variety of ways to justify a wide variety of ends. This characteristic, of widely differing uses and interpretations, marks stewardship as a strong and complex example of polysemous language: what Robin Jensen defines as "language containing multiple meanings as intended by authors or interpreted by audiences."[20] And these polysemous qualities mark stewardship as a point of tension, an evolving argument that carries in it and with it these competing views.

Central to my point here is that studying texts in actual ecologies and embodied contexts reveals multiple dimensions and relations not otherwise apparent through text. To understand the capacities and limitations of a term like stewardship, and to understand its very real stakes, it becomes essential to engage with this and a cluster of related *topoi* by engaging with the people and policies that mobilize it and with the landscapes it impacts. Crucially, I am interested in stewardship because its capaciousness marks it as a possible point of intervention. In other words, because stewardship can be mobilized so variously, it serves as a springboard for the sort of intervention that something like an applied rhetoric of science can level.

An American Mandate to Feed the World

The contemporary debate about stewardship and agricultural production emerges in the context of the Green Revolution—the dramatic increase in crop production through fertilizers, pesticides, and high-yield crop varieties beginning in the mid-1940s—with Iowa-born agronomist Norman Borlaug serving as its patriarch. Borlaug's pioneering work on specialty crop varieties, coupled with his tenacity in exporting his innovations to the developing world, marked the beginning of the modern era of agriculture. Borlaug framed the innovations that garnered him the 1970 Nobel Prize for Peace in terms of an ongoing war against hunger, summoning America's farmers as an "army of hunger fighters," as Borlaug referred to them, who would be his "companions in arms" in the Green Revolution.[21] Borlaug created the shared national project of feeding a growing global population, and he argued for management, efficiency, and productivity for the sake of a growing nation in an increasingly powerful global position. This was a vision of stewardship that many farmers were understandably eager to inhabit, both then and now.

The farmers I came to know in the Clear Creek watershed were born into the policies, practices, and discourses of Borlaug's Green Revolution. They inhabited Borlaug's mandate to enlist in "the army of hunger fighters" who would do their civic duty by exporting grain to the developing world. And that message was sustained by the advertising all around them. During my field seasons in Clear Creek, for instance, Monsanto's home page greeted visitors with a large, rotating banner at the top of the page. Monsanto's message flashed in front of four crisp photos of America's farmers:

The world's population is growing /
To keep up with population growth, farmers will have to produce
    more food . . . /
More food in the next 50 years than in the last 10,000 years com-
    bined. /
America's farmers will meet this challenge.[22]

Monsanto hails this vision of agricultural stewardship, entreating each visitor to embrace his (typically "his") role as one of America's farmers and participate in the national project by purchasing Roundup and Roundup Ready seed to answer this call because the fate of the world depends on it.

Monsanto's farmers know that the use of herbicide and genetically modified seed is an integral part of the national project: stewardship through increased production for the sake of the world's growing population. As Monsanto's farmers literally gaze into the distance, not the foreground, the local landscape disappears; the global scale and the demand to participate in a national agricultural project take precedence. And the time, they are told, is now. This *topos* of the moral imperative travels throughout agricultural chemical company discourse, calling farmers to "mak[e] a difference in the world" by ensuring that "no individual goes hungry."[23]

Again and again, farmers and landowners are told that the embrace and economic support of synthetic herbicides and genetically modified seed is essential to meeting this "moral imperative" to feed the world's population, a moral imperative they acutely feel. This language is persuasive because its taps into farmers' existing motivations and desires. They want to perform the role of agricultural steward. They want to play a role in feeding the world. They want to do what is best for their global neighbors. And to do that, they need to keep pace with production. But several of the farmers I spoke with in Clear Creek were concerned that this version of stewardship comes at an environmental cost.

Discourses of Stewardship Enter the Fray

In their foundational work on the rhetorics of agricultural conservation and stewardship, Tarla Rai Peterson and Cristi Horton described Texas ranchers as firmly connected to a myth of stewardship, perceiving themselves as stewards and protectors of the land, suggesting that stewardship might serve as an important touchstone for identification.[24] Following Peterson and Horton, I anticipated that Clear Creek's farmers and landowners—seemingly immersed in the images and arguments of stewardship circulating in speeches, commercials, and outreach materials—would have completely bought into the myths of stewardship with little awareness of the contradictions and conflicts in both theory and practice the term manifests: incorporating both Wendell Berry's ecological philosophy and DuPont's broad-spectrum insecticide.[25]

But given my interests in *agôn*, tension, and friction, in discomfort as both methodology and lens, I was quick to attend to and pick up on the particular tensions that emerged in the discussions with my interviewees in Clear Creek: not only the tensions that I observed but also that my informants clearly articulated and inhabited. What I found in Clear Creek differed from Peterson and Horton's findings and elucidated some of the tensions of competing visions of stewardship occurring in printed texts.[26] Being there in my study watershed allowed me to see that my interviewees did, indeed, seem invested in something like Peterson et al.'s definition of stewardship as "personal responsibility to consider the interests of others when managing one's private property."[27] But the contradictions that Peterson and Horton identified were not lost on my informants, as these farmers and agricultural landowners were quick to point out.[28] When it came to the discourses of the Green Revolution, both Russell, a successful middle-aged farmer in the watershed, and the landowner he rents from, Harlan, a retired farmer in his early 80s, echoed the language of "feeding the world," but each problematized this version of stewardship even as he supported it.

During our interview, Harlan demonstrated an encyclopedic knowledge of the conservation practices he had installed on his farmland and of the myriad (and incredibly confusing) government programs that fund such practices. When asked about the conservation work done on his farm, Harlan consulted a tidy notebook that cataloged the variety of practices installed on his farmland—buffer strips along the creek, terraces, basins, a standpipe, grassed waterways—an impressive amount of work on two hundred acres. Harlan was persuaded to adopt a variety of conservation practices thanks to his identification with a rhetoric of stewardship that focused on care at the local scale, with his connection to a specific place. It mattered to Harlan that he was present on his farm: as he put it, he took "a really big interest"; he wanted to "know what's going on." He stayed in close contact with his renter, Russell, who, Harlan explained, chose to take over the farm because: "I knew what kind of a farmer he was . . . he does things right. We have good communication. And, uh, he just does everything according to the conservation programs that we're in, and just overall does a good job." For Harlan, it mattered that Russell practiced good conservation and carried out the long-term vision that Harlan had for his farm: that "he does things right." Though Harlan no longer farmed the land himself, he took an active interest in its care, and, in turn, he expected his renter, Russell, to do the same; Harlan felt a responsibility to the land he inherited from his father and wanted to carry out that legacy for the long-term to, as he described: "Save the soil for future generations." But when I asked Harlan what he was most proud of about his land, he paused for a moment and then replied: "I like owning some land that you're feeding the world." Despite Harlan's interest in best management practices on his farm for the sake of his present neighbors and future generations, Harlan's adoption of this Borlaugean version of stewardship betrays a concurrent sympathy with a national project that can be complicit with environmental degradation. Significantly, for Harlan, this rhetoric of "feeding the world" is not an empty slogan. He was proud of his lifelong role in the global food economy. After detailing the specific practices that he has installed on his land, Harlan pointed to "feeding the world" as the accomplishment he was most proud of.

And this national agricultural project of "feeding the world" has served to define the role of heroism for American farmers for over a half century, offering farmers a tangible project with which to identify. While American agriculture underwent drastic changes throughout the twentieth century, this national project of feeding a hungry and growing world offered farmers a measure of stability unavailable elsewhere. It offered a project they could believe in: a validation not only of their jobs but also of their very selves. It is a highly persuasive rhetoric. But even while Harlan identified with and acted upon this strong rhetoric of stewardship, of assuming responsibility for alleviating global hunger, this argument had not eclipsed his concern for local, emplaced soil and water conservation. Harlan saw stewardship as a motivator for the adoption of best management practices. But stewardship, for Harlan, was also connected to post–Green Revolution global production and "feeding the world." These are conflicting imperatives. This is a friction, a tension, an instance of *agôn* that Harlan, importantly, seemed well aware of.

Harlan recognized the tense symbiosis between the rhetorics and practices of a seemingly environmentally positive version of stewardship (the adoption of best management practices for his two hundred acres) and a potentially ecologically damaging one, the demand to care for the world's population through intensive row-crop production: "I think people, some people, think we're cropping too much, but with the increase in population, we're going to have to raise more out of every acre to feed the world." He recognized the criticism voiced by advocates of a "more sustainable" version of stewardship, but, for Harlan, "rais[ing] more out of every acre to feed the world" mattered most. His conservation actions were a palliative, relieving the short-term pain inflicted on his land without a long-term solution to the underlying problems posed by intensive production.

Harlan's renter, Russell, expressed even more discomfort than Harlan with the fraught relationship between intensive production and conservation. After describing improvements in hybrid crop varieties and chemicals from his thirty years of farming, Russell checked himself: "Chemicals are still chemicals. I mean, they're not hundred percent good, but they're not as bad as what they used to be. They're bad, but not as bad. You know, I wish we didn't have to use 'em at all. But if we're gonna feed everybody we gotta do some stuff that we probably shouldn't do all the time." As Russell clearly articulated, there are moments when his identifications with various rhetorics of stewardship, of feeding the world and conserving his soil, come into conflict. Russell wanted to care for his local land (both his own farm and the land he farmed for Harlan); he felt a sense of connection and duty to the land he had inherited from his father, grandfather, and great-grandfather. But he also felt compelled to manage that land for maximum efficiency and profit. He felt a duty to his role as an American farmer who is expected to produce for a growing national and global population and to support his family while doing it. His identification with these competing versions of stewardship is complicated even further by material factors: by agricultural subsidies; by the availability of chemical fertilizer; by consumer demand for cheap food; by widespread flooding; by a growing global population.

Russell clearly wanted to participate in the project of "feed[-ing] everybody." He saw his work on the fifteen hundred acres he farmed as having a positive effect on the wider world. But Russell recognized that this work came at a cost: that his basins and waterways would not fully ameliorate the effects of the widespread chemical application that intensive row crop agriculture demands. His identification with and enactment of a version of stewardship that advocates for maximum production come at a recognized cost: Russell had to "do some stuff that we probably shouldn't do all the time"; stuff that Russell recognized could not be fully ameliorated by existing government-supported conservation practices.

By enacting a particular version of stewardship, meeting the perceived needs of this global population, Russell made decisions about chemical use that he recognized were not necessarily in the best interests of the local landscape, "But if we're gonna feed everybody we gotta do some stuff that we probably shouldn't do all the time." For Russell, stewardship presented a tension: to feed the growing population and to take care of his grandfather's farmland on behalf of his sons. It is the tension between a powerful and appealing universal rhetoric to "feed the world" and the situated, environmental practices and consequences that undermine that universally agreeable mandate. He was held between the two competing demands by the economics of agriculture. For Russell: "If we want cheap food, we have to do this. I mean, that's kinda flustrating for other people to hear that . . . but we have to if we wanna have cheap food. That's what people want." Russell felt the acute pressure placed on him by the global economy. As he saw it, the world demanded that he produce cheap food, and he delivered, no matter the cost to his farmland and his watershed. He sacrificed his local landscape for the benefit of a global population.

Both Russell and Harlan supported, mobilized, and acted upon competing versions of stewardship: of soil and water conservation; of feeding a hungry planet; of widespread chemical application. At times, each man supported a version of stewardship that seemed a far cry from that of Monsanto or DuPont. At others, they embodied the role of one of Borlaug's hunger fighters. At still others, their language seemed plucked from the pages of a Monsanto advertisement. And they seemed well aware of these tensions; still, they never went so far as to criticize the entire system. Instead, they lived with this tension, and in it.

In some ways, these tensions are reflected in the competing ways that stewardship is mobilized in some of the written texts cited above. But critically, in practice, those competing visions of stewardship coalesce in particular speakers, bodies, landscapes, and lives. It is not that Harlan's view of stewardship competes with Russell's view, which competes with Monsanto's view. It's that Harlan's own view and Russell's own view are internally fractured, and knowingly so. These farmers are in a rhetorical, economic, and biophysical bind. And they live that bind every moment of every day. But that acute tension would not have become apparent if I hadn't spent time with them, listened to them, walked their land, drank coffee at their tables, saw the family pictures on the wall, heard stories of their grandparents and great grandparents first arriving in Iowa and their children departing it. Only then does that tension become apparent, real, consequential. Urgent. And these tensions mark a potential point of intervention for a rhetorician interested in something like an applied rhetoric of science: in, as Herndl and Cutlip offer, "mov[ing] us from a focus on saying and representing to a concern for doing and intervening."[29]

This is the difference between criticism that unpacks logics or arguments and their breakdowns, identifies contradictions, and critiques and decenters, and one that examines the situatedness of why those arguments, logics, and breakdowns exist and exist for very reasonable rationales at the human scale. These are reasons, conflicts, fractures that cannot be hammered out. They are embodied, consequential, visceral, and must be attended to if you want to not only study public rhetoric in these shared public problems but also offer tentative hopes for intervention.

But what would I intervene in? What I hoped to do in Clear Creek was to use my rhetorical training and rhetorical sensibilities to intervene in both the damage to water quality prompted by farmers' decisions about fertilizers, pesticides, livestock management, and erosion and the pain and discomfort in farmers' lives as they grappled with these competing visions of stewardship and the socioeconomic and biophysical factors that sustained them.

Attending to Vibrant Matter: The Material Stakes of Rhetorics of Stewardship

How conservationists, farmers, landowners, public figures, and private companies talk about stewardship matters deeply for the agricultural landscape. The United States's current level of and approach to agricultural production, both despite and because of varying arguments for stewardship, has had dire consequences for the landscape of the Upper Midwest and beyond. Iowa has long been planted virtually corner to corner in soybeans and corn thanks to its climate, topography, and exceptionally fertile soils. And the scientific advances of the Green Revolution allowed Iowa to cash in on an exponential boom in commodity crop production over the last sixty-plus years. A remarkable 89.5 percent of Iowa's land area is privately owned farmland, and that high intensity of agricultural production has come with an environmental cost.[30] As P. A. Matson et al. describe in their study of the ecological impacts of contemporary US farming: "It is now clear that agricultural intensification can have negative local consequences, such as increased erosion, lower soil fertility, and reduced biodiversity; negative regional consequences, such as pollution of ground water and eutrophication of rivers and lakes; and negative global consequences, including impacts on atmospheric constituents and climate."[31] The type of farming that rules the State of Iowa can have damaging effects at the local, regional, and global scales. The type and intensity of farming that most Iowans do seems not to be, in the most good sense way, sustainable; regardless of the wider environmental cost, Iowa's soils likely cannot continue to support it.

Intensive agricultural practices—the widespread application of chemical fertilizer, the disappearance of headlands and stream buffers, the practice of clean tillage, and so on—have hastened soil erosion on Iowa farms, pushing soil loss above the T value (tolerable soil loss), the maximum annual amount of loss that soil can tolerate without an adverse effect on productivity.[32] Soil loss due to erosion has choked Iowa's creeks and streams with sediment that carries high levels of nitrogen and phosphorous from chemical fertilizers.

The problems caused by sheet and rill erosion in Iowa's watersheds spread well beyond the state. Nutrient saturated runoff from the Upper Mississippi River Basin is cited as the major contributor to the growing hypoxic zone, also called the "dead zone," in the Gulf of Mexico.[33] Post–Green Revolution intensive agriculture in Iowa is depleting Iowa's soils and choking its waterways with sediment and excess nutrients, and this impact continues downstream. Despite these near- and far-reaching consequences, the force of American agricultural policy, combined with fluctuating grain prices, have meant that Iowa's farmers have had to overlook these environmental problems in the face of both real and perceived demands of increased production. These competing demands are at the heart of the tensions identified here in the polysemous nature of stewardship. These are the deeply real consequences for these conversations. Soil, streams, humans, fish, nutrients, livelihoods, families, and industries are bound up and at stake.

"Ease His Pain": Everything Is More Complicated than It Seems

There is a moment in W. P. Kinsella's classic Iowa novel *Shoeless Joe*, where the main character, Ray, hears a voice from his Iowa cornfield whisper, "Ease his pain." In the novel, it turns out that the voice seems to be referring to J. D. Salinger, and later, to Ray's father, and finally, to Ray himself. Ray obsesses over the voice: "This one idea has run like a colored thread through all my thoughts for all these months. 'Ease his pain. Ease his pain.' I have repeated it ten thousand times, in my dreams, in my fantasies, to my wife, to my daughter, to myself as I drove my tractor over my black fields."[34] I admit that I repeated it, too. I couldn't shake the whispered phrase, "Ease his pain," over the years I worked with farmers and landowners in Iowa.

I entered my field site thinking of these farmers as the enemy. If only they "got it," I thought. If only they would make the "easy" choice to practice in more environmentally sustainable ways. For me, it seemed like an easy choice. But, of course, everything is more complicated than it seems, and fieldwork is one of the best ways to understand that, see that, live that. I came out the other side of this fieldwork with deep ambivalence: I still see the ecological damage caused by current agricultural practices—prompting erosion, sedimentation, nutrient enrichment, fecal coliform bacteria, hypoxia, among other things—and I work to combat it. But, as a responsible (post-)critic, I also see and feel the lived realities these farmers face and within which they struggle. My experience in the fields and farmhouses in Clear Creek offered irreplaceable lessons about stewardship and humility. It knocked my arrogant argument off its foundation and encouraged me to look more closely at the ways I might, with the help of a rhetorical perspective, attend to farmers' pain. Even if I ultimately can't fix that pain, there is power in humbling oneself: listening; attending; bearing witness; learning; hoping; trying.

Polysemous mobilizations of the term stewardship, and the socioeconomic and biophysical structures that support and are supported by those multiple meanings, serve as founding tensions in the lives of farmers in Clear Creek and throughout the American Heartland. In some ways, those tensions felt hopeless. Farmers seemed irrevocably caught. And maybe they are. But I suggest that this friction offers possibilities for an applied rhetoric of science: for providing tangible, rhetorically based recommendations to conservation staff.

In Clear Creek, I was able to suggest to conservation staff that they consider the reality that farmers, at least the farmers with whom I spoke in the watershed, want to, as so many of them put it, "do the right thing." But the question comes down to defining what that "right thing" is or could be. Farmers and landowners in Clear Creek were born and bred into the Green Revolution. They came to define themselves through the language of Norman Borlaug and Monsanto. They changed their farming operations in light of the new technologies of the 1960s and suffered through the economic turmoil of the 1980s Farm Crisis. They have taken seriously Thomas Jefferson's mandate to prove themselves as God's chosen people: taking responsibility for the health and security of their households and nation and now their increasingly global worlds.

The Green Revolution helped to establish a very particular heroic opportunity for American farmers, one that the residents of the Clear Creek watershed have spent their lives working to embody. But in working to fulfill that role by producing as much as possible on their land, concerns with soil and water quality have taken a back seat. And so, even when highly respected conservation staff approaches Clear Creek farmers and asks them to adopt conservation measures on their property for the sake of the creek, conservation staff is working against a lifetime of rhetorical and ideological baggage that has defined the agricultural hero not as someone who installs a terrace to help prevent erosion, but as someone who farms every available inch of his land for the sake of high yields for a growing global population.

I argued that this must change. I suggested to conservation staff that in order to make conservation a viable option for America's farmers, they needed to create new opportunities for heroism that are consistent with the goals of soil and water quality: reframing conservation as the noble choice without eschewing the very real tensions that farmers and landowners face.

This rhetorical work was illuminative for conservation staff, and it was illuminative for me: forcing me to consider the productive possibilities of tension and the uses of field methods for accessing, theorizing from, and acting on those tensions. My engagement also prompted an ethical connection to the group with whom I researched and worked. It made me empathetic: made me want to find ways to make use of rhetoric's constructive capacities to "ease his [and her and things'] pain," while I also worked to exercise rhetoric's strategic, relational, and ecological dimensions to make changes to farmers' socioeconomic and biophysical conditions.[35]

My interest in consequential intervention, shared by other proponents of applied rhetoric of science, demands a methodology that illuminates the ways competing rhetorics are called on, created, and enacted in everyday life. Here I have suggested that agonistic methodology—rhetorical field methods coupled with *agôn* as both subject matter and methodology— offers a robust path forward for applied rhetoric of science. Field methods place rhetoricians in uncomfortable and productive positions from which to theorize and create. And these uncomfortable paths, and the humility and (post-)critical attunement they can provide, offer incomparable insights for science, for rhetoric, and for praxis.

Notes

1. Alan G. Gross, "The Roles of Rhetoric in the Public Understanding of Science," *Public Understanding of Science* 3, no. 1 (1994): 3–23; Leah Ceccarelli, "To Whom Do We Speak? The Audiences for Scholarship on the Rhetoric of Science and Technology," *Poroi* 9, no. 1 (2013): 7; Carl G. Herndl and Lauren Leigh Cutlip, "'How Can We Act?' A Praxiographical Program for the Rhetoric of Technology, Science, and Medicine," *Poroi* 9, no. 1 (2013): 9.

2. Herndl and Cutlip, "Praxiographical Program."

3. Anna Lowenhaupt Tsing, *Friction: An Ethnography of Global Connection* (Princeton, NJ: Princeton University Press, 2005), 270.

4. My work in the watershed is described in Caroline Gottschalk Druschke, "Watershed as Common-Place: Communicating for Conservation at the Watershed

Scale," *Environmental Communication: A Journal of Nature and Culture* 7, no. 1 (2013): 80–96; Caroline Gottschalk Druschke and Silvia Secchi, "The Impact of Gender on Agricultural Conservation Knowledge and Attitudes in an Iowa Watershed," *Journal of Soil and Water Conservation* 69, no. 2 (2014): 95–106; and Sarah Varble, Silvia Secchi, and Caroline Gottschalk Druschke, "An Examination of Growing Trends in Land Tenure and Conservation Practice Adoption: Results from a Farmer Survey in Iowa," *Environmental Management* 57, no. 2 (2015): 318–30.

5. Gottschalk Druschke, "Watershed as Common-Place."

6. Gottschalk Druschke and Secchi, "Impact of Gender"; Varble, Secchi, and Gottschalk Druschke, "Land Tenure and Conservation Adoption."

7. Debra Hawhee, "Agonism and Arete," *Philosophy and Rhetoric* 35, no. 3 (2002): 186.

8. Jane Bennett, *Vibrant Matter: A Political Ecology of Things* (Durham, NC: Duke University Press, 2009).

9. I explored some of these connections in Gottschalk Druschke, "Watershed as Common-Place."

10. Paul Willis and Mats Trondman, "Manifesto for Ethnography," *Ethnography* 1, no. 1 (2000): 5.

11. Johan Pottier, *Anthropology of Food: The Social Dynamics of Food Security* (Malden: Polity Press, 1999); Tsing, *Friction*.

12. Tsing, *Friction*, x; 270; 5.

13. Ibid.

14. Michael Carrithers, "Why Anthropologists Should Study Rhetoric," *Journal of the Royal Anthropological Institute* 11, no. 3 (2005): 579; Herndl and Cutlip, "Praxiographical Program."

15. Ralph Cintron, "Democracy and Its Limitations," in *The Public Work of Rhetoric: Citizen-Scholar and Civic Engagement*, ed. John M. Ackerman and David J. Coogan (Columbia: University of South Carolina Press, 2010), 110; Sharon Crowley and Debra Hawhee, *Ancient Rhetorics for Contemporary Students*, 3rd ed. (New York: Pearson Longman, 2004); Gottschalk Druschke, "Watershed as Common-Place," 94.

16. For references to God-terms and trump arguments, see Kenneth Burke, *A Grammar of Motives* (Berkeley: University of California Press, 1969); Caroline Gottschalk Druschke, Nadya Pittendrigh, and Diane Chin. "Community-Based Critique: No Walk in the Park," *Reflections: A Journal of Writing, Service-Learning, and Community Literacy* 6 (2007): 151–68. I am indebted to Ralph Cintron for the trump argument idea.

17. Wendell Berry, "Private Property and the Common Wealth," in *Another Turn of the Crank* (Washington, DC: Counterpoint, 1995), 54.

18. Richard Worrell and Michael C. Appleby, "Stewardship of Natural Resources: Definition, Ethical and Practical Aspects," *Journal of Agricultural and Environmental Ethics* 12 (2010): 264.

19. Leah Ceccarelli, "Polysemy: Multiple Meanings in Rhetorical Criticism," *Quarterly Journal of Speech* 84 (1998): 395–415.

20. Robin E. Jensen, "Sexual Polysemy: The Discursive Ground of Talk about Sex and Education in U.S. History," *Communication, Culture & Critique* 1 (2008): 396.

21. "Norman Borlaug-Acceptance Speech," NobelPrize.org, delivered December 10, 1970, http://www.nobelprize.org/nobel_prizes/peace/laureates/1970/borlaug-acceptance.html.

22. Monsanto, accessed December 5, 2009, http://www.monsanto.com (ellipsis in original).

23. "DuPont leader says increasing food production a moral imperative: Both biotech and native traits needed to sustainably feed growing population," Pioneer Seed, released September 8, 2009, http://www.prweb.com/releases/DuPont/FoodProduction/prweb2842924.htm.

24. Tarla Rai Peterson and Cristi C. Horton, "Rooted in the Soil: How Understanding the Perspectives of Landowners Can Enhance the Management of Environmental Disputes," *Quarterly Journal of Speech* 81, no. 2 (1995): 139–66.

25. Peterson and Horton, "Rooted in the Soil," 158–59.

26. Ibid.

27. M. Nils Peterson et al., "Views of Private-land Stewardship Among Latinos on the Texas-Tamaulipas Border," *Environmental Communication: A Journal of Nature and Culture* 4, no. 4 (2005): 407.

28. Peterson and Horton, "Rooted in the Soil."

29. Herndl and Cutlip, "Praxiographical Program."

30. United States Census Bureau. (2009a). Table 344. Land and water area of states and other entities: 2000. 2009 Statistical Abstract: The National Data Book; United States Census Bureau. (2009b). Table 797. Farms—number and acreage by state: 2000 and 2007. 2009 Statistical Abstract: The National Data Book.

31. P. A. Matson et al., "Agricultural Intensification and Ecosystem Properties," *Science* 277 (1997): 504.

32. Richard Cruse et al., "Daily Estimates of Rainfall, Water Runoff, and Soil Erosion in Iowa," *Journal of Soil and Water Conservation* 61, no. 4 (2006): 191–99.

33. Donald Scavia and Joan Iverson Nassauer, "Introduction: Policy Insights from Integrated Assessments and Alternative Futures," in *From the Corn Belt to the Gulf: Societal and Environmental Implications of Alternative Agricultural Futures*, ed. Joan Iverson Nassauer, Mary V. Santelmann, and Donald Scavia, 1–9 (Washington, DC: Resources for the Future, 2007), 1.

34. W. P. Kinsella, *Shoeless Joe* (New York: Houghton Mifflin, 1982), 84.

35. Caroline Gottschalk Druschke and Bridie McGreavy, "Why Rhetoric Matters for Ecology," *Frontiers in Ecology and the Environment* 14, no.1 (2016): 46–52.

2

Historiographic Remembering and Emotional Encounters

Possibilities for Field-Based Rhetorical Research

HEATHER BROOK ADAMS

The expanding questions and methods of rhetorical study encourage scholars to pursue inquiry related to how discourses emerge, circulate, and function within and across moments and spaces, current and historical. My own work engages in one such project. I investigate the rhetorical forces at play during the mid-twentieth century and later that colluded to create a cultural mandate whereby white and unwed pregnant women were systematically shamed, silenced, and urged to deny their identity as mothers. To contribute to an ever-changing map of what rhetoric is and what rhetoric does, particularly in relation to issues of gender, sexuality, and power, I contend that "unwed mother" was an identity that, for some women during midcentury and later, provoked rhetorics of shame that invoked the impure mother as shame-bearer and shame-carrier. The history of unwed pregnancy during this era is marked by poignant rhetorical practices in which families hid their daughters' unwed bodies from the view of friends, neighbors, and even other family members. The culmination of this hiding often resulted in mothers surrendering their "illegitimate" child for adoption in an effort to permanently remove all traces of the pregnancy.

My research, then, explores this part of US women's recent history to gain better understanding about the context from which these arguments and practices of hiding unwed motherhood emerged. This history resides primarily in the memories of those who have lived it, since the erasure of unwed motherhood—in fact, the erasure of unwed mothers themselves through acts of hiding—means that sparse written accounts of this history exist despite the ubiquity of this response to unwed pregnancy among certain groups of women. I also account for why these extreme practices were so widely embraced, since frequently the only explanation offered for this history is "that is just the way things were." Although some memoirs have been written by women who experienced hiding and surrender, these texts do not recount the everyday rhetorics and cultural logics that contributed to the incredible illusion, an intricately coordinated effort, of disappearing an illicit pregnancy. Going to the field has provided me an opportunity to seek out unrecorded narratives by interviewing women to collect memory texts, the reminiscences of memoried experiences and recollections of everyday rhetorics, that have helped me reconstruct "going away" as a fraught process of gendered shaming and rhetorical violence with life-changing implications for many mothers.

In this chapter, I reflect on my experiences with what I have come to call field-based historiography, share the insights I have gleaned from working largely with memory texts, and detail the dispositional and research design adaptations that I have made as a result. I first focus on the considerations for and implications of working at the nexus of historiography and rhetorical memory, particularly when writing rhetorical history makes semipublic memory accessible and (hopefully) understandable to new audiences. Validity of research findings, memories' relationship to temporality, rhetors' dimensionality, and the sociality of memory are aspects of historiographic remembering that have shifted my dispositions and research design. The second half of the essay discusses the implications of historiographic remembering by arguing for greater attention to the emotional and/or felt aspects of field encounters. Situating this focus alongside a methodology of the history of mentalities and more recent work by ethnographer Sarah Pink and rhetorical scholar Jamie Landau, I argue for systematically noting and responding to "intensities," or points of affective or emotional salience, that are experienced during fieldwork. I propose recalcitrance, an attitude of openness toward being corrected, as a framework for replacing a pursuit of historical accuracy with the goal of remaining critically responsive to emotional intensities that may enrich historiographic remembering. Throughout, I draw on my research with unwed mothers to illustrate my evolving methodological awareness and to suggest its implications for my findings.

Historiographic Remembering

Learning about experiences of once-unwed and pregnant women in hiding has led me to investigate mothers' memories as rhetorical texts that I encounter in the field and to consider mothers as rhetors in dynamic relationship with their memories. Part of this meta-focus on rhetorical memory stems from the unique quality of mothers' testimony in relation to *public memory*, or what Jessica Enoch describes as the "vernacular presentation of the past composed specifically for the purposes of the present."[1] Public memory—or memory that, most simply, has in some way "become public,"[2] as Kendall Phillips describes—is a textured site of rhetorical examination. For instance, when taxonimizing public memory that "occurs in several different ways,"[3] Edward S. Casey emphasizes that a memory becomes a public memory when it is "understood right away, without hesitation or interpretation, in its basic signification."[4] This definition helps explain why mothers' memories occupy a convoluted form of "publicness." The general knowledge that young, mostly white, middle-class women "went away" if they became pregnant was shared by peers and adults during what Karen Wilson Buterbaugh refers to as the "Baby Scoop Era," extending from roughly 1945 to the early 1970s.[5] Despite the fact that elaborate secret-keeping strategies were put in place to uphold the ruse explaining a young woman's absence (from school, home, etc.), the practice of hiding unwed mothers—and, by extension, denying the existence of unwed pregnancies—was known to happen. That is, a schoolmate might not know where his or her peer had gone or any of the details of a pregnancy, but "a girl who went away" was code, even if only thought or only spoken in hushed voices, for a girl who "got herself in trouble." Such furtive but otherwise "public" knowledge was infrequently, if ever, acknowledged openly, and young women who "went away" were urged to never speak of their experience and to forever deny their identity as a mother. Given the systematic exclusion of these women's experiences from public memory, the only way I could learn what happened to them as once-unwed mothers was to listen to their stories.

In cases, therefore, when the primary extant "texts" relating bygone practices are the living memories of those who experienced them, what I label historiographic remembering, questions can and should arise as to the nature of these texts and their relationship to research that seeks to heighten both awareness and rhetorical understanding. In other words, focusing on memories as texts warrants exploration of *how* memories are rhetorical and *how* this rhetoricity figures into historiography as a method and product of research. As Phillips claims, a "study of memory" as "largely one of the rhetoric of memories"[6] is not new. Neither is a distinction between memory (Phillips's "multiple, diverse, mutable, and competing accounts of past events") and history (an implied singular and accurate or authentic version of the past).[7] But even as scholars develop theories for understanding memory as rhetorical, there exists a continued need to grapple contextually and methodologically with memories (with all the dynamism they entail) that are encountered during field research, particularly when the research aim is to compose rhetorical history. As Phillips reminds, frequently "hegemonic tendencies" exist that work to "inscribe memories . . . in stone and fix them in seeming immutability."[8] Field-based historiography, the product of historiographic remembering, such that I encountered in conversations with once-unwed mothers, provides one opportunity to consider how memories figure into writing rhetorical history.

Drawing on memories to serve as qualitative data for rhetorical analysis and historiography requires us to expand and challenge our conceptions of validity and historical accuracy or, at any rate, to consider the invaluable historical and experiential meaning nevertheless contained in memories that may not perfectly correspond with accurately recalled detail. For example, my necessary reliance on mothers' recollections as the primary entry point into my research offers both more immediate access to "going away" in terms of experience (e.g., through first-hand accounts) and simultaneously renders the memory texts themselves less temporally proximal and, thus, more "vulnerable" to rhetorical reconstruction (i.e., less "accurate"). The potential "loss" of validity in this type of historiographic work will not be a grave concern to feminist historiographers who recognize the pursuit for objectivity to be wrongheaded, not to mention impossible.[9] When considered for its affordances, field-based historiography can encourage inquiry into the "discursive practices" of memory and "diverse memory work" that enables some public memories to be recognized and trusted—a more useful pursuit than that of validity itself.[10] In light of these considerations, I have tasked myself with being attentive to the kinds of "memory work" I am encountering in the field and also with considering what dispositions and research design choices I can make based on the historiographic remembering I engage.

Mothers' rhetorical and "imperfect" memory texts suggest that a disposition that adopts a fluid orientation toward temporality can behoove an historiographer gathering memory texts from participants. Michelle Ballif asserts that memory brings into view a "haunted temporality" that "summons a historiographical practice that lives on border lines."[11] In relation to my scholarship, these borders include those of the tangible and collectable, on one hand and the re/collected, on the other, as well as the temporal artifact (e.g., the pregnant body) and the (semi) enduring artifact (the memory). Insofar as memory making is a cognitive function, psychology can help us theorize this borderland. Psychologists' notion of "autobiographical remembering" empirically demonstrates that there is a distinction between a "present self that is remembering and the past self that is remembered."[12] Yet a more discursive and culturally minded approach, such as that of psychologist Jens Brockmeier, advocates understanding memory as one portion of an inter-animation between remembering and forgetting that courses through the "modalities of past, present, and future," which, themselves, are "multi-temporal configuration[s] of experience."[13] Brockmeier contends that it is most "productive to conceive of memory as a movement within a cultural discourse that continuously combines and fuses the now and then, the here and there."[14] Thus, by foregrounding mothers' relationships to their personal history as memoried and rhetorical, I lean into the notion that historiography is discursively constructed, recalled, and reconstructed, when told to me during my field-based research.

Another such disposition has involved responding to Enoch's call to approach memory "as a rhetorical act in and of itself," so that we can go on to "explore how rhetors remember and to what uses these memories are put."[15] In terms of my research on unwed motherhood, this has meant not just listening for a story, but taking into account the shape and contours of each story, or the varied ways that mothers-as-rhetors have remembered. Specifically, the women with whom I have spoken have notably varied relationships with these memories prior to their interview with me: some had shared the stories openly, many had shared only with friends, family, and/or in a support group, and several had hardly spoken of their experience to anyone, including a spouse or child. Each memory shared was certainly true for the mother sharing it, although the time lapsed since having gone away, as well as the mothers' various experiences with telling (or not telling) their story to others, are undeniable aspects of these rhetorical and shaped memories. Field-based historiography has, for me, included the experience of sharing physical space with these women and listening to their stories, some which are effortless at this point from being shared so often and others which are delivered more falteringly as distant memories activated in real time. The stories of these stories, then, are still being created by the women who choose to rhetorically reconstruct their memories so that I can listen to them, learn from them, and share them with others, whether this sharing extends mothers' voices further or encourages new stories to be heard. The pastiche of history, memory, story, and affect (the latter which I will discuss more below) present in such field-based scholarship enhances my historiographic research by allowing me to share a richer rhetorical account of the implications of silencing, of silences held, and silences broken.

The mothers I interviewed presented dynamism in their memoried self-representations, drawing upon multiple iterations of the self to recount their experiences; such awareness aids in tracing the dimensionality of participants-as-rhetors. Narrators use memory from the present to recall a past self and to represent their current notion of self, which is surely shaped by the past. More simply, each interview invokes at least two persons, the unwed mother then and the adult woman now, through a single narration. The dissonance between these two selves calls attention to itself in mothers' stories as they grapple with their younger and older senses of being. For example, Deborah, a young unwed mother who went to a maternity home in Manhattan, describes to me the growth that she has experienced by being able to distinguish her present self from her past self: "I know women who have been married for forty years and have never told their husband that they had another child. But they [eventually] did and it turned out to be okay. Because they're, they're still looking at it through those eighteen-year-old eyes. They haven't—because they haven't processed it, they are still back there, then. Being told that—They haven't gone through a critical thinking process. Thinking, so wait a minute, maybe this wasn't so bad. That I was *made* to feel that way." Memory, for Deborah, seems to be a way of accessing a portion of her past that she can now see from a different perspective, one that enables her to narrate her story with a double consciousness.

Such "simultaneous habitation,"[16] as Malea Powell explains, of present and past selves calls attention to the intellectual effort and distance that some once-unwed mothers likely needed to free themselves from the silencing power of rhetorics of shame, a direct contradiction to the assurances they received from social workers, parents, and others who told them they would simply forget about the experience of hiding and giving birth. The double window through memory that Deborah's realization illuminates in the case of unwed mothers is what anthropologist Beoña Aretxaga refers to as the "twin elements of agency and subjection."[17] Young unmarried women who "got pregnant" were positioned as being responsible for conception and thus punished into "making" the often life-altering "decision" to relinquish a child for adoption at a time when they were systematically denied the responsibility/ability to act on their own behalf. And for some women, in Deborah's estimation, subjection has permanently arrested opportunities for agency. Mothers shared their stories with me because, as more than one woman told me, they were ignored, overlooked, and not listened to for so long. But in recalling their experiences, mothers not only recounted a past experience but also demonstrated how contrastive memories, those pulled from various points of their lives, helped to explain how their own sense of identity evolved over time and against the mentalities and experiences of their youth. Memories, in this way, can be studied for how they have "made a difference in people's lives, and how [they have been] enacted on the local and private level."[18]

Finally, realizing the mothers' disparate relationships to their semipublic memories, I situate their stories as rhetorical artifacts that function simultaneously as individual memories and social memories, a dispositional shift that has come to affect my research design. According to Casey, individual memories are those that come from a singular viewpoint and that can provide information, explanation, and perspective.[19] Social memories are shared by groups of individuals with a particular affiliation or proximal relationship, even if the memory is not publicly known.[20] As individual experiences, I have learned much from what mothers have shared with me. But I also have been struck by mothers' frequent claims of not finding much strength or comfort in their shared confinement in maternity homes, where women were typically housed with others in the same circumstance. I repeatedly heard from mothers that their experience of hiding was one of "loneliness" and "isolation." Their memories of hiding, then, do not function as "collective episodic memory," which is the type of recollection of a group experience that is spatially and temporally contextualized and that, significantly, contributes to the group's identity.[21] Nevertheless, some mothers shared with me their experience of reading Ann Fessler's *The Girls Who Went Away: The Hidden History of Women Who Surrendered Children for Adoption in the Decades before "Roe v. Wade"* or participating in support groups with other mothers in recent years as ways of coming to terms with these practices of hiding and surrendering and dealing with mixed feelings of frustration, regret, anger, and helplessness at their own part in this history.

In terms of research design, this awareness encouraged me to rethink my practice of requesting individual interviews, a default that, I realized, might replicate the isolating experience of "going away" by oneself and in secret, even if a one-on-one interview in a mother's home offered the value of safety and discretion. After being invited to attend one support group meeting for such mothers, I initially considered a focus-group style conversation to be an acceptable convenience for both participants and me, since we would already be in a safe and discreet location (the regular support group meeting site) and given that the participants knew one another and had shared at least some memories with one another. In this first group session, mothers and I were seated in a circle. I asked each participant to share her story, and each mother spoke in turn, moving around the circle. This format worked well and encouraged me to ask the additional members of the same support group to reconvene later for additional conversation. In this situation, I asked mothers to share their individual stories but also asked questions that were open for more general discussion, such as "What role did shame play in your experience of going away?" The group setting activates what Casey refers to as one key location of individual memory: the "intersubjective nexus that is at once social and collective, cultural and public."[22] Choosing to forsake individual interviews for group conversations has historically presented research concerns about validity given the potential for group think.[23] Asking mothers to embrace an opportunity for shared historiographic remembering, however, encourages researchers to spend less energy worrying about the "distortions" of remembering and more on enabling an accretive capacity for linkages, recall triggers, and, perhaps most importantly, awareness that stems from intersubjective experience. Such a design celebrates what Bradford Vivian refers to as "acts of recollection": a conception of memory that is valuable *because* of and not in spite of the fact that memories "invariably transform the nature of memory"; that "memory's changing incitements and purposes ensure that we remember in different ways, even if we remember the same event"; and that this remembering can function "in the service of diverse social interests."[24]

In sum, field-based rhetorical work aligns with conceptual and methodological perspectives related to public memory studies while also encouraging nimble and reflective deployment of these perspectives when writing field-based rhetorical history. Focusing on memory texts as rhetorical offers a valuable meta-exploration of historiographic remembering while also helping to bring memories into wider public circulation.

Intensity, Emotional Encounters, and Recalcitrance in the Field

The second way in which my field encounters have shaped my thinking about the rhetorical memories mothers shared involves the significant and varied roles that sensory experience plays in the interviews and in the recall of memory itself. This sensory focus has emerged through my engagement with memory texts as they have been shared with me in one effort (i.e., via my scholarship) to make them more public and understood contextually and collectively.[25] Actively contributing to the public circulation of memories renders an historiographer complicit in a shared assumption that public memory is, as Carole Blair, Greg Dickinson, and Brian L. Ott describe, "animated by affect," because more than standing as historical record, public memory "embraces events, people, objects, and places that it deems worthy of preservation, based on some kind of emotional attachment."[26] It remains my responsibility as a field-based historiographer who relies heavily on memory texts, then, to explore the sensory (e.g., affective, emotional, felt)[27] dimensions of this work. Here, I borrow from Pink's notion of using the senses as a "route to knowledge"[28] and exploring sensory "sites of embodied knowing" that are part of field encounters.[29] While the preceding section of this essay aligns with Pink's call for researchers to seek the "meanings and nature of the memories that research participants recount, enact, define or reflect on for researchers,"[30] in this section, my focus shifts to consider how the sensory aspect of memory texts can complicate methodologies related to historiographic remembering.

I came slowly into the practice of noticing and attending to the sensory aspects of my research, a gradual shift that exemplifies Pink's assertion that analyzing the "sensorial and emotional dimensions" of qualitative research is most frequently taken up in "intuitive, messy and serendipitous" ways.[31] As noted above, early in my research, having read what little I could find *about* once-unwed mothers, I decided to talk *with* them and ask them to help me, someone much closer in age to their children, understand the cultural logics of a past era. I went into my earliest interviews with a schedule of questions concerning the contours of the experience of going away, the space of the maternity home, the conversations with other mothers and with family members, and so forth. Most often, however, I found myself listening to stories punctuated by the shame of unwed pregnancy, the loss of a child relinquished for adoption, and the ongoing ebb and flow of feelings, memories, and experiences that carried forward from a long-ago, but never forgotten, pregnancy. Thus, rather than collecting data in the way that I had originally imagined, a practice that I now recognize as mostly being in service of pursuing historical accuracy, I found myself listening intently and interjecting at key moments to ask for clarification that would help me more fully understand the rhetorical context of the moment invoked. For instance, I learned to ask mothers about the euphemistic expressions that once performed discursive compression and elision: "went away," "just the way things were," "bad girls," "shameful." I had to slow down the participants and ask them to help me unpack these concepts, to articulate the assumptions encased in such phrases.

Through this process of listening to stories in order to discern cultural logics, the centrality of rhetorics of shame in this history became apparent. Shame is an emotion and sensation that winds through rhetorical practices configured through language, within space, and on bodies in informal (e.g., kinship) and formal (e.g., legal, institutional) networks. Because hiding an unwed pregnancy was a practice meant to erase the shame of its illicitness, to expunge the pregnancy and the resultant baby altogether, I did not encounter shame as the rhetorical lynchpin of these histories until I sat with mothers, listened to them, and asked questions of them when they tried to articulate their lack of autonomy as unmarried, pregnant teenagers. On a practical level, references to shame were recurring discursive *topoi* in my interviews, overwhelmingly present in all but one of these conversations. For example, for Deborah, shame was felt and internalized, heightening her sense of powerlessness based on the comments she heard from parents and adults at the maternity home that interpolated her as a non-mother: "Um, there was so much shame in that you are not good enough—you're not good enough to be a mother. And how would you—well, how dare you bring a baby into this? You know, there was no, there was no celebration of life—that this was a new life. It was, 'This is, this is a huge shame.' And I just felt that, well, um, they all knew better than I did, you know?" Deborah's comments move back, through memory, to her experience of shame while pregnant, providing a memory text that helps to reconstruct this history from her lived experience.

Shame also presented itself as a sensation-rich, often nondiscursive rhetorical force (rather than a logical argument) in multiple participants' experiences. I needed to pay attention to shame as it was expressed in mothers' stories, accounting for its sundry appearances during these conversations. Although participants *named* shame as an emotion that they felt, and that as "errant" women they were ostensibly supposed to feel, shame was expressed in other ways, too: the meaningful silences some participants used to gather their thoughts, the pain (often manifesting in tears) that these memories inflicted upon mothers who shared them, and the recollection, often vocal reenactment, of biting insults such as being called a "slut" by a loved one. I found myself also listening for clues as to how shame was enacted in everyday practices. One such example is the stories I heard from several mothers about how postcards and letters were routed through a maternity home other than the one they were living in so that the postal cancelation on the mail would be from the "right" city, the city they were allegedly living in or visiting. This type of elaborate secret-keeping strategy comprises a complex if indirect type of rhetorical action that was premised on the shame of an unwed pregnancy. Hearing about mothers' shame provided a salience I could not deny or ignore, adding a dimensionality to these "data" that I would have never grasped if not in the mothers' presence.

Historiographically, attention to remembered emotional states and presentation of sensation through shared memories aligns with a "history of mentalities" approach to learning about the past. Emerging from twentieth-century French historians and most prominently embraced by Michel Foucault, histories of mentalities examine "the attitudes of ordinary people toward everyday life" through investigations of "the psychological realities underpinning human conceptions of intimate relationships, basic habits of mind, and attitudes toward the elemental passages of life."[32] Historians have theorized this approach without articulating a precise method, although a culture of mentality is thought to be located by, as Robert Mandrou describes, "reconstructing the patterns of behavior, expressive forms and modes of silence into which worldviews and collective sensibilities are translated."[33] A history of mentalities, then, identifies deep mental and "affect structures" that are resistant to change that can be indexed through discourse as well as, I would argue, extra-discursive communication.[34] Such histories can enable rhetorical scholars to recover and rearticulate a synchronic value system, the mentalities that, as a cultural logic, made perfect sense at a moment in time. In my experience, these mentalities can be discerned through conversation with those who lived during that time, conversation that, through participants' stories and movement forward and back through memoried time, provides a diachronic perspective. For rhetorical scholars, mentalities can help to identify the motivations and pieties that enable identification and persuasion, a useful tool when trying to recontextualize epistemologies and arguments that seem foreign, even if they reside in the recent past.[35]

Opening oneself more fully to these "context[s] of interaction" affords an opportunity to pivot away from pursuit of historical "truth" to what Jenny Edbauer refers to as "*affective ecologies* that recontextualiz[e] rhetorics in their temporal, historical, and lived fluxes."[36] My time with mothers led me to reflect upon how their physical and embodied sharing (through laughter, tears, silence, etc.) were part of the stories they told, both individually and, later, in the group settings that I mentioned above. In terms of my research, affective ecologies emerged most vividly when mothers spoke about their experiences with rhetorics of shame, the component of their stories that has most fully helped me identify the way that memories of the past connect to ongoing rhetorical practices and constructions of the self that the mothers inhabit today. My methodological adaptations, which stemmed in large part from my emerging realization of the function sensation held in my interactions with participants, provide an exigence for suggesting more proactive and sensory-responsive methods for fieldwork and analysis. The remainder of this essay conceptualizes one such strategy, while also acknowledging that true engagement with affect precludes prescriptive methods and design.[37]

Refiguring exchanges with participants as something other than opportunities to gather and record data can enhance the possibilities for sensory-rich exchanges. Here, Pink's proposal to see an interview as an "emplaced" social encounter and "multisensory event" is instructive, as she emphasizes the dialogic quality of such an event, the opportunity to attend to materiality and place during the experience, and the benefits of mutual listening between participant and researcher.[38] I extend this frame by suggesting that during and after such events, scholars might actively notice and note the sensory qualities of an exchange, what I would call "intensities," that are perceptible (at least to the researcher), no matter their shape or potential signification. Naming these sensory happenings "intensities" encompasses affect ("nonconscious," and "embodied" reactions that do not signify and that are not "semantically or semiotically ordered," as Brian Massumi describes[39]), and/or emotions that are symbolic and thus more likely fold into narratives and sensory logics. Although I reflected personally on the emotional weight of my interviews after I met with these mothers, I lacked the awareness and tools necessary to systematically examine the intensities involved in these exchanges. Through inductive coding, I identified references to shame but ultimately lacked an orientation and framework for more dimensional, affect-inclusive analysis. What deeper exposure to cultural logics might I have been able to appreciate if I were poised to respond to intensities present during an interview? And, what responses might be most appropriate, ethical, and useful in the context of rhetorical research? For instance, I might have noted intensities as such in my field notes, which likely would have helped me couple my analysis of discursive *explanations* of shame with nondiscursive moments when the residue of shame resonated but did not result in a specific verbalization. My later group conversations would have greatly benefitted from this approach, given the increased number of intensities present when mothers were speaking with and to one another, not just with me, thus increasing the intersubjective quality of their memory sharing. During my interviews, I could have taken a different approach when experiencing signals of intensity from others or even my own embodied response (e.g., the sense of dread I felt, manifest on the surface of my skin, when listening to a mother's experience). I chose to remain quiet during the most emotional moments as a sign of respect and to allow participants to set the pace of resuming a discussion. While I do not advocate pressuring those who are experiencing the trauma of remembering, in such instances I could have replaced my "pause-and-resume" approach by, when seemingly appropriate, inviting a participant to reflect on such intensity, thus enabling a further exploration of it rather than figuring it as something to be moved beyond.

These considerations echo Jamie Landau's field method of "feeling rhetorical criticism," which calls for "analyzing emotion words captured by rhetorical critics and analyzing affective bodily sensations that are felt by rhetorical critics but for which they struggle linguistically."[40] It also builds on Frank Farmer and Margaret M. Strain's call to capture silences in oral history narratives to develop a "repertoire of discernments" that can help interpret participants' various silences in meaningful ways.[41] An intensity-focused approach supplements these contributions to rhetorical study and responds to an emerging suite of interdisciplinary methods for sensory-attuned field methods.[42] It is also applicable given the temporal flux inherent in historiography primarily reliant on memory texts. Massumi theorizes intensity as being "associated with nonlinear processes," such as "resonation and feedback which momentarily suspend the linear progress of the narrative present from past to future."[43] Thus, by more fully and intentionally minding intensity in the interview event, a practitioner of field-based historiography can assume a ready stance for "mutation" that comes with the "nomadic" quality of remembering,[44] which infrequently follows chronology or other rational organizational structures.

Engaging with affective intensities encountered during fieldwork can perform a sort of recalcitrance, Kenneth Burke's notion of processes of resistance or "revisions" that complicate, or correct, one's view on reality.[45] According to Lawrence J. Prelli, Floyd D. Anderson, and Matthew T. Althouse, rhetorical critics can reveal "zones of recalcitrance" by enacting a "dialectic that brings under-stressed or muted perspectives into contact with dominant, over-stressed, or insular points of view."[46] Such recalcitrance can occur in the process of engaging with participants when such zones "at least partially, open the universe of discourse by enabling expression of a wider range of voices that—through revising, reshaping, rephrasing, and correcting—could ultimately yield a more mature, more encompassing, and less reductive orientation toward a situation."[47] For the purposes of this essay, recalcitrance names a strategy for replacing a search for historical correctness with an openness toward a fuller multisensory experience, a rhetorical emplacement, that yields to the intensities of such exchange. A recalcitrant disposition can afford greater understanding as well as deeper insight into mentalities as sites of power that hold rhetorical significance. One example from an interview illustrates my point. In telling me her story, Fran recounted that she went to a maternity home in 1959 to receive medical care for her unborn child and for herself, care that she was prepared to pay for with money she had earned from a job she held during summer breaks from college. "I never walked through that door [of the maternity home] wanting to put my child up for adoption. I walked through that door because I wanted medical care," Fran explained. Her statement aligns closely with sentiments delivered by Judi Dench in her portrayal of the once-unwed mother Philomena Lee in the film *Philomena*: "I did not abandon my child. He was taken from me." Both Fran's commentary and *Philomena's* filmic, based-on-a-true-story depiction of an Irish unwed mother function to correct audiences' likely assumption that white unwed mothers of the 1950s and later willingly *chose* to surrender their child for adoption. Literally hearing the resonance of these two iterations—as well as Fran's emphatic, punctuated, and purposeful delivery of the words, "I wanted medical care," which I can still hear her speaking to me—helped me grasp the urgency of this corrective move.[48] This moment, what I now would label an intensity, impressed upon me the centrality of this part of Fran's story to her larger understanding of her experience as an unwed mother. Many of the mothers with whom I spoke emphasized the problematic language of "choice" and "giving up" a child for adoption, but my interaction with Fran helped me *feel* how important it was to draw attention to the false narrative of agency and situational control that the mothers simply did not experience. Recalcitrance helped to guide me back through my previous interview materials to draw connections around this point of salience.

Conclusion

In his contribution to *Framing Public Memory*, Charles E. Scott reminds us that "there is no available, original reality called cultural or public memory toward which we can make our way as though toward a timeless essence."[49] This essay has attempted to take seriously such a claim and to overlay it with considerations of rhetorical remembering and the emotional encounters that can take place when a researcher pursues field-based historiography. Memory is a knotty site of rhetorical energy, signification, and affective significance. Such richness provides a valuable site for theorizing the nature of rhetorical history that is particularly reliant on memory but also urges historiographers to train their gaze not only on the history that they are writing, but also on their own dispositions and practices in light of this complexity.

Notes

I would like to thank editors Candice Rai and Caroline Gottschalk Druschke for their invaluable and ongoing support of this project, which has benefitted greatly from their intellectual labor as well as the feedback of two anonymous reviewers. Additional thanks to Clare Dannenberg and to Jennifer Mallette for their ideas and support. My thinking about sensory rhetorics, memory, and fieldwork was also deepened by conversations at the 2015 Rhetoric Society of America Summer Institute seminar on "Rhetoric and Sensation" led by Debra Hawhee and Vanessa Beasley. I am also grateful to interview participants who shared their stories of unwed pregnancy with me.

1. Jessica Enoch, "Releasing Hold: Feminist Historiography without the Tradition," in *Theorizing Histories of Rhetoric*, ed. Michelle Baliff (Carbondale: Southern Illinois University Press, 2013), 62.

2. Kendall R. Phillips, "Introduction," in *Framing Public Memory*, ed. Kendall R. Phillips (Tuscaloosa: University of Alabama Press, 2004), 3.

3. Edward S. Casey, "Public Memory in Place and Time," in *Framing Public*

Memory, ed. Kendall R. Phillips (Tuscaloosa: University of Alabama Press, 2004), 17.

4. Ibid.

5. "What Was the 'Baby Scoop Era'?" The Baby Scoop Era Research Initiative, accessed 18 May 2017, http://babyscoopera.com.

6. Phillips, "Introduction," 2.

7. Ibid. See also Carole Blair, Greg Dickinson, and Brian L. Ott, "Introduction: Rhetoric/Memory/Place," in *Places of Public Memory: The Rhetoric of Museums and Memorials* ed. Greg Dickinson, Carole Blair, and Brian L. Ott (Tuscaloosa: University of Alabama Press, 2010), 8–9.

8. Phillips, "Introduction," 10.

9. Cheryl Glenn, *Rhetoric Retold: Regendering the Tradition from Antiquity Through the Renaissance* (Carbondale: Southern Illinois University Press, 1997), 6–8.

10. Bradford Vivian, "'A Timeless Now': Memory and Repetition," in *Framing Public Memory*, ed. Kendall R. Phillips (Tuscaloosa: University of Alabama Press, 2004), 207.

11. Michelle Ballif, "Historiography as Hauntology: Paranormal Investigations into the History of Rhetoric," in *Theorizing Histories of Rhetoric*, ed. Michelle Ballif (Carbondale: Southern Illinois University Press, 2013), 149.

12. Lisa K. Libby and Richard P. Eibach, "Looking Back in Time: Self-Concept Change Affects Visual Perspective in Autobiographical Memory," *Journal of Personality and Social Psychology* 82 (2002): 177.

13. Jens Brockmeier, "Remembering and Forgetting: Narrative as Cultural Memory," *Culture and Psychology* 8 (2002): 21.

14. Brockmeier, "Remembering," 21.

15. Enoch, "Releasing," 65.

16. Malea Powell, "Rhetorics of Survivance: How American Indians Use Writing," *College Composition and Communication* 53 (2002): 426.

17. Beoña Aretxaga, "Strip-Searching of Women in Northern Ireland," in *History in Person: Enduring Struggles, Contentious Practice, Intimate Identities*, ed. Dorothy Holland and Jean Lave (Santa Fe, NM: School of American Research Press, 2001), 40–41.

18. Alon Confino, "Collective Memory and Cultural History: Problems of Method," *The American Historical Review* 102 (1997): 1394.

19. Casey, "Public Memory," 20–21.

20. Ibid., 21–22. A third category of public memory, collective memory, involves a shared and distributed experience not dependent on relationship, such disparate people's ability to remember where they were or what they were doing at the time of some national tragedy. See Casey, "Public Memory," 23–24.

21. David Manier and William Hirst, "A Cognitive Taxonomy of Collective Memories," in *Cultural Memory Studies: An International and Interdisciplinary Handbook*,

ed. Astrid Erll and Ansgar Nünning (Berlin: Walter de Gruyter, 2008), 257.

22. Casey, "Public Memory," 21.

23. Jimmie Manning and Adrianne Kunkel, *Researching Interpersonal Relationships* (Los Angeles: SAGE, 2014), 76–77.

24. Vivian, "Timeless Now," 190.

25. My thinking about the relationship between memory and rhetoric relies on the assertion that one defining aspect of rhetoric is its publicness and that contemporary memory studies are defined by an investigation of memory as collective. See, Blair, Dickinson, and Ott, "Introduction," 2–3, 5.

26. Ibid., 7.

27. As I share in my discussion of "intensity," I find definitions of affect (nonsymbolic), emotion (symbolic), and feeling/sensation (perception) generative as categories but not as mutually exclusive as Jamie Landau does. See, Jamie Landau, "Feeling Rhetorical Critics: Another Affective-Emotional Field Method for Rhetorical Studies," in *Text + Field: Innovations in Rhetorical Method*, ed. Sara L. McKinnon, Robert Asen, Karma R. Chávez, and Robert Glenn. (University Park: Penn State University Press, 2016), 76.

28. Sarah Pink, *Doing Sensory Ethnography*, 2nd ed. (Los Angeles: SAGE, 2015), xiv.

29. Ibid., 13.

30. Ibid., 44.

31. Ibid., 141.

32. Patrick H. Hutton, "The History of Mentalities: The New Map of Cultural History," *History and Theory* 20 (1981): 237.

33. Mandrou, qtd. in Confino, "Collective Memory," 1389.

34. Hutton, "History of Mentalities," 238–40, 248, 252.

35. I rely on Burke's (1941) notion of motivation and pieties. Pieties refers to a desire to uphold associations among distinct things that collectively form a whole. In Burke's words, recognizing a piety refers to having "the sense of what properly goes with what." See, Kenneth Burke, *Permanence and Change: An Anatomy of Purpose*, 3rd ed. (Berkeley: University of California Press, 1941), 74.

36. Jenny Edbauer, "Unframing Models of Public Distribution: From Rhetorical Situation to Rhetorical Ecologies," *Rhetoric Society Quarterly* 35 (2005): 9.

37. Landau, "Feeling Rhetorical Critics," 77; Pink, *Doing Sensory Ethnography*, 5.

38. Pink, *Doing Sensory Ethnography*, 73.

39. Brian Massumi, "The Autonomy of Affect," *Cultural Critique* 31 (1995): 85.

40. Landau, "Feeling Rhetorical Critics," 77–78.

41. Frank Farmer and Margaret M. Strain, "A Repertoire of Discernments: Hearing the Unsaid in Oral History Narratives," in *Silence and Listening as Rhetorical Arts*, ed., Cheryl Glenn and Krista Ratcliffe (Carbondale: Southern Illinois University Press, 2011), 232.

42. Pink, *Doing Sensory Ethnography*, xi–xiii.

43. Massumi, "The Autonomy of Affect," 86.

44. Vivian, "Timeless Now," 201.

45. Burke, *Permanence and Change*, 255–61.

46. Lawrence J. Prelli, Floyd D. Anderson, and Matthew T. Althouse. "Kenneth Burke on Recalcitrance," *Rhetoric Society Quarterly* 41 (2011): 116–17.

47. Prelli, Anderson, and Althouse, "Kenneth Burke," 117.

48. To listen to a published audio version of Fran's story, see Heather B. Adams, "The Story of Fran and Priscilla: An Oral History of Unwed Motherhood," *Peitho* 18, no. 1 (2015): n.p.

49. Charles E. Scott, "The Appearance of Public Memory," in *Framing Public Memory*, ed. Kendall R. Phillips (Tuscaloosa: University of Alabama Press, 2004), 151.

3

What's a Farm?

The Languages of Space and Place

CARL G. HERNDL, SARAH BETH HOPTON, LAUREN CUTLIP,
ELENA YU POLUSH, RICK CRUSE, AND MACK SHELLEY

> This puzzle can be stated very simply: the Greeks made one invention too
> many! They invented both democracy and mathematical demonstration.
> . . . We are still struggling, in our "mad cow times," with this same quan-
> dary, how to have science *and* democracy together.
> —Bruno Latour, *Pandora's Hope*

Early in this century, scholars across the humanities, social sciences, and
biophysical sciences sought ways to bring citizens and scientists together
to make better science, technology, and environmental policy. Critics such
as Harry Collins and Robert Evans articulate a theory of experience-based
expertise to better manage citizen participation in science and technology policy. Latour calls for a materialist project that moves away from critique and brings people and things together to compose a better world in
the face of impending ecocide. Herbert Simons calls for a "reconstructive
rhetoric" that moves beyond critique toward a rhetorical practice of judgment and collective action.[1] Meanwhile, in science studies, planning, medicine, and sustainable development, participatory risk assessment and technology development that brings diverse people together to develop policy
are well-established practices.[2]

Despite these calls for citizen participation, we still struggle, as Latour
says in the epigraph, to "have science *and* democracy together."[3] As climate

change and the necessity for mitigation and adaptation become increasingly pressing, the need for citizen participation only becomes more urgent. But integrating the expertise of citizens with those of technical experts is not easy. Better understanding of the rhetorical challenges present when citizens participate in the making of technology or environmental policy is key for well-intentioned researchers and activists hoping to avoid the traditional technocratic, top-down model of decision making. This chapter responds to programmatic statements by Latour, Collins and Evans, and Simmons by exploring the rhetorical activity that arises when citizens and scientists alike contribute to the making of science and environmental policy. Our goal is to better understand the rhetorical dynamics that can make such collaborations difficult when, in our case, scientists and farmers talk about farms as two very different things.

Despite the emphasis in science studies, applied science, medicine, and sustainability on citizen participation in decision making, very little of this work considers how rhetoric might contribute to more democratic science and technology development. Many studies categorize the range of mechanisms for citizen participation and evaluate participatory mechanisms on a variety of procedural and outcome-based criteria.[4] While the consensus is that mechanisms that facilitate dialogic communication—such as citizen juries, planning cells, and focus groups—are better, these studies do not examine the talk involved in dialogic participation. Matthew Harvey, Robert Futrell, and Gail Davies are rare voices that call for a more careful analysis of the role of language in citizen science and participatory processes.[5]

This conjunction of disciplinary interests in citizen participation and expertise presents a unique opportunity for rhetoric. While scholars in science studies have called for participatory mechanisms but overlooked the role of language, rhetorical scholars have argued with renewed vigor that rhetoric should re-engage with the public sphere and with scientific activity.[6] In this chapter, we argue that rhetorical research can move this interdisciplinary effort forward by exploring the specifically rhetorical aspects of citizen participation in science policy. As S. Scott Graham et al. argue, the "long-standing problem of inclusion may be long-standing because the focus has been so exclusively on how to get more (or the right) people to the table. In the absence of an attendant focus on procedures after arrival, the democratization of STEM policy decision making may fail."[7] As Graham et al. suggest, we need to focus on what happens after the right participants arrive for the STEM policy discussion.

This chapter presents a case study of a rapid technology assessment project focused on cellulosic biofuel that examines what happens once the participants arrive at the table. While business has made ethanol from corn grain for some time, the technology to make ethanol from the cellulosic material in woody plants such as corn stalks is emergent. Unfortunately, the cellulosic ethanol industry is rapidly developing to meet federal renewable fuel guidelines before careful, long-term scientific studies can be conducted. As such, our research team conducted workshops with scientists and farmers to gather and analyze what these diverse experts know about the emerging technology and make that knowledge available to policy makers.

We analyze the transcripts of three rapid technology assessment workshops, one with scientists and engineers, two with farmers. Using both qualitative analysis as well as semantic network analysis (SNA), we make two interrelated arguments. First, integrating the local knowledge of non-credentialed experts with that of credentialed experts is complicated by specific rhetorical and discursive differences. As both Gerard A. Hauser and Robert Danisch argue, the vernacular necessary for participation in emergent publics conflicts with the dominant technical discourse.[8] Our analysis of workshop transcripts identifies specific patterns of discursive differences, interpreting them as issues of space and place. Drawing on Latour, Annemarie Mol, and Andrew Pickering, we suggest that the problem is not that scientists and farmers have different perspectives on the same environment and therefore produce competing epistemic claims, but that their material practices enact different farms. Thus, integrating the knowledge of the two groups is not a matter of evaluating and combining two distinct perspectives, but of calibrating the enactment of two different farms that emerge from the everyday material practices of distinct lifeworlds.

Our second claim is methodological. Given the rhetorical complexity of citizen participation, we suggest that SNA, which uses network displays to visualize relationships between concepts, is a powerful addition to our analytic repertoire that helps us better represent and investigate rhetorical knowledge. For example, SNA can represent a thematic analysis of the technology assessment workshop with one group of farmers in the study (figure 3.1), illustrating a relationship between the prominence of terminology and the "context" of related terms through node size and proximity to other terms. The larger the node, the more times the word occurs in the text, demonstrating its importance or salience.

Rhetorical scholars have begun to use techniques for managing big data,

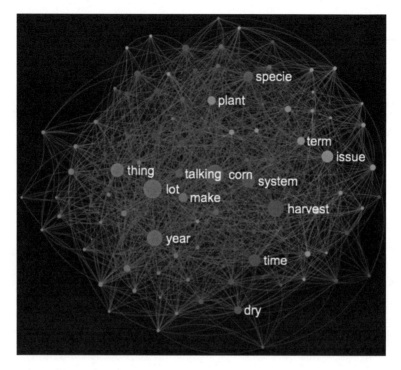

Fig. 3.1. Network graph using Textexture to visualize transcripts of the farmers' group 1 discourse.

but the utility of this methodology remains underdeveloped.[9] Our case study demonstrates that SNA can "map" the rhetorical practices of two or more groups, identifying similarities and differences in discourses. While our corpus is small, we argue that SNA can be integrated with traditional qualitative methods in ways that confirm and extend qualitative findings. Further, since SNA can manage vast data sets, it provides rhetorical studies a powerful new tool for analysis.

The Case Study: The Matrix Project

In the first decade of this century, the ethanol industry emerged as an alternate fuel source that supplemented traditional fossil fuels. This development was not without controversy.[10] As biofuels developed, researchers and policy makers considered cellulosic biofuels an alternative to ethanol derived from corn grain. Cellulosic biofuel is made by processing materials containing high concentrations of cellulose, roughly the woody material in corn stalks, wheat straw, perennial grasses and trees. In 2009, federal policy mandated that renewable fuels contribute thirty-six billion gallons to the national fuel supply by 2022. Of this, 21 billion gallons were to be derived from cellulosic sources but, as of 2011, there were few commercial facilities producing cellulosic biofuels.[11] The cellulosic biofuel industry would have to emerge very quickly to meet federal mandates, presenting a significant challenge and an opportunity for researchers, farmers, policy makers, and citizens. In the Midwest, interest in cellulosic biofuel was spurred by the Department of Energy's "Billion-Ton Report" in 2005, which estimated that a billion tons of cellulosic stem and leaf plant materials were unused annually, most from corn stover (stalks and leaves left after corn grain harvest). While offering an untapped source of biomass for conversion to biofuels, the material presented a challenge. Removing biomass such as corn stover, storing it, transporting it, and converting it to biofuels could have major impacts on soil and water resources, communities, rural infrastructure, and farmers.[12] The "matrix" project, the object of our analysis here, emerged as a response to this situation.

The rapid development of the cellulosic biofuel industry required that policy makers and industry planners make decisions before rigorous scientific research to assess long-term environmental and social consequences could be completed. It can take a decade or more to produce the agroecological data necessary to evaluate the consequences of removing corn stover.[13] By the time data are collected and analyzed, the industry would already exist. One research approach for guiding industry development in such situations is the "rapid assessment" project, which draws on distributed expertise to gather the best extant knowledge about an emerging issue to guide decisions that must be made without scientific consensus. These "participatory assessment" projects sometimes include a range of stakeholders.[14]

The rapid technology assessment project designed by our research team brought together a group of fourteen scientists with expertise in various aspects of cellulosic biofuel production, as well as two groups of Iowa farmers who had what Collins and Evans call "non-credentialed" expertise. To gather the expert opinion of these three groups, we conducted three day-long workshops: one with the scientists and one with each of the two groups of farmers. These workshops were organized by a research instrument we called the "system configuration matrix" (figure 3.2), hence the nickname of the project. The matrix combines two pairs of variables (centralized vs. distributed facilities and single input vs. multiple input processing) to present four potential structures for the emerging cellulosic biofuel industry. Broadly, cellulosic biofuels can be produced in large centralized facilities or in smaller facilities distributed across the landscape and closer to the source of "feedstock" that would be processed into ethanol. The second variable is whether the production facility processes only corn stover as a feedstock or whether it can process a range of cellulosic materials from a variety of plants. Thus, the industry can be built around large centralized facilities that process only corn stover, large centralized facilities that process several feedstocks, smaller facilities distributed across the landscape but which process only corn stover, or, finally, smaller distributed facilities that process a range of cellulosic feedstocks. The thirteen criteria or metrics that make the rows of the matrix are important measures of the sustainability of each potential industry configuration. For example, if a potential industry configuration such as the centralized, single feedstock option caused significant soil erosion, that configuration is probably not sustainable over time.

The workshop for "credentialed experts" included fourteen researchers among them chemical engineers, agricultural economists, wildlife specialists, and so forth. Each participant was a university researcher and a specialist in one of the evaluation criteria. There were six farmers in the first farmer workshop and eight farmers in the second farmer workshop.[15] These farmers represented farming operations ranging from small, two hundred-acre farms, to large operations that rented significant tracts of land. The farmers also represented significant geographic distribution, coming from all over central Iowa. Most importantly, all the farmers had extensive, often lifelong, farming experience. After a brief introduction by the research team, workshop discussions were structured by the matrix.[16] In the scientists' workshop, discussion of each metric (e.g., soil erosion, rural development, wildlife habitat) was led by participants with expertise in that specific criteria. After each specialist identified the key issues, there was an open group discussion. Then participants were asked to fill out the matrix for that metric, "voting" whether each of the four potential configurations was likely to be sustainable in terms of that criteria.

The workshops with the farmers were similarly structured by the matrix. The farmers discussed each potential industry configuration and how that structure might affect their farms and the individual evaluation criteria. For example, farmers used their experience and their familiarity with their own farms to discuss whether soil erosion would be better or worse if the industry relied on only corn stover or an industry that processed multiple kinds of feedstocks. Unlike in the scientist workshop, there were no presentations by specialized experts. Rather, farmers contributed as they felt comfortable or

Fig. 3.2. The Matrix: Biorenewable System Evaluation Worksheet. Participants were given the following instructions: "For each cell in the worksheet, please mark 'red' (black) if a configuration 'suggests major challenges will likely occur'; 'yellow' (light grey) if a configuration 'suggests a caution is advised or if insufficient information is available to draw a reasonable conclusion'; 'green' (medium gray) if the configuration 'currently offers or will likely offer a favorable opportunity,' and 'blank' if 'no opinion or not applicable for you.' Your responses will remain anonymous and no identifying information will be used when analyzing and reporting results. Thank you for sharing your views."

Functionality Metric	System Configuration				
	Centralized Processing		Distributed Processing		
	Single sp (corn)	Multiple sp.	Single Sp. (corn)	Multiple Sp.	
Will lead to **high and stable levels of feedstock production.**					
Development of required and producer acceptable **feedstock conversion** technology is likely.					
Transportation requirements can be met and will be acceptable to producers and the industry.					
Labor needs for feedstock harvest and processing can be met.					
Required **feedstock** storage is reasonable, manageable and acceptable.					
A favorable and acceptable **energy balance** is likely.					
A favorable and acceptable **carbon balance** is likely.					
Farm net income will benefit.					
Water quality will be affected favorably.					
Soil erosion will be affected favorably.					
Soil carbon sequestration will be affected favorably.					
Wildlife habitat will be affected favorably.					
Rural development will be affected favorably.					

when they had questions. And, unlike the scientist workshop, the farmers asked the lead researcher technical questions to which he offered succinct responses.[17] Each workshop was digitally recorded and later transcribed. The transcripts of these workshops comprise the data for the rhetorical and discursive analysis of this chapter.

Qualitative Analysis of the Matrix Transcripts

This chapter is motivated by our concern for what was left unrepresented within statistical and thematic analysis about celluslosic ethanol policy from an earlier publication of this research,[18] which involved interpreting the differences between the farmers' judgments and those of the scientists represented by the matrix.[19] While the statistical analysis in that earlier publication helped identify significant differences in how the farmers and scientists evaluated the sustainability of elements of the matrix, and the thematic analysis helped explain how the farmers and the scientists understood the problems involved in cellulosic biofuel production, we were not able to fully explain why they disagreed or how we might negotiate those differences without qualitative research. This chapter builds on the Iowa team's (Herndl, Polush, Cruse, Shelley) earlier belief that these different communities of practice had different ways of conceptualizing and talking about farming and sustainability that were as significant as the statistical differences. If these differences make public participation problematic, then the rhetorical analysis of workshops such as these becomes a valuable tool for the project of fostering citizen participation in science and technology development and decision making. An analysis of these ways of talking can help us understand the sources of these differences and might suggest ways to address them.

The workshop transcripts with farmers consist of 180 pages from sixteen hours of conversation. The scientists' workshop transcripts include 106 pages, representing seven hours of conversation. The analysis of these transcripts here is an extension of earlier work developed by the Iowa team. After the workshop with scientists and the first workshop with farmers, the Iowa team noticed that the two groups evaluated the criteria on the matrix differently. This was subsequently confirmed by the statistical analysis of the data. They also began to notice, however, that the two groups talked about farming, sustainability, and the different elements of cellulosic biofuel processing in very different ways. Following Barney G. Glaser and Anselm L. Strauss's concept of grounded theory, the research team compared its assumption that the farmers' expertise and knowledge could contribute to policy deliberations with the data emerging through the conversation.[20] How does one integrate the knowledge of the two groups when they are conceptualized and expressed in such different ways?

Aware of the different patterns of talk after the first two workshops, the Iowa research team was again struck during the final farmers' workshop by how differently the farmers conducted their discussions. Immediately following this final workshop, the Iowa team articulated a series of differences between the ways the farmers and the scientists talked about cellulosic biofuels, farming, and sustainability. For example, members of the Iowa research team pointed out that the scientists talked in abstract and hypothetical terms whereas the farmers told narratives about particular experiences on their farms. Scientists talked about farming systems as a collection of variables, but farmers talked about farms where they lived and worked. The lead author recorded this informal analysis and the contrasts in the participants' talk in his field notes, which provides the basis for the coding and analysis here.

Two of the authors read the complete set of transcripts using the list of contrasts the Iowa team saw between the ways the farmers and scientists talked as an interpretive frame. After agreeing on a common set of codes, the two readers coded a significant section of the transcripts independently. Where they coded differently, they discussed the differences and refined their coding process. When the two readers learned to apply the codes consistently, one reader coded the whole set of transcripts using the common coding scheme.[21] The coding included the following contrasting themes which are salient to the current discussion: (1) general versus specific, (2) abstract versus concrete, (3) global versus local, (4) formal versus personal, and (5) active versus passive.

Questions of Definition and Differentiation

The scientists' conversation is characterized by a shared insistence on technical accuracy, rules, order, precise definitions, and methodological clarity. They demanded *specificity* and precision. In addition to defining what counts as fuel, for example, scientists discussed the definition of the distributed versus centralized industry configurations that structure the columns on the matrix; they distinguished the term processing as referring both to "partially energy densified" and "processed completely"; and they questioned "what we mean by a biorefinery." One scientist even asked for a distinction between the distributed processes for single species of feed-stock such as corn stover and multiple species of feedstock: "I got a question more related to the distinction between distributed and centralized," one scientist asks. "I was wondering where do we draw the line on this thing. Are we talking about distributed as soon as we get to a radius of 20 miles or less?" The scientists thus began their discussion by meticulously delineating the objects under consideration. They often broke concepts down into their component parts, so that a discussion of "climate change" became a discussion of "adaptation" and of "mitigation." Finally, the accuracy of terms was strictly adhered to and self-enforced by the group.

The scientists' concern for clear definitions of terms is echoed in their great care and precision when discussing data, figures, and measurements. If a figure had to be discussed that was not known with certainty, the scientists struggled with the imprecision. This can be seen in a discussion about distribution related to the cost of a bale of corn stover: "I realize that this is not very precise, but the definition of 'distributed' is going to depend on cost per bale, and a distributed system is going to function [differently] if you are paying $35.00 as opposed to $65.00. So if you can live with imprecision we are going to have to ask you to do that" (Scientist Speaker). The farmers' conversations, by contrast, were carried out in *general*, rather than strictly defined, terms, and tended to focus on the issues rather than definitions. For example, the farmers did not discuss the distinction between centralized and distributed systems, nor did they discuss the intricacies of the terms carbon balance and carbon sequestration. They used these terms in their discussion, but the definitions were assumed to be understood by the group and were not explicitly expressed. They made general assertions like "it's a moving target figuring out what the gain versus loss is," and "the soil loss in Iowa has to go up again." They used imprecise figures like "thirty-some dollars" or "x dollars." Unlike the scientists, the farmers were comfortable with vague and nondefinitional terminology. For example, one farmer said, "I think it's going to come to the point where government or policy makers, the EPA, whoever, is just going to look at that producer and say, 'You know what? You're above *this* level and, and *here* you're fine,' and I think that's where the road will end up going down to [in] my honest opinion"—where the terms "this" and "here" refer to imaginary unknown figures.

System Analysis and Concrete Issues as Systems

When the farmers talked about a farm, they talked about the crops, the feed, tilling, harvesting, selling, taking care of the land, and they thought of these activities in relation to themselves. The scientists, however, discussed these same issues differently. They discussed a farm, for example, as a system for which they "have to create the parameters for decision metrics." Perhaps not surprising from a group that speaks precisely, the scientists often discussed concrete issues in terms of *components* that can be arranged in a variety of ways. For example, the scientists saw decisions related to biofuels as determinable by sets of parameters and metrics regarding the farm "system" and the different ways that the system can be arranged.

This distinction between a "farm" and a "system," two terms used to refer to the same thing, illustrates the powerful change in thinking that corresponds to changes in terminology. In sustainability science, systems analysis or life cycle analysis takes a whole network extended in time and space as its object of analysis. A single farm considered in isolation obscures the system-level analysis sought by sustainability science. For the farmers, however, farm is a tangible place where you stand on the grass, sit on the ground, and dig your hands into the soil. It has a material and affective reality that can be seen, felt, and loved. A system, however, is a not a place— it is an abstract thing to be analyzed. You can't visit a system; you can only talk about it.

Talking Globally, Locally, and Using Analogies

Perhaps because the scientists talked about "systems" not "farms," they tended to talk about issues on a larger scale than the farmers, and applied outside knowledge to a localized situation. This can be broadly characterized as a "global versus local" way of speaking and thinking. For example, when discussing bio-fuels in Iowa, the scientists discussed situations, materials, and practices all over the world. One scientist described, "a guy from [the] Peace Corps in Canada [who] developed a process where you actually put urea into the bio-oil and made a super fertilizer." They described practices conducted in various places like Oregon, Wisconsin, Illinois, Minnesota, Louisiana, Australia, and Africa, as well as possibilities garnered from Monsanto and the *Journal of Agronomy*. When discussing the densification of fuels and the issue of economies of scale, they even compared biofuel processing to the production of iPods.

Where scientists discussed production with abstract principles garnered from many, often distant, cases, farmers discussed practices they have used personally or seen used in nearby farms. For example, the farmers made statements like "One of the things that we do where I'm at from Michigan . . . ," "I guess one of the things that we see in southwest Iowa is . . . ," and "I see it every single day at my job." Another farmer talked about transportation from his own perspective, saying, "Being from Boone, we'll have to put in four or five rails to transport this stuff all over." This personal, experiential evidence framed how farmers saw larger processes. Farmers tended to use anecdotal evidence and local analogies to discuss local circumstances, whereas scientists applied a wide range of data from the global to the local more readily.

The Abstract, the Concrete, and the Emotional

Scientists' talk of systems and global perspectives led them to talk in abstractions and in analytic, unemotional ways. Farmers, by contrast, talked about specific, concrete things and often about the affective values associated with issues. For example, a driver and his time, driving distance, and truckload are all components that can be described by the single term "transportation." This term can then be applied to a number of scales—it can be scaled outward to apply to a broader system, or inward for a focus on the smaller, but still collapsed, system components—as one scientist speaker broke it down, "From the transportation side we are looking at both two things. One is the cost issue and there is also the labor issue." Here, "the cost issue" and "the labor issue" are abstractions; they were framed as problems to be resolved. Speaking and thinking in this way caused the scientists to talk of actions as what should "be done," a passive way of speaking, rather than the more active "what a person does." The groups' different ways of talking about "issues" also suggest different ways of thinking and being in the world. The scientists used collapsed terms like "labor" and "logistics" to characterize actions and processes that the farmers, in contrast, spent time discussing in detail. Where a scientist talked about land use using phrasings like "the logistics of the field," farmers named those logistics, using phrasings like "I don't know how they can get a plow that close to a fence." Similarly, the farmers described the "distance issue" of transportation, more concretely, as "a lot of trips with a truck."

The difference between scientists' and farmers' talk showed a significant affective distinction. The "cost" of system components as opposed to the "cash" required for farmers to operate is a clear example. For the scientists, money was *a variable* in an equation where, for example, the costs of fuel production were considered in hypothetical scenarios to solve mathematical problems. Such talk lacked a personal valuation. In contrast, farmers tended to talk about money in terms of figures and in emotional terms, saying things like "I can't imagine the cost." Money, to the farmers, was more than a figure—it was a mortgage payment; it was a livelihood. They used words like "outrageous" and "ridiculous," whereas the scientists rarely utilized emotional diction. Farmers tended to talk about biofuel costs with statements like "The ideal would be to make a high-value product from what we're growing and the organic residue that comes from that enriches the soil as well of our wallets." Farmers asked questions like "If all this corn is going towards exports and for fuel, what's it going to do to your grocery bill?"

Talking about Uncertainty: What May Happen vs. What Will Happen

Both groups talked about the future of the cellulosic biofuel industry a great deal. But their ways of talking were quite distinct, with scientists talking about what *may* happen and farmers talking about what *will* happen. Scientists looked at potential futures, at what may happen under given conditions (variables). Farmers were more interested in knowing "What is going to happen?"

The different ways of framing the future can be seen through the contexts in which both groups use the word "happen." The farmers never used the phrase "may happen," and the scientists never used the phrase "will happen." The farmers discussed "happenings" *here*, not there. The farmers wanted to know what will happen, what was happening, and how this affected them in their location. Unlike the scientists, the farmers positioned these issues personally, in terms of themselves. The scientists, for example, never said things like "What happens if I . . ."

The farmers did not discuss possible outcomes objectively, as neutral potential scenarios under discussion. Instead, they discussed them personally and emotionally in terms of their *hopes* about what may happen. One participant mused, "they're doing some research with double cropping, which is, I think, far-fetched in Iowa, I do really think, but it sounds like it actually could happen." The farmers also used this "may/could happen" construction to characterize their *fears* about what could happen. Uncertainty for the farmers was emotionally charged and unmeasurable; for them, uncertainty tended to be a "yes" or a "no," either black or white, not shades of gray, "Is it going to matter then?" (or not?)

The scientists, however, discussed levels of uncertainty more comfortably. They discussed uncertainty as a means to an end. For example, when discussing whether farmers will cooperate with corn-cob biofuel production (a subject of uncertainty), the scientists broke down the uncertainty into parts, analyzed each part, and moved on. They first discussed the issue in the context of "current policies." Then they discussed a scenario in which policy change gives the farmers the incentive to "move away from corn based ethanol," which removes the factor of "willingness," a main source of uncertainty, from the analysis and allowed them to continue the discussion. Next, they considered the uncertainties of plant availability and petroleum alternatives. This approach allowed the scientists to effectively work through the issues of uncertainty and incorporate them into their discussion.

What Can Computerized Data Analysis Contribute?

While traditional qualitative analysis, like that provided above, provides rich understanding of discursive activity, the time-consuming coding methods limit researchers to relatively small data sets. Like Graham et al. and Karen Gulbrandsen, we think that computer-based data analysis can open up new sites, data, and audiences for rhetorical analysis. Our work in this section is exploratory and comparative, and asks two questions: What can semantic network analysis (SNA), a technique often used to analyze large sets of data, tell us about our data? And how do these findings relate to or enhance the traditional analysis we have offered above?

For rhetoricians, the applications of SNA are multiple: SNA can recover subtle structures within a text; visualize and read *inter*textually; enhance distant reading and writing of volumes of texts; quickly summarize, profile, or diagram texts for comparison; and profile a text's tenor, tone, or sentiment. Other studies have used SNA methods to classify the similarity of documents; improve text indexing and retrieval to analyze changes in topics over time; and to predict citations.[22] We are particularly interested in whether network analysis methods validate, enhance, or contradict qualitative research developed entirely by humans.

In semantic and social network analysis, nodes in the network represent words or actors and the links between them represent some kind of relationship. Social network analysis such as Nicholas A. Christakis and James H. Fowler's can tell us much about how humans interact, how communities form or dissolve, and how information and opinion diffuses across time and space.[23] Similarly, SNA graphs the relationships between *words* instead of actors. Semantic networks tell us not just what a text says, but also how texts and individual units within a text are related and what their relative importance within a system of words and ideas might be. For example, we

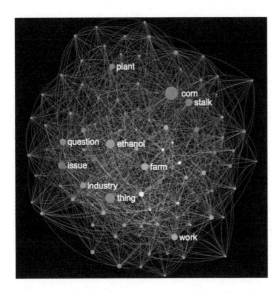

Fig. 3.3. Network graph using Textexture to visualize transcripts of the farmers' group 2 discourse.

can see that the word "system" is central to the scientists' discourse but not to the farmers' discourse (figures 3.1–3.4). In addition to tracking the occurrence of individual terms like "system," SNA can identify clusters of singular or grouped concepts that form a context, and contexts can be qualitatively themed or described.

For example, the term "system" is a concept central to the discourse because of the size of the node and the number of other concepts to which it is connected (figure 3.4). Though it is difficult to see without drilling into the network, "system" is connected to many other concepts. This means that the term "system" also serves as a junction of meaning; it is a term around which other terms are clustered, forming a context or community or theme that is qualitatively significant. A "context" is a subnetwork within the larger semantic network. Contextual clusters point to the "semantic path," the associated words and concepts through which a specific term like "system" achieves its explanatory power.

Though the tools used to analyze volumes of unstructured text offer affordances that traditional methods lack, SNA does not follow one straightforward sequence of rules. There are many ways to visualize a network, each telling a slightly different story, and most of the foundational and current research in semantic network analysis suggests such work requires a subject matter expert, someone who can interpret, identify, and validate patterns of significance within the network.[24] This is analogous to the strategy

Table 3.1. Comparing parts of speech used by farmers versus scientists

	Adjectives	Adverbs	Nouns	Verbs
Farmers 1	11,048	8,687	31,052	20,251
Farmers 2	8,297	6,507	22,802	14,865
Scientists	9,002	6,648	23,948	14,950

of member checking in traditional qualitative analysis. In our case, the lead author filled this role, having worked with this research project and the participants for many years.

At a more technical level, the use of tools like Textexture in SNA is relatively straightforward. Each transcript file was combined to represent the complete account of the discourse from each workshop. These text files were then loaded into Textexture, where "stop words," insignificant words like "a" or "uh," were removed automatically. The remaining words were encoded as nodes and each node's co-occurrence value was calculated. Every word in the corpus is a node. Co-occurrence values represent the number of times terms appear as a pair in a text, and is significant because it suggests that a specific concept or idiomatic expression only makes sense when the two words appear together. For example, the word "explanation" may appear in a text by itself, but when it co-occurs with "unnecessary," it becomes a significantly different concept. We then used AutoMap, a text analysis product that extracts information, like parts of speech. For corpus statistics and categorization dictionaries, we used WordStat. Finally, we used Textexture, a nonlinear distant reading and text network visualization tool developed by Nodus Labs to quickly "read" and visualize the interview transcripts as networks of words and concepts, using these tools to check our findings and interpretations against each other and see what the differences and similarities are.

The complexities of SNA and the software used to do the computations present rhetorical analysis with two major challenges: how to define and identify the objects of analysis and how to interpret the visualizations that result. The first challenge is illustrated by the SNA analysis of the distinction between abstract and concrete terms in the farmers' and scientists' workshops. The second challenge is illustrated by the key terms or "nodes" in the respective workshops.

Defining Objects for Analysis: The Abstract, the Concrete, and the Emotional

One way to check whether scientists were more abstract in their discussions and farmers more concrete is to track the use of abstract and concrete nouns across texts. To do this, we used AutoMap to generate a *parts-of-speech* file, which extracts each word and identifies it with the appropriate linguistic tag—noun, verb, adjective, and so on. The parts of speech were then sorted in Excel and exported into WordStat's categorization dictionary against which each of the discourses were then compared. If adjectives are considered "emotional" because they are descriptive, then indeed the farmers' discourse is more emotional than the scientists' but these categorization dictionaries are crude, and to truly support the observation that the farmers' discourse is more *emotional* further disambiguation of terms is required. The same is true to determine and compare concrete and abstract nouns.

Another way of mapping the differences and similarities in the ways that farmers and scientists talk about issues is to drill down into one specific concept, like "farm," and investigate and compare the words that co-occur. Though the single lexical item "farm" occurs sixty-two times in both the farmers' and scientists' discourse (an unusual coincidence) the word is co-located with the word "income" ten times in the scientists' discourse creating the phrase "farm income" but only four times in the farmers' discourse.

Comparatively, the article or pronoun is often co-located to the term "farm" in the farmers' discourse (e.g., "*his* farm" or "*the* farm") suggesting for the farmers "the farm" as a concept is personal; it is a system, but one meant to support *people*. Drilling deeper into the text to look at related words like "farmer" and its plural "farmers" finds the terms occurring ninety-seven times in the farmer discourse, and fifty-four times in the scientist discourse, suggesting that in-group identification is stronger among the farmers. Conversely, the term "science" or "scientist" occurs only ten times in the scientist discourse, and never occurs in the farmer discourse.

The challenge of interpreting the visualizations produced by the analysis is illustrated by the figures below that display the semantic "nodes" in the two discursive networks, indicating the centrality of specific concepts. In these network representations, the size of the node denotes its relative importance in the network and within its cluster or "community" of contextual terms. Nodes are not linked because they are next to each other in a sentence, but because they are central to a "window" of context-dependent words. This "node-edge" structure is encoded and visually represented as a graph using the open source network visualization tool, Gephi.

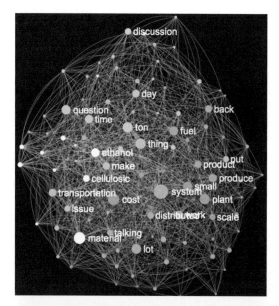

Fig. 3.4. Network graph using Textexture to visualize transcripts of the scientists' discourse.

Fig. 3.5. Key contexts, scientists.

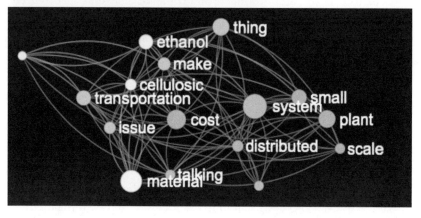

The larger the node, the more times the word appears in the text, making it more important or salient. Colors (not reproduced here) denote a cluster or context of topics that are related to one another, so if we drilled into green nodes and links, for example, we would find that the concepts "specie" and "corn" and "talking" were closing related, likely operating in sentences spoken multiple times by multiple speakers. The size of the nodes in the network graphs depends on the network calculation called "betweenness centrality," a standard network measure that accounts for how often the shortest path between two randomly chosen nodes appears in a network.[25] In SNA, betweenness centrality is an important measure because

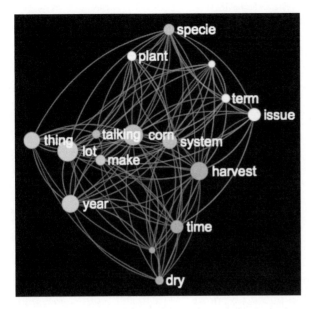

Fig. 3.6. Key contexts, farmers' group 1.

words that measure high on this scale often appear at the *junctures of meaning* such as the term "system" above (figure 3.4). A "juncture of meaning" is an area of the graph that visualizes a significant relationship, an exigency. In other words, the nodes at a juncture of meaning are not just frequent, but influential. Nodes can have high betweenness centrality within *clusters* of concepts, too, making them influential terms within a specific context or subsystem of ideas. For example, the term "system" is the central term in the scientist discourse, but it is also key within a context or community structure of terms, forming a contextual cluster. Both the central term and the contextual cluster structure the circulation of meaning in the transcripts. In other words, when the scientist transcripts are read, the word "system" will play an important role in establishing meaning for the text, as well as its interpretation.

In figure 3.4 (above), which represents the scientists' discourse, "system" has the highest betweenness centrality, confirming the qualitative assessment that scientists talked about systems. Furthermore, within the scientists' discussion of farm-as-system, there are concepts unique to their discourse: *distributed, centralized, processing.* Figure 3.5 is a "drilled into" context that offers a closer look at what terms are connected to one another in the scientific discourse. Here, the term "system" is important (as denoted by its size) and is connected to (which means it frequently co-occurred with) "distributed" and "talking."

Table 3.2. Variation in paragraphs, sentences, and words used by farmers versus scientists

	Paragraphs	Sentences	Words
Farmers 1	872	2137	44,834
Farmers 2	958	1826	34,269
Scientists	588	1622	35,450

Though farmers also talked about farms as a system, the term "system" did not have as high a betweenness centrality measure in the farmers' dialogue. Thus, "system" was not a concept that organized meaning in their discussions. Instead, as figure 3.6 shows, "word/node" "corn" had a high betweenness centrality, suggesting that farmers' meanings were organized by the crop, the *thing that composes the system*, which is more important than the system itself. The contrast between these two visualizations supports the qualitative finding that scientists often described the farm as a system and that system was distributed.

Corpus Statistics and Politeness

It is difficult to generalize these findings because there are so many variables at work here and because this experiment was not initially set up with SNA in mind. That said, one of the first observations to make about the corpus is variation in size. In statistical terms, there is significant variation in the number of paragraphs and words spoken per paragraph, which generally corresponds to turn taking. The numbers suggest that though fewer scientists talked, they spoke about ten to fifteen words *more* than farmers did. Another interesting observation involves the number of words *excluded*. One might think because farmers are more conversational and use lay terms, they would use more extraneous words, like "um," but the words excluded, those that made the "stop lists," including the word "um," were about the same with one significant difference. The word "yeah" dominates the farmers' discourse, appearing seventy times in the second farmer workshop and ninety times in the first; however, in the scientist discourse, it appears only forty times. This quantitative finding supports the qualitative

Table 3.2 *continued*

Words excluded	Words per sentence	Words per paragraph	Nodes	Edges
31,716	21.0	51.4	100	1641
24,290	18.8	35.8	100	1448
23,608	21.9	60.3	100	1526

observation that farmers are somewhat deferential to one another. They were polite and affirming of each other's ideas and thoughts and experiences. This affirmation of lived experience was integral to creating the ethos that guided the farmers' discourse, an ethos that was reflected in the scientists' discourse in the use of specific terms and definitions.

Questions of Definition, Differentiation

One final comparison of SNA and the traditional qualitative analysis concerns the finding that questions of definition and differentiation were central to the scientists' discussion. Particularly noteworthy is the scientists' concern with defining terms like "distributed" in at least three different points of the conversation, whereas the term "define" or "definition" doesn't appear in the farmers' discourse at all. This impulse toward precision and specificity is demonstrated with the use of other terms, too, like "economies of scale," a term that occurs on nine separate occasions in the scientists' discussion, but does not appear in the farmers' discourse.

The scientists not only used this economic jargon, but also indicated that the theme of economics was important to them, as signified by the volume of time spent talking about it. An economic term occurs thirty-seven times in the science discourse versus twenty-two times in the farmer discourse, which is a significant ratio considering the farmer transcripts are significantly longer. The scientists' discourse leans to the particular in other ways. The term "soil carbon," for example, appears fourteen times in the scientist discourse, but only three times in the farmer discourse, and the tri-gram (a phrase composed of three words but counted as one term) occurs eleven times in the science discourse and never in the farmer discourse (figures 3.7, 3.8).

Understanding These Different Ways of Talking

As both the qualitative analysis and SNA above demonstrate, the scientists and farmers in the workshops talked very differently. To generalize, scientists strove for precise definitions, talking in abstract, global terms about systems and their components as variables in possible scenarios to analyze. For the farmers, the future was a personal and affectively charged challenge rather than a site of manipulation. The farmers lived on their land. It was their family past, their social identity, and the source of their future wellbeing. The scientists were not tied to specific pieces of land and their future. The scientists' knowledge could be scaled up or down and was transferable to other sites. The farmers' knowledge was neither scalable nor transferable. It was embedded in a specific piece of land and an affectively charged lifeworld.

The very different material relationships the scientists and farmers have to the object of their analysis shapes both that object itself, the system or the farm, and the language through which the two groups construct that object. Using Pierre Bourdieu's work on objective social science, Henri Lefebvre's work on the construction of space, Thomas Gieryn's work on place, and Graham's "praxiography of representation," we argue that the scientists' language emerges from practices that enact a farm as an abstract space while the farmers' language emerges from practices that enact a farm as a lively place of practical activity.[26]

Bourdieu offers a critique of objective social science that suggests a practical and material explanation of the differences we see in the discourse of the workshops. For Bourdieu, the social scientist is an observer, distanced from the practice he observes because he is "excluded from the real play of social activities by the fact that he has no place (except by choice or by way of a game) in the system observed and has no need to make a place for himself there."[27] Because social scientists do not experience practical activities directly, they reduce them to an objective set of rules that captures the tacit knowledge of the native's lived experience. The scientists in our workshops were distanced from the farmers' lived experience not only as disciplinary language speakers but also as observers, positioned outside the lifeworld of the farm.

Rather than the social scientists' set of rules, the scientists in our workshops created abstract systems composed of components and variables. They talked about scenarios and models, speculating about future scenarios

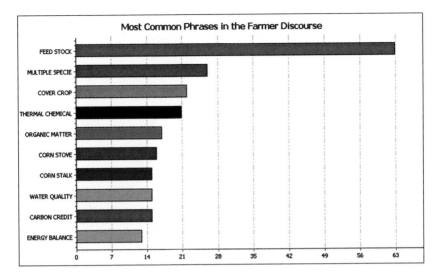

Fig. 3.7. Common phrases from farmer discourse.

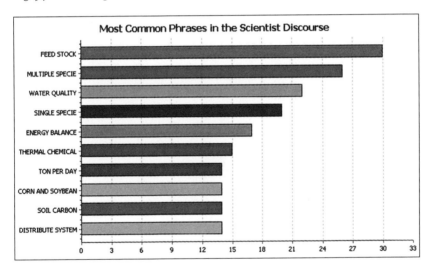

Fig. 3.8. Common phrases from scientist discourse.

for the biofuel industry and the farms that provided the feedstock. These models could be populated with different inputs and produce different outcomes, some more sustainable than others. The farmers, by contrast, rarely talked about scenarios, hypothetical situations, or alternative data sets. They spoke about concrete situations rather than abstractions. They talked about the past on their specific farms and about present conditions. The future was something to be prepared for and concerned about, but not the object of play and manipulation through the efficacy of models. As Bourdieu suggests, one experience is structured by "axes of the fields of potentialities" while the other is structured by a system "linked unalterably to our [the farmers'] bodies."[28]

The difference between the abstract space of the scientists and the practical space of the farmers is a product of what Lefebvre calls the production of space. In tracing the concept of space, Lefebvre argues that the philosophical and scientific tradition has side-stepped the way it "bridges the gap between the theoretical (epistemological) realm and the practical one, between mental and social, between the space of philosophers and the space of people who deal with material things."[29] This gap between the theoretical and practical realms captures the distinction between the scientists' and farmers' relationship to the system/farm traced in the qualitative analysis above. This gap and the different languages it separates is a fundamental challenge facing attempts to integrate the expertise of credentialed and noncredentialed experts, the knowledge of scientists and farmers.

Lefebvre's conception of how space is produced allows us to understand the gap between mental and practical space and the rhetorical differences it both produces and is produced by. Lefebvre identifies three types of social space, all operative in our case: spatial practice or space as "perceived"; representations of space or space as "conceived"; and representational space or space as "lived." Each of these spaces is produced through a distinct social activity, characterized by a particular relationship of the subject to the surroundings, and each is constituted in and expressed by a distinct code or language practice.[30]

The practical activity of scientists as analytic observers and the farmers as affectively engaged producers create two different kinds of space. Representations of space are the space of science, architecture, and engineering. They identify what is lived and perceived with what is abstractly conceived as the object of knowledge. This is the dominant space in society and tends to be associated with a highly regulated system of verbal or written signs. For the scientists with whom we worked, language is highly paradigmatic and metaphorical, moving from model to model, scenario to scenario, where an abstract model is identified with the whole. Representational space, by contrast, is lived by the inhabitants of space and full of symbolic and affective meaning. It is alive. Representational space is qualitative, fluid, dynamic, felt, often inconsistent and incoherent, and highly localized.

For the farmers, the language is strongly metonymic, fluid, and associative among often affectively charged statements and ideas.

Lefebvre's third type of space, spatial practices, captures the patterned ways we move in and through space. These are repetitive and typically unconscious movements that tend to follow established routes and routines. We perceive or make space through our familiar movements within it. Spatial practices are dialectic because our physical movements through space both follow existing pathways and establish new pathways and patterns. Spatial practices involve the body's capacity to do things.[31] We perceive our bodies by using them to do things. In our case, spatial practices emerge when a farmer talked about practical activities rather than "logistics," such as "I don't know how they can get a plow that close to a fence." Where the scientist calculated the economic cost of transportation, the farmer took a lot of trips in a truck. Representations of the body, by contrast, emerge from the accumulated sciences of anatomy and medical physiology that define the body as an external and, following Foucault, transparent object of the knowing gaze. In our case, the representation of space emerges when scientists debated about the precise distinction between centralized and distributed processing systems or when they broke the question of transportation into "the cost issue and the labor issue." Where the scientist calculated the economic cost of transportation, the farmer took many trips in a truck.

We can generalize these different ways of constructing space in our case study by suggesting that the scientists analyze a space while the farmers occupy a place. The sociological literature on place distinguishes the abstract space of science from the lived, affective, and meaningful place of the people who live in a space. Gieryn puts it succinctly: "First, place is not space-which is more properly conceived as abstract geometries (distance, direction, size, shape, volume) detached from material form and cultural interpretation (Hillier & Hanson 1984). . . . Put positively, place is space filled up by people, practices, objects, and representations."[32] Gieryn distinguishes place and space by suggesting that a census tract, so useful in sociological study, is merely a "bundle of analytic variables" used to distinguish neighborhoods.[33] It does not tell you how the residents of the neighborhood understand themselves as inhabitants, what their neighborhood means to them, or how they use space or feel as they move through it. To summarize, the distance between the scientists and their object allows them to constitute a representation of the space of agriculture while the farmers' immersion in the activity allows them to constitute what Lefebvre calls a representational space and Gieryn understands as place.

Lefebvre argues that there are distinct discourses with unique terms associated with the ways groups occupy and produce space.[34] "Codes" or ways of speaking about space are dialectical; different kinds of space embody the different relationships between subjects and their surroundings, and these in turn are expressed in very different languages. The practical activity of observing and analyzing, distant from the lifeworld, produces a *representation of space* with its characteristic way of talking: fine distinctions; refined definitions; talk of variables, scenarios, and systems. Similarly, the practical activity of farming immerses the subject in the lifeworld and produces a *representational space* with its way of talking and thinking. Emotional language, synecdotal associations, personal anecdotes, and opinion constitute the farm as a place. Talking about spaces and talking about places are two distinct activities.

Lefebvre pinpoints the question of how to integrate these two spaces and the different knowledge of scientists and farmers, credentialed and noncredentialed experts. Lefebvre's driving question concerns the relations between and potential intercourse among these three spaces: "The question is what intervenes, what occupies the interstices between representations of space and representational spaces."[35] Put more directly and pragmatically, Lefebvre questions what intervenes between the representational practices of science and of farming.

A Tale of Two Farms

To return to the motivating issue of citizen participation in science and technology policy, ours is not merely a question of integrating the knowledge of farmers and scientists expressed in two systematically different forms of language use. Ours is a tale of two farms. In discussions of expertise and knowledge, the expertise of credentialed and noncredentialed experts is typically seen as additive. We make better decisions when we combine the knowledge of both groups. This is the driving motive of Collins and Evans' theory of experience-based expertise as continuous with and potentially contributory to the expertise of credentialed scientists. It is also the hope of rapid technology assessments that include noncredentialed experts such as our farmers. But as Sheila Jasanoff, Ari Rip, and Brian Wynne argue, the expertise and knowledge of groups like the farmers and scientists in this case are not merely additive.[36] There is more at play than what Wynne refers to as "propositional" knowledge.[37] As Jasanoff maintains: "This [that farmers and radiation experts possessed different but complementary knowledge] is certainly a piece of Wynne's story, but more significant is that these discrepancies were rooted in different life worlds, entailing altogether different perceptions of uncertainty, predictability and control. The knowledges stemming from these divergent experiential contexts were not simply additive; they represented radically 'other' ways of understanding the world."[38] The representational space of a farm as an affectively rich place of identity and dwelling is not continuous with the representation of the space that makes a farm system a scalable model populated by data points and useful for scenario analysis. The prominence of the Farm-Aid movement and benefit concerts of the 1980s suggests that the space of a farming system and the place of the family farm are two different things.

Following the new materialist arguments of Mol, Latour, Pickering, and Graham, we suggest that Jasanoff's "radically 'other'" ways of understanding the world of space and place in our study emerge from the different ways scientists and farmers realize or enact different farms.[39] For example, Graham traces the way pain is made real in different ways by neurosurgeons and psychologists who not only talk differently but treat the patient differently. The warranting concept of these new materialist analyses is that different material practices ontologize or realize different things. For Graham, pain as the result of nerve damage in neurology is measured, diagnosed, and treated as a different thing than pain as the result of cognitive representation diagnosed, measured, and treated in psychology. We suggest that the material practices of studying a farm system—of gathering data points, calculating economic benefits, defining distributed and centralized systems—create a different entity than the farmers' daily actions on the farm, such as tilling the soil, driving a truck, and paying the mortgage. Where Lefebvre argues that representations of space and representational space had different codes, Graham insists that, "Practices stage modes of being that in turn encourage participants to talk about truth and knowledge in ways that are operationalized by the underlying ontology."[40]

Understanding this case as a tale of two farms captures the difference between space and place and explains why the representational practices are so different and such a challenge to integrate. It is almost literally a case of apples and oranges. Seeing these as two different entities, a system or representation of space as opposed to a farm as a representational space or a place, however offers practical benefits. The knowledge of the scientists and farmers is not in competition; they are not competing or even complementary propositions about the same thing. As such, there need not be an epistemic hierarchy between two forms of knowledge, one typically accepted as more authoritative than the other.[41] While this does not solve the problem of what to do after we get the right people to the table, it does explain the nature of the difference and suggest some practical ways forward.

In our earlier project, the Iowa team integrated the contributions of the scientists and farmers through what Graham calls "calibration by detour."[42] Graham adapts Mol's metaphor of calibration to describe how pain practitioners managed the differences among the different pains to improve patient care. Calibration does not resolve differences or determine which claims are correct, better or more authoritative. Calibration preserves and manages difference, integrating two different experiences, by detour, in medical care in pragmatic ways. In Graham's case, neuroimaging acts as a black box to calibrate subjective patient reports of pain with neurological diagnosis so that neither is dismissed. The two enactments of pain are integrated through the agency of a third party, the powerful black box of neuroimaging that legitimizes the subjective patient report through its own authority. In our case, the experience and knowledge of the scientists and farmers is calibrated through the black box of our matrix instrument and its assessment function. Our statistical analysis of the assessment results identified significant differences in the two assessments without privileging one over the other.

Moving Forward with Engaged Research

The question of how to include citizens in decision making about science, technology, and development does not have a single or simple answer. In our case, scientists and farmers enacted two different things, systems and farms, and talked about them using distinct representational practices. Our analysis does not tell us how to integrate a vernacular discourse of place with a professional discourse of space. It does, we think, clarify the rhetorical dimensions of the problem and open new ways of managing it. Graham concludes his analysis of pain and cross-ontological management of pain by describing various modes of calibration and authorizing resources that offer rhetorical and institutional strategies for accommodating different ways of enacting pain or farms and making productive use of both forms of experience. Together these strategies contribute to what Graham calls a "praxiography of representation": "a praxiography of representation focuses not so much on what people say or what texts mean, but rather on how representational activity circulates within and contributes to a deeper ecology of practices in which those acts of representation are embedded. Cross-ontological calibration is one form of representational practice that serves to navigate the boundaries among different ontologies."[43] Rhetoricians engaged with science-based projects might see their work as cross-ontological calibration, the practical understanding and management of different representational practices that intersect in a policy or decision-making space. A praxiography of representation helps rhetoricians navigate the boundaries and differences among practices and ontologies to improve deliberation, decision making, and policy formation. To answer Lefebvre's earlier question, the practice of calibration intervenes and so does the rhetorician as praxiographer.

Finally, many discussions of climate change, technology development, or policy happen in very local settings such as that of our case study. But the context that shapes a community's practices is also extended in space, time, and media. Farmers talked about a sense of place, but that place is itself embedded in a larger context and conversation. The way citizens in Iowa conceptualize climate change, interpret information, and make decisions is embedded in national and global discourses that are too large and distributed for fine-grained rhetorical analysis. As our exploratory work here suggests, big data analysis such as SNA can reproduce some of the results of traditional qualitative and rhetorical analysis. We found that SNA confirmed the qualitative finding, for example, that scientists talk about farms as systems where farmers talk about places. Besides confirming traditional findings, SNA can provide our qualitative results a quantitative element that carries considerable cultural capital. Unfortunately, there is no commonsensical or natural way to develop these analytic capacities. Rhetoricians who can do so, however, will have a powerful research tool that opens new data for analysis. SNA might be seen as a calibration by detour that authorizes more traditional forms of rhetorical analysis. Further, this research tool can warrant analytic claims in ways that will provide rhetoricians membership in large, externally funded interdisciplinary projects in ways that are very rare at the moment.

Notes

1. Harry M. Collins and Robert Evans, "The Third Wave of Science Studies: Studies of Expertise and Experience," *Social Studies of Science* 32, no. 2 (2002): 235–96; Bruno Latour, "Why Has Critique Run Out of Steam?" *Critical Inquiry* 30 (2004): 225–48; Latour, *The Politics of Nature: How to Bring the Sciences into Nature* (Cambridge: Harvard University Press, 2004); Latour, "An Attempt at a 'Compositionist Manifesto,'" *New Literary History* 41 (2010): 471–90; Herbert Simons, "The Rhetoric of Philosophical Incommensurability," in *Rhetoric and Incommensurability*, ed. Randy A. Harris, 238–68 (West Lafayette, IN: Parlor Press, 2005).

2. See Daniel Fiorino, "Citizen Participation and Environmental Risk: A Survey of Institutional Mechanisms," *Science, Technology and Human Values* 15, no. 2 (1990): 226–43; Frank Fischer, *Citizens Experts and the Environment: The Politics of Local Knowledge* (Durham, NC: Duke University Press, 2000); Julia Abelson et al., "Deliberations About Deliberative Methods: Issues in the Design and Evaluation of Public Participatory Processes," *Social Science & Medicine* 57 (2003): 239–51; Barbara Murdock, Carol Wiessner, and Ken Sexton, "Stakeholder Participation in Voluntary Environmental Agreements: Analysis of 10 Project XL Case Studies," *Science, Technology and Human Values* 30, no. 2 (2005): 223–50.

3. Latour, *Pandora's Hope: Essays on the Reality of Science Studies* (Cambridge: Harvard University Press, 1999), 218.

4. There is a long history of studies that categorize participatory mechanisms. See Dorothy Nelkin and Michael Pollak, "Public Participation in Technological Decisions: Reality or Grand Illusion?" *Technology Review* 81 (1979): 55–64; Peter M. Wiedemann and Susanne Femers, "Public-Participation in Waste Management Decision-Making: Analysis and Management of Conflicts," *Journal of Hazardous Materials* 33, no. 3 (1993): 355–68; Bretta Maloff, David Bilan, and Wifreda Thurston, "Enhancing Public Input into Decision Making: Development of the Calgary Regional Health Authority Public Participation Framework," *Family and Community Health* 23, no. 1 (2000): 66–78; Gene Rowe and Lynn. J. Frewer, "A Typology of Public Engagement Mechanisms," *Science Technology Human Values* 30, no. 2 (2005): 251–90. For studies that evaluate participatory mechanisms on procedural and outcomes-based criteria, see Deborah S. Carr and Kathleen Halvorsen, "An Evaluation of Three Democratic, Community-Based Approaches to Citizen Participation: Surveys, Conversations with Community Groups, and Community Dinners," *Society and Natural Resources* 14, no. 2 (2001): 107–26; Caron Chess and Kristen Purcell, "Public Participation and the Environment: Do We Know What Works?" *Environmental Science and Technology* 33, no. 16 (1999): 2685–92; Edna F. Einsiedel, Erling Jelsoe, and Thomas Breck, "Publics at the Technology Table: The Consensus Conference in Denmark, Canada, and Australia," *Public Understanding of Science* 10, no. 1 (2001): 83–98.

5. While there are not rhetorical analyses of talk in participatory mechanisms in the literature on science studies or policy management, some studies do recognize the importance of language in these mechanisms. See Matthew Harvey, "Drama, Talk and Emotion: Omitted Aspects of Public Participation," *Science, Technology & Human Values* 34, no. 2 (2009): 139–61; Robert Futrell, "Technical Adversarialism and Participatory Collaboration in the U.S. Chemical Weapons Disposal Program," *Science, Technology, & Human Values* 28, no. 4 (2003): 451–82; Gail Davies, "The Sacred and the Profane: Biotechnology, Rationality and Public Debate," *Environment and Planning* 38 (2006): 423–43.

6. Robert Danisch, *Pragmatism, Democracy, and the Necessity of Rhetoric* (Columbia: University of South Carolina Press, 2007); Stuart Blythe, Jeffrey Grabill, and Kirk Riley, "Action Research and Wicked Environmental Problems: Exploring Appropriate Roles for Researchers in Professional Communication," *Journal of Business and Technical Communication* 22, no. 3 (2008): 272–98; John Ackerman and David J. Coogan, eds., *The Pubic Work of Rhetoric: Citizen Scholars and Civic Engagement* (Columbia: University of South Carolina Press, 2010); Celeste Condit, "Rhetorical Engagements in the Scientist's Process of Remaking Race as Genetic," in *Public Work of Rhetoric*, 119–36; Carl Herndl and Lauren Cutlip, "How Can We Act: A Praxiographical Program for the Rhetoric of Technology, Science and Medicine," *POROI* 9, no. 1 (2013), http://ir.uiowa.edu/poroi/vol9/iss1/9/.

7. Scott Graham et al., "Statistical Genre Analysis: Toward Big Data Methodologies in Technical Communication," *Technical Communication Quarterly* 24, no. 1 (2015): 38.

8. Gerard A. Hauser, *Vernacular Voices: The Rhetoric of Publics and Public Spheres* (Columbia: University of South Carolina Press, 1999); Robert Danisch, "Political Rhetoric in a World Risk Society," *Rhetoric Society Quarterly* 40, no. 2 (2010): 172–92.

9. Two significant early uses of big data analyses in rhetorical research are Graham et al., "Statistical Genre Analysis"; and Karen Gulbrandsen, "Revising the Technical Communication Service Course," *Programmatic Perspectives* 4, no. 2 (2012): 243–54.

10. Adam Liska et al., "Biofuels from Crop Residue Can Reduce Soil Carbon and Increase CO_2 Emissions," *Nature Climate Change* (May 2014), doi: 10.1038/nclimate2187; David Laborde and Siwa Msangi, "Biofuels, Environment, and Food: The Story Gets More Complicated," *2011 Global Food Policy Report* (Washington, DC: International Food Policy Research Institute), http://www.ifpri.org/node/8439.

11. Robert D. Perlack et al., "Biomass as a Feedstock for a Bioenergy and Bioproducts Industry: The Technical Feasibility of a Billion-ton Annual Supply," 2005, DOE/GO-102005–2135 ORNL/TM-2005/66, http://www.fs.fed.us/research/; Council for Agricultural Science and Technology (CAST), "Convergence of Agriculture and Energy: II. Producing Cellulosic Biomass for Biofuels" (Ames, IA: CAST Commentary QTA2007–2. CAST, 2007).

12. Brent D. Yacobucci and Randy Schnepf, "Ethanol and Biofuels: Agriculture, Infrastructure and Market Constraints Related to Expanded Production," *Congressional Research Service Report to Congress*, 2007, Order Code RL33928; Rick M. Cruse and Carl G. Herndl, "Balancing Corn Stover Harvest for Biofuels with Soil and Water Conservation," *Journal of Soil and Water Conservation* 64 (2009): 286–91.

13. The time scale difference between policy making and scientific research is a long-standing problem in the relationship between science and policy. For discussions of the problem, see, Shelia Jasanoff, "Contested Boundaries in Policy-Relevant Science," *Social Studies of Science* 17 (1987): 195–230; Bryan Norton, *Sustainability: A Philosophy of Adaptive Ecosystem Management* (Chicago: University of Chicago Press, 2005); Richard M. Cruse, Michael J. Cruse, and Don Reicosky, "Soil Quality Impacts of Residue Removal for Biofuel Feedstocks," in *Advances in Soil Science: Soil Quality and Biofuel Production*, ed. Rattan Lal and B. A. Stewart (New York: CRC Press, 2009), 45–62.

14. R. W. Howarth et al., "Rapid Assessment on Biofuels and Environment: Overview and Key Findings," in *Biofuels: Environmental Consequences and Interactions with Changing Land Use*, ed. R. W. Howarth and S. Bringezu, Proceedings of the Scientific Committee on Problems of the Environment (SCOPE) International Biofuels Project Rapid Assessment, 22–25 September 2008, Gummersbach Germany, Cornell University, Ithaca NY, 1–13, http://cip.cornell.edu/biofuels/; Government Accountability Office, "Expert Opinion on the Economics of Policy Options to Address Climate Change," *A Report to Congress Requesters*, 2008. GAO-08–605; Sherri Goodman, "National Security and the Threat of Climate Change," (Alexandria, VA: CAN Corporation, 2007); Tara G. Martin et al., "The Power of Expert Opinion in Ecological Models Using Bayesian Methods: Impact of Grazing on Birds," *Ecological Applications* 15, no.1 (2005) 266–80.

15. In the published report, only one farmer workshop is described. Because participants in the two farmer workshops were selected by different criteria, that report only included results from the first workshop. Those participants attended an earlier presentation of this project by the lead investigator. Since the current analysis concerns the rhetorical forms used by the participants and not their technical knowledge, the distinction between the two farmer groups is irrelevant here.

16. A detailed presentation of the research methodology, including the conduct of the workshops and the data analysis, is available in Rick Cruse et al., "An Assessment of Cellulosic Ethanol Industry Sustainability Based on Industry Configurations," *Journal of Soil and Water Conservation* 67, no. 2 (2012), 67–74.

17. The results of this project were published in the *Journal of Soil and Water Conservation* and in a technical report to the Aldo Leopold Center for sustainable agriculture, which partially funded the research.

18. The qualitative analysis in this section draws heavily from Lauren Cutlip, "Talking About Talk: The Problem of Communication as an Object of Study in

Public Participation Research" (master's thesis, University of South Florida, 2012). The transcripts of the Iowa workshops served as raw data for her analysis, and the lead author was the subject matter expert who provided explanations and interpretation of the salient features of that data.

19. Cruse et al., "An Assessment of Cellulosic Ethanol."

20. Glaser, Barney G., and Anselm L. Strauss, *The Discovery of Grounded Theory: Strategies for Qualitative Research* (New Brunswick, Canada: AldineTransaction, 2009).

21. A more thorough discussion of the coding and analysis appears in Cutlip, *Talking About Talk*, 2012.

22. David M. Blei and John D. Lafferty, "A correlated topic model of science," *The Annals of Applied Statistics* (2007): 17–35; Jonathan J. Chang and David M. Blei, "Hierarchical Relational Models for Document Networks," *The Annals of Applied Statistics* (2010): 124–50.

23. Nicholas A. Christakis and James H. Fowler, "The Spread of Obesity in a Large Social Network over 32 Years," *New England Journal of Medicine* 357, no. 4 (2007): 370–79.

24. Mark Granovetter, "The Strength of Weak Ties," *American Journal of Sociology* 78 (1973): 1360–80; Ronald S. Burt, *Brokerage and Closure: An Introduction to Social Capital* (Oxford: Oxford University Press, 2005); Kathleen M. Carley, "Coding Choices for Textual Analysis: A Comparison of Content Analysis and Map Analysis," *Social Methodology* 23 (1993): 75–126; Roel Popping, "Knowledge Graphs and Network Text Analysis," *Social Science Information* 42 (2003): 91–106; M-L. Ryan, "Diagramming Narrative," *Semiotica* 165, no. 1 (2007): 11–40.

25. Linton Freeman, "A Set of Measures of Centrality Based on Betweenness," *Sociometry* 40 (1977): 35–41. doi: 10.2307/3033543.

26. Pierre Bourdieu, *Outline of a Theory of Practice* (Cambridge: Cambridge University Press, 1977); Henri Lefebvre, *The Production of Space*, trans. Donald Nicholson-Smith (Oxford: Blackwell, 1991); Thomas Gieryn, "A Space for Place in Sociology," *Annual Review of Sociology* 26 (2000): 463–97; S. Scott Graham, *Politics of Pain Medicine: A Rhetorical-Ontological Inquiry* (Chicago: University of Chicago Press, 2015).

27. Bourdieu, *Outline of a Theory*, 1.

28. Ibid.

29. Lefebvre, *Production of Space*, 4.

30. Ibid., 38–46.

31. Ibid., 40.

32. Gieryn, "A Space for Place," 465.

33. Ibid., 466.

34. Lefebvre, *Production of Space*, 17.

35. Ibid., 43.

36. Responses to and by Collins and Evans appear in a special issue of *Social*

Studies of Science from 2003: Sheila Jassanoff, "Breaking the Wave of Science Studies: Comment on Harry M. Collins and Robert Evans, 'The Third Wave of Science Studies,'" *Social Studies of Science* 33, no. 3 (2003): 389–400; Ari Rip, "Constructing Expertise: The Third Wave of Science Studies?" *Social Studies of Science* 33, no. 3 (2003): 419–34; Brian Wynne, "Seasick on the Third Wave? Subverting the Hegemony of Propositionalism: Response to Collins and Evans (2002)," *Social Studies of Science* 33, no. 3 (2003): 401–17.

37. Wynne, "Seasick on the Third Wave,"402.

38. Jasanoff, "Breaking the Wave," 392.

39. Annemarie Mol, *The Body Multiple: Ontology in Medical Practice* (Durham, NC: Duke University Press, 2002); Bruno Latour, *Reassembling the Social: An Introduction to Actor Network Theory* (London: Oxford University Press, 2005); Andrew Pickering, *The Cybernetic Brain: Sketches of Another Future* (Chicago: University of Chicago Press, 2010); Graham, *Politics of Pain*.

40. Graham, *Politics of Pain*, 84.

41. Mol, *The Body Multiple*, 63; Graham, *Politics of Pain*, 120–21.

42. Graham, *Politics of Pain*, 117–44.

43. Ibid., 69.

4

Rhetorical Cartographies

(Counter)Mapping Urban Spaces

SAMANTHA SENDA-COOK, MICHAEL K. MIDDLETON,
AND DANIELLE ENDRES

When residents describe Omaha, they typically reference three geographic areas—North Omaha, South Omaha, and West Omaha[1]—that reveal both material disparities and perceived value, as well as imply the presence (or lack) of social, economic, and political capital of the residents. As with most urban areas, these rhetorical boundaries are marked by streets that reveal the lived divisions of the larger community: Dodge Street divides North and South Omaha (figure 4.1); West Omaha describes the area west of 72nd Street that continually expands as a result of Omaha's urban planning and annexation policies. These rhetorical boundaries also map onto Omaha's demographic segregation, which starkly illustrates Omaha as one of the most racially and economically segregated cities in the country.[2]

Popular perceptions of Omaha reinforce the material and demographic realities that support these rhetorical, racial, and socioeconomic divisions. South Omaha is known by residents and represented by demographic data (e.g., The Racial Dot Map) as an economically disadvantaged place where immigrant populations (most prominently Latino/a but also Italian and Czech) settle. This is a place where Latino/a markets and restaurants and the sounds of Spanish being spoken abound. North Omaha, in local perceptions and discourse, is characterized by its high crime rate, primarily African American population, and economic disenfranchisement. Nationally, headlines like, "Omaha, Nebraska: The Most Dangerous Place in America

To Be Black," emphasize the problems that residents in North Omaha face.[3] By contrast, West Omaha is known by residents as primarily white and affluent, as marked by high-end shopping areas (such as Ann Taylor, Anthropologie, Borsheim's Fine Jewelry, Pottery Barn, and Williams-Sonoma) and wealthy housing developments. While census-based demographic data for Omaha are not broken out for each of these specific areas of the city, fine-scale, block-level demographic data seem to support these broad categorizations. Further, participant observation and analysis reveal rhetorical constructions of these areas of the city that matter to the way they are understood by residents and outsiders.

Figure 4.1 offers a close view of our study area in the older, Eastern part of the city, at the juncture of North and South Omaha. Although the map shows the location of four of the major points of reference in our chapter, the map elides other key neighborhoods in the city. Although these boundaries appear clear-cut through geographic demarcations, demographic data, and local perceptions, features such as highways, rail lines, and decaying business districts create gaps between some neighborhoods while others overlap, yielding places that challenge the widely perceived boundaries of Omaha described above. Particular areas of the city within these broad geographic areas have atmospheres of their own that may reinforce or challenge the perceptions of North, South, and West Omaha. Furthering the ambiguity of spatial boundaries, navigating through Omaha, like many cities, can introduce changes from street to street. With surprising suddenness, a pedestrian can quickly go from feeling safe to vulnerable.

Gifford Park, for example, exists about half a mile north of Dodge Street on the cusp of North Omaha. Gifford Park has had a reputation as a dangerous neighborhood with high crime rates and extensive drug-related activities, but recent initiatives by Gifford Park's multiracial, middle-class residents (e.g., creating community gardens in abandoned lots) have attempted to reconstruct this area into a more positive, livable, and community-centered neighborhood, while keeping it affordable.[4] Across Dodge Street, a few blocks south of Gifford Park, a comparatively new shopping and residential district called Midtown Crossing has completely gentrified. These examples, and the tensions that develop between them, demonstrate not only how boundaries and movement patterns shift as neighborhoods themselves change in material ways, but also that these changes come with rhetorical consequences for current and future residents.

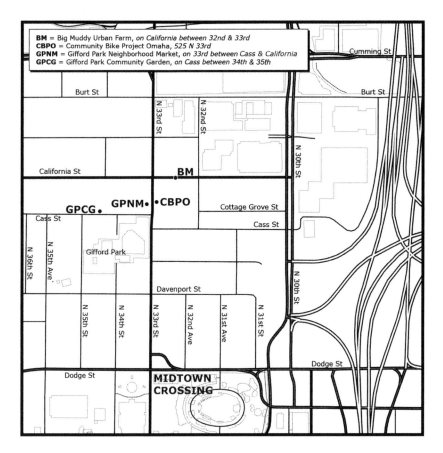

BM = Big Muddy Urban Farm, *on California between 32nd & 33rd*
CBPO = Community Bike Project Omaha, *525 N 33rd*
GPNM = Gifford Park Neighborhood Market, *on 33rd between Cass & California*
GPCG = Gifford Park Community Garden, *on Cass between 34th & 35th*

Fig. 4.1. Study sites in Omaha, Nebraska.

We conceptualize the ongoing urban development and change in Omaha as an example of place-in-process. As Tim Cresswell notes, places are not static, but are always being "made, maintained and contested" through material, embodied, and emplaced rhetorics.[5] Before unpacking the processual nature of places, it is important to define place and its relationship to space. Following Greg Dickinson, Carole Blair, and Brian L. Ott, space and place are mutually constitutive with space being more general than place.[6] Space can be thought of as a broad concept, recognizing patterns and practices that extend beyond one location whereas place is a localized, semibounded, instantiation of spatial practices. Endres and Senda-Cook explain it this way: "Place refers to particular locations (e.g., a city, a particular shopping mall, a park) that are semi-bounded, a combination of material and symbolic qualities, and embodied," whereas "space refers to a more general notion of how society and social practices are regulated (and sometimes disciplined) by spatial thinking (e.g., capitalist mode of production or gendered notions of public and private space)."[7] Both space and place are imbued with meaning. As such, place is particularized or localized whereas space is more general but not without meaning.[8]

Given their mutually constitutive relationship, we understand space and place as entwined in an ongoing process of producing space/place (as opposed to a conception of place producing space or space producing place). Our interest is with Omaha neighborhoods and regions, particular places that are inextricably connected to larger spatial patterns, such as urbanization and gentrification. Building on rhetorical scholarship about the rhetoricity of space/place, we focus on the ongoing embodied and emplaced rhetorical performances that (re)make Omaha's neighborhoods as living and evolving spaces/places.[9] Thinking about the processual nature of Omaha highlights how the localized, everyday, rhetorical performances of space/place affect changing meanings, (re)constructions, and tactics of resistance.

Mapping is one important way that people conceptualize, engage with, and perform in place.[10] Unlike studies of particular places—museums, malls, and even cities—that focus on the rhetorical construction and consequentiality of these places, we use the concepts of cartography and mapping to redirect our critical focus to *in situ*, embodied mappings of space/place that reveal how places are much more than any one map. They are dynamic places-in-process, wherein embodied and emplaced performances select, reflect, and deflect place through the experiences of those who interact with the place. In this way, mapping can be an active process of moving through and engaging with place, as opposed to a static visual representation of place. To understand the dynamics of place-in-process in urban areas, specifically Omaha's changing neighborhoods, through the concept of mapping, we build on Walter Green and Kevin D. Kuswa's notion of *rhetorical cartographies* as a way to focus on how people engage with and map out spaces/places, and how those mappings perform rhetorical functions.[11] While Greene and Kuswa use rhetorical cartography exclusively as a critical tool that rhetoricians can use to make sense of a place and its uses, we contend that participants themselves can enact practices of rhetorical cartography as a tactic for (re)creating places that (re)negotiate power locally.[12] For us, rhetorical cartographies describe the dynamic processes of making, conceptualizing, and enacting, both materially and symbolically, the space/

place in which one lives, works, or otherwise experiences daily. By (re)mapping physical places, participants alter both the performances of the places and the practices that people engage while inhabiting them. In doing so, community members can map these places in a variety of (un)conventional, even resistive, ways. People challenge and support the normative cartographies of space/place by (re)articulating them through tactics of enacting material change, engaging in practices that establish vernacular boundaries, and establishing (new) patterns of movement. In this case, rhetorical cartographies describe tactics that emerged directly from the techniques deployed by people in Omaha's communities. That is, while Greene and Kuswa conceptualize rhetorical cartography as a critical analytic that scholars can use to understand the significance of the ways in which members map their communities,[13] we view it as a broad category of emplaced and embodied rhetorical tactics that (sub)populations can use to remap space/place with (alternative) meanings and uses.

In this chapter, we begin by introducing the case study and our critical approach. Then, we illustrate three tactics of rhetorical cartographies that emerged from our field-based participatory case study in Omaha: enacting material change, undoing boundaries, and moving through the city. These three tactics are not meant to be exhaustive or mutually exclusive but rather offer a starting point for further theorizing rhetorical cartographies as a category of embodied and emplaced rhetorical practice.[14] For each tactic, we present theoretical grounding followed by our analysis of how each is performed in midtown Omaha. Finally, we articulate three implications of this conceptualization of rhetorical cartography. In terms of our understanding of space/place, rhetorical cartographies invite us to view performances of space/place and mapping as processual, dynamic experiences that align with the maps people make as they live within space/place. Rhetorical cartographies also add to a growing movement to theorize practices of participatory critical rhetoric.[15] Finally, this analysis informs conversations about urbanization by making salient the role that perception plays in categorizing a place as gentrified or gentrifying (or as resisting such efforts toward economic "development").

Midtown Omaha: A Case Study

We focus our case study on midtown Omaha, which straddles the line between North and South Omaha, two economically disadvantaged and racially diverse areas on the city's eastside. This area is a place-in-process undergoing material and symbolic changes, such as repurposing run-down buildings. Like many cities (and reflecting changing preferences among white, economically advantaged people), there is a movement to "reclaim" the inner-city. Some call this gentrification and others call it community improvement (often depending on the relative benefits they do or do not experience from such reclamation efforts). Regardless of intentionality and consequence, the changes taking place in midtown Omaha demonstrate both the fluidity and firmness of formations of space/place that are subjected to acts of rhetorical cartography by the communities that inhabit them. Recall: we define rhetorical cartographies as ways that people challenge and support official uses or interpretations of places by remaking places and engaging in practices that establish boundaries and patterned movement.

To understand how people enact rhetorical cartographies, we examined a variety of public and field-based artifacts, the latter drawn from participatory field methods engaged in by one of us, Samantha Senda-Cook. Having lived in Gifford Park for four years, Samantha used knowledge gained from her own experiences and informal conversations with Omaha residents from a variety of neighborhoods to select sites for this case study. She conducted approximately seventy hours of participant observation of community interactions at the Community Bike Project Omaha, Gifford Park Community Garden, Gifford Park Neighborhood Market, and Big Muddy Urban Farm, as well as eight, hour-long semistructured interviews that sought to understand how people (re)create urban space to challenge or reinforce dominant place meanings.[16]

Through analysis of the texts produced from participant observation and interviewing, we noticed that materiality and embodied practices significantly impact how people experience places and how they attempt to remake the meanings and uses of those places. Therefore, we also analyzed material places in Omaha such as buildings, parks, empty lots, roads, sidewalks, and paths. Similarly, we attended to embodied and emplaced practices, both witnessed and reported in interviews, that relate to these material places. Examining these practices allows for reflection on how people who regularly use places understand and engage with them. Finally, we investigated documents associated with an art project called *The Department of Local Affairs,* developed by Chloe Bass. Bass and about twenty students from an art class hosted by The Bemis Center visited different sites around Omaha and asked people to provide advice, maps, reviews, or pamphlets about local places. These artifacts provide another window into how people conceive of, move in and through, and personally connect to Omaha. Taken together, these artifacts provided a set of perspectives on how Omaha is (re) mapped alongside everyday interactions and encounters between communities and the places those communities inhabit.

Most specifically, our focus on midtown Omaha features the Gifford Park neighborhood. For many years, Gifford Park had a reputation as a dangerous place. Even though it still has that reputation among outsiders, some residents see material changes like the Gifford Park Community Garden, the Community Bike Project Omaha, Big Muddy Urban Farm, and the Gifford Park Neighborhood Market as evidence that the neighborhood is overcoming its reputation and becoming safer and more desirable for stable, long-term residents, newcomers, and short-term residents. These changes have affected the character, boundaries, and movement options within and around the neighborhood for residents. Summoning both the positive and negative connotations of the word, this neighborhood is in the midst of gentrification. For those who previously considered the neighborhood a nondestination, the emerging and embodied rhetorical cartographies of this neighborhood have morphed, in both material and intangible ways, its boundaries and the activities to which it plays host. It has gone from a place to move through as quickly as possible to one where the decreased threat of violence invites lingering. For those who call Gifford Park home, these emerging cartographies likewise contribute to reshaping the opportunities and challenges of living in Gifford Park. Before we turn to the changing rhetorical cartographies in this neighborhood, we provide some background on the widespread perception of this neighborhood as dangerous and undesirable.

When Samantha first moved to Omaha, an acquaintance told her about his experience living in Gifford Park and moving out after being mugged twice in one night. This anecdote represents deeply seated perceptions about Gifford Park by nonresidents, former residents, and current residents. To combat such negative perceptions and street realities, residents formed the Gifford Park Neighborhood Association and started a watch group about twenty-five years ago. According to one original member, they would walk around the neighborhood and mostly stand on 33rd Street between Cass and California Streets (the heart of the neighborhood) to "try to disrupt open air drug dealing" that happened most frequently in a few apartment buildings. Another original member reported that there were "people killed, children killed, in those buildings." And, because kids had to walk "past this crap" to get to school, the association organized for a safer, more community-focused neighborhood.

Since these efforts began, the crime rates have dropped significantly, according to members of the community. Long-time residents perceive positive results from their work, a neighborhood where significant changes have taken place to improve the community. In the words of one resident, "people care more about community than having a nice lawn." For example, a resident, who moved in about a year ago, said he feels connected with people who are passionate about building the neighborhood into a place that does what is best for the residents. He explained that there is a mix of people who are passionate about building a positive community in the neighborhood, which has a history of multiracial business owners and residents.[17] He gave the example of neighbors, Ben and Abdi,[18] working together at the community garden and local market. Ben, a middle-aged white man who is sometimes called the "unofficial mayor of Gifford Park" bought the properties that now house the community garden, the bike shop, and Big Muddy. Abdi, a fifteen-year-old recent immigrant from Kenya who actively volunteers at the bike shop and the community garden, has been recognized by the neighborhood association that gave him the Youth Volunteer of the Year award in 2013. Both Ben and Abdi are enthusiastic representatives of the kinds of people who live and work in the neighborhood and who strive to reshape it into a different space/place.

Many residents perceive Gifford Park as a diverse and inclusive neighborhood.[19] Tina, who is the market manager and lives in a bordering neighborhood to the northwest, describes Gifford Park as, "Friendly, inclusive, diverse. There are many incomes, races, [and] ages represented." In addition to community-building and diversity, residents see the neighborhood as a model of localized, city living. For instance, one resident says he "couldn't imagine living in any other part of Omaha" because "it's easy to not have a car." While many nonresidents view the neighborhood as dangerous, participant observation and interviewees consistently confirmed that residents— long-term and new, of different racial backgrounds and income levels—view it as a positive place where they are building community out of diversity and inclusion. Ongoing neighborhood changes illustrate a form of embodied rhetorical cartography wherein people devise tactics of material reconstruction, draw new boundaries, and develop ways of moving through the city that reinforce and/or challenge the meaning of places.

Theorizing Rhetorical Cartographies

In recent years, the material turn has led rhetorical scholars to emphasize the intersections between rhetoric and the physical spaces/places where rhetorical activity occur. For example, Blair has argued for the importance of "being there" as a critical means by which rhetorical critics can grasp the rhetorical influence of the material contexts in which rhetoric is encountered.[20] Similarly, Endres and Senda-Cook have explored how places of protest can reinforce, challenge, and influence the means, effectiveness, and rhetorical force of protest rhetoric.[21] Other scholars have focused on the rhetorical dimensions of material places themselves, highlighting how spatial design can evoke feelings of nostalgia, foster performances of class status, and create a sensibility of how communities relate to the environment.[22]

We aim to join and extend the conversation about the intersections between rhetoric and material space/place. Like other rhetoricians, we are interested in how space/place influences, constrains, enables, and constitutes various types of rhetorical activity, and we share an interest in how the meanings of space/place both influence and are influenced by the rhetorical practices of their inhabitants. The particular argument that we advance in this essay, however, focuses on the creation of rhetorical cartographies by those who live in, make use of, and aim to reimagine space/place, especially urban space/place. Communities reimagine space/place through (vernacular) rhetorical practices that challenge official interpretations and establish unofficial boundaries and patterns of movement. They create new maps of space/place through their embodied and emplaced performances and practices. Rhetorical cartographies as a conceptual term supplements the hermeneutic focus of extant rhetorical theorizing of space/place, generally (and rhetorical cartographies, specifically), by uncovering the rhetorical tactics community members utilize to materially and symbolically remap their community. By approaching rhetorical cartographies with a participatory critical rhetorical lens, we can unpack the interactions inhabitants have in particular places and the rhetorical implications of the maps produced through those encounters.

Gifford Park is one exemplar of these rhetorical practices; however, our focus on an urban setting should not suggest that rhetorical cartography happens only in urban environments. Rather, urban space/place, owing to the intensity of the interactions between inhabitants and specific locales and the acute civic and economic regulations that shape it, provides an example of what is at stake in the construction of place and residents' attempts to remake place via the material (and discursive) practices they deploy.[23] Commenting on the tensions at play in the regulation of space/place, Talmadge Wright argues that places, urban and otherwise, often confront their inhabitants with "polarized topographies."[24] This means that such places are organized and disciplined via numerous discourses—that is, media, development, planning, policing—that invest places with meanings, define their appropriate uses, and associate them with appropriate identities, which can leave others "out-of-place." However, where Wright usefully posits that "urban spaces are not 'neutral' backdrops," but instead "polarized topographies" that define "disciplinary spaces,"[25] in this essay we identify some of the tactics by which community members act with the space/place to develop emergent rhetorical cartographies, which in turn remake the idea of urban space in particular places. In doing so, we illustrate how urban communities can productively engage what Deborah Kaplan describes as the "political struggle" of urban life.[26] Disciplining uses of space/place can happen both discursively by referring to areas as a "wasteland"[27] and materially by denying basic maintenance and police services, for example. By enacting material changes, undoing boundaries, and moving through the city, inhabitants can remap places, thereby challenging disciplinary/dominant conceptualizations of space/place that aim to categorize and enforce distributions of certain people in certain spaces/places. The residents of Gifford Park are attempting to reclaim and restore community value to a neighborhood that many consider to be one of the city's "refuse" spaces.

Enacting Material Change

Space/place is made disciplinary both by economic processes and cultural practices, and civic policies that complement and sustain these processes and practices.[28] One means by which emergent communities challenge the disciplining of urban (and other) spaces/places is by enacting material changes within particular places. While these are often temporary reconstructions, by engaging in deliberate, long-term, and repeated efforts to materially reconstruct urban places, such places can be invested with new meanings and reshaped to invite new practices. For example, the contemporary movement toward establishing urban gardens on abandoned lots invites those gardens to become associated with new rhetorical practices and material places within an urban landscape. Whereas abandoned urban sites may initially be established as locations of urban decay and illegal activity, over time the construction and maintenance of urban gardens reshapes places, makes them central to collective community-based activity, and contests their association with negative dimensions of urban life.

In other words, repeated reconstructions of urban space/place provide a means by which place-as-rhetoric can foster new ways of thinking about and doing community. In some instances, these practices take the form of ongoing efforts toward gentrification that convert places by making them more exclusive to an affluent populace. For others, the reverse is true; the uses made of places mark them as off limits to "proper" citizens. Such instances are often communicated through references to "the wrong side of the tracks" and other aphorisms that communicate racial, cultural, and economic difference. However, in our analysis of repeated reconstructions of place in Gifford Park, we highlight how these repeated reconstructions can also be used to create new forms of inclusivity in the urban environment. We deploy an understanding of place-as-rhetoric to identify how urban space/place can be reconstructed to forge new identities and foster new rhetorical and material practices in those places.

About fifteen years ago, three white, middle-aged men who had grown up in and near Gifford Park realized that they could begin reconstructing the neighborhood through property ownership and community-based development. By buying properties in the area, they influenced the residential environment and uniquely built community. Taking advantage of low property values, they provide cheap leases (e.g., $1/year) on their properties for what they see as positive, community-centered efforts. Part of the rental agreement between the property owners and tenants is that renters take responsibility for maintenance and any improvements to the properties. The property owners stay financially solvent through income from full-time jobs, in two cases, and by renting other properties at market value, in the third. This strategy of buying property, fixing it up, cleaning it out, and then either using it for residences or renting it to positive community movements is itself a remapping practice initiated by these three men. The strategy works in part because it has buy-in from residents and community organizations taking advantage of the inexpensive leases and the services provided in the leased spaces. Ben, one of the property owners, has three parcels between two streets, which includes the space for the community garden. Owning the property between these two streets has, in his words, "allowed me to do things right." By that, Ben means investing in quality materials and expanding the garden into backyards while renting out houses at the front of the property.

When Ben first bought the property for the garden, he was worried about the landowners next to him environmentally contaminating the site. Lawrence, one of the three, told Ben to "just buy it." This is possible in this neighborhood because property values have been and continue to be among the lowest in the city. Ben now owns his house and the houses around him as a way to "control [his] environment" by removing lead-contaminated topsoil (emissions from Asarco, a lead refinery, contaminated about fifteen thousand residential properties in Omaha until 1997, when it closed)[29] and lease this land to the Gifford Park Neighborhood Association for $1/year for a community garden. Lawrence said he knows that it sounds easy to say this even though most people do not have the financial resources to make it possible. But, he advocates it as a remapping strategy that most people and organizations do not consider in urban areas.

Similarly, the community garden is a good example of how rhetorical cartographies change over time and through material efforts by a few individuals. In 2001, when Ben and his wife, Nancy, bought the abandoned lot on which two houses used to stand, it was full of "tires, junk trees," and was a "wasteland." Ben said, "We can do better." The houses had burned down forty to fifty years ago and the lot sat abandoned for thirty years or so. They made improvements like installing copper pipes for watering stations throughout the property, leveling out the land, and trucking in topsoil. They expanded it into the adjacent backyards, started an herb garden, erected a shed, and made a chicken coop. Now, the community garden hosts annual youth programs, potlucks, and a place to grow food and flowers.

Around 2003, Lawrence and his brother, Pat, bought an abandoned lot in which some Gifford Park business owners parked their cars and dumpsters. Lawrence said, "I liked it because no one cared about it." He wanted the opportunity to shape a positive neighborhood, to "develop" a neighborhood with a community instead of a monetary focus. Around 2006, they started the neighborhood market. According to him, there was a "great little business district with no business." Lawrence had a friend who grew sweet corn, and they started to sell that on Saturday mornings. By his logic: "We didn't see the need to get a peddlers permit to sell corn when people are selling drugs right down the street." His approach was to "just do it. And, if we break a few laws, OK." They saw this as a way to create community and encourage people to reconsider this "refuse" as a place.

Fig. 4.2. Gifford Park Neighborhood
Market residents at the 33rd Friday
Block Party and Multicultural Event.
Photo by Samantha Senda-Cook.

The market has grown significantly, now hosting about eight tents selling products like locally made cards, aprons, bacon, cosmetics, mole sauce,
and pickles in addition to food grown in the neighborhood at Big Muddy
Urban Farm. It now happens on Friday evenings, and they now have a ped-
dler's permit. As figure 4.2 shows, the market also brings community members together, especially during the 33rd Friday Block Party + Multicultural
Event. Some residents like that the market makes the neighborhood more
"self-sufficient." One person said that he thinks it ensures that we are not
"as affected by external factors." One respondent to Bass's Department of
Local Affairs touted this explicitly, "The Gifford Park Neighborhood Market on Fridays is not to be missed. Takes cash, card, and EBT [Electronic
Benefit Transfer, a.k.a SNAP]. Organic produce, pickled things, and sewn
scarves, and bags proliferate." One interviewee said, "I think the GPN Market is another great way to cultivate a food community and just strong community in general. It is a place for people to gather, socialize, experiment
with entrepreneurial projects and ideas, and a healthy activity to have in the
neighborhood." And, Tina said, "The market has proven to be a safe place
and we are constantly striving to make it more comfortable for all. When
you take the time to make a place welcoming for people, I think our community responds and takes ownership in that." Her comment about people responding to and taking ownership of welcoming places demonstrates
the degree to which residents can successfully reconstruct even places with

existing, entrenched meanings when they see positive changes happening. The market brings people to the business center of Gifford Park because it is directly across the street from the bike shop and is close to both Big Muddy and the community garden. The efforts of Lawrence and Pat and all of the vendors alter personal maps that people develop of places and impact the kinds of practices in which they engage.

When Ben saw that Lawrence and Pat had bought the lot for the market, he got in touch with them and said that he would be interested in "going in on" more projects with them. From that unification came the location for the bike shop and the central site for Big Muddy Urban Farm. Instead of targeting abandoned lots, next, Ben, Lawrence, and Pat focused on the occupied buildings referenced above, where "children were killed." They attempted to recraft the story of this neighborhood by repurposing these buildings, which had functioned as drug distribution and prostitution centers and sat in the center of Gifford Park. The building that now houses the bike shop used to have six small apartments. They thought that if they changed this building, the rest of the neighborhood might follow. Lawrence reports that when they went to look around, "The people in there were sad; it was scary inside." When they bought the building, they displaced residents and connected them with social service representatives to find different housing. But, in starting what they consider "a positive movement" for the neighborhood, they excluded people who relied on those buildings as economic centers. The remapping happening in this neighborhood came from diverse, long-term residents and is motivated by altruism, but it seeks to eliminate activities that they felt made the neighborhood dangerous. Their efforts have only been partially successful, which is why property values are still very low. But, the bike shop has become a place where children and adults congregate, as shown in figure 4.3.

Some residents see their neighborhood changing from a fearful place to one that promotes community involvement, while remaining diverse. On a typical morning, one might see college students driving to school, middle-aged people biking to work, school buses picking up children, delivery trucks unloading products, and people walking home with a six-pack of tall boys in a plastic bag. The difference now is that more people perceive walking as a possible form of transportation through the neighborhood's core. Little by little, place by place, people are reconstructing Gifford Park through material changes. By buying buildings and renting them cheaply to organizations that invest in the community, landowners have created a

Fig. 4.3. Three community members work on bikes at the Community Bike Project Omaha. Photo by Samantha Senda-Cook.

place that maintains the neighborhood's character by remodeling old buildings and that feels safe and positive for new and old residents alike. While materially changing a place can produce new rhetorical practices in the place, it also enacts a rhetorical cartography that both dismantles old and erects new material and perceptual boundaries. This can open community members to more inclusive forms of engagement across community boundaries, or further stratify social groups.

Undoing and Critiquing Boundaries

Another tactic by which rhetorical cartographies are enacted is by undoing or blurring the boundaries between the polarized topographies that constitute lived spaces. Wright argues that urban space, in particular, is organized into pleasure spaces (e.g., spaces whose aesthetic invites the circulation of capital, such as shopping centers), refuse spaces (e.g., marginal spaces where citizens are "refused" recognition and services, such as abandoned buildings), and functional spaces (e.g., spaces through which people move on their way to other destinations, such as transit centers).[30] For Wright, the experience of (urban) space is motivated by efforts to sustain these boundaries as a means of organizing communities and establishing a hierarchy of value for communities within a particular shared place. That is, according to Wright, as space/place becomes overlaid with the maps of class difference, racial difference, and neoliberal governance those spaces that cater to affluent populations (e.g., pleasure spaces) are viewed as more desirable, while spaces that are inhabited by less affluent populations (e.g., immigrants, the homeless, and other minority populations) become configured as "the bad part of town." Once urban space/place is configured as such, it further reifies hierarchical urban space/place (e.g., more aggressive policing versus more community investment).

However, these boundaries can be undone; Wright argues, "as one crosses the border from one site into another these subjective and often physical borders are often those areas subject to the greatest community struggles" focused on "who will define their uses, where are they to be placed, and who will benefit or suffer from their location."[31] In what follows, we examine how communities engage in these unforeseen uses of Omaha's refuse places and how, in doing so, they create a rhetorical cartography that redraws the boundaries and the sorts of rhetorical and material practices that can be engaged by its inhabitants.

Adjacent to Gifford Park is another place that has changed significantly in the last ten years. Mutual of Omaha, an insurance company, developed a shopping and residential district called Midtown Crossing, which itself functions like a neighborhood. Before this development, there might have been some question about where Gifford Park ended and another neighborhood began. But after, it is clear, as one participant put it, that "Dodge Street certainly divides the two." Midtown Crossing offers shops, restaurants, bars, a hotel, condos and apartments, a grocery store, a movie theater, and a park. Unlike the example of more bottom-up community revitalization of Gifford Park, Midtown Crossing is driven by top-down revitalization and gentrification.

After Mutual of Omaha built Midtown Crossing, the buildings created an obvious barrier between Gifford Park and the Turner Park neighborhood, both of which used to be considered dangerous. By erecting buildings that close off the center of the space, the developers ensured that people walking from the north would have to walk around buildings to get anywhere in the development. While Farnam Street has storefronts on both sides of the street and on-street parking, Dodge Street has a massive building wall that effectively closes off Gifford Park residents. For example, Wohlner's Grocery is the closest store to Gifford Park. And, for the many impoverished residents, walking there is easier than getting elsewhere. However, William, the former shop manager at the community bike shop, explained that people feel it is expensive and inaccessible. Therefore, some people still do not go there. The door located at 33rd and Dodge (and most accessible for Gifford Park residents) is locked and labeled as an emergency exit. One community member observed the rhetorical effect of this barrier to movement for residents of Gifford Park. Instead of making that door accessible, the barrier makes people walk "half way down the block." One interviewee summarized the feelings of many community members, noting that "it seemed like they turned their back on North Omaha."

The material changes in Midtown Crossing remapped the way that residents of the adjacent neighborhood, Gifford Park, experience this place. For instance, walking across Dodge Street between Turner Boulevard and 33rd Street is difficult because there are no lights or crosswalks. If people from Gifford Park want to go to a free concert in Turner Park, a semipublic place, they need to either walk up the hill to 33rd to the crosswalk (or run across the major thoroughfare between cars). The materiality of this place works to enact a rhetorical cartography that communicates not only a boundary, but also a barrier between this expensive development and the changing but still somewhat dangerous neighborhood of Gifford Park.

Semipublic places can also reinscribe dominant ways of being in the city. In one example, formal boundaries between a city-owned public park (the Gene Leahy Mall near the Old Market) and a privately owned public park (Heartland of America Park owned by ConAgra Foods) do not exist. Therefore, movement between the two is easy, yet the rules are different in part because a private security firm patrols Heartland of America Park. An avid bike rider reported, it "looks like public space," but he had been ejected for riding his BMX bike there. Caught on camera, he said a security guard "comes out and makes you leave." In a review of these parks from Bass's art project, one participant wrote, "The park is really pretty. [. . .] You can run, walk, slide down the slides or just lay down. But you can't sleep here because you could get in trouble." By creating a place seemingly open to the public, ConAgra invites some kinds of behaviors and not others. It attempts to control the area by enacting a rhetorical cartography that constructs boundaries that invite and discourage different citizens from traversing and dwelling in these parks. In other words, rhetorical cartography and the tactics by which such mappings are enacted highlight performances/practices of place-in-process that can both uphold and transgress dominant norms. ConAgra, therefore, advances a rhetorical cartography for one purpose while others may use similar tactics for contradictory, or even resistive, purposes.

Moving through the City

A final tactic by which rhetorical cartographies are constructed is through the ways inhabitants move in the city. As suggested above, boundary-crossing between polarized topographies reveals the disciplinary borders between different types of urban space. And, the constraints on movement, whether those be difficulty city inhabitants find engaging in movement because of the lack of transportation or privileged routes of movement, likewise create material realities that shape the experience of urban dwellers. However, the improvisational remappings of urban space, as Michel de Certeau argues, potentially "constitute a 'wandering of the semantic' produced by masses that make some parts of the city disappear and exaggerate others, distorting it, fragmenting it, and diverting it from its immobile order."[32] Rhetorical cartographies, therefore, also emerge from the ways communities interact with space/place to create different material experiences of the city by emphasizing some dimensions while erasing others. For example, the ways of traversing urban space/place adopted by parts of a broader community can act as a critique of both the dominant modes of movement (i.e., established modes of transit, such as cars) and the hierarchy of urban space those dominant modes construct (i.e., privileged destinations, such as pleasure spaces that align with dominant economic interests).

The means by which people move through cities reveal self-constructed rhetorical cartographies, personal maps that not only reflect but also implicate various shifting rhetorical constructions of urban space/place. These transportation practices demonstrate both routinized movement and fluid patterns that respond to and construct the shifting boundaries that unfold as neighborhoods undergo material changes. When people travel to the same places over and over, they develop their own patterns of getting there. As represented in Chloe Bass's *Department of Local Affairs* art project that asks people to map their experiences of Omaha, one participant created a map on which she drew the places that constitute most of her trips: work, shopping, and running. The roads on the map only connect where her experience tells her they connect. When they get further from her route, she stopped drawing them. Visually, the roads on her map do not connect up with anything else and do not even go to the edge of the page. She has places marked on the map: "food," "gas," "work," and "lake." She also includes a picture of a house that seemed to signify her residence. This person is taking advantage of the infrastructure in expected, normalized ways. She probably goes to the lake to run. It could be that she runs to work, but the fact that she included the gas station indicates that she probably drives. Modes of transit such as running or driving affect an area in different ways, which can (re)make rhetorical cartographies and change broader social perceptions of an area. Examining where people walk and how they traverse "refuse spaces" (or not) provides examples of practices that remap space.

Many interviewees see Gifford Park as walkable now. William explains that Gifford Park is well connected, describing how many people who come to the community bike shop walk from the Sienna Francis House (a homeless shelter and drug rehabilitation center) to the community garden without a lot of trouble. Additionally, the neighborhood creates opportunities for relationships that might not otherwise be possible. William says that as one goes further away from Gifford Park, this walkability dissipates. The owner of Big Muddy offered another perspective, explaining that when people walk past the urban farm, "from Creighton [University] to Cali Taco," they ask the farmers what they are doing. Seeing the place and people working there "prompts something in the mind," according to him. It provides an education both for the new farmers and for the community that sees the land being used to produce food. By contrast, the woman who lives across the street from Big Muddy said that a few years ago: "We realized we were winning the battle when some drug dealers said, 'Well, we can't go down 32nd because the bike people are there, we can't go to the park because the neighborhood association is there, we can't go here because there are police there.' That's when we realized we were winning the battle." In other words, she interpreted the restricted movements of criminals to indicate more freedom for those who wanted to build community and walk without fear.

Yet, fear persists for people who do not drive cars through Omaha; one reason is because "refuse spaces" (or "dead zones") lack businesses and housing. Throughout downtown Omaha, rail lines and underpasses cut off parts of the city, deterring walking and biking. For example, one participant noted that the 13th Street underpass is "covered in bird shit and not nice to walk through." Although a boundary like a rail line is obvious, others are more nebulous, such as when the occupied buildings become farther apart. These fluid boundaries expand and contract as different property owners move in and out. Parking lots and abandoned light industrial buildings also create boundaries between what feels safe and dangerous. To get from one area to another, people often must travel through some "refuse space" that "feels creepy," as one participant put it.

A volunteer at the bike shop gave an example of a coworker who does not drive a car. The woman, who is in her fifties, lives about a mile away but will go to Film Streams only to see a matinee because she has to cross several isolated areas to get to the movie theater. The overpass she has to walk under is poorly lit, and downtown is mostly abandoned at night. She says that the difference between the populated areas and the unpopulated ones happens so fast; two blocks can be totally different. This is one reason people perceive walking and biking as dangerous in Omaha. According to William, drivers assume that pedestrians and bikers are weird. The volunteer agreed; she thinks it will be a "very, very, very long time before the populace thinks of cyclists as anything other than freaks who aren't in their right minds." The material spaces of Omaha render one form of transportation sensible while marginalizing others as dangerous and foolish. Through structures, lack of population density, and dominant practices some urban spaces become more recalcitrant to the tactics of rhetorical cartography, while others shift in response to inhabitants' rhetorical engagements.

Specific points in midtown and downtown Omaha demonstrate the fluidity and firmness of rhetorical cartographies. Remaking material places in Gifford Park and Midtown Crossing have influenced not only how people experience these areas, but also their personal movements through and around them. They function as material manifestations of cartographic constructions of places, indicating dedicated efforts to control one's environment. The ways people traverse places also demonstrate their concepts of places and call attention to dominant perceptions and ways of being in those spaces. We conclude by considering how investigating space/place can contribute to rhetorical theory by articulating how material places manifest in everyday life.

Conclusion

The enactment and production of rhetorical cartographies is not limited to the three tactics examined in this chapter. We offer them as a productive subset of the (re)mapping practices that encompass the embodied and emplaced processes of place making rather than looking at space/place as finished products or texts. As a set of (rhetorical) tactics, rhetorical cartographies help people imagine ways of mapping and recreating actual spaces/places where they live, work, and play. They can also function as analytics by helping us see and unpack certain aspects of urban space and its (re)makings. The three tactics of rhetorical cartography that we discussed in this chapter—material changes, (un)making boundaries, and practices of movement—are united in their emphasis on the processual nature of space/place and offer an important view into how we go about studying spaces/places as they manifest. In addition to building on this concept, we see three significant implications from our concept and case study.

First, we see rhetorical cartography as adding further nuance to the already-sophisticated understanding of the rhetoricity of space/place. Previous work on space/place focuses on semipermanent material structures or snapshots of places and spaces in particular moments—such as a museum, a shopping mall, or memorial—as rhetorical artifacts. This work is invaluable in establishing the rhetorical dynamism of things that were once seen as context or unrhetorical physical structures. Building from this, an additional dimension of the rhetoricity of space/place comes from examining its processual nature as people move within and experience it. If creating personal maps is one way that people engage with and experience space/place, then a critical analytic can reveal not just how a particular place is rhetorical but also how the process of production is valuable because it moves us toward understanding the role of mapping in everyday experience with space/place. For example, our analysis highlights how places and people actively reinforce and create anew the boundaries of their neighborhoods, the movements through a city, and perceptions of places through rhetorical cartographies. These conceptual, but also embodied and emplaced, (counter)mappings of a place can expand our understanding of how space/place is always in process and emergent, always performed and practiced.

Second, the concept of rhetorical cartography has implications for the recent moves toward incorporating participatory methodologies in rhetorical criticism.[33] Rhetorical cartography not only offers a theoretical lens for examining *places of persuasion* but also has implications for other critical approaches. Accessing the tactics by which rhetorical cartographies are produced involves being present in the space/place through participatory field methods as well as engaging with those doing the place making (in the form of interviews, for example). This situates rhetorical cartography within the use of rhetorical field methods. However, more than just situating it within these participatory approaches, rhetorical cartography points to the direct relationship between fieldwork and theories of space/place.

Finally, in relation to the specific focus of this chapter on midtown Omaha and urban experience, this case study and the concept of rhetorical cartography nuances how we classify gentrification. While both Gifford Park and Midtown Crossing are in the process of gentrification and both exclude some residents, Gifford Park remains open and available to most people, and Midtown Crossing contributes physical barriers to traversing the city. Additionally, we demonstrate that people understand places differently. For example, to those living outside of Gifford Park but still in Omaha, it may appear that few changes have occurred. This is why Gifford Park still feels "edgy" and dangerous, according to one interviewee. To people who hear only about the community garden, the bike shop, the neighborhood market, and Big Muddy, it seems that Gifford Park already gentrified. But, to many residents, the neighborhood is a safe yet affordable place. The place-making processes associated with rhetorical cartographies that are ongoing in Gifford Park reveal how gentrification itself is open to interpretation.

Notes

1. While there is technically an East Omaha as displayed on Google Maps, locals do not usually refer it to. East Omaha on Google Maps is not a residential area but the airport. The Missouri River prevents further eastward extension.

2. Dustin Cable, "The Racial Dot Map," The Weldon Cooper Center for Public Service, http://demographics.coopercenter.org/DotMap/index.html.

3. Palash Ghosh, "Omaha, Nebraska: The Most Dangerous Place in America to Be Black," *International Business Times*, http://www.ibtimes.com/omaha-nebraska-most-dangerous-place-america-be-black-1548466; "Radio Controversy," WOWT 6 News, last modified October 3, 2006. http://www.wowt.com/news/headlines/4301982.html.

4. Carol Bicak, "A Midtown Project That Builds Bikes—and Communities," *Omaha World-Herald*, last modified July 5, 2014, http://www.omaha.com/living/a-midtown-project-that-builds-bikes-and-%20communities/article_76472967-e8ee-5f99-b62b-736edefe9364.html; Josh Egbert, "Gifford Park Keeping Neighborhood Safe," KMTV, last modified July 26, 2013, http://www.scrippsmedia.com/kmtv/news/Gifford-Park-Keeping-Neighborhood-Safe-217178181.html; Cindy Gonzalez, "Renovated Gifford Park Apartment Building is Now a 'Cool Property,'" *Omaha World-Herald*, last modified November 9, 2013, http://www.omaha.com/money/renovated-gifford-park-apartment-building-is-now-a-cool-property/article_f3e23749-8e0a-5cc1-986d-568f67fe2210.html; Lindsey Theis, "Gifford Park: Diverse, Safe, Unique," KMTV, last modified August 12, 2015, http://www.scrippsmedia.com/kmtv/news/Gifford-Park-diverse-safe-unique-321597752.html.

5. Tim Cresswell, *Place: A Short Introduction* (Malden, MA: Wiley-Blackwell, 2004), 5.

6. Carole Blair, Greg Dickinson and Brian L. Ott, "Introduction: Rhetoric/Memory/Place," in *Places of Public Memory: The Rhetoric of Museums and Memorials*, ed.

Greg Dickinson, Carole Blair, and Brian L. Ott, 385–402 (Tuscaloosa: University of Alabama Press, 2010).

7. Danielle Endres and Samantha Senda-Cook, "Location Matters: The Rhetoric of Place in Protest," *Quarterly Journal of Speech* 97 (2011): 259–60. See also, Danielle Endres, Samantha Senda-Cook, and Brian Cozen, "Not Just a Place to Park Your Car: Park(ing) as Spatial Argument," *Argument and Advocacy* 50 (2014).

8. While some humanist geographers, such as Yi-Fu Tuan (2001), define place as space imbued with meaning, we draw from critical/cultural geographers who see meaning in both place and space (see Doreen B. Massey, *For Space* (Thousand Oaks, CA: Sage Publications, 2005). For more, see Danielle Endres and Samantha Senda-Cook (2011) and Danielle Endres, Samantha Senda-Cook, and Brian Cozen (2014).

9. Carole Blair, "Contemporary U.S. Memorial Sites as Exemplars of Rhetoric's Materiality," in *Rhetorical Bodies*, ed. Jack Selzer and Sharon Crowley, 16–57 (Madison: University of Wisconsin Press, 1999); Greg Dickinson, Brian L. Ott, and Eric Aoki, "Spaces of Remembering and Forgetting: The Reverent Eye/I at the Plains Indian Museum," *Communication and Critical/Culture Studies* 3 (2006): 27–47; Candice Rai, "Positive Loitering and Public Goods: The Ambivalence of Civic Participation and Community Policing in the Neoliberal City," *Ethnography* 12 (2011): 65–88; Caroline Gottschalk Druschke, "Watershed as Common-Place: Communicating for Conservation at the Watershed Scale," *Environmental Communication* 7 (2013): 80–96; Ralph Cintron, *Angel's Town: Chero Ways, Gang Life, and Rhetorics of the Everyday* (Boston: Beacon Press, 1997).

10. Bernhard Klein, *Maps and the Writing of Space in Early Modern England and Ireland* (New York: Palgrave, 2001); Denis Wood, *The Power of Maps* (New York: The Guilford Press, 1992).

11. Walter Greene and Kevin D. Kuswa, "'From the Arab Spring to Athens, From Occupy Wall Street to Moscow': Regional Accents and the Rhetorical Cartography of Power," *Rhetoric Society Quarterly* 42 (2012): 271–88. For an extension of this theory, see Heather Ashley Hays, *Violent Subjects and Rhetorical Cartography in the Age of the Terror Wars* (New York: Springer, 2016).

12. See Michel de Certeau, *The Practice of Everyday Life*, trans. Steven Rendall (Berkeley: University of California Press, 1984).

13. Greene and Kuswa, "From the Arab Spring to Athens."

14. For more on rhetorical practices, see Samantha Senda-Cook, "Rugged Practices: Embodying Authenticity in Outdoor Recreation," *Quarterly Journal of Speech* 98 (2012): 129–52.

15. See Aaron Hess, "Critical-Rhetorical Ethnography: Rethinking the Place and Process of Rhetoric," *Communication Studies* 62 (2011): 127–52; Michael K. Middleton, Samantha Senda-Cook, and Danielle Endres, "Articulating Rhetorical Field

Methods: Challenges and Tensions," *Western Journal of Communication* 75 (2011); Michael K. Middleton, Aaron Hess, Danielle Endres, and Samantha Senda-Cook, *Participatory Critical Rhetoric: Theoretical and Methodological Foundations for Studying Rhetoric In Situ* (Lanham: Lexington Press, 2015).

16. Samantha interviewed six people who lived in Gifford Park between one and fifty-three years. Three were relatively new (ten years or less) and three were long term (over ten years). Some of interviewees participated in community-oriented projects. Some did not. She also interviewed two people who did not live in Gifford Park but worked there. The interviews started from a few general questions such as: How long have you lived here? What are routes you usually travel to get from place to place in Omaha? What is safe and what is dangerous? Based on participants' answers, she asked a variety of follow-up questions. While formal fieldwork happened over the course of about three and half months, Samantha has drawn from insights, observations, and conversations that extend throughout her six years of living and volunteering in the neighborhood.

17. Eva Swanson and Chris Foster, *History of 33rd & California*, Gifford Park Neighborhood Association.

18. We used culturally consistent pseudonyms for this essay.

19. Firm demographic statistics are not accessible because Omaha does not collect neighborhood demographics; however, no one during participant observation or in interviews mentioned a significant shift in demographics. A few mentioned the long-time diversity as a desirable characteristic. Additionally, a random sampling of property tax information, available through the Douglas County Treasurer's website, reveals that property values have both increased and decreased in this neighborhood in the past five years.

20. Carole Blair, "Reflections on Criticism and Bodies: Parables from Public Places," *Western Journal of Communication* 65 (2001): 271–94

21. Endres and Senda-Cook, "Location Matters."

22. Greg Dickinson, "Memories for Sale: Nostalgia and the Construction of Identity in Old Pasadena," *Quarterly Journal of Speech* 83 (1997); Jessie Stewart and Greg Dickinson, "Enunciating Locality in the Postmodern Suburb: FlatIron Crossing and the Colorado Lifestyle," *Western Journal of Communication* 72 (2008): 280–307.

23. Soja (2010) argues that urban space is also a useful analytic for understanding suburban, rural, or other spaces.

24. Talmadge Wright, *Out of Place: Homeless Mobilizations, Subcities, and Contested Landscapes* (Albany: State University of New York Press, 1997).

25. Ibid., 6.

26. Deborah N. Kaplan, "Dispatches from the Street," *Journal of International and Intercultural Communication* 1 (2008): 269–89.

27. See, Danielle Endres, "From Wasteland to Waste Site: The Role of Discourse

in Nuclear Power's Environmental Injustices," *Local Environment: The International Journal of Justice and Sustainability* 14 (2009): 917–37.

28. Henri Lefebvre, *The Production of Space*, trans. Donald Nicholson-Smith (Oxford: Blackwell, 1995).

29. "Superfund Program Implements the Recovery Act: Omaha Lead Superfund Site," United States Environmental Protection Agency, last modified December 15, 2011, www.epa.gov/superfund/eparecovery/omaha.html.

30. Wright, *Out of Place*, 101–11.

31. Ibid., 99–100.

32. de Certeau, *Practice of Everyday Life*, 102.

33. Blair, "Reflections on Criticism and Bodies"; Phaedra C. Pezzullo, *Toxic Tourism: Rhetorics of Pollution, Travel, and Environmental Justice* (Tuscaloosa: University of Alabama Press, 2007); Hess, "Critical Rhetorical Ethnography"; Middleton et al., *Participatory Critical Rhetoric*; Middleton, Senda-Cook, and Endres, "Articulating Rhetorical Field Methods"; Gottschalk Druschke, "Watershed as Common-Place."

5

Bus Trip Named Desire

Doing Fieldwork in the Balkans

Ralph Cintron

I am riding a gaily decorated bus from Prishtina, capital of Kosova, to Mitrovica, one of the last remaining hotspots from the 1990s Yugoslavian breakup.[1] The bus is all flashy reds and yellows with Albanian music piped through the sound system. A bus trip to almost any point in Kosova costs typically three euros or less, providing most Kosovars without means a way to travel. The bus makes many stops in cities, villages, and sometimes along the open road. It's February 2008 and coldish. But the bus is warm, packed, and very friendly, and I think of the sudden change the newest passengers must feel as they leave the damp, cloudy weather outside.

We don't know it yet, but exactly two weeks after this bus trip, February 17, 2008, Kosova will declare its independence. It will appear like the apparition of independence, nothing quite recognizable, for independence may no longer exist as imagined in the eighteenth and nineteenth centuries, as something innate and inevitable rising up from a "people," that is, as the self-recognition of a nation justifying a war or a revolt, and leading in time to a political reality called sovereignty, and finally a bureaucracy managing internal and external affairs in the name of a specific population. In two weeks, this modernist tale will generate enthusiastic celebrations, but underneath, as one of my younger political science colleagues at the University of Prishtina put it: "something different is being born, but we do not know what it is."

The city that we are headed to, Mitrovica, split in half by the Ibar River, seems to summarize the dilemma. The northern half of the city and surrounding region has become a largely Serbian enclave with specific legal and financial ties to Serbia; however, according to another set of arguments, the entire region belongs to Kosova, a country that is majority Muslim. The southern half of the city and running to Kosova's southern border with Macedonia is ethnically Kosovar Albanian, but even in this expanse there are, again, Serbian enclaves. Parallel structures have emerged in which pockets of Serbian density retain a degree of autonomy from Kosovar rule and maintain legal, political, and financial relationships with Serbia. The enclave where this sentiment is strongest is northern Mitrovica and the surrounding region, hence, this area is one of the most volatile in all of Europe.

"Something different is being born." Since 1999, the Kosovar government has been internationally supervised by UNMIK (United Nations Mission in Kosovo), and then by EULEX (European Union Rule of Law Mission in Kosovo).[2] Both entities have had their hands full, for most of the Serbs living in the enclaves have not recognized Albanian Kosova, claiming instead to belong to Serbia. Serbia and Russia back their claim, refusing to recognize the independence of what they call the "so-called country of Kosovo." Indeed, many countries hesitate to recognize Kosova because of their own Serbian ties or because they renounce the legality of breakaway territories. In these disputes regarding what counts as a legal state, we seem to encounter the competing rhetorics of a deeply felt sense of a people (whether Serbian or Kosovar Albanian) who have named themselves as a nation, versus the calculative rhetoric of the international order that measures historical and legal precedents against future consequences. The first logic follows nineteenth-century cornerstone virtues such as the right to resist oppression or the right to revolt or declare independence; whereas the second logic adheres to another virtue, the globalization of international law and systems of management. The latter in particular looks like a kind of international governmentality ironing out an otherwise patchwork of national laws and regulatory policies that slow down, among other things, international trade. The term "nomosphere," which pulls spatial and legal matters together and suggests the spread of a legal liberal order that attempts to occupy all surfaces of the planet with the principles of sovereignty, property, and ownership, might also be applicable here. Seemingly, we have been moving, in fits and starts, from Romanticism to management. Arguably, in today's most highly developed, bureaucratized nations the siren call of nationalism may be a kind of stylization rousing the memories of a "people" for their fictive nation. Typically, these sentiments are in the minority (excepting, of course, the recent British vote to exit a powerful symbol of globalization, the EU). But among more peripheral nations, such as Kosova, that most feel the muscle of nationalism—because, perhaps, they have for too long been in the global backwater—such rhetoric is central. A few weeks after the bus trip and soon after the declaration of independence, the owner of one of my favorite restaurants in Prishtina said to me, "I feel I have my own state now. Until now I have felt like an orphan. When people ask where I am from, I have not been able to explain this place. Now I can. Now I am somebody. I am equal to them."

But, first, back to that bus, and its wall-to-wall desire. The riders are mostly young people, rural kids. The young men bunched into different clusters, both sitting and standing, are out of their league, intimidated by the young women huddled here and there. Despite little capital, the women have cultivated a kind of hip surface, a rather aggressively sexualized version of international fashion. Chinese-made shoes selling for five-to-ten euros have made international fashion available to the poor, driving out the resigned cobbler who explains: "Who wants to pay three euros to repair old shoes when new ones can be purchased for ten?"[3]

The women, as I will soon substantiate, have turned the tables of a class-positioned marriage market. They manage their sexuality to break control of the male—their fathers, brothers, or potential boyfriends—and, at a deeper level, to break their class position by entering the marriage market of the class directly above. (Kenneth Burke's analysis of rhetoric and courtship come to mind: "The vocabularies of social and sexual courtship are so readily interchangeable, not because one is a mere 'substitute' for the other, but because sexual courtship is intrinsically fused with the motive of social hierarchy."[4]) But these women are caught in an uncomfortable tension: even as they transcend the country males on the bus through the power of their style and its aesthetic capital—despite the fact that they, too, have no real capital behind their performance—they seem reluctant to abandon their admirers, for they are enjoying male attention and, besides, they best not treat these guys too badly because no one can tell who will fail or who will ascend.

It seems these males simply do not know what to do. They have been out-smarted in more ways than one, and they seem to know it. Some former position that was granted to them for no other reason than their maleness, family name, or village has been taken away. While Yugoslavian communism did not rupture village traditionalism and its patriarchal structures,[5] these women, the young males' peers, are collapsing some of these structures and leaving them behind, wielding sexuality and aesthetic capital as new forms of mobility. In contrast, these males don't know how to look hip, much less middle-class or educated. They seem to be sinking into themselves, and what they are left with is very little: their glances, their eagerness, their intimidation, their desires.

My closest Kosovar acquaintances have talked endlessly about the rapid changes occurring among Kosovar youth. They argued that, at its root, Kosova's social structure, economy, and gender relations have been agrarian, and even its Muslim practices were determined by that. They explained that Kosovar patriarchy was also agrarian, and that even those families that did not observe religious practices exhibited a style of authoritative patriarchy pertaining to land. The new bride entered the enclosed compound of the husband's family, and was placed under the patriarchal, agrarian thumb. Her purpose was to keep domestic order and produce children to secure future landholdings. But a more global economy was replacing this agrarian economy and social structure, and the effects of the transition were everywhere: the local green grocers replaced by supermarkets, the erosion of craft industries. This transition was particularly mirrored in youth culture and its desires. Youth who could not move directly into the employment of the global market could at least adopt its aesthetics.

Hence, if the rural women on the bus had fundamentally ruptured the agrarian marriage market, it also meant that they did not have any solid footing, like their male counterparts, as professionals in the global economy. Without this opening, liberation from the agrarian could not be completed. Their dependence on the male gaze spoke to the very problem of not being able to enter the global market as career women: finally, being reduced to marriage markets and reproductive labor. Indeed, a feminist friend of mine, and anthropology graduate student in Italy, had found her own way toward a similar conclusion: "these women have no role models to symbolize how to dress because there are no professional women to imitate." The women on the bus made a dramatic, bold move, breaking patriarchal, agrarian control with a global aesthetic bought on the cheap. But this aesthetic signaled, with a degree of irony, and maybe even sadness, their lack of education and training and, therefore, their dependence on marriage markets.

At least that is one way to read their subjectivities, but these readings are fraught with complications. Some readers may have little patience for my own male gaze. Furthermore, I am risking a controversial interpretation, namely, that these young women, intentionally or not, were breaking agrarian gender rules and class positioning. Can one really extend to the rest of Kosova this slice of youth culture that just happened to ride a bus one day to Mitrovica? Like most ethnographers, I am haunted by stuff like this: Carey Wolfe quoting Niklas Luhmann: "reality . . . is what one does not perceive when one perceives it."[6]

The rapidly changing rules governing gender relations and sexuality, with this particular emphasis on the young female, is a pervasive topic across Kosova. Journalists, imams, and families are eager to weigh in. My devout but very tolerant Muslim friend Bekim, twenty-four years old, explains it this way: "Look at the dress styles. It is the Europeanization of Kosovar fashion. And pornography on TV. I do not approve of women wearing short skirts. Women think it is a sign of being modern. But it is also individualism—is individualism a good thing? Youth and contemporary morals—these are some of the main subjects discussed at the mosque. Globalization and modernization—where is it taking us? After the war the foreigners brought many things with them, but before the war many families had members abroad sending money, so the changes are coming from both sides."

There is general agreement that a fundamental change is unfolding in Kosovar society. Most see the negatives: the moralists disparage the recent opening to the West and its seduction of Kosovar youth. But they do not wish to return to any past; they are just unhappy with the present. Young feminists claim some women have simply succumbed to the cheapest fashion styles, dispensing with dignity and bowing to male desire. But within feminism another interpretation is possible, namely, that changes within gender relations correspond with broader patterns of change, leading to a stronger democracy, an improved economy, women's rights, and finally, to integration with the EU. The question here is whether the sexualization is necessary in order to get everything else, and the short answer is probably no. Though prone to sensationalism, my journalist acquaintance, Baton, interprets Kosova through the eyes of Jean Baudrillard: "Kosova is a ritual society; we imitate everything badly and produce nothing. You know Baudrillard? We cannot tell the difference between virtual and real life. We live off TV, our fashion life is TV. When the Ottoman Empire fell, it was because half of the population was ignored, women. That is still our problem. There are three reforms that must occur: reform of language, reform of women so that they participate in society and stop this nonsense of the fashion plate, and the reform of education. These reforms would transform us from virtual life to real life."

Together with Zanita, a young professional woman working with a local NGO devoted to issues of sex work and HIV/AIDS, I talk with a group of five males and five females between the ages of seventeen and twenty-one one afternoon. A young woman captures something everyone agrees with:

> You want to know about equality between the sexes? My boy friends think that the time is over for men to be over women. Maybe men thirty years old or more still think that way, but not my friends. In our house, my mother and father are fairly equal. Labor should be divided equally. Men maybe do not agree with all this equality as much as women do. Maybe men believe that they should do this and this, but then they don't really like it. I think women are the key persons to change these attitudes. If the women keep saying that they will do what the men require, then the men will not change. So, the women will change things.

What Do Statistics Add Up To?

Is there some way to "see" more broadly beyond the voices of these women, that is, to "see" the population more generally? Would data on poverty, unemployment, education, and gender "speak" the same conclusions as these women came to? Statistics are supposed to perform that sort of "seeing" or "speaking." After the Yugoslavian wars ended in Kosovo in 1999, this small region became one of the most internationally observed places in the world. Suddenly the World Bank, IMF, foreign government agencies, NGOs, and the United Nations started combing Kosovo's institutions and population in order to understand the "structural impediments to the advancement of ____." The blank here could be just about anything: economic development, democracy, civil society, ethnic relations, women's issues, human rights, rule of law. Their focus on the intersections of unemployment, youth, and gender provides a backdrop for my accidental bus ride to Mitrovica.[7]

At the time of the bus ride, in 2008, no complete, reliable census had occurred in Kosova since 1981. In 2011–2012, a census was conducted, but the northern Serbian region, including north Mitrovica, decided to boycott and do their own census led by Belgrade. Having an accurate census was, of course, important for both the international managers and the Kosovars.[8] It would lead to good governance, for, as the World Bank well knew, without a census there is no baseline and little sense of what constitutes a representative sample.[9] But the ability to take a census was also a sign of the competency of Kosovar sovereignty, a major concern of all the Kosovar government bureaucrats that I had talked to. Kosova simply had no "numbers," or, at best "unreliable numbers," and this was a sign of a more general condition, namely, backwardness or an endemic failure to complete modernization, a sense in which the practices of life run ahead of the state's capacity to measure, understand, and manage the affairs of its society. Census figures and statistical data in this sense negotiate the rhetorical relationship between the visible and invisible. That is, they produce knowledge that is not visible through any other means, for it is not as if a total population or the totality of the poor versus the wealthy can be witnessed. These are foundationally invisible to any naked eye, but through the statistical arts they become formidably visible to that same eye. Consider how statistics in particular function as a type of synecdoche (part to whole). In order to make the necessary representative sample (the part), it needs to strip away contextual "noise." In this sense, the visibility of the part is produced by producing invisibility. It is a kind of rounding off. Through such means, the part acquires the power to point to an abstracted whole—voilà! The "nation" becomes visible.

The nation's visibility through statistical representations takes us to an important point that bears on both the state's capacities, which were of enormous concern to Kosovar government officials, but also to the establishment and success of democracy throughout Eastern Europe. Among these populations, democracy did not necessarily win the day on its own merits. Of course, the entire complexity of democracy is more than this essay can manage. Rather than attempting that, I want to focus on the local scene in which democracy seemed to represent a vast hope competing against a nostalgia for Yugoslavian communism. The nostalgia was most evident when people compared the former security of pension funds, state employment, and health care against market precarity and the disciplining of daily life through the rule of law. Hope regarding the new, nostalgia regarding the past, in other words, people could both fetishize democratic life and remain suspicious of it.

At any rate, for liberal theorists, such as Jürgen Habermas, liberal democracy seems more idealized, for it can serve to legitimize the state, tame its potential for authoritarian power and compel it to serve the interests of the people. But something slightly different was manifesting in the region and perhaps was widespread in Eastern Europe. The region seemed to be saying that it is state capacity that legitimizes democracy, that proves democracy's efficacy and makes it persuasive to those disposed, as some were in Kosova, to communist nostalgia. Consider: democracy in the eyes of most would not have moral superiority over any rival political theory, such as communism, if a specific state capacity failed to deliver goods, services, and what might be called the expansion of life. A Pew Research Center made this very point in 2009, claiming that "the initial widespread enthusiasm about these [democratic, capitalist] changes has dimmed in most of the countries [of Eastern Europe] surveyed; in some, support for democracy and capitalism has diminished markedly. In many nations, majorities or pluralities say that most people were better off under communism, and there is a widespread view that the business class and political leadership have benefited from the changes more than ordinary people."[10]

State capacity in these regions, then, could make or break a democratic regime and create the conditions for the persuasiveness of democracy. It seems to me that this is a very materialist understanding of democracy and not an idealized one. In sum, life under democracy must be seen and felt as substantively ethical, and not just abstractly ethical, that is, as having material consequence (improving human relations, enabling happiness, adjusting economic levers to maintain some sort of standard of living); and it is state capacity as a mechanism of deliverables that most clearly marks this transformation toward a substantive, persuasive ethicality.

So, the numbers that were being gathered during my fieldwork seemed to indicate the fragility of the state. According to the World Bank, the population was economically and socially vulnerable[11]: poverty was at 45 percent (with 15 percent deemed "extremely poor," defined as having difficulty meeting basic nutritional needs,[12] or 37 percent, depending on the source).[13] Kosova has been the poorest country in the Western Balkans, a region in Eastern Europe notable for poverty. (Conflicting poverty data at the time reflected the difficulty of measuring the impact of the informal economy.[14]) The World Bank Report seems to seize the central point—no matter what the actual figure, a large fraction of the population hovers "just around the poverty line," which means "a shock that reduces incomes by 25 percent could send an additional 18 percent of the population below the poverty line." A positive shock, however, might lift an equivalent number out of poverty. Poverty, therefore, may have been widespread, but it was also shallow.[15]

How did this connect to my fellow bus riders? Kosovars were both poor and young. Sixty percent of Kosovars were between the ages of fifteen and twenty-nine, 50 percent were below the age of twenty-five, and 40 percent under eighteen. Approximately half of Kosova's population of two million consisted of young people; the birthrate was the highest in the Balkans. Fifty-seven percent of those facing extreme poverty were under twenty-five, while 22.4 percent of the extremely poor were between fifteen and twenty-four. Women were a complicated piece of the puzzle. At the time, 60 percent of women were unemployed compared to 38 percent of the men; however, women's unemployment was a different matter in Kosova than in Western Europe because families did not necessarily expect independent incomes from their wives or daughters. In rural areas, it was estimated that "one in four women has very limited knowledge of reading and writing." According to one estimate, in 93 percent of cases "household decision-making remains with the man. . . . As a result, young women are almost completely excluded from participation in social, political and economic life. Although the situation among the better-educated group is slowly changing, the overall social patterns are still discriminatory towards women."[16] Low levels of education for women discourage employment, which, in turn, leads to dependency on and reinforcement of patriarchal structures.

The portrait of Kosovar youth that emerged from such statistics seemed accurate enough to anyone living in Kosova. And, they added, the hopes of youth will not improve anytime soon. Economic stagnancy, as the World Bank describes it, was pervasive: "The prevailing macroeconomic conditions do not provide the platform for significant poverty reduction. The prospect for improved growth is uncertain."[17] Indeed, stagnancy was a felt experience anytime I took a visit with my friend Kreshnik or someone else to villages to talk to farmers or others. The reason they weren't farming, they told us, was that inputs cost too much, which meant in blunt terms that they were subsistence farmers as opposed to selling volume on the market.[18] Literally nothing was happening, until school let out in the early afternoon and there was a rush of children, so many that we could not believe that such stagnant places could produce all of them. But there they were.

An essential question at this point is: have things gotten better in the interim (2007–2008 to the summer of 2016, the moment of this writing)? For instance, is stagnancy, at least as imaged by statistical data, still pervasive? The conclusions are a mixed bag. Kosova is frozen politically, meaning that 109 UN member countries have recognized Kosova's independence but 84 countries have not, and this latter number includes two permanent members of the UN Security Council.[19] Serbia and the Serbian enclaves in Kosova keep pulling all international strings possible, which means that the Serbian rhetorical label, "the so-called country of Kosovo," has engineered a significant political reality that should last for a decade or more while simultaneously scaring off international investment. Here is rhetorical force working at its highest pitch, a kind of Serbian fantasy manufacturing real, but, at the same time, fantasies of independence contained in the name "The Republic of Kosovo." "Independence" remains rhetorically seismic as it counters Serbian interests, but independence in Kosovo only functions through layers of internationalism, particularly a legal order not so much determined by any "people." That is, every major international agency has an office in Kosova charged with helping the country and its people become "EU ready," because there is little choice. The report, like prior ones, offers a fantasy of independence within a reality of international control, or, switching it up, the fantasy of functioning within an international order while enduring the crushing reality of going nowhere in this "Republic."

The best news is that the 2007 projection that "the prospect for improved growth is uncertain" turned into something slightly better by 2016. Indeed, Kosova was "one of only four countries in Europe" to record "positive growth rates" every year since 2008. Between 2011 and 2014, the average growth rate was 3.5 percent, which compared well to the region but "slightly below the global average." Still, these positive growth rates reflect Kosova's isolation from the global economy, and, significantly, they depend on aid and remittances to bolster consumption. The report is clear: "the current growth model is unlikely to be able to sustainably support Kosovo's future development or EU ambitions." Meanwhile, both companies and agricultural production are not yet competitive in either regional or international markets. Perhaps the clinching argument here is that during the winter of 2014–2015, "5 percent of Kosovo's population (mostly without the required visas)" fled to the EU countries: "The migration pressure" reflected "widespread pessimism about the rule of law and economic prospects."[20]

In sum, Kosova remains "one of the poorest countries in Europe." Using the threshold of $5 per person per day, the poverty rate is "about 80 percent"; using a domestic calculation of poverty set at "€1.72 per day (2011 data)," 29.7 percent of its "1.8 million are considered poor." Unemployment continues to be bothersome (35.3 percent in 2014), and for fifteen- to twenty-four-year-olds, unemployment "exceeds 61 percent." The fact that Kosova continues to be exceedingly young explains the mass exodus.[21] And what of the women, has their situation changed? Hardly. According to a labor force survey from 2012, "women in Kosovo face higher rates of unemployment (40 percent) than men (28.1 percent). In addition, only 17.8 percent of working age women are economically active" in the labor force "compared to 55.4 percent of men."[22]

So, along with a sense of economic and political stagnancy that seems to have endured across moments of jubilation (the end of the 1999 war; independence in 2008), there is another felt experience: namely, the dynamism of desire and fear among these young people. There are no statistical numbers that claim access to the psyche, and one wonders how to measure such a thing. Nevertheless, I had a distinct impression: even as the young people destroy convention, they passionately adhere to it. Consider again the young women on our bus trip named desire, and my earlier claims about marriage markets, agrarian patriarchy, and class aspirations. Consider the overwhelmed young men, their ruralness, and likely unemployment alongside their likely sense of responsibility, the psychic weight of being the provider with few chances in a stagnating economy, their unpreparedness and deep fear of being displaced by whatever it is that is churning up in Kosova, indeed, "something different is being born, but we do not know what it is." Are the young women here seizing rights, rebelling, becoming self-sufficient agents? I suspect it has more to do with desperation, fear, longing, exhaustion, and maybe some fun, alongside a curious duality in which even as the "structures of oppression" come undone, the need remains to find one's way in an increasingly complicated marriage market, the chance, even if slim, to snag a guy with opportunities, someone worldly, even wily, because it may be hard to get ahead otherwise, but still unafraid to share the labors of house and family. The latter quality is important, for with the dissolution of the subsistence economy so goes the extended family, and all this is what integration into the EU implies. Calling it the "advancement of rights" fits a particular kind of rhetoric, but its felt experience, I suspect, is less noble and more mundane. Call it adjusting oneself to the social machinery of one's moment.

And then there are the women, unlike the riders of my bus, who seem not at all ensnared by this marriage market, young professionals like Zanita, Luljeta, and Julietta, who describe a different version of this theme in which convention remains rooted in the midst of the unconventional. Somehow, they say, we have advanced beyond males in so many things; we are so much smarter, and we understand independence and equality, but still we have our "daughterly duties" (their phrasing). So, they return home almost every weekend, as if their independent lives in Prishtina were constantly checked by parental expectations, and how the wedding, if it ever arrives, will be done in traditional dress. In some sense, they can't stand any of it, and yet they say that these little affections for family and convention mark them as "Kosovars" compared to the "loose" and uprooted internationals. They say they are grateful for these differences; in sum, different class inflections of social change through which propriety is both destroyed and displayed.

What about the young males riding the bus? Historically, their status depended on family name and village. Today it depends increasingly on their ability to market themselves according to newer rules of meritocracy, which demand certain skill sets: language skills (particularly English), education, technological skills, personal skills, such as the potential to become "professional," and so on. Underlying the idea of a meritocracy is the ability to make the self into a competitive product in the market place. The fear that one may never acquire such skills and thus get left behind as modernity plows ever deeper into Kosovar social structures is one way to characterize how our bus-riding young males seemed to be sinking into themselves as they faced their female bus mates: symbols of what they desired yet symbols of their displacement.

Meritocracy, Corruption, and Where Does the Nation-State Exist?

What does a meritocracy amount to? Consider one internationally produced report on corruption in Kosovo. Ostensibly about public procurement, it also captures the development themes repeated in report after report regarding the evolution toward a legitimate public sphere, a civil society, democratic institutions, a healthy economy, fill in the blank. It explains that corruption must be wrung out of Kosovar institutions and values through regulation before good governance can manifest: "A Public Procurement Regulatory Body (PPRB) is situated in the Ministry of Finance to develop procedural guidelines, train personnel, monitor the tendering function, and review complaints—essentially, to serve as a regulatory mechanism." This report details "several alleged procurement irregularities at the municipal level as well as at the Ministerial level," including kickbacks, standards mistakes, alleged irregularities, and missing documents, many of which went unprosecuted despite strong evidence.[23] Or, consider how the World Bank put it in 2016: "Weak institutional capacity, unclear property rights, and a complicated and fragmented licensing and inspection regime continue to create disincentives for formal private sector activities. *Fair competition is not necessarily ensured*, for several reasons: First, the large informal economy significantly distorts the market and harms those businesses that comply with the laws. Second, regional, family, or political connections have an important impact on market outcomes, weakening the informative powers of the price and quality signals that emanate from the marketplace."[24]

The engineering of a marketplace with properly functioning price signals and the engineering of competent and honest civil servants are at the heart of the liberal rule of law and, thus, at the heart of these reports. The entire bureaucratic apparatus hangs in the balance of writing good laws and developing the capacities of enforcement, of training professionals who are able to translate law into effective guidelines, monitor the functions of agencies, review complaints; in sum, regulate the actions of public life. But the social engineering that is at stake here runs deeper, for there is also a sense in which a certain kind of subjectivity is being urged along, that of a civil society by which the population becomes competent actors demanding the improvement of governance and economic well-being. Implied in these reports, then, is a vision of what constitutes democratic modernization characterized by rule of law, property rights, and respect for difference. At the center of these reports, almost always written by internationals, is the specter of the well-governed society that the authors do not necessarily detail but that is confidently known, as are the techniques for getting there.

There is something extraordinarily ironic here: these rules for "good governance" seem to have no history, no sense that they themselves evolved in a hit or miss, give and take, and often tumultuous atmosphere in which, it is hard to believe, anyone could have grasped them as a totality, significant and efficacious in their ability to transform the human worst. If these rules at their moments of origin in Western history resembled something like pragmatic guesses, today they have fundamentally lost those qualities in order to acquire a new one: sanctioned certainty. These international reports, every single one of them, embody a central rhetorical characteristic: mask the contingency, proliferate the certainty. Moreover, every time I sat in on official meetings between the international advisers and the Kosovars, this same dynamic structured the interactions. Behind the smiling, extraordinarily polite faces of the internationals and their supposed certainties, I kept thinking of the unfolding recession appearing in the United States and Europe at that exact moment in 2007–2008. If their economic engineering was so smart, why was that happening? And what of Brexit in 2016 and the fact that in 2007–2008 becoming EU ready was seemingly the *only* solution to stagnancy? The "certainties" of the international order that prop up the game of development start looking like cruel jokes.

Framed slightly differently: These neat and tidy reports are informative and helpful because they represent a sum of "best practices," acquiring their coherence and assuredness as an artifact of becoming part of an international system whose target is the outlier. Outliers cause damage. They drain resources. Their people flee and become refugees or undocumented workers in the EU, and sometimes they suicide-bomb the international system. With so much at stake, the rules cannot afford to be anything except authoritative, coherent, total, and abstracted from locality. In terms of the fetishization of democracy and the expansion of life, the outlier is the negative force, the disorder that modernity also gave birth to, that solidifies the call for democracy as the only moral choice. Without the outlier, democracy does not achieve its commonsense. But this commonsense is not quite adequate, for democracy is no pristine actor here but part of the DNA of the outlier itself.

Here we arrive at the deepest issues: what does this conception of the outlier tell us about the international system, which still relies on the nation-state form as its cornerstone, despite the proliferation of supranational institutions, the globalization of investment and debt, and the creation of a common security apparatus? The outlier is the raw material that has never been socially engineered into the nation-state form, or was once so shaped and then lost. In either instance, the nation-state remains the fallback position simply because the management of peoples is too daunting a project for the international system. It must delegate that management to the individual nation-states. That is, if the international system wants few outliers, wants a smooth horizon of stability, it lacks the ability to make it happen. Such a horizon comes with too large a price tag or requires too much apparatus. Lacking the ability to do what it wants, the international system capitulates to the familiar and known, that is, the nation-state form. What the reports embody, then, is the codification of that form, the how-to procedures for its realization. Indeed, it is in the reports where Delaney's notion of the nomosphere achieves its greatest virtue, where the nation-state form most exists as something seamlessly total and possible, whereas in the real world what exists is the extraordinary amount of repetitious labor that builds and rebuilds an ideological project that constantly breaks down.

The Nation-State Form and Three Principles of Stability

Post-Westphalian in character, the nation-state has been a slowly evolving idealization of the organization of mass social life built on three main principles: (1) sovereignty, (2) politics increasingly defined as democratic, and (3) economics. Each principle has vertical and horizontal dimensions: the verticality of hierarchy versus the horizontality of equality. The principle of sovereignty is, first, a spatial demarcation of territory and marked borders. Horizontally, each nation-state is conceived as equally sovereign and subject to a legal structure that delineates a system of rights and freedoms, for instance, the right to self-defense and freedom from the meddling of other nation-states. Hence, war as the most organized act of aggression becomes tamed by legal procedures that frame the start of war through a declaration that constructs a rationale for going to war and concludes said war by treaty. Of course, alongside such "legal" wars, there is a long history of secret wars conducted by government. Vertically, the idea of equally sovereign nations succumbs to the fact that some nation-states are far more powerful than others, meaning, for instance, that some states can grant themselves the right to violate the sovereign rights of other states (the infamous Bush doctrine) while weaker states can be punished for similar actions (Iraq's invasion of Kuwait). At first glance, what is at stake in these instances are competing notions of transcendence, namely, the transcendence of sovereign rights can be trumped by the transcendence called democracy, but not that thing called totalitarianism. Or at least this is the game of logic that is played. More realistically, it is force, the fact that Iraq could be punished, and that the United States cannot, tells us that verticality has the ultimate "right" to intervene in matters of horizontality (equality).

The second principle, the political, has at one point or another been dictatorial, communist, or fascist but increasingly liberal democratic. The horizontal dimensions of democracy consist of a shared language, culture, and values by which representability becomes possible. Representability means, in simplest terms, the emergence of a coherent sovereign people equal as an electorate that legitimizes rulership; that is, rulership and lawmaking move into the hands of an "equalized people" as opposed to the powerful. Legitimacy is of enormous significance because it comprises the struggle by which authority aspires to virtue; that is, the virtue of monarchical authority rests on divine right whereas the virtue of political authority in the modern nation-state rests on an equalized people exercising their choice in "free and open" elections. Both monarchs and elected officials need legitimacy, which suggests, finally, that divine right has not so much disappeared as moved from the ultimate authority of God to that of the "people." However, the horizontal equality of the electorate is persistently strained by the oligarchic, vertical tendencies of power: the ways, for instance, in which representability is determined by US redistricting; or how political parties, not the people, first choose the candidates to run for office; or how legislators need expert advice more than voters when determining complex, technical matters; or how political parties rely on lobbyists for both information and funding. Do the poor have a lobby? These are instances in which verticality and horizontality negotiate a truce.

The third principle is an economy that brings prosperity to the citizens living inside the nation-state. Its classic depiction is Adam Smith's *The Wealth of Nations*, which articulates the rules and laws that underpin prosperity in national terms. Smith's vision of the nation's centrality continues to be ours because the nation-state form will remain for some time the only unit capable of managing both wealth making and its distribution, a polarization that can upend social order.[25] In sum, economic stability buttresses territorial and political stability to create the nation-state form as an ideological projection, a mapping of the world, which has enabled in some places but disabled in others the pragmatic management of populations. A premise of these mutually reinforcing stabilities is that populations will be able to stay in place because their respective nation-states can provide for their needs. (Toward the end of this essay I will label this tension as the politics of stasis versus the politics of movement.) By staying in place (stasis) populations can accomplish some very important transformations: the cultivation of national traditions, a sense of belonging and loyalty, and the coherence that leads to the legitimation of democratic governance.[26]

But asylum seekers, brain drains, and undocumented workers (movement) represent the breakdown of the premise, particularly of the economic principle. Consider the impact of NAFTA (the North American Free Trade Agreement) on subsistence corn farmers in Mexico during the 1990s. Over two million left agriculture, "a drop of more than 25 percent," because they could not compete against the flood of cheap, subsidized American corn, and this movement of people helped spike the numbers of undocumented workers moving to the United States.[27] The differences in scale between these two competing economies has meant, thus far, that Mexico has been the loser,[28] which means that the economic principle, as one of the imperatives of a stable nation-state, is also in the hands of larger forces and not just under domestic control. (Something similar may be unfolding in the agriculture sector between the European Union and subsistence farmers in Kosova. Recall the general complaint in the reports that too many small landholdings prevented scaling up. The development solution, then, would seem to be some version of industrial farming and selling agricultural produce on the international markets.)

At any rate, the movement of populations—that is, peoples following their desires and wants, enabled by technologies that have ruptured the limitations of space/time (airplanes, remittances, Internet, and other forms of media)—has become a powerful force. The sheer forcefulness of movement, which interrupts the emergence of a sameness of national culture, suggests that the nation-state form, as a paradigm that *ought* to be stable (otherwise why should it command our loyalty?) is ontologically unstable. So, despite the fact that today the nation-state is the only pragmatic solution for population management, its inadequacy has become the beginning of rhetorical invention, a search for another paradigm that might not stigmatize movement but remake a new norm at the heart of a political stability differently imagined. But this is the nation-state as it ought to be, not what it is. As an ideological project, the nation-state requires a tremendous labor to be realized. The sheer energy needed to build and maintain such a grand thing is hard to sustain.

Meritocracy and Corruption One More Time

In Kosova, internationals work to engineer a different subjectivity, while many Kosovars desire to establish this "modern" subjectivity. All this is set against a backdrop of meritocracy versus corruption. The advantage of framing these two terms in a loose dialectical relation is that they acquire paradigmatic functions beyond their more exact and restricted meanings and represent competing subjectivities and motives. Hence, as the international system engineers corruption out, it establishes the paradigm of meritocracy understood now as both a subjectivity and a whole host of bundled "best practices" that will lead to broad changes in social relations.

"Corruption" in these documents has at least two understandings that seem to adhere to the public/private split. Corruption as a public matter is "generally understood as the *misuse of public office for private gain*. Within this definition, corruption can take many forms: bribery, speed money, extortion, fraud, embezzlement, influence peddling, favoritism, and nepotism, among others."[29] A variety of other terms attempts to capture private illegality such as the "illegal economy," "unreported economy," or "informal economy." Such terms attempt to label private initiatives that circumvent tax laws[30] and the costs, benefits, and rights "incorporated in the laws and administrative rules covering property relationships, commercial licensing, labor contracts, torts, financial credit and social systems."[31]

I conflate both understandings in order to understand these practices under the broader heading of *ethos*. Implied in the concept of meritocracy is a particular *ethos* and imperative. Meritocracy, acting as an *ethos*/imperative that favors the public good at the expense of friends and family, competes with corruption. Corruption is an *ethos*/imperative that favors duty to friends and family at the expense of the larger public good. The first is the subjectivity that the internationals want to engineer and many, but not all, Kosovars want, for it promises the hope of prosperity and EU integration. The first might be understood as fairness to strangers while the second as fairness to intimates. The first is associated with democratic modernity; the second with social systems based largely on intimates. The first may require a painful sacrifice of the second, that is, a sacrifice of those others who have helped us become who we are, if the democratic project is to be realized. Ironically, however, the first has never eliminated the second, even in the most "advanced" democracies—hence, the Bush clan, the Kennedy clan, the Clinton clan, the function of the Ivy Leagues in the structuring of both American and global political power and wealth, the cycling of Goldman Sachs executives into government positions in different countries, United States inheritance laws that encourage multigenerational concentrations of wealth, and so on. There is much to be said in defense of maintaining stable wealth (yes, for the larger public good) through an *ethos*/imperative that permits intimates their connections, loyalties, and favors. Hence, resisting the extremes of an *ethos*/imperative of meritocracy and transparency may not be perversion but preservation.

In noting this constant rubbing of one *ethos*/imperative against another, I have offered a small opening by which to understand how the dynamism of social change disturbs our youthful bus companions, their country, and places like it. The two *ethoi*/imperatives are sufficiently different so that when the stabilities of the older system are disrupted by the newer, many may be left with few connections, loyalties, and benefits. They are abandoned on a marketplace that demands credentials and skill sets that the poor struggle to acquire. This is one reason why Kosova saw a boom in private universities between 2004–2008: thirty private universities opened mostly in the capital city to confer over twenty thousand students with questionable degrees.[32] Eventually, the Ministry of Education shut down this private awarding of degrees, putting an end to the proliferation of chaos. This scramble for degrees, which was also a scramble for money, spoke not just to the general conditions of poverty described earlier and the weaknesses of public education, but also to the insecurities inaugurated by new rules for getting ahead. The imperatives of meritocracy, credentialing, and the rule of experts were forming a different subjectivity, which produced a black market of marginal degrees. Similar things were happening throughout the entire region.

Much of Eastern Europe is a raw playing field in which the *ethos*/imperative of meritocracy moves against and with the *ethos*/imperative of loyalty to intimates (otherwise known as corruption, or the informal economy, by those not sympathetic to the human grip of loyalty). One intention of the EU as it spreads into Eastern Europe is the eradication of corruption in politics, for the combination of a weak economy and a corrupt political order seriously undermines the democratization-stability of the region. The nation-state form, whose guiding principle is the management of desire, anger, and chaos, is the edifice of these presumptions. At the time of my fieldwork, a Pew Center (2009) poll of nine Eastern European countries ranked the economy as the top national problem, with eight ranking corruption as the second or third most significant problem.[33] But corruption and its companion, the informal economy, represent a curious problem, particularly when they are not about pure individual greed. They often compensate when the capacity of the state is weak or the economy is dysfunctional. Hence, it is a serious question whether their eradication might be positive in the long run but negative in the short.

Consider the brilliance of anthropologist Carolyn Nordstrom's inquiry into the informal economy and its dense connections with the "formal" economy in *Global Outlaws*. Through interviews with smugglers, money launderers, and international police, she arrives at a conclusion similar to mine. From an interview with a Scotland Yard detective, she hits the same notes I have already played:

> The bottom line in all this is that if you can't trust the system in late capitalist society, it's chaos. The capitalist system is terrified that people will lose trust in the system. If they don't trust it, they will move to what they do trust, to bartering, to another system. The vibrancy of the economy as a whole, its adaptability to pressures and change, often comes from the nonformal sector. Of course, it's only those at the bottom that get caught. As people work their way up the system, they become more and more divorced from the 'illicitness' of the system. Those higher up are protected by layers and layers of laundering, organization, and seeming legitimacy.[34]

Corruption and the informal economy are not just compensating mechanisms filling in gaps produced by the formal economy, as when high-grade pharmaceuticals unavailable in the hospitals of poor countries get sold by street vendors more cheaply than by legitimate pharmacies. Informal and formal economies are wholly integrated, meaning, for instance, that multinationals, according to Nordstrom, routinely engage in smuggling by stuffing shipping containers with more product than declared to avoid taxes, and this integration constitutes a fuller picture of "capitalism" than any reduction of capitalism to formal or legal economy. In short, two scenarios may come into place: (1) Corruption and the informal economy may function as necessary compensating mechanisms for the whole economy to evolve into broad economic growth, leading to greater state capacity and the passage and enforcement of law. Corruption and the informal economy thus lead to their own demise. Or (2) corruption and the informal economy may cement themselves so thoroughly into daily practice that nothing gets done without them, and this may not be all bad. Of course, as we read earlier, the World Bank does not see it this way: corruption and the informal economy "distorts" the transparency of price signals.

Some further examples drawn from Kosova but relevant to the rest of Eastern Europe: During a dinner at a friend's house, a well-placed international with expertise in the management of electric companies described the pervasiveness of the "corruption" he was trying to clean up: "Twenty-two percent of the electricity is stolen [through illegal lines]. Seventeen percent goes as uncollected bills. But the mafia also gets involved when they pay for 10 percent of usage because that is the amount that the meters record. Eighty percent of the buildings do not have all the permits for one thing or another. [In some places] two floors are metered, but the rest of the electricity just flows through to the other parts and disappears from accounting. And then meter readers can be bribed."

On another occasion, my friend Naser and I talked to owners of medium-sized businesses who complained that political parties favored some businesses while punishing others connected to rival parties. Inspections at the border or elsewhere were a primary device by which a political party in power could exert its will over another. Political parties under these conditions resemble protection rackets. In one instance, owners laughed at my left-leaning inquiry about free trade and the need for some level of government involvement. They replied with subtlety and irony: Yes, they liked free trade, real free trade, where politicians stay out of the business of interfering with business. Indeed, my question had not imagined governance as a protection racket. Governance here is crude power busily creating and reinforcing oligarchic structures that protect some and destroy others. (And there were instances when the supervisory "over-state" so to speak, first UNMIK and now EULEX, was occasionally, if not systemically, a participant.)

We see a deep irony: the multiparty system considered a hallmark of a strengthening democracy evolves into oligarchic structures or protection rackets for disseminating rewards and punishments. In these settings, a struggle to control the police may ensue, for political parties in these instances are looking for the most effective enforcement arm, individuals willing to do the dirty work. The counterforce in both Kosova and the rest of Eastern Europe, as far as I can tell, is the conviction that EU integration will eventually deliver more prosperity than weak states with weak economies and multiparty systems functioning as oligarchic entities. As long as this conviction remains in place, *and does not reveal itself as a cruel joke*, there will be enough public will to sanitize local governance in order to realize integration with the EU.

Approaching the same issues from another angle, an astute observer of Kosovar life, a very well-known owner/editor of a powerful media company, answered my questions about the emerging entrepreneurial class and the new semiotics they were constructing on the open lands around Prishtina:

Who are they? One, they reflect the heightened social mobility of the post war [post 1999]. The post war opened up space without planning. And there is no sense of a collective organization. Two, it reflects the rapid movement of villagers toward the city. Drinitza Valley people came here because of the political power. Three, Prishtina is becoming the capital of a state. There is economic movement linked to politics. These people are linked to PDK or AUK. Also LDK. [Three major political parties.] The Grand Store on the way out to Skopje [Macedonia] is connected to LDK. These people aspire to the networks of power. Political thinking has been poor. No party talks about development. They fight over turf: real estate, privatization, etc. About two years ago I gave a speech about the economy. We had then about 1100 petrol stations in 10,000 sq. kilometers. This is probably the highest percentage in the world. This is not a free market where people compete with each other—otherwise many of these would go under. They function as money laundering, contraband, and political favors.

Choosing Movement

What choices are there for the large number of unemployed youth, assuming that they are indeed unemployed and not a part of the informal economy or benefiting from the structures of corruption? For a number of years, the Kosovar government has tried to attract foreign investment in order to create jobs and allow the local economy to merge with the global. But, according to one of the best sources for news and analysis of the region, BalkanInsight.com, foreign investment fell in Kosova postindependence.[35] At the time, a pro–business/global economy publication blamed this lack of foreign investment on the global recession but also pointed to reasons why foreign investors stay away: endemic corruption; an uneducated workforce compared to Western Europe; weak property rights; weak infrastructure; and a lack of international consensus over the 2008 declaration of independence.[36] (Again, still familiar themes in 2016, as we have seen.) Another publication concluded ominously that: "In light of these ongoing developments, we maintain our view that Kosovo will remain the least developed economy in the region through 2014, with real GDP expanding by 3.3% in 2009, followed by an average annual rate of growth of 4.4% between 2010 and 2014."[37] Again, we can ask if these projections materialized. Comparative markers between Serbia and Kosova, whether accurate or not, are part of the political wars. Thus far, the growth rates suggest that neither country is racing ahead of the other, but if Serbia should race ahead, it would represent a dagger driven into the heart of Kosova.[38] For if the Serbian economy starts to deliver more than Kosova's, the Serbian enclaves in Albanian Kosova will have no reason to abandon their allegiance to Serbia. In contrast, if the Kosovar economy starts delivering, then Serbian independence inside Kosova's borders would become increasingly foolish and archaic. Everyone reads signals such as these to determine their actions, as they did, for instance, during the mass exodus from Kosova in 2014–2015.

Statistics like these function as figures of speech in the making of truth statements. They suggest stories of dire need or stories of well-being that encompass the whole of the nation. With these statistics and their stories in mind, I want to return to my accidental companions. A very real possibility for the young male riders would be migration, with papers or not, to the EU. Indeed, a major global answer to weak national economies is migration and the sending back of remittances. These actions have consequences for the nation-state form. Mimoza Kusari-Lila, the head of the American Chamber of Economy in Kosovo at the time of fieldwork, thought of remittances as a sign of a weak national economy: "The fact that Kosovo is very much dependent on the remittances of its diaspora tells us that we don't have a sustainable economy."[39]

But the global impact of remittances seems profound. In many developing countries, remittances have become a significant proportion of a country's GDP. In Kosova, for instance, remittances, by one estimate, accounted for approximately 14 percent of GDP between 2005–2007,[40] 2.7 percent more than Kosova's exports.[41] These estimates are probably low, for many remittances bypass the banking system.[42] At the time of fieldwork, approximately 30 percent of Kosovar families had at least one family member living abroad who was benefitting the family.[43] Riinvest Institute insightfully described remittances as payments for a country's exported labor, as well as "psychic benefits to the giver."[44] But we might also say that remittances act as broad wealth transfers from richer to poorer economies. This transfer often occurs on the backs of laborers, rich and poor. We do not know the percent of laboring poor who are transferring the capital of richer economies directly to poor family members. But are these the ones who are evening out the wealth divide on a global scale? If so, it proceeds unconsciously during small electronic transfers by which the poor take matters into their own hands. The totality of their actions, characterized surely by anxiety and obligation, and a source of profit from fees charged by international money transfer firms, has now surpassed the amounts provided by international businesses and governments. If our bus riders seemed not very cosmopolitan and lacked opportunities to make money, one way to break those patterns was through their very movement: through migration and remittances. If choosing migration is a good answer, it is also a painful one, another sign that even if individual capacity is in place, the nation-state form is unable to absorb the talent and eagerness of its population. Choosing movement, then, signals this lack, while the remittances themselves seem to signal a modest filling up of that lack.

Here ultimately is the deep irony that seemed to underpin my fieldwork, an irony that has not disappeared as of 2018. The irony is not just Kosova's but has different articulations in a variety of places. The politics of stasis versus the politics of movement seems to summarize, on the one hand, the nation-state ideal constituted through democratic principles and a viable economy, while, on the other hand, the politics of movement summarizes the choice that occurs when the ideal wobbles. As we saw in the restaurant owner's words described earlier, the desire to become an independent nation-state and the hope of using that structure to enable individuals to achieve democratic equality and economic well-being, and thereby to step onto the global stage, was a central driver of the Kosovar imaginary. Besides, the international order could not permit any other choice because the continued co-existence of Muslims within the Serbian state would have surely resulted in a Muslim/Orthodox conflict in Europe, causing more displacement, more movement. But the irony was that despite all the international energy and even good will that helped feed Kosovar hope, the emergence of a viable state and economy was proving very difficult to engineer. The nation-state, in effect, requires a politics of stasis to hold it together, that is, a people who gladly choose to stay in place because they are being well served. To see stasis giving away to movement felt like an emerging betrayal, and the young, eager men on the bus ride that day seemed to sense both the vitality of change and opportunity that was all around them and how unprepared they were.

When I talk, then, of a bus trip filled with desire, it is more than young men and women stealing glances at each other. It is also about an historical lack, indeed, a profound desperation, to acquire some of the solutions to human want that modernity has proffered. These solutions have become today's sovereign nation-state, democracy, and a functioning economy. Modernity has as one of its central concepts the "finding of solutions" and, therefore, modernity must produce "solutions," practical ones whose failure rates must be lower than their success rates. If those rates flip, modernity loses credibility. If the inventions of modernity, such as the nation-state, are unable to satisfy the desperations of human want, if want seems so fundamental and impervious to the mechanisms of the nation-state—or if the mechanisms themselves by creating solutions produce another round of wants—that is, if want is permanent, all pervasive, and boundless, so that it will always reappear like a balloon that we keep trying to drown in water, well, what then? The current global crises regarding migration have much to do with the fact that we are trying to preserve a politics of stasis in the face of complex weaknesses in our systems of stability. Choosing movement is a reasonable response, but the international order has yet to develop a politics of movement that might compensate for the shortcomings of the politics of stasis.

Out the window of the bus, the February landscape is littered with plastic, reminding me of a riddle I enjoyed while in Kosova: "What is the national bird?" "A plastic bag sailing on the wind." "What is the national tree?" "A bush in the middle of nowhere with lots of national birds." On my side of the window, an engaging display of desire and longing. On the other side, something similar, the nation's desire to become an equal player in the game of import/export, consumption/production, wealth making. Now in the midst of playing that game, some successes were becoming minor horrors. The state lacked the capacity to absorb the waste that appetite creates. On both sides of the window, the vagaries of desire.

Notes

1. Much of this essay was written in 2009–2010, when I was a Great Cities Institute Faculty Scholar at the University of Illinois at Chicago. It's now 2017, and I have updated the economic data where feasible. The essay draws on fieldwork conducted in 2007–2008 while I was a Fulbright Scholar at the University of Prishtinë, Kosova's major university. I did sporadic fieldwork in Kosova from 2001–2007. I use the English spelling of the Albanian Kosovë (Kosova) instead of "Kosovo," which is the Serbian pronunciation and standard international spelling. Such differences in spelling are no small matter, a point made abundantly clear by Yael Navaro-Yashin, *The Make-Believe Space: Affective Geography in a Postwar Polity* (Durham, NC: Duke University Press, 2012). These spellings evoke the fiercely competing sovereignties that date at least to the nation-building projects of nineteenth-century Europe.

2. EULEX replaced UNMIK in 2008 with the aim of helping Kosova "develop its justice system and [deal] with sensitive cases of organized crime, corruption, and war

crimes." EULEX's mandate officially expired on June 14, 2016, but the Kosovar government passed amendments to "prolong the mission" for two more years. See "Mandate of EU Kosovo Mission Expires," Radio Free Europe, Radio Liberty, June 15, 2016.

3. This comes from 2008 interviews in Prishtina with cobblers, tinsmiths, tailors, and other craftspeople. Petrit Collaku describes a similar trend: "Today the craft society has 35 crafts on its books, about nine of which are on the brink of extinction. . . . This has happened because of new trends in Kosovo, said [Enver] Pakashtica, blaming cheap imports and modern lifestyles for the change." "Kosovo's Last Blacksmiths Fade from the Scene," *Balkan Insight*, October 19, 2009, http://www.balkaninsight.com/en/article/kosovo-s-last-blacksmiths-fade-from-the-scene.

4. Kenneth Burke, *A Rhetoric of Motives* (Berkeley: University of California Press, 1969), 217.

5. At University of Prishtina, my graduate students and I discussed this fusion of traditional patriarchy to other political orders. We concluded that patriarchy (headmen passing out goodies in return for security) was the dominant political form that functioned under the Ottoman Empire, continued below the surfaces of communism, and, more recently, underneath democracy and free markets. We also wondered whether "mature" democracies incorporate patriarchal structures. Consider: US senators and representatives must secure "pork" for their constituencies if they are to secure campaign funds.

6. Carey Wolfe, *What is Posthumanism?* (Minneapolis: University of Minnesota Press, 2010), xix.

7. World Bank, "Kosovo Poverty Assessment, Vol. I: Accelerating Inclusive Growth to Reduce Widespread Poverty," Report No. 39737-XKm, October 3, 2007.

8. Linda Karadaku, "Kosovo Completes 2011 Census Without Data from North," *Eurasia Review: A Journal of Analysis and News*, October 17, 2012, http://www.eurasiareview.com/17102012-kosovo-completes-2011-census-without-data-from-north/.

9. World Bank, "Kosovo Poverty Assessment," 37–38.

10. *End of Communism Cheered but Now with More Reservations: Two Decades After the Wall's Fall*, Pew Research Center, November 2, 2009. This Pew research does not necessarily contradict my argument about the fetishization of democracy in the region, for there was also substantial support for democratic principles. What the research reinforces is the argument that the state's capacity, democratic or otherwise, to serve people's needs is what proves the legitimacy of governance.

11. World Bank, "Kosovo Poverty Assessment," 1.

12. Ibid., i–ii.

13. Ibid., 6; *Youth: A New Generation for a New Kosovo*, United Nations Development Programme Kosovo, 2006, 3.

14. A study published by the reputable Rinnvest research institute estimated unemployment at 49 percent in 2003, but qualified that number by noting the

difficulty of counting agricultural labor such that informal employment ranged between 15 to 22 percent. See *Labour Market and Unemployment in Kosova*, Riinvest Institute, January 2003, 38, 42.

15. World Bank, "Kosovo Poverty Assessment," i.

16. Ibid., 1–7.

17. Ibid., 7.

18. Our interviews were reinforced by The World Bank and Statistical Office of Kosovo: "When farmers were asked why they let the land fallow, about 30 percent reported low economic profitability, which suggests low productivity agriculture. Not surprisingly, the agricultural production is still predominantly subsistence oriented so that smaller farms reported that 70 percent of output is devoted to households needs in 2005," World Bank, "Kosovo Poverty Assessment," 3. A 2016 report from the World Bank shows that not much had improved: "The agriculture sector is predominantly subsistent/semi-subsistent . . . characterized by fragmented landholdings averaging 1.5 hectares each . . . outdated farm technologies . . . a lack of adequate investments in irrigation, limited access to credit . . . limited market access," and neighboring states that subsidize their farmers' exports. "The World Bank in Kosovo: Country Snapshot Program," *Trading Economics*, 2016, 8.

19. "The World Bank in Kosovo: Country Snapshot Program," *Trading Economics*, 2016, 1.

20. Ibid., 1–3.

21. Ibid., 4–5.

22. *Kosovo Human Development Report 2014: Migration as a Force for Development*, United Nations Development Program, 2014, 47.

23. Bertram I. Spector, Svetlana Winbourne, and Laurence D. Beck, *Corruption in Kosovo: Observations and Implications for USAID*, Washington, DC: United States Agency for International Development, July 10, 2003, 17.

24. "The World Bank in Kosovo," 4, emphasis added.

25. Adam Smith, *The Wealth of Nations* (New York: Bantam Classics, 2003).

26. The other two principles of stability, sovereignty and liberal democracy, are problematic, but the economic principle seems profoundly so. On the one hand, the notion of "creative destruction," which is most pronounced in industrial and post-industrial nation-states, creates powerful instabilities. On the other, the contemporary complaint about the "outsourcing" of jobs and the demand on the government to create jobs is a call for the economic principle to stabilize the nation-state. This call is nothing less than a counter response to creative destruction. Consider the popularity of the Trump presidential campaign (2016) upon the white and right-leaning working classes opposing the creative destructions of globalization.

27. Timothy A. Wise, "Reforming NAFTA's Agricultural Provisions," *The Future of North American Trade Policy: Lessons from NAFTA* (Boston: Boston University, The Frederick S. Pardee Center for the Study of the Longer-Range Future, 2009), 35.

28. "When more highly industrialized, high-input agricultural systems, with many negative externalities, are brought into direct competition through trade with more sustainable low-input systems, with their positive externalities, the effect is what has been referred to as the globalization of market failure," Wise, "Reforming NAFTA's Agricultural Provisions," 39.

29. Spector, Winbourne, and Beck, *Corruption in Kosovo*, 5.

30. According to one, albeit old, estimate (2003), 34.3 percent of Kosova's "entrepreneurs do not pay taxes for their employees," *Labour Market and Unemployment in Kosova*, Riinvest Institute, 37.

31. Guillermo Vuletin, *Measuring the Informal Economy in Latin America and the Caribbean*, International Monetary Fund, April 2008, 3.

32. Steve Bristow and Stephen Vickers, *Kosova Accreditation Project Report* (London: The British Accreditation Council, 2008), 7, 16.

33. *End of Communism Cheered but Now with More Reservations: Two Decades After the Wall's Fall*, Pew Research Center.

34. Ibid., 152–54.

35. Lavdim Hamidi, "Foreign Investment Falls in Kosovo for Second Year," *BalkanInsight*, January 12, 2010.

36. "UK-Kosovo Investment Forum: A Necessary First Step," *Business Monitor Online*, November 27, 2009.

37. "Energy Shortages to Weigh on Growth," *Business Monitor Online*, October 19, 2009.

38. Kosova's GDP per capita moved steadily from $2,270 in 2006 to $2,863 in 2014. During that same time Serbia's GDP per capita moved unevenly from $3,716 to $4,246. See, "The World Bank in Kosovo: Country Snapshot Program," *Trading Economics*, 2016, http://www.tradingeconomics.com/kosovo/gdp-per-capita.

39. Lavdim Hamidi, "Diaspora Remittances Fall by 8 Percent," *BalkanInsight*, August 5, 2009.

40. Muhamet Mustafa et al., *Forum 2015: Diaspora and Migration Policies* (Prishtina, Kosova: Riinvest Institute, 2007), 16.

41. Hamidi, "Diaspora Remittances."

42. Hamidi, "Foreign Investment."

43. Mustafa et al., *Forum 2015*, 39.

44. Ibid., 20.

6

Belonging to the World

Rhetorical Fieldwork as Mundane Aesthetic

BRIDIE MCGREAVY, EMMA FOX, JANE DISNEY, CHRIS PETERSEN, AND LAURA LINDENFELD

> We need to have a much more material, much more mundane, much more immanent, much more realistic, much more embodied definition of the material world if we wish to compose a common world.
> —Bruno Latour, "An Attempt at a 'Compositionist Manifesto'"

> Does this mean that we have to take seriously the real and sometimes exquisitely small differences between the many ways in which people "achieve the social"?
> I'm afraid so.
> —Bruno Latour, *Reassembling the Social: An Introduction to Actor-Network-Theory*

Introduction

We begin with a small and mundane difference, a trace from our rhetorical fieldwork. This trace illustrates how a mundane aesthetic orientation to rhetorical ethnography offers standpoints for becoming sustainable through fieldwork. The text we share emerges from the territory for our research, an area once called clam gathering place (Man-es-ayd'ik) by Wabanaki

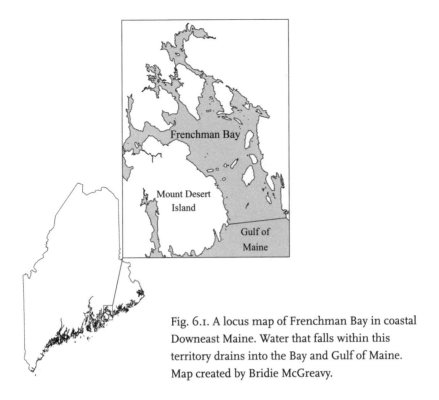

Fig. 6.1. A locus map of Frenchman Bay in coastal Downeast Maine. Water that falls within this territory drains into the Bay and Gulf of Maine. Map created by Bridie McGreavy.

inhabitants and now inscribed on maps as Frenchman Bay, Maine (figure 6.1). The quotation we share below was produced from words spoken during one of twenty-two interviews we conducted with the Frenchman Bay Partners, a group of researchers, shellfishers, municipal officials, business owners, and others working on a conservation action plan in the Bay. Our ethnographic research studied and shaped the development of this plan.

In this interview, we asked clam diggers for feedback about conservation priorities. The interview was originally scheduled with one digger for 6:00 PM, an hour before a monthly shellfish committee meeting in a rural town hall in Lamoine. When we arrived, the first digger (Clam Digger 1) had invited another to join (Clam Digger 2). As we stood outside on a warm March evening, wind and traffic sounds layered over voices on the recording. Because of the time and place, as we neared the end of the interview, another joined us (Clam Digger 3). This is what we transcribed from the digital audio recording:

Clam Digger 3: Don't know why they closed [that mudflat]. There ain't no more houses there than there ever was.

Clam Digger 1: There's uh, I think that's one of the leaky septic systems.

Clam Digger 3: Well there ain't no more houses there than ever was. Because the State . . .

Clam Digger 1: Well I don't know about that.

Clam Digger 2: The State is going by and really looking into a lot of these places that have been shut down for years.

At this moment, Clam Diggers 2 and 3 start a side conversation, and Clam Digger 1 continues to direct his comments to the interviewers. The recording becomes layered with two conversations. This layering is further textured by traffic sounds as other diggers start to pull in to the parking lot for the meeting. There is also the flow of a light wind across the microphone. "Close" indicates conversation directed at interviewers holding the digital recorder. "Far" indicates a side conversation that arose between Diggers 2 and 3 and that, in some places, layered on top of the closer exchange.

Clam Digger 2 (far): I think it still is, and I don't know why that is either.

Clam Digger 1 (close): That'd be, we'd like to get money somehow to try to improve some of these water quality areas. Like that one down in Trenton there. It's kind of a mess. It's a property that's been . . .

Clam Digger 2 (far): They can get that way if you don't keep on them. You know, I don't know, what's in there, like in Egypt Stream, that's . . .

Clam Digger 1 (close): . . . that's closing down a pretty good area down here where there's some nice clams. It's just the one septic system. And, if there was such year after year after year, and we can't dig the clams because of one system.

This artifact from our fieldwork was once spoken words, shifting bodies, and wind that became inscribed to the recording device, an uploaded audio file, and now written words that emerge from this clam gathering place on a warm March evening in Lamoine. The wind, as it flowed across the recorder's microphone, and the diggers, as they shifted into two conversations where their words layered on top of each another, emerged from a set of interactions that shaped the words just read and reterritorialized anew.[1] In their actualization they, too, were material: wind to recorder, voice to ear drum, and other atomic dynamisms not visible, beyond perceptible for us, yet still actual entities.[2]

The texts we compose from our rhetorical fieldwork are traces of innumerable material relations like these. How do we account for the materiality that produces and shapes these traces? In this chapter, we argue that a mundane aesthetic orientation to rhetorical ethnography helps attune to, address, and work with materiality in the production of rhetorics from fieldwork. We begin by describing how the mundane aesthetic grows from a sustained interest in vernacular discourse in rhetorical fieldwork.[3] Interest in the mundane or vernacular arises from the recognition of how rhetoric occurs through everyday interactions that shape lived experiences, communities, and polities. We take up this first and more common association with the mundane to emphasize the everyday and ordinary interactions, like the conversation about septic waste running into a stream in rural Maine, that enliven rhetorics. However, an exclusive focus on mundane as ordinary or banal risks ignoring the roots of mundane: *mundanus*, the worldly belonging from which all else emerges.[4] This second sense of the mundane emphasizes the creative and transformative potential of deeply belonging to the world. This approach to mundane calls attention to the role of affect, materiality, and ambient rhetorical capacity; how agency is distributed through human and nonhuman assemblages; and how the world is always in process and flux.[5] Given these characteristics, we build from the quotation introduced above to develop three specific standpoints within the mundane aesthetic to (1) attend to vibrant matter, (2) adopt a mode of experimentalism, and (3) enact an ecological form of trust in what we become from what we do. We develop these standpoints by working through an extended example drawn from our rhetorical fieldwork in Frenchman Bay and conclude with a reflection on how these standpoints allow us to become sustainable through fieldwork.

Mundane as Everyday Belonging to the World

The clam diggers' discussion of water quality and leaking septic systems exemplifies the discourse that becomes available in rhetorical fieldwork. Rhetoricians who seek this type of discourse express an interest in the mundane. Michael Middleton, Samantha Senda-Cook, and Danielle Endres demonstrate this when they describe the "mundane rhetorical experience[s] for which rhetorical field methods are also well suited."[6] Interest in the mundane also corresponds to Kent Ono and John Sloop's discussion of vernacular discourse and Robert Hariman's description of mundane rhetoric as occurring within daily routines that appear banal and dull, things like campaigning, legislating or, in our case, writing conservation plans and tracking down municipal problem forms for broken septic systems.[7] These discussions of the mundane evoke its most common associations: everyday, ordinary, banal.

But, as Hariman argues, this banality is often accompanied by "visions of affirmation, acts of beauty, and moments of collective consummation" that are produced through the "continual oscillation between these two poles of ordinary, predictable detail work and extraordinary experiences of transformation."[8] Similarly, when Steve Woolgar and Daniel Neyland explore mundane governance within waste management, traffic patterns, and air travel, they demonstrate that a "striking feature of dealing with the mundane is the hugely divergent ways in which it is apprehended."[9] They contrast mundane as ordinary, inconsequential, and unremarkable with it also being profound, extraordinary, and highly political. We call attention to both associations within the mundane, the everyday, and the extraordinary, not to privilege one over the other but to highlight how the two are always already enmeshed.

How can something as seemingly ordinary as the mundane articulate such a potent set of dialectics? We argue that this potency, and resulting creativity, arises by remembering that mundane is first *mundanus*, a material belonging to the world. It is in the space of belonging to the world from which all else emerges. This space is the *aesthetic*. The aesthetic depends on affectability, cohesions, and creativity as the world gathers together and composes itself.[10] This gathering occurs within what Alfred North Whitehead calls *organism*, which is not a living body but a mode of abstraction that seeks to maintain wholeness and avoid the supposed rift between words and things, theory and practice, material and immaterial rhetorics. This aesthetic orientation to organism acknowledges that even though we may understand that the Earth revolves around the sun, we "may still miss the radiance of the sunset. There is no substitute for the direct perception of the concrete achievement of the thing in its actuality."[11] Perceiving every *thing* in an aesthetic space of enactment is impossible. For instance, there was a lot more happening in that parking lot in Lamoine than what ended up on the recorder. Organism is an active recognition of that fact. For example, from our standpoint, the sun set while we conducted the interview and the sky turned a dusky pink. From another perspective, the sun setting is an actualization of the Earth turning on its axis, which we do not perceive from where we stand. Organism is thus an attunement to wholeness, a commitment to the direct perception of the things in their actuality—mudflats, clams, parking lots, wind, words spoken, recorded, transcribed, read once, and then again—and the recognition of myriad other things that elude direct perception yet are still actual in their own achievement.

In this aesthetic orientation to apprehending organism, appreciating the radiance of a sunset is therefore not a simple recognition of beauty. Radiance as "creativity is the principle of novelty," whose "sole appeal is to intuition."[12] This creative process occurs as an entanglement, a gathering together or concrescence, of actual entities made possible by intuition.[13] It is through these dynamic entanglements that things come to matter as things draw together to become themselves, like clams in clamflats and wind in early spring across a microphone.

These moments of gathering do not follow one after the other "like beads on a string."[14] Instead, patterns cohere and draw out as events, or recognizable strains made possible by the conditions of their emergence. One way we visualize this series of events is as wave action-formed ridges in the surface of mud: (dis)continuous ripples across space and time that still draw out in a recognizable pattern when observed from a specific standpoint. When clam diggers articulate an interest in intertidal mudflats and fixing leaking septic systems, these materialities become inscribed by the audio-recording device and move as written transcriptions that inform the technical report to the planning group, the discussion in the subsequent conservation action planning session that rearticulates an interest in fixing leaking septic systems, the grant proposal that requests funding to address these issues, and so on. Just as it is impossible to acknowledge all of the entities that were participating in that parking lot in Lamoine, it is equally impossible to account for all the entangled threads that weave a pattern, like conservation action planning as a recognizable pattern of action, in time and space. Attempting to do so is not only incomplete; it also risks slipping back into representationalist thinking wherein the description is meant to be taken as the real.[15] Instead, the mundane aesthetic orientation to rhetorical fieldwork provides standpoints that allow rhetoricians to attend to how a host of living and nonliving entities shape these patterns, how we might actively work with the world to encourage patterns to emerge in particular ways, and how, so attuned, we can learn to trust what we become from what we do.[16]

Becoming Mundane through Fieldwork

It was in the countless moments exemplified in the parking lot in Lamoine where we encountered a need to attend to the materiality that so fundamentally shaped the production and patterns in our subsequent texts. The mundane aesthetic orientation to rhetorical fieldwork is thus grounded in our ethnographic research with the Frenchman Bay Partners in Downeast Maine. Drawing from the growing body of literature on rhetorical ethnography,[17] we initially designed our research in Frenchman Bay to ask questions like: How do the Frenchman Bay Partners identify conservation priorities? Whose knowledge counts, and in what ways is this knowledge incorporated in the plan?

Yet, as we showed up asking these questions equipped with pens, paper, digital recorders, laptops, and cameras, we observed events that did not quite fit our research frame. For example, we noticed how the tides actively participated in all aspects of our planning. The tides in this region cycle twice per day at varying times and with a mean tidal range of about eleven feet. The ocean is always on its way out or rushing back in again, and in the process inundates or exposes a stretch of coastal mud and rock known as intertidal mudflat. Frequently, low tide work in the intertidal zone—activities such as planting eelgrass, surveying mudflats for clam abundance, and conducting water quality monitoring—was planned months in advance by pouring over tide charts. Planners would schedule conservation fieldwork for days and times when the pull of the moon would heighten Earth's watery bulge and create "low-low" tides ideal for extending the amount of time we could be out in the intertidal.

As we began paying more attention to how the tides and other materialities shaped our work, we saw that our study was not exclusively focused on rhetorics *of* and *about* conservation action planning. Rhetorics of conservation planning do not, as Thomas Rickert says, address "more fundamental insights into an a priori enmeshment of person and world."[18] He goes on to offer an alternative, encouraging rhetoricians to "explore how the material environment itself matters for how life is conducted."[19] When tides washed up in ways that we as rhetors did not expect, we were provoked to grapple with rhetoric's more-than-textual materiality.

The mundane aesthetic helps us do this by attending to vibrant matter, adopting a mode of experimentalism, and promoting ecological trust in collective becoming as distinct standpoints for rhetorical fieldwork. We want to emphasize from the outset that these three standpoints are not intended to serve as an interpretive device or heuristic. Instead, we see these standpoints as aesthetic modes of enactment to guide subsequent choices about practice, including practices of interpretation. This is in line with a praxiographic approach[20] that "comprises a variety of ethnographic methodologies and focuses on the study of practices, as opposed to the study of cultures" and attempts to account for the "effects, rather than the hermeneutics of representation."[21] Calling for a method that allows a rhetor to acknowledge and work within multiple ontologies, Graham advocates that rhetorical ethnographers attend to consequences of representational strategies and to how rhetorical techniques shape modes of power and materiality. The standpoints we describe here are yet another way of "calibrating" to help rhetorical ethnographers ecologically account for the "what" and "how" that, together, shape research practices and the making of multiple worlds.[22]

Territory and Practices of Fieldwork

Our rhetorical fieldwork occurred over three years (2011 to 2014), during which we studied and shaped the Frenchman Bay Partners' conservation action planning process. The Partners are composed of those who *work the tides* in Frenchman Bay. Some Partners work when the tides are out: digging clams, planting eelgrass, and surveying clam populations with shellfishermen and students. Others work when the tides are in: working with boats to harvest mussels, trap green crabs, and measure bacteria levels so people don't get sick when they swim or eat shellfish. Working the tides became an organizing metaphor for the Partners, corresponding with Caroline Gottschalk Druschke's analysis of how rhetorical landscapes shape the ways symbols and materials come together in conservation activities.[23] For her, "watershed" is a rhetorical landscape that promotes identification across difference. For us, working the tides influences identification, too, because the ocean tides along Maine's coast shape a suite of practices that produce identifications, like clam diggers, mussel harvesters, and eelgrass ecologists. In quotations we share throughout the essay, we label human participants by how they *work the tides*, like "Clam Digger" above, to draw attention to the practices and identifications that shape their relative participation in the planning.

The initial group of Partners noticed changes in the Bay and identified a need for coordinated action. For example, eelgrass, an aquatic plant that is important in marine ecosystems, has virtually disappeared in much of Frenchman Bay over the last two decades.[24] Further, though the Clean Water Act has resulted in significant improvements in water quality, more than two thousand total acres of intertidal mudflat in the Bay remain closed to shellfishing due to persistent sources of bacterial pollution like leaking septic systems, waste water treatment plants, and other land uses.

Given these and other changes, the Partners initiated a conservation action planning process and created the mission to ensure that the Frenchman Bay area is ecologically, economically, and socially healthy and resilient in the face of future change. The first author was invited to participate as a rhetorical ethnographer, and she collaborated with the other authors to do this work.[25] Conservation action planning follows a set of open standards developed by Conservation Measures Partnership for Success.[26] The open standards use a conceptual modeling process to help participants identify and achieve conservation goals. Miradi, the conceptual modeling software, organizes how participants identify ecological and social targets related to the goals, threats to targets, and strategies to address threats. Through sustained effort to learn how to use the software, compile information, and identify and deliberate priorities, the group creates complete results chains to finalize the plan.

Our primary method in this context consisted of observations, interviews, and focus groups over the three-year period. We observed steering committee meetings, conservation planning retreats, monthly shellfish committee meetings, meetings with municipal officials, and annual meetings. We audio-recorded yearly meetings and, at more routine, task-oriented, or public meetings, conducted real-time transcription where we recorded as much of the spoken dialogue as possible and took detailed field notes. We conducted two focus groups with fifteen participants in September 2011. We interviewed thirteen Partners involved in the steering committee from February through May 2012 and a subset of the initial group again in March and April 2013, for a total of twenty-two interviews. Interviews lasted approximately one hour and were audio-recorded and transcribed. As our research proceeded, we developed several projects to support the conservation action plan. Here, we highlight the 610 Project, which sought to make progress on opening 610 acres of closed clam flats in the Bay. Two or more observers participated in most meetings, and we regularly discussed and compared observations through field notes, presentations, and writing projects.

In the following section, we share excerpts to develop the three standpoints in the mundane aesthetic. From standpoint 1, we account for how vibrant matter shaped the conservation action planning process. From standpoint 2, we describe how we actively worked with specific types of objects to intentionally shape the plan. Finally, from standpoint 3, we describe our belonging to the always-unfinished work of becoming sustainable in the Bay.

Standpoint 1: Accounting for Vibrant Matter

The first standpoint helps us acknowledge how *vibrant matter* capacitates rhetorics, and how those rhetorics then continue to matter as the world becomes itself.[27] Calling our attention to assemblages of vibrant matter, Jane Bennett asks us to remember that "What is at work here on the page is an animal—vegetable—mineral—sorority cluster with a particular degree and duration of power. What is at work here is what Gilles Deleuze and Felix Guattari call an assemblage."[28] From this standpoint, we address the constituents of this assemblage and how our words on this page are a material cluster dependent on other sororities for production and continued performances. As organisms, we can never fully account for every thing in the production of rhetorics but this does not diminish the relative thing-power of the materials that participate.

The quotation in the introduction and the one provided below demonstrate the power of things like parking lots, traffic, wind, spoken words, shifting bodies, and recorders in the production of texts. The quotation in this section was produced from an audio-recorded planning session on October 17, 2011, where a conservation action planning "CAP" facilitator introduced conceptual modeling and the software. This event was held in a large meeting room at the Schoodic Institute just south of Winter Harbor, Maine. The CAP facilitator displayed the Miradi software on a large screen at the front of the room and participants sat at tables arranged in a U-shape around the screen (figure 6.2):

CAP Facilitator: So, good conceptual models should present the picture of the situation of the project site . . . but you also don't want to go too far. I mean, if you are like in the Galapagos working to protect sharks, well it's really the demand for shark fin soup in China and Hong Kong that's the real driver for why people are capturing these sharks and cutting off their fins. And, so, you need to take that into account even if it's way outside of your geographic region. Um, so it's a bit subjective: what should and should not be included?

(pause) So, how do you develop a conceptual model? Well you start with your scope. You add your conservation targets. You then add your direct threats and in some cases you may want to include the stresses that describe the biophysical impact of the threat on the target. . . . but in a lot of cases we find that including a lot of the stresses can make the conceptual model really messy. So, it's more a matter of, you know, if you feel it really needs to be in there to clarify what's going on.

As can be observed in the quotation and the photograph (figure 6.2), participants gathered around the software to define priorities and plan actions. Miradi software affected how other things assembled, including the group formation and the selection of targets. This software provided a gathering place for identifications to occur and relationships to form. Miradi created spaces, *rhetorical exigencies*, in which collaborators identified what they cared about and explored how their priorities differed from others. The software made a "space to discuss shared and divergent meaning, and to move forward on shared action."[29] In this space, the CAP facilitator described the scope for the planning, where the territory of Frenchman Bay conditioned the emergence of subsequent symbols like mudflats, water quality, and leaking septic systems—not sharks and shark fin soup.

From an aesthetic perspective, we resist an absolute split between symbols and materials. Instead, from this standpoint, we address how territory and mobility shape symbols and materials in their modes of (re)production. Symbols produced through fieldwork trace the territories of their production and actively compose new territories through their movement. The symbol is constituted materially through interactions that are then continually reterritorialized in ways that influence how the world is composed.[30] For example, the words "clam" and "mudflat" as symbols can intervene in

Fig. 6.2. Territory and assemblage in the first conservation action planning retreat showing Miradi software displayed on the screen and Partners arranged around the conceptual modeling tool. Photo by Bridie McGreavy and retouched to maintain confidentiality.

ways that clams and water as materials cannot. "Mudflat" is a material entity characterized by inscriptions that are connected to but can move independent of the *actual* mud. In a restricted sense, then, symbols can move independent of territory. We come to this realization by asking, as Latour does, "What is behind a [rhetorical] text? Inscriptions. How are these inscriptions obtained? By [working with] instruments."[31] Here, we replace Latour's terms "science" and "setting up" to draw attention to the practices that produce texts and our relationships to instruments and objects that coproduce them.

The preset options in Miradi guided the Partners in their selection of five targets, including eelgrass, mudflats, migratory fish, ocean bottom, and working waterfronts. A "mudflat habitat target" is a material entity characterized by symbolic inscriptions connected to—but capable of moving independent of—*actual* mud. The production of mudflat as habitat target forecloses other possible foci in the plan. Based on the facilitator's recommendation, the group limited its number of targets to five. With salt-marsh and estuarine wetlands as numbers six and seven on its initial list, some mud became a different matter of concern than mud in other places. This standpoint acknowledges how things like mudflats and water quality articulate *"matters of concern,* not only *matters of fact."*[32] Mudflats became a different matter of concern than saltmarsh and estuaries by how these materials showed up and became inscribed.

This standpoint also attends to how the vibrant matter within the performance makes subsequent interpretations available. The above quotation is a verbatim transcript from a digital audio recording of this event. Because of the things involved in the production of this text, we were able to include pauses, verbal fillers, and repetitive phrases. The repetitive use of the word "so" in the above quotation creates a persuasive rhythm. This rhythm can be experienced again, yet differently, when the quotation is read aloud. Further, when we compare the text from the parking lot in Lamoine to this one from a meeting room at the Schoodic Institute, there is a noted contrast in participants, as the voices and place-based sounds were differently produced in each situation. These patterns show how mundane differences, such as who shows up and how they participate—wind, clam diggers, facilitators, computer softwares, and more—matter for patterns that emerge within and from fieldwork, a difference we carry forward in the next section.

Standpoint 2: Experimenting with Objects

The first standpoint accounts for how vibrant matter capacitates rhetorics and how the specific territory and movement of symbols shape the emergence of subsequent materials and patterns of order. In vibrant assemblages, we do not ultimately control the participation of other things. As posthuman perspectives have long acknowledged, we operate within a distributed set of agencies.[33] The second standpoint grapples with how we perform our fieldwork when we as rhetors are no longer the center of the rhetorical action. We do this through a commitment to experimentalism,[34] a dynamic space of play between materials, recognizably human and otherwise, in the production of rhetorics. Studies of science as practice and of boundary objects have helped us grapple with things as phenomena/process.[35] This is in line with Graham's multiple ontologies approach, which offers a "theory of doing and being: The reality you engage is determined by the kinds of actions you habitually perform and the material contexts in which you act."[36] Adopting this second standpoint and actively experimenting with objects is a practical commitment to acknowledge how multiple worlds are made through our enactments with each other and with entities.

Approximately one year after the first planning retreat, the Partners held a second one, a six-hour goal-setting session on November 8, 2012. In this session, the CAP Facilitator participated on the phone and a second Process Facilitator was in the room. This quotation was produced from a real-time transcription where the researcher acts like a stenographer to record as much of the spoken dialogue as possible. Words in [brackets] were added to improve interpretability. In addition to highlighting the vibrant matter that capacitates rhetorics, the following quotation shows active experimentation with objects, observable in the moment when the Process Facilitator directs the group back to Miradi in a way that changes how specific things, like mudflats closures, come to matter:

Restoration Ecologist: If a clam flat is healthy enough to support clams, it should be healthy enough to support mussels.

Marine Biologist: We're using "healthy" in a weird way. It's not an ecological question. We're talking about human pathogenic problems, I think, when we're talking about clam flats and harvestability.

Restoration Ecologist: In the long term, our view of Frenchman Bay includes economic as well as ecological health.

Marine Biologist: Maybe you want individual areas like Kilkenny stream. Or open up two areas over the next five years. Or choose an acreage. [Clam Digger], we have 610 acres [of closed clam flats]. Where do we think closures are on the scale?

Clam Digger 1: Too much.

Marine Biologist: Okay, then we can label it as "Poor."

Clam Digger 1: You take clams. When they spawn, it goes into the water column for 3 weeks. Tide and winds take it and after 3 weeks it sets down. We brush to help bring [the seed] down. I think if we looked at all those cycles, like [Mussel Aquaculturalist] was saying, I think we're getting in over our heads.

Process Facilitator: So, back to Miradi. Maybe we want to focus on health closures.

CAP Facilitator: Under water quality, I have shellfish bed closures and I have number of mussels and clams per acre separated under productivity.

From standpoint 1, we call attention to the vibrant matter that capacitated this text. Because this was a real-time transcript, the production was shaped by the continuous transformation of words spoken in this meeting to words written in the process of hearing. If our bodies and technologies are an assemblage of instruments, in Latour's sense, then the inscription of this written text was likely influenced by how well we could hear participants who were on the other side of the room or on the phone; fatigue from continuous typing compounded by hunger just before lunch; the mediating effect of caffeine on said fatigue and hunger; the speed of our respective computers and our typing skills; among other possible influences.[37]

Given all this productive uncertainty, why not record the meeting to fill in missed words, verbal fillers, and other details? This was what we intended to do but when we tried to upload the audio to our computer the file would not play. This makes a difference for the verbal pattern of speech as inscribed here and for the analytic process, which relied in part on the text typed during the meeting. It is a mundane fact of fieldwork that sometimes our instruments do not work in the way that we intend. Accounting for the material shaping of texts allows an analysis of small differences that shape what becomes available within a pattern. It matters that the audio file would not play and therefore some territorialized symbols and sounds were not available for inscription. In the first two sets of quotations, the recording allowed the emergence of territorialized symbolic inscriptions to indicate body movements near and far and other mundane differences and a rhythmic persuasive repetition. Above there is no indication of body movements nor differences in sound between, for example, the facilitator in the room and the one on the phone. Though we could include a note about how it was more difficult to hear the facilitator on the phone, that difference is differently available for this particular transcription because of the materials involved in the production.

From the second standpoint, we examine how we actively worked with objects to shape texts and related patterns that emerged *as* conservation action planning. Our interaction with Miradi shows active experimentation with objects as processes. This experimentation was in line with Sarah Whatmore's imperative "to supplement the familiar repertoire of humanist methods that rely on generating talk and text with experimental practices that amplify other sensory, bodily and affective registers and extend the company and modality of what constitutes a research subject."[38] Discussions of boundary objects extend Whatmore's experimentalist stance, providing ways to organize and examine diverse participation within fieldwork. Boundary objects are not stable, fixed entities but flexible and open-ended practices through which agents compose relationships and produce knowledge, social order, and material assemblages.[39]

At the moment when the clam digger expressed concern that group members were getting in over their heads by trying to address complex ecological interactions within the Bay, Miradi and the facilitator intervened, shifting the discussion about mudflat and shellfish ecology to one focused on concerns about human health impacts associated with poor water quality. This shift occurred through the entanglement of facilitator and Miradi and how the two came together in that space of enactment. One consequence of this entanglement was the continued separation of clam and mussel productivity as distinct realities and, eventually, the selection of clams as a focal area for continued action.[40]

There were countless examples of how boundary objects like maps, technical reports, the Frenchman Bay Atlas, food at meetings, eelgrass, and the grids on which they were tied shaped conservation action planning as a pattern. A full discussion of boundary objects is beyond our scope, but one subtler example of the role of boundary objects appears in the clam digger's reference to "brushing," in the quotation above. Brushing is a practice whereby clam diggers stick cut brush in the mudflat, usually from a conifer that has ample needles for creating small eddies or swirls around the branches. These swirls help draw clam seed suspended in the water down into the mud so it can settle and start to grow. Brushing may help increase the amount of clam seed in the mudflats and is an active intervention to try to make the world different. Knowing how, when, and where to brush requires attunement to the tidal cycles and to the quality of mud. It doesn't work to simply stick brush in the mud anywhere in the intertidal zone. This second experimental standpoint helps us attune to the respective capacities of the objects involved and pursue ongoing redirection as things/processes continue to change.

Standpoint 3: Belonging to the World

Vibrant matter and experimentalism acknowledge the limits of human perceptibility and control. The third standpoint addresses how we trust what we become from what we do.[41]Acknowledging vibrant matter and experimenting with objects relies on a form of trust that flows through and connects but does not reside in a single body. It is a trust that emerges from belonging to the world. Isabelle Stengers recommends that we learn to trust "by paying attention as best [we] can, to be as discerning, as discriminating as [we] can about the particular situation."[42] The first two standpoints help us do this by directing our continual search for "the possibility of finding 'more' in nature than what is observed in it at first glance" and maintaining stances that are "mobilized by the concept of nature have the vocation of resisting the power of words that contradict this trust."[43]

We return to our situation in Lamoine to illustrate this organismic trust. At the moment when there was a slight shift in bodies, the assemblage changed and the "Far" diggers talked among themselves about Egypt Stream in Hancock, saying that they did not know what was causing the mudflat closure. The "Close" digger directed his comments to the ethnographers, expressing an interest in getting money to fix the leaking septic in Trenton. As we will describe, we ended up getting a grant and the Trenton closure became a central focus where the closure in Hancock did not. Should we have focused on Egypt Stream instead? Maybe. But when we remember these unavoidable constitutive exclusions that occur within organism, we succeed in "creating a plan able to welcome, without privilege or hierarchy, the plurality of what we are aware of" where trusting is never a guarantee or stable foundation for discernment.[44] Instead, organism "conveys the difference between two modes of 'trusting': the implicit one presupposed by our certainties and habits, and the riskier one, which exposes the thinker to adventure."[45] Our creative adventure in trust occurs etho-ecologically: through bodies in all their relations and multiplicities. This third standpoint also recognizes that when we are attuned to organism, there is always an unfinished quality to trusting what we become from what we do.

As tempting as it is to trace a simple linear pattern from one event to the next, Karen Barad cautions against making claims about causal relationships because "effect does not follow cause like hand over fist." Interactions matter in how "each one reconfigures the world in its becoming— and yet they never leave us; they are sedimented in our becoming, they become us."[46] Instead of looking for causal relationships, a mundane aesthetic approach examines how materials shape conditions of possibility in ongoing processes of becoming. This orientation looks for the ways in which belonging to the world occurs as a gathering-together of different types of bodies, a gathering enabled by etho-ecological trust. This bodily and ecological trust occurs as "a way of shaping that is always individual, limited, obstinate, and a wager on an environment that confirms and nourishes it," where belonging to the world is both ordinary and transformative.[47]

From this third standpoint, we consider how comingling materialities conditioned how mudflats came to matter. The computer technology shaped what became available for subsequent action, like the moment when the group identified the "mudflat habitat target," which then became a territorialized symbolic inscription. Our practices of rhetorical fieldwork posed questions shaped by the interactions in the first planning meeting that produced the symbol "mudflat habitat target." We asked these questions of the clam digger in the Lamoine parking lot who expressed an interest in getting "money somehow to try to improve some of these water quality areas." The expression of this interest conditioned the participation of this same digger in the next planning meeting, who through interactions with Miradi, the facilitator, and the others in the room identified the goal of opening 610 acres of closed clam flats. These traces conditioned the eventual development of a successful grant to the Maine Community Foundation to create the 610 Project, itself is an expression of the wager we have made within our milieu and the constitutive exclusions that have occurred in doing so. Accounting for vibrant matter and attending to the agency of objects as we coproduce the world is also a commitment to pay attention to these requisite exclusions and the possible consequences for the worlds we make.

The following intends to illustrate how we become mundane in our everyday belonging to the world and how, in this belonging, we may begin to enact a bodily trust in what we become from what we do. Once funded, the 610 Project created an advisory board composed of representatives from Partner groups. The board meets on a regular basis, with all the mundane details that reflect the material entanglements of project planning and implementation in Frenchman Bay. These details include scheduling meetings according to the tide charts and sharing project information in ways that correspond with ecological practices for working the tides, an ecology that may or may not include e-mail and thus requires communication through multiple instruments like phone and letter writing. The routine of scheduling meetings, making budget decisions, writing meeting minutes, producing technical reports, reporting outcomes to funders, and following up on ordinary grant-related tasks highlights the everydayness of this effort. However, as Hariman describes, it has been our experience that these everyday routines are accompanied by moments of creative transformation from our collective striving, temporary as these moments may be.[48]

For example, in October 2014, after months of meeting, we learned that water samples from the mudflat we had prioritized in Trenton had bacteria counts below the closure threshold. All signs indicated that this area, which is easily accessible to clam diggers and where estimates indicated approximately thirty thousand pounds of clams, would open soon. Then bacteria flourished again and the possibility of opening this area diminished. In response, shellfish committee members decided to allow a company from southern Maine to conduct a depuration dig. This is a type of harvest where clams are dug from a pollution closure and then put through a treatment process that makes them safe to eat. In towns where shellfish committees are not actively working to address pollution closures, the depuration company can freely dig in these areas. Because of the ongoing work in the 610 Project, the Maine Department of Marine Resources allowed the shellfish committee to decide whether it wanted to allow the depuration harvest to occur. In this case, the 610 Project created a decision space that it would not have otherwise had, and gave us a brief sense of accomplishment when we felt our efforts supported the committee's work. The shellfish committee then announced at its next monthly meeting that anyone present at the meeting could sign up to participate in the depuration dig. Those who were not at the meeting were excluded from signing up for the dig, which prompted frustration from other license holders in the ordinance. Conflict escalated within the group, and our sense of accomplishment faded again. Co-incidentally, the winter of 2015 was exceptionally cold and long, and much of the Maine coast remained locked in ice well into April. The depuration company missed the window in which it intended to dig the closure and decided it would wait until December 2015. At the same meeting where we learned that the depuration harvest had been postponed, we also learned that the Town of Trenton had received money to fix its septic system. We thought this system had been fixed, but as it turns out the town never got the grant money to help the landowner pay to fix it, which partly explains how the bacteria gained a foothold again. If the leaking septic system is fixed, water quality could improve once again, and we might open this area sooner than expected, again.

A Conclusion in Process

A letter that shellfish committee members wrote to request municipal support for the 610 Project states, "We are striving for clean water." This striving is the essence of an etho-ecological trust in belonging to the world. It is a process that has no end point. So, this will not be a tidy wrap-up describing our success in achieving sustainability in the Bay. Offering such an ending would contradict the mundane aesthetic approach to rhetorical fieldwork. Instead, we end with attunement, and more striving.

Though there are many questions we could ask from our choices as we composed this work, we pose just one to highlight the contingent questioning that vibrant matter, experimentalism, and etho-ecological trust requires. Tracing across the texts that weave a story about water, clams, mudflats, leaking septic systems, water quality tests, grant funding, and so forth, our concluding question asks: what about the bacteria? As the marine biologist pointed out in the second planning meeting, our use of the term "healthy" is anthropocentric, not ecological. Our striving for clean water is a striving that seeks to *deny* bacteria an ecological foothold in the world. Their foothold is conditioned by human waste moving into places where it can cause sickness and degrade livelihoods. This, for us, is the sense of rights and responsibilities we bring to our striving. The bacteria remind us that a "delicate tissue of ethicality runs through the marrow of being. There is no getting away from ethics—mattering is an integral part of the ontology of the world in its dynamic presencing."[49] Our fieldwork is based on choices with consequences, at the very least for bacteria, and acknowledging this fact is an attempt at organismic enactment.

We will never achieve sustainability. We can only belong to the world and trust in our continual and collective striving as organism. The mundane aesthetic approach to rhetorical fieldwork opens a mode of questioning that serves a necessary part of the creative and ethical adventure of sustainable world making. The standpoints within the mundane aesthetic orient rhetorical ethnographers to address vibrant matter, find ways to experiment with objects, and belong to the world. These standpoints help us respond to Latour's call that we become more mundane and, in doing so, more embodied and more realistic as we continually compose sustainable worlds.[50] Like the mud and tides, the mundane aesthetic offers fluid ground for sustainable becoming: by belonging to the world through fieldwork.

Notes

1. Gilles Deleuze and Felix Guattari, *A Thousand Plateaus: Capitalism and Schizophrenia* (Minneapolis: University of Minnesota Press, 1987), 126–27.

2. Alfred North Whitehead, *Process and Reality*, ed. David Ray Griffin and Donald W. Sherburne, 18–29 (New York: The Free Press, 1978).

3. Robert Hariman, "Terrible Beauty and Mundane Detail: Aesthetic Knowledge in the Practice of Everyday Life," *Argumentation and Advocacy* 35, no. 1 (1998); Gerard A. Hauser, "Vernacular Dialogue and the Rhetoricality of Public Opinion," *Communications Monographs* 65, no. 2 (1998): 83–107, doi: 10.1080/03637759809376439; Michael K. Middleton, Samantha Senda-Cook, and Danielle Endres, "Articulating Rhetorical Field Methods: Challenges and Tensions," *Western Journal of Communication* 75, no. 4 (2011): 386–406; Kent A. Ono and John M. Sloop, "The Critique of Vernacular Discourse," *Communication Monographs* 62 (2005): 19–46.

4. Steve Woolgar and Daniel Neyland, *Mundane Governance: Ontology and Accountability* (Oxford, UK: Oxford University Press, 2013), 37.

5. Thomas Rickert, *Ambient Rhetoric: The Attunements of Rhetorical Being* (Pittsburgh, PA: University of Pittsburgh Press, 2013); Jane Bennett, *Vibrant Matter: A Political Ecology of Things* (London: Duke University Press, 2010); Karen Barad, *Meeting the Universe Halfway: Quantum Physics and the Entanglement of Matter and Meaning* (Durham, NC: Duke University Press, 2007); Isabelle Stengers, *Thinking with Whitehead: A Free and Wild Creation of Concepts*, trans. Michael Chase (Cambridge, MA: Harvard University Press, 2011); Whitehead, *Process and Reality*.

6. Middleton, Senda-Cook, and Endres, "Articulating Rhetorical Field Methods," 396.

7. Ono and Sloop, "The Critique of Vernacular Discourse"; Hariman, "Terrible Beauty."

8. Hariman, "Terrible Beauty," 6.

9. Woolgar and Neyland, *Mundane Governance*, 260.

10. Whitehead, *Process and Reality*.

11. Stengers, *Thinking with Whitehead*, 199–200.

12. Whitehead, *Process and Reality*, 21–22; Stengers, *Thinking with Whitehead*, 257.

13. Ibid.; see also, Stengers, *Thinking with Whitehead*, 261.

14. Barad, *Meeting the Universe Halfway*, 394.

15. Barad articulates a nonrepresentationalist approach that focuses on phenomena and practices that she calls "agential realism," 56; see also, Paul Feyerabend and Eric Oberheim, *The Tyranny of Science* (Cambridge, UK: Polity Press, 2011).

16. Stengers, *Thinking with Whitehead*, 164.

17. Danielle Endres and Samantha Senda-Cook, "Location Matters: The Rhetoric of Place in Protest," *Quarterly Journal of Speech* 97, no. 3 (2011): 257–82; Aaron Hess, "Critical-Rhetorical Ethnography: Rethinking the Place and Process of Rhetoric," *Communication Studies* 62, no. 2 (2011): 127–52: doi: 10.1080/10510974.2011.529750;

Michael K. Middleton et al., *Participatory Critical Rhetoric: Theoretical and Methodological Foundations for Studying Rhetoric in Situ* (Lanhman, MD: Lexington Books, 2015).

18. Rickert, *Ambient Rhetoric,* 252.

19. Ibid.

20. Annemarie Mol, "Ontological Politics: A Word and Some Questions," in *Actor Network Theory and After,* ed. John Law and John Hassard (Oxford, UK: Blackwell, 1999), 74–89; Annemarie Mol, *The Body Multiple: Ontology in Medical Practice* (Durham, NC: Duke University Press, 2002), 53–54, 121.

21. S. Scott Graham, *The Politics of Pain Medicine: A Rhetorical-Ontological Inquiry* (Chicago, IL: University of Chicago Press, 2015), 83–85.

22. Graham, *Politics of Pain,* 85–88.

23. Caroline Gottschalk Druschke, "Watershed as Common-Place: Communication for Conservation at the Watershed Scale," *Environmental Communication: A Journal of Nature and Culture* 7, no. 1 (2013): 80–96.

24. George W. Kidder, Shannon White, Molly F. Miller, Wendy S. Norden, Theodore Taylor, and Jane E. Disney, "Biodegradable Grids: An Effective Method for Eelgrass (Zostera marina) Restoration in Maine," *Journal of Coastal Research* 31, no. 4 (2015): 900–06. Jane Disney and George Kidder, "Community-Based Eelgrass (Zostera marina) Restoration in Frenchman Bay," *The Bulletin: MDI Biological Laboratory* 49 (Bar Harbor, MN: Mount Desert Island Biological Lab).

25. Our longer list of authors intends to call attention to the politics of authorship when we produce research with community partners. We encourage rhetorical ethnographers to explore collaborative writing with those community members who would benefit from and find value in coproducing rhetorical scholarship.

26. Richard Margolius, Caroline Stem, Nick Salafksy, and Marcia Brown, "Using Conceptual Models as a Planning and Evaluation Tool in Conservation," *Evaluation and Program Planning* 32 (2009): 138–47.

27. Bennett, *Vibrant Matter.*

28. Ibid., 23.

29. Greg Wilson and Carl G. Herndl, "Boundary Objects as Rhetorical Exigence: Knowledge Mapping and Interdisciplinary Cooperation at the Los Alamos National Laboratory," *Journal of Business and Technical Communication* 21, no. 2 (2007): 151.

30. Deleuze and Guattari, *A Thousand Plateaus.*

31. Bruno Latour, *Science in Action: How to Follow Scientists and Engineers Through Society* (Cambridge, MA: Harvard University Press, 1987), 69.

32. Latour, "Compositionist," 478.

33. Donna J. Haraway, *Simians, Cyborgs, and Women: The Reinvention of Nature* (New York, NY: Routledge, 1991); Latour, *Reassembling the Social;* Andrew Pickering, *The Mangle of Practice: Time, Agency and Science* (Chicago, IL: University of Chicago Press, 1995).

34. Isabelle Stengers, "Including Nonhumans in Political Theory: Opening Pandora's Box?" in *Political Matter: Technoscience, Democracy, and Public Life*, ed. Bruce Braun and Sarah Whatmore (Minneapolis: University of Minnesota Press, 2010); Sarah Whatmore, "Materialist Returns: Practising Cultural Geography in and for a More-Than-Human World," *Cultural Geographies* 13, no. 4 (2006): 600–09, doi: 10.1191/1474474006cgj377oa.

35. Graham, *Politics of Pain*; Pickering, *Mangle of Practice*; Susan L. Star and James R. Griesemer, "Institutional Ecology, 'Translations' and Boundary Objects: Amateurs and Professionals in Berkeley's Museum of Vertebrate Zoology, 1907–39," *Social Studies of Science* 19, no. 3 (1989) 387–420; Wilson and Herndl, "Boundary Objects."

36. Graham, *Politics of Pain Medicine*, 31.

37. Latour, *Science in Action*, 69.

38. Whatmore, "Materialist Returns," 49–50.

39. Pickering, *Mangle of Practice*, 101–102, Star and Griesemer, "Institutional Ecology."

40. Barad, *Meeting the Universe Halfway*, 309; See also, Graham, *Politics of Pain*; Mol, *Body Multiple*.

41. Isabelle Stengers, "Introductory Notes on an Ecology of Practices," *Cultural Studies Review* 11, no. 1 (2005): 183–96; Stengers, *Thinking with Whitehead*, 164.

42. Stengers, "Ecology of Practices," 188.

43. Stengers, *Thinking with Whitehead*, 37.

44. Ibid., 59.

45. Ibid.

46. Barad, *Meeting the Universe Halfway*, 394.

47. Stengers, *Thinking with Whitehead*, 164.

48. Hariman, "Terrible Beauty."

49. Barad, *Meeting the Universe Halfway*, 396.

50. Latour, "Compositionist," 488.

7

Rhetorical Life among the Ruins

John M. Ackerman

When people occupy the house of the other; when we expropriate as we invariably do the material conditions of lives adjacent to and preceding ours; and when we take up the spoils of conquest and calamity to launch the next campaign, or turn our gaze elsewhere as if nothing happened—in all of this, we participate in ruination. Ruination maps the fields upon which shattered buildings and landscapes, broken social bonds, public distrust, and sustained apprehension circulate. "Ruination is an *act* perpetrated, a *condition* to which one is subject, and a *cause* of loss"[1] though the authority, circumstance, volume, and duration within ruinous acts will vary. Ruination as a circumstance and force within local communities appears to unravel the social tissue that binds households, neighborhoods, and regions together. Yet, after moments of extreme and subtle forms of violence go their way— by military incursion; or by violence in the street, in the home, and through institutions; or by insidiously unequal economic redistribution—after all these forms of violence upon one's land and soul, the unraveled social tissue holds true in a local sense. It recombines and reconditions: life not only goes on; it makes do with what is at hand, and one motive for writing this essay is to understand how this could be so, and then to propose a standpoint for qualitative rhetorical studies of late-industrial communities or any milieu that reveals the visible, palpable signs of duress.

A related motive for writing was a gnawing discomfort, long after my fieldwork was over, with how society at large and academic scholars, in particular, refer to the social and economic circumstances of neighborhoods: in *late liberalism*, the *latter stages of advanced capitalism, uneven distributions of wealth,* the *post-industrial society,* and so forth. These are biting yet pastoral themes that cast light on such neighborhoods but only in an epiphenomenal sense. As a critical reader of theory, I could assign a relation between historical and ideological differences, but the residences I have studied and lived in exceeded the imagined circumstances of those theories. Once one commits to a participatory study of residential economic practices in locale—indexed through local policy debates, economic prognoses, and on behalf of comparatively silenced voices—pastoral theoretic accounts tend to obscure the grittiness of everyday life of a more granular or "textured" scale, as Robert Hariman puts it.[2]

J. K. Gibson-Graham confronted the same conundrum in their advocacy of local economies by considering the space between "small facts" (on the ground) and "large issues" (in the conceptual air) mediated, they propose, by turning to "weak" theories of vital, local economies. A weak theory points to moments of "transformation" in an "undecidable" terrain.[3] A weak theory does not presuppose "any one direction for economic change but is alert to the ways in which crisis and stability are experienced differentially across the heterogeneous practices that constitute an 'economy.'"[4] Weak theories are pliable, capable of "bend[ing] any method away from abstraction and toward a more engaged encounter with particularity."[5]

This essay began years ago when I noticed that textbook treatments of qualitative and rhetorical methods and my studies of local economies were not bending enough. Generally, my studies of post-industrial neighborhoods[6] did not provide an explanatory register equal to the affectability within abject societal conditions. I introduced for discussion the difference between creative and cultural economies to try to get closer, but there simply was more creative circumstantial engagement, more *metis,* more *making do,* in the neighborhoods where I studied and lived than theories allowed. Not only did the subaltern speak; it also made things out of neighborhood remnants and vacant lots, things that worked, lived, thrived. The making and making do exceeded the capacity to speak or reflect; words were often muffled or came forth as a stutter or a sigh. I turn to ruination, as a weak theory, because other economic signifiers failed to name the capaciousness of residential life in the after-effects of violence, whether that violence was directly felt like the National Guard gunning down students at Kent State in 1970 or more ephemerally as economic inequalities absorbed by that community forty years thereafter.

Across my scholarship, I have labored with inadequate terminology whenever the neighborhoods I frequented were hailed as *post-industrial* or the *rust belt* or in *economic decline* or as sites of *public trauma* or in need of *gentrification, redevelopment,* or *renewal,* or even as the locus for *counter-publicity.* None of those terms, nor the epistemological formations sanctioning them, can identify the catalytic potential alive in the after-effects of racial and economic violence, nor capture the more "protean connectionism" that irrepressibly surfaces in times of economic peril and social unrest.[7] Expressions of relevance, of connections, tend not to be shouted by protesters or recorded by journalists; these are more intimate, more immediate. Yael Navaro-Yashin's ethnography of the after-effects of ethnic violence and incursion in Cyprus, a study that introduced me to the concept of a "ruined" neighborhood and region, featured the immediacy of ruination over time as "an intimate involvement with the abject or abjected material."[8] For this essay, I argue that ruination is a likely candidate for a weak theory of economic diversity and vitality in local communities across the United States and beyond. I hope to show that in both principle and practice, ruination carries within its conditions as much persuasive capacity as other more modern and progressive framings. To consider that capacity, I turn primarily to anthropologists who have rethought and remade ruin as a tangible, lively, remembered process of ruination in the affairs of the state and foremost in the affairs of people who recuperate their daily lives in residence.

Ruins and Ruination

The ruin in Western society, as Tim Edensor explores, remains in place with shades of its originating economic content, devoid of the originating desire and appeal for economic consumption.[9] Edensor's focus is on industrial ruins left to rot as "wastelands" although they do not remain so for very long. As many have noted, Detroit and other "rust belt" communities in the industrial Northeast and elsewhere can and must be repurposed whether by scrapping clean an abandoned factory or retail site or by turning them into a monument to progress or a museum of the past.[10] In the communities that I've studied, remnants of a former economic life, for example the Flats and the warehouse districts in Cleveland, are sampled for posterity, saving remnants of iron bridges, barges, and heavy machinery. Economic ruins as artifacts and zones of new economic potential are the inevitable consequences of economic expansion, yet for every tattered neighborhood or decimated industrial park, the remains play an allegorical role. For Edensor, ruins offer a "rebuke to visions of progress," and though they may be categorized by a city investment zone, or by property owners as vacant, they "contain within them stimuli for imagining things otherwise."[11]

An economic ruin, therefore, may be set aside with a residual capacity to be re-categorized and monetized for a different role in the market place. The ruin as remainder may also be set aside for public reflection and recreation in the way that some industrial parks are turned in historical monuments or the narratives and artifacts curated in a dedicated space. Increasingly, rhetorical scholars have looked to "places of memory" to describe this rhetorical capacity, in a sense, of ruins from a previous regime: prisons (Alcatraz), military endeavors (Nevada atomic weapon test sites), sport and civic figures (Joe Louis monument), and natural history (the Draper Natural History Museum).[12] These places might celebrate, or rebuke, the affairs of the state; they might honor virtuous people and triumphal events, or implicitly dishonor those deemed less worthy of public commemoration.[13] Yet if ruins carry within them, as Edensor proposes, "stimuli for imagining things differently," then there exists a capacity within their material form that holds a collective potential, beyond immediate economic possibilities, for those who live nearby or pass through. "Hidden in ruins," as Edensor argues are "forgotten forms of collectivity and solidarity, lost skills, ways of behaving and feeling, traces of arcane language and neglected historical and contemporary forms of social enterprise."[14]

The interdependence of the ruin to ruination has caught the eye of cultural anthropologists concerned foremost with the political life of the subject within the peaks and valleys of imperial conquest. The ruin could be a designated remnant of past progress, a landmark, a vacant field, or a curation, but ruination, as a weak theory, captures "actual imperial residues and remnants that may elude our (critical) chartings."[15] Ruination gains ontological force through an inclusive array of objects, structures, and spaces, often ordinary in their registration, enlivened by a quotidian sensorium that enables an embodied, collective memory of what happened and then an image of what is possible. Ruination provides an adjacent history and relocates the more formal historical record within "sites and circumstances of dispossession that imperial architects disavow as not of their making, in violences of disenfranchisement that are shorn of their status as imperial entailments that go by other names."[16]

Violence can be etched into the material tableau of a community, such as the physical traces of violence from the Guardsman's volleys at Kent State in 1970,[17] or through more indirect forms of economic decline and racial intolerance left in place long after a traumatic event. In *Space and the Memories of Violence*, Estela Schindel and Pamela Columbo describe the after-effects of state violence as an erasure of the "determinant topography," leaving residents to reconfigure their livelihoods from indeterminate conditions that circulate as the "haunting effects emanating from buildings and the practices of living" even when the "material remnants seemingly remain untouched."[18] In other words, violence can be swift, leaving a gaping hole of trauma, or can be insidiously slow in the manifestation of indifference and inequity that "saturate the subsoil of people's lives and persist . . . over a longer duration."[19]

The ruin as artifact can invite different degrees of attention: a ruinous scene might reveal itself as a process, a texture, a trace, of degradation and decomposition. Gastón Gordillo's ethnographic study of the Chaco region of Argentina differentiates state-owned ruins from the ruination that constitutes daily living in the countryside because monuments, museums, churches, statues, histories, and policies reconstitute the past as a "unified object that elite sensibilities often treat as a fetish that ought not be disturbed."[20] The state's ruination becomes "petrified" and furthers an already existing "estrangement" to the spaces, matter, and artifices that constitute daily living.[21] An applied, cultural theory of ruination became necessary for Gordillo when he saw his informants paying little heed to the memory apparatus of the state and chose instead to turn official, material remains into "rubble." His informants from the Chaco region tore stones from the walls of sacred buildings because they better served them as paving stones; far better to walk across them than to respect them as commemorations to the powerful.

The ruin decomposed to its core elements opens a subaltern space, a topology such that raw materiality is pried loose from its imperial heritage. Instructed by the stories, gestures, and actions of those in residence, Gordillo discovered within the rubble of ruin a negative dialect between the "elite mind" and the "subaltern body" that pivots on the "positivity of the given" such that an obdurate social imaginary finds the potency of eventual use.[22] Negative dialectics, for Elizabeth Povinelli, are often criticized by the intellectual elite because they offer no pathway forward. They presume that a critical analysis of displaced people or inequitable agencies must be accompanied by a just plan for what to know and what to do. In contradiction, she proposes that negative dialectics shift the analytic lens from the question of how normative identities, dispositions, and policies are maintained by the state or resisted through strident insurrection to the question of their "background," their making, their constitution to make "visible the nonidentity between claims of social unity and claims of social difference and diversity.[23] Once these identity claims and static histories are set aside for the interpretive moment, different capacities and agencies, memories and strategies, reveal themselves as "quasi-events that provide the preconditions in which some new social content might be nurtured."[24]

Whereas rubble for the peasants of Chaco obliterates the artifice of a controlling regime, the people I have lived with and studied would look at rubble differently if it were a broken street or buildings in need of repair. My informants, quite often my neighbors, knew the cycles and events of violence in their lives better than history would tell, and they expressed the desire for a better life, one that exceeded their most immediate economic circumstances. I believe that they knew, better than the critic, the verisimilitudes of their homelands, the basis, as Henri Lefebvre has long argued for a "critique of everyday life" that constitutes a material dialectic in residence and, therefore, within the "residuum" of everyday life. The residuum can be considered a ruin of modernity, a "remainder" after all forms and gestures of progress and achievement come to pass. They are the "remnants, the remains" of "thinking, circulating, dwelling, dressing" that offer for living and contemplation, for critical thought and political action "their common measure, their fertile or barren soil, their resource, their common site or ground."[25]

The liveliness of ruination as a condition appears, at times, to lurk between language and matter, as a "hangover,"[26] or as hauntings or melancholy that sustains a "cruel" optimism granted by elite and powerful institutions, including those from the left, that in turn requires a more "absorptive awareness"[27] of the precariousness of life that may, in time, translate into what Navaro-Yashin terms a "local moral discourse."[28] That discourse may eventually lead to policy debates or social protest but appears through its most immediate reception fragile and sometimes incoherent, requiring an affectively charged attunement to dwelling in residence. This attunement, as I will demonstrate, augments current rhetorical scholarship on place and memory by shifting our attention from artifact to artifice to reinvest in the "familiarity" of everyday materiality, a familiarity that undercuts an official "hylomorphism" that grants authority foremost to forms, and thus to long histories of formalism that render vital matter "passive and inert."[29] If the rhetorical gaze shifts away, at least momentarily, from iconic texts, exemplary performances, monumental structures, and ideological positions, then the backgrounds of habitation shift to the ontological foreground to reveal a deeply textured precarity as a counter-space within modernity's "ceaseless advancement toward an optimistic future," as Ralph Cintron conjures, a future that transcends the economic "tropes" and "calculations" used to name and measure ruinous conditions around the world.[30]

Ruination as a condition does not lessen the obligation to hold people or institutions accountable, but the premise of ruination as a constant, comparative condition for living could help people understand the sense making that ensues, given the residues of war, violence, conflict, or decline that remain long after a cataclysmic event. If we approach ruination this way, as a commonplace circumstance, we—as residents, as researchers—may learn to find ourselves alive among the ruins, less dissociable from the communities we study and the burdens that people carry there.

Cosmopolitan Legibility

Ruination, along with the potential to find rhetorical life among the ruins, offers a contrastive standpoint and field of reference for critical and cultural analysis and, to the point of this collection, a methodological commitment to capture and characterize violence meted out in different signatures of time, events, intensities, texture, affected territories, sensory engagements, and embodiments. Ruinous forces, at this moment in Western history, impel the critic and the resident to look more closely at one's homeland; yet, as Ann Stoler summarizes, the commitment to locality must be coupled with an awareness that imperial forces leading to ruination circulate on a global scale: "a focus on 'ruins of empire' is not about a gaze but a critical vantage point on one. Asking how people live with and in ruins and articulate those conditions redirects the engagement elsewhere: to the politics animated, to the common sense such habitations disturb, to the critiques condensed and disallowed, and to the social relations vividly coalesced or shattered around them. What material form do ruins of empire take when we turn to shattered infrastructures, polluted places, dispersed families rather than to the leisure of evocations? . . . Imperial ruins are, not least, racialized markers on a global scale."[31] Throughout Stoler's writing on ruination, she separates the "material form of the ruin" from postcolonial critiques of imperial domination. The scholarly enterprise of postcolonialism has oversold its ability to clarify the difference between a colonial legacy of ownership from the "trace" and textures in the remnants and residues of daily living.[32] These residues, textures, traces, and gestures take material form capaciously to include, in the neighborhoods I study, degradations in the urban form, polluted rivers, loss of economic fortitude, divisive attitudes, and postures toward race, status, and economic success, and, then, a more general malaise over the uncertainty of the future.

In this next section, I turn to my fieldwork as sites of ruination. This involves recollection and retracing more than careful documentation because I did not begin these studies with a "weak" theory of economic difference in mind. I, therefore, propose that a reading or rereading of an urban scene requires of the critic, the resident, and the observer, a cosmopolitan legibility. To read a city, to find it legible for rhetorical inquiry, enlists one in the discovery of a neighborhood's textures and contours, its performances and rituals. One must look beyond the textual record to comprehend a neighborhood's expressive (therefore rhetorical) potential within material and historical complexity; to read a city in these ways is an established (if not traditional within the discipline) methodological commitment. As others have done, I've turned to scholars such as Greg Dickinson in rhetorical studies, Ash Amin and Nigel Thrift in critical geography, Michel de Certeau in quotidian analysis, and Kevin Lynch in critical architecture, to learn how to read the city's tableau, and to other scholars such as Kathleen Stewart and Sara Ahmed whose reading of city spaces tracks the ways that bodies orient within common spaces.[33] All of these scholars help establish an active, interpretive process of reading the contours, movements, bodies and (at times) discourse that constitute daily living in urban spaces.

If legibility can be accepted as a qualitative pursuit, then a cosmopolitan vantage point frames legibility in purposive ways. First, it invites, as I strive to demonstrate here, an openness to "theoretical cosmopolitanism," advanced by Robert Craig as "the willingness and ability to participate in more than one theoretical conversation."[34] And, second, a cosmopolitan legibility, in addition to intellectual pluralism, refracts the open, ontological brightness of affectability in all circumstances of habitation and home life. In *Inessential Solidarity*, Diane Davis argues for the rhetorical precondition of territories of affectability that constitutes a "fundamental structure of exposure." The legibility of exposure in turn depends on an "irreparable openness to affection/alteration" that I take quite literally to mean the

material and immaterial textures of ruination on display in a local neighborhood for residents that can be overlooked by more broad-based cultural
criticism.[35] Davis concerns herself with subjectivity, and her hospitality does
not require a fixed, textured explication of doorways and dinner tables, road-
sides and industrial river ways, but she does turn to Jacques Derrida, who
says "In order to constitute the space of a habitable house and home . . .
you need an opening, a door or windows."[36] There must be passage ways
for others to enter and enough ownership and security, enough sovereignty over one's residence, to allow hospitality and habitation to occur in their
most cosmopolitan sense.

Thirdly, the ruins of imperial domination frame cosmopolitanism not as
an ideal but as a necessity for discovering habitation and hospitality through
the lingering effects racial, ethic, and economic violence played out with
striking similarity in households around the world, even though people live
in striking different circumstances. The Kantian ideal of "a kingdom of free
rational beings, equal in humanity, each of them to be treated as an end,
no matter where in the world he or she dwells"[37] is obsolete because, and
with painful irony, globalization has made us strikingly similar as the con-
suming subjects. We are, as Wendy Brown would put it, "*homo oeconomic-
us*" within the neoliberal economic apparatus and as subjects in a global
war on terror.[38] To counter these sorts of sameness, a cosmopolitan legibility would be intellectually plural, open to affections, and would attend to
habitation in the everyday, that is, as "mediated through various particular,
more local solidarities."[39]

The conditions of ruination are expressed through the intimacies of
"what remains, to the aftershocks of empire, to the material and social afterlife of structures, sensibilities and things."[40] A cosmopolitan legibility would
attend to these intimacies of daily living traceable to global patterns and
structures of violence and indifference. It would yank the expressions and
textures of intimacy from the "privileged sign of liberal interiority or domes-
ticity" to be reconstituted as "residual" and "emergent" through "scenes
of close connection in relation to a global geography."[41] Such intimacies
could be expressed as vacant landscapes, or piles of refuse, or unmaintained
buildings, or unrequited loss, grief, melancholy or regret. Intimate ruin-
ations can be heard or felt as a shared breadth of common air or a lingering afterthought. As Ahmed explains, "Breathing does not establish territory or fix the relation between self and other, and yet breathing is that which
allows the one and the other to live in a co-inhabitance that is not premised

on the commonality of a bond, but on the intangibility of air."[42] Paul Gilroy offers his case for a "vulgar" cosmopolitan legibility:

> The challenge of being in the present, of synchronizing difference and articulating cosmopolitan hope upward from below rather than imposing it downward from on high provides some help in seeing how we might invent conceptions of humanity that allow for the presumption of equal value and go beyond the issue of tolerance into a more active engagement with the irreducible value of diversity within sameness. . . . In sharp contrast with recipes for good governance that have been pronounced from above, this variant might be described as "vulgar" or "demonic" cosmopolitanism [and] finds civic and ethical value in the process of exposure to otherness . . . [and] in response to the xenophobia and violence that threatened to engulf, purify or erase it.[43]

Bending ruination and a cosmopolitan legibility toward a methodological practice can begin, as Craig suggests, with an openness to different scholarly traditions and, therefore, an openness to comparable scenes of ruination. What follows is a pointed comparison between my site work in the greater Cleveland area and the fieldwork of Navaro-Yashin located on the island of Cyprus.[44] Both communities suffered different waves of violence in the early 1970s, and both communities are bound by their ethnic, economic, and geographic differences. Yet, a cosmopolitan reading of these communities reveals the affective grounds for recovery, as something common to different communities, a basis to remake the habitus from the residues of violence. From her career-long ethnographic study of the aftermath from the 1974 ethnic war in Cyprus, Navaro-Yashin urges those who study and live in sites of conflict to rethink the obviousness of ruination as the consequence of violence and to yank the term out of its negative connotations of pointless loss, debris, decline, or trauma and to reinvest in ruination as a commonplace condition for survival and renewal. Ruination on Cyprus manifests forty years later and constitutes "the material remains or artefacts of destruction and violation, but also [as] the subjectivities and residual affects that linger, like a hangover, in the aftermath of war or violence."[45] They linger because the spoils and debris of war transmogrify, eventually, into a basis for a local economy and a political doctrine; they seed the ground to engage and resist the state's apparatus because it, too, evolves after the shock of violence. After the battles subsided late in 1974, the Turkish-Cypriots found themselves awash in the collateral objects of war, things that belonged to someone else, that held histories and uses unfamiliar, and that now carried extraordinary meaning as "loot." Suitcases thrown by the side of the road, table settings without diners, and houses without occupants slipped from object status to "thing-ness," as Jane Bennett would describe the shift from inanimate to animating objects.[46]

My two field sites are neighborhoods: one on the Near West side of Cleveland and the other between two residential and economic zones in Kent, Ohio. Both neighborhoods reside in the Lakes industrial region of the United States, the *rust belt*, as some would say. Both neighborhoods owe much to the production of steel and the fabrication of parts. Both neighborhoods historically depended on river trade: Kent, Ohio, grew in the nineteenth century along the connection to river trade along the Cuyahoga in the eighteenth and nineteenth century. The regional economic histories for these two neighborhoods are important but are written, as histories can be, to be dimensionally hollow when it comes to the zones of affect potential in daily living. To step out of your car, onto a sidewalk, away from your screens, and into these worlds might well call forth sensations of economic ruin and feelings of melancholy because the streets, houses, schools, and playgrounds plainly display the tattered edges and barren spaces of economic decline. Everyone I spoke with, from city planners to local families, wanted economic renewal of one kind or another, but a causal basis for decline that might affectively complicate a process of recovery was outside most everyone's local moral repertoire, including mine. The Orchard community in Ward 17 has been subdivided so many times through redistricting that the ward boundaries bore no resemblance to the historical circumferences of the city, or to the contours of river valleys, and is now nothing like the neatly subdivided geographies of intermountain west cities like Phoenix or Salt Lake. The older housing stock correlates with a dwindling tax base. The typical civic and economic markers of public buildings or food chains were nowhere to be found. The affective center of the Orchard community in Ward 17 in Cleveland was an invented park, a site of local, moral organizing through play and celebration on official land reinvented for unofficial use.

The affectability of Kent does not center at the May 4 Memorial and archive on campus, not in the sense of daily living with ordinary objects in melancholic repose. The center was instead a stretch of boulevard that divided the campus from the city's business center. The melancholic reservoir in

Kent spans forty-two years from the May 4, 1970, when students were shot dead by the National Guard to a recent redevelopment project that, on the surface of history, paved over the residues of violence and broken trust in the city. When I lived in Kent, and well before this redevelopment, a prominent visitor asked, after taking an evening stroll, "Why is the town so silent on its political history?" with no signage, no commemorative gestures in the township proper, except for a series of dead end streets and under-developed commercial sites along the boulevard that bisects town and campus. Recent redevelopment in both Orchard and in Kent has provided economic relief by increasing property values and adjusting the visual landscape. Yet I find that melancholy still resides in both communities in the residuum of economic and political aggression that shaped their late-twentieth century identities and twenty-first century futures.

Navaro-Yashin documents everyday life after the partitioning of Cyprus, following the 1974 invasion of Cyprus by Turkish troops. Turkey invaded Northern Cyprus, occupying Greek-Cypriot lands, with the announced purpose of defending Turkish-Cypriots who lived in the south. The Turkish incursion, however, left no one safe from dislocation because each group was coerced through invasion to occupy the territories and everyday artifacts of the other. The Turkish-Cypriots escaped to the north, where they were allocated Greek-Cypriot land and property, while the Greek-Cypriot refugees fled south, making do with what was left: both communities found themselves living among the ruins of the other such that the daily practices of working, raising a family, and remaking a familiar way of life depended entirely on the sense and use one could make of someone else's belongings, and this after thirty years of a structured coexistence with little visitation and participation in the other's affairs.[47]

By necessity, the homes of others were looted, but as these objects were expropriated for daily life, they carried the memories of sociability and an imagination for how others, arbitrarily cast as "enemy," made use of them. It is from these memories and imaginaries that Navaro-Yashin identifies the invention of a "local moral discourse" such that "looting" (*ganimet*) shifts its reference point from the bounty of conquest to "self-reprimand . . . 'everyone's hand has been dirtied by plunder.'"[48] Morality depends on ruination, and *the enemy* has as much claim to morality as we do. Navaro-Yashin's informants spoke about a melancholy attached to postwar "rusty and dusty surfaces." Rust and dust (clutter and damage) have a commemorative, affective potential that opens space for moral commentary on habitation and community identification that in turn sanctifies a "new political system . . . formed by way of assuming the abject."[49]

The residuum of economic aggression is not an idle place to live, but it is where many of us live most of the time. To reside, to hold residence, to be addressed within the residuum takes account of the material remains from violation, a remainder constituting objects and subjects with affect "lingering," to borrow Navaro-Yashin's language. To reside this way offers moments of reflection, a pause along the way, if not an explicit argument for change. These pauses might identify the moments of "impasse" that can, as Lauren Berlant suggests, shift our purposive attention to an "optimism of attachment" within the residual lives you lead. The two moments in two neighborhoods for me are unforgettable in this way. The Orchard community was forty-five minutes away from Kent on Cleveland's Near West side. I drove from campus, leaving town over the Haymaker Bridge proposed before May 4 and built shortly thereafter. My entrance to scholarship was a tour of the Cuyahoga river drainage along an Interstate highway that ended in the Cleveland industrial trade zone and Lake Erie. The approach followed the contours of the river valley and cut through the former sites of heavy industry, principally steel mills and manufacturing. My exit off of I-90 in Cleveland cut through empty warehouses, broken sidewalks, and aging intersections, until I arrived at 41st and Bailey Avenue, the site of the (then) Orchard middle school. Leaving my car, invariably I heard children playing or laughing in the street or schools or at the neighborhood handball court, drawn by chalk against the north wall of the schools. If I was noticed at all, on my way to an interview, or meeting or the next round of photographs, pensive looks were shared, neither of us knew why exactly I was there. I dropped a name; someone recognized my face; I was consistently welcomed into this neighborhood. We spoke of a shared desperation in being noticed and the desire to protect oneself and family. These sentiments were tagged to the physical, visual apparatus of a neighborhood with no organizational center. What stood in for meeting halls, town squares, and commerce was the triangulation of porches, pick-up games on parking lots, and the north perimeter of the school.

In Kent, my approach to research was daily, residential, and ordinary: getting up in the morning, looking outside a window, driving across the bridge and along Haymaker Boulevard, past the broken lanes ("College" and "Erie" streets) that used to connect campus to city. Since 1970, the city planners have looked at the Boulevard as a design problem, a structured social and physical impasse. I have archived the planning documents, including the "South Central Bridge Project" that was commissioned before May 4, 1970, and finished shortly thereafter. Five planning cycles later, in all cases the city tried either to reassemble Haymaker Boulevard to reconnect the city and campus or at least to beautify it with greenery, benches, and crosswalks. The Boulevard remained in the residuum, an object of adversarial design. Its original purpose was to spirit people and cars across the river, without the interference of local traffic, but from May 4, forward, its object state skipped the technical bounds of transportation to assume the role that Carl DiSalvo calls "adversarial . . . that express or enable a particular political perspective, known as *agonism*" (italics his).[50] Affect theory grants agency to objects, whether on the debris fields of Cyprus or a post-industrial city and this particular affect field metastasized for forty years after horrific events and the ensuing irreconciliation of trust between a city and a campus that saw its economic futures elsewhere in the state.

Not for a moment would I suggest that Orchard and Kent in the US late-industrial Northeast had the same object fields, nor the exact same public imaginaries, nor would they share the objects and imaginaries strewn across the war-tattered plains of Northern Cyprus. What they do share is an abject, affect field of potential nested in the aftermath of violence. What they share is the desire, if not fully articulated, to escape the impasse that *hangs in the air*, collecting as dust, debris, and stifled speech rooted in public ambivalence. The impasse and the will to escape that impasse animated through objects—burned fields, someone else's kitchen, an adversarial bridge project—that reside in the poetics of the common on roughed surfaces that are preconditional for any sort of local moral discourse for the sake of inclusive habitation or for economic progress. Stewart performs and then narrates the performance of affect upon her body and affiliations to offer the reader a "poetics" of the commons, an "ordinary affect in the textured, roughened surface of the everyday" that hails an "intimate public of onlookers [to] recognize something in a space of shared impact."[51] A local moral discourse does not, it seems, self-generate through discourse alone; there is rather a slow syncopation between rough surfaces and smooth commentary at odds with the late-modern desire to compress time and to scrape away the past to make way for the new through precise assertions.

When Navaro-Yashin steps onto the plains of Cyprus, many years after the Turkish incursion, she feels something akin to the remorse felt by those who were "allocated" land property from someone else. At the precise moment of qualitative recollection, she stands at a midpoint, between two halves of an island, between affected awareness and critical reflection, and between her comprehension of ruined lands and those shared by local authorities, someone who lives literally in the house of the other. Her apprehension enables the speech of her informant, and his enables hers. In one direction are barren plains, incinerated by war and marked by "cemeteries of used cars," while in the other direction are the bland, militaristic structures of occupation, the new residences for the families of Turkish officers. Little is cared for and the green fields of "fruit trees, carob, police and pine" as her Turkish confident, Hasan, remembers ushers in an "immense melancholy."[52] The formerly Greek plains of Cyprus, and Hasan's remembering, bring forth a "sense of melancholy" in the anthropologist as well.

Whatever the epistemological differences between Navaro-Yashin and myself, we both step out onto places of abjection and depend on local residents to point the way. Both communities thrive in ruination, and for both communities, the discernment of a way forward is fraught with desire to escape and not repeat the past. Cruel optimism, if left unchecked, fosters a return to much the same conditions that fostered pain, loss, violence, and dislocation in the first place. Barbara Biesecker assigns a similar kind of cruelty to an "ambivalent possession of an impossible ideal" solicited by the Bush administration after 9–11; the exchange mechanism for this cruelty is subjectively discursive, a proselytizing of "a democratic way of life."[53] Rhetorical melancholy would circulate within a historical sensorium taking the form of a precarious public sphere. The rhetorical melancholy that escapes the impasse would seek out and celebrate an "intimate public of subjects who circulate scenarios of economic and intimate contingency and trade paradigms for how best to live on."[54] Ethno-rhetorical fieldwork indexed by the melancholic impasse would find the ordinary utterances, fields of occurrence and objects that hold a promise for a more equitable public life that reverses, ever so slightly, the spoils of war and conflict so that "those whom you would think of as defeated [are] living beings figuring out how to stay attached to life from within it, and to protect what optimism they have for that."[55]

The Fieldwork of Ruination

To this point, I've proposed ruination as a counter-space in contrast to the tapestries of economic progress that rely on the constancy of renewal, a counter-space that hangs in the air and is etched into the fabric of a local community. Ruination takes the form of things more tattered that one might hope, less useful than the prevalent political economy might desire and therefore less valorized by society. These matters are open to critical, empirical analysis; they can be imaged, mapped, and logged into field notes: the anthropologists I've turned to in this essay talk with residents, travel to sites, and record their impressions. Their exposures, however, tend to mingle with those of the residents to the point that the critical distance built into canonical, qualitative metrics gives way to cohabitation as a methodological and ethical concern, to a shared exercise of cosmopolitan legibility. This exposure grants the observer, as resident, a powerful skein for ethno-rhetorical work: a debris field, housing stock, pots and pans, a handball court—the list is endless—constituting the topological exposure of residential life in the residuum. Ruinous circumstances could be studied from afar, sampled from historical events and after-effects, but the veracity nearer the surfaces of ruination, closer to the conditions for survival, invites the observer to pay attention to the textures of life *in vivo*. Over a four-year span in Gordillo's fieldwork, the original goal of studying the decimation of the countryside by global agribusiness gave way through such exposures to become a study of rubble, "not abstractly but spatially and ethnographically. . . . I was forced to rethink what space is and how it is produced, how it is destroyed, and what is created by this destruction."[56]

Exposure over time, thus, weighs heavily in ruination as a qualitative, rhetorical concern. There was no immediate ethnographic present that would reveal the slow expression of a local moral discourse for Navaro-Yashin, no obvious pace of renewal in Stewart's study of the accumulation of decay in the coal-mining region of West Virginia.[57] History in the linear sense is held in abeyance; it "trembles" waiting for some master stroke of resolution and retribution.[58] "The shock of history, then, is not the end of the story but its ground and motivation. Things do not simply fall into ruin or dissipate in the winds of progress but fashion themselves into powerful effects. . . . 'History' digs itself into the present."[59]

The historical events of the Kent State shootings dug into the present, earmarked by cycles of planning efforts before May 4, 1970, that never resolved the lapse in trust between a campus and its community forged in a moment of violence. On February 5, 2013, *The New York Times* published an article in its commerce section that announced a successful partnership among the city, the campus, and developers, after forty years of waiting. The city had waited with apprehension for something good to happen, and tried to reimagine itself, and this new development helped to "heal the psychic worlds" in a city that, by this telling, "neglected, if not deliberately retreated from, its history as a college town and its place in the annals of the Vietnam War era."[60] The normative assumption is that healthy, progressive cities do not retreat from trauma, and if they do, they do so in defeat. Yet, ruination as conditional to renewal might suggest that solutions to complex problems respond in different time signatures such that public designs and designations cannot be fabricated faster than the capacity that the residuum allows. Not if public designs are supposed to last. Stewart continues, "History, then, we might say, arises in the present. . . . The question of 'meaning' finds itself caught in a signification that is at once contingent and receptive, overwhelming and inconclusive, tactile and uncertain."[61]

A rhetorical sensibility might be predisposed to look for how a local moral discourse arises from history in the present. Navaro-Yashin found a local moral discourse, but she did not intervene in its making as one might in the pursuit of "communication design."[62] Once she recognized this local moral discourse, she was able to track its trajectory through figures of melancholy that hung in the air and nested in expropriated homes and fields. "Ganimet," or looting the house of the other, over time, became an ideograph for the country as a whole. Cyprus became, discursively, a "ganimet state," a figurative term with wide circulation no matter where one lived, north or south on the island. In my studies, the local moral discourse in Orchard emanated from an expropriated parking space on the north side of a middle-grade school. It never achieved ideographic status, but it was mobilized as a cultural economy made of passion, of moral sentiment, of local knowledge and trust that spoke back to gentrification. Kent, I argue, denied itself a local moral discourse to counter the disaffiliations of campus and the city; it took over forty years and different leadership from outside the community to give form to a latent desire to heal its own wounds under the rubric of economic revitalization.

Preceding and substantiating a local moral discourse, then, are the biologics of decay that become the circumstances that allow people to make do as they see fit in their local communities. The value of a weak theory of ruination, as I began this chapter, lies in the conviction that people struggle daily with their local circumstances such that a people collectively "disidentify" with capitalism as a unified, historically consistent force.[63] Rather, any sort of local "language of economic diversity" depends foremost on the comprehension of an economic landscape rooted in geologies, geographies, physical structures, long-lived identities, and treasured rituals that enable discursive invention. The biologics of everyday life are discovered to be, what they already were, in relation to a hegemonic cultural system; they are "queered" as they become "unfixed" from cultural and capital centrism.[64]

The biological foundation to ruination as process of recovery resurfaces as a place of persuasion. In reference to catastrophe, but also applicable to ruination as a condition within late modernity, Cintron finds "nature and the human . . . fully braided together . . . textured."[65] They become the motive and mechanisms of modern life; when one spectrum collapses—a city neighborhood, a shoreline—the other spectrum responds. There exists then a constancy within any built environment, from the newest production neighborhood (that I live in today) or older first-tier neighborhoods built midway through the twentieth century, a constancy of nature's return. I do not suggest that nature will return in some grand triumph over capitalist intrusions into the countryside but rather that there is a palpable, visceral ambivalence between natural and built worlds that hums within ruination. Buildings in decline, maintenance budgets eclipsed by infrastructural decay, underfunded school systems, struggling small businesses with tattered facades all point to a different source of memory recuperation between the built and the natural. Buildings hold the urban collective together, momentarily in a false sense of secure domination over farmlands and river valleys, but also in a more sustained way as "mode of memory," where the "endurance of stone over time, and through time, is both nature and history at once."[66] I think this is why peasant farmers picked through the carcass of a rotting Jesuit church in the Chaco region, without remorse, to transform walls first into rubble and then into material for reconstruction. I think this is why Orchard residents paid little attention to the legal, prescribed boundaries between a schoolyard and a city street to invent a social space for recreation. Those who live within ruins (all of us to one degree or another) reside in a close, tangible relation to the generative potential within the eventual collapse of our surroundings. We know it's there, and we are more willing and able to take matters into own hands because the magisterial subject eventually will lose interest in our wellbeing. The sovereign state will search for other forms of conquest elsewhere, such that cracks in sidewalk can offer clues to a different sort of solidarity at least as much as they signpost the inevitability of excess and decline.

Notes

1. Ann Stoler, *Duress: Imperial Durabilities in Our Times* (Durham, NC: Duke University Press, 2016), 11.

2. Robert Hariman, "Introduction," in *Catastrophe and Rhetoric: The Texture of Political Action*, ed. Robert Hariman and Ralph Cintron (New York: Berghahn Press, 2015).

3. J. K. Gibson-Graham, "Rethinking the Economy with Thick Description and Weak Theory," *Current Anthropology* 55, no. 9 (2014): 149.

4. Ibid.,151.

5. Hariman, "Introduction," 9.

6. John Ackerman, "Rhetorical Engagement in the Cultural Economies of Cities," in *The Public Work of Rhetoric: Citizen-Scholars and Civic Engagement*, ed. John Ackerman and David Coogan, 76–97 (Columbia: University of South Carolina Press, 2010).

7. William Connolly, *The Fragility of Things: Self-organizing Processes, Neoliberal Fantasies, and Democratic Activism* (Durham, NC: Duke University Press, 2013), 154.

8. Yael Navaro-Yashin, "Affective Spaces, Melancholic Objects: Ruination and the Production of Anthropological Knowledge," *Journal of the Royal Anthropological Institute* 15, no. 1 (2009): 5.

9. Tim Edensor, *Industrial Ruins: Space, Aesthetics and Materiality* (Oxford, UK: Berg Publishers, 2005).

10. For a panoptic view of the American industrial ruin, see Greg Grandin, "Empire's Ruin: Detroit to the Amazon" in *Imperial Debris: On Ruins and Ruination*, ed. Ann Stoler (Durham, NC: Duke University Press, 2013).

11. Edensor, *Industrial Ruins*, 167.

12. For an account, see Carole Blair, Greg Dickinson, and Brian Ott, "Introduction: Rhetoric/Memory/Place," in *Places of Public Memory: The Rhetoric of Museums and Memorials*, ed. Dickinson et al., 1–49 (Tuscaloosa: University of Alabama Press, 2010).

13. Though ruination favors the material remainder to index social difference and latent persuasive force, sites may well also index displaced local histories. See Greg Clark, "Rhetorical Experience and the National Jazz Museum," in Dickinson et al., *Places of Memory*.

14. Edensor, *Industrial Ruins*, 167.

15. Ann Stoler, "Imperial Debris: Reflections on Ruins and Ruination," *Cultural Anthropology* 23, no. 2 (2008): 192.

16. Ibid., 193.

17. A bullet hole remains in the Don Drumm sculpture, Solar Totem #1 near Taylor Hall on the Kent State Campus.

18. Estela Schindel and Pamela Columbo, eds. *Space and the Memories of Violence: Landscapes of Erasure, Disappearance and Exception* (New York: Palgrave Macmillan, 2014), 4.

19. Stoler, "Imperial Debris," 192.

20. Gastón Gordillo, *Rubble: The Afterlife of Destruction* (Durham, NC: Duke University Press, 2014), 6.

21. Gordillo, *Rubble*, 116.

22. Ibid.

23. Elizabeth Povinelli, *Economies of Abandonment: Social Belongings and Endurance in Late Liberalism* (Durham, NC: Duke University Press, 2011), 190–91.

24. Ibid., 191.

25. Henri Lefebvre, *Critique of Everyday Life*, Volume III (Brooklyn: Verso Press, 2005), 11.

26. Navaro-Yashin, "Affective Spaces," 5.

27. Lauren Berlant, "Cruel Optimism," in *The Affect Theory Reader*, ed. Melissa Greg and Greg Seigworth, 93–117 (Durham: Duke University Press), 4.

28. Navaro-Yashin, "Affective Spaces," 3–4.

29. Tim Ingold, "Toward an Ecology of Materials," *Annual Review of Anthropology*, 41 (2012): 432.

30. Ralph Cintron, "Conclusion: What Next?" in *Catastrophe and Rhetoric: The Texture of Political Action*, ed. Robert Hariman and Ralph Cintron, 232–39 (New York City: Berghahn Press, 2015).

31. Stoler, *Duress*, 353.

32. Ibid.

33. I offer these sources as representative of different ways to read cities discursively and phenomenologically: Greg Dickenson, *Suburban Dreams: Imagining and Building the Good Life* (Tuscaloosa: University of Alabama Press, 2015); Ash Amin and Nigel Thrift, "The Legibility of Everyday Cities," in *Cities: Reimagining the Urban*, 7–30 (Cambridge, UK: Polity Press, 2002); Michel de Certeau, *The Practice of Everyday Life*, trans. Steven Randall (Berkeley: California Press, 1984); Kevin Lynch, *The Image of the City* (Cambridge: The MIT Press, 1960); Kathleen Stewart, *Ordinary Affects* (Durham, NC: Duke University Press, 2007); and Sara Ahmed, *Strange Encounters: Embodied Others in Post-Coloniality* (London: Routledge Press, 2000). I offer the term of "oscillation" to account for the synapse between a physical sensation of an environment and the "jump" to a discursive interpretation. See John Ackerman, "Walking in the City: The Arrival of the Rhetorical Subject," in *Tracing Rhetoric and Material Life: Ecological Approaches*, ed. Guy McHendry et al. (London: Palgrave Macmillan, in press).

34. Robert Craig, "Minding My Mental Model, Mending Myers," *Communication Theory* 9 (2001): 236.

35. Diane Davis, *Inessential Solidarity* (Pittsburgh, PA: University of Pittsburgh Press, 2010), 3.

36. Jacques Derrida, *On Cosmopolitanism and Forgiveness*, trans. Mark Dooley and Michael Hughes (New York: Routledge Press, 2001), 121.

37. Martha Nussbaum, "Kant and Cosmopolitanism," in *The Cosmopolitan Reader*, ed. Garrett Brown and David Held (Cambridge: Polity Press, 2010), 33.

38. Wendy Brown, *Undoing the Demos: Neoliberalism's Stealth Revolution* (Brooklyn: Zone Books, 2015).

39. Craig Calhoun, "The Class Consciousness of Frequent Travelers: Toward a Critique of Actually Existing Cosmopolitanism," *The South Atlantic Quarterly* 101, no. 4 (2002): 873.

40. Stoler, "Imperial Debris," 194.

41. Lisa Lowe, *The Intimacies of Four Continents* (Durham, NC: Duke University Press, 2015), 19.

42. Ahmed, *Stranger Encounters*

43. Paul Gilroy, *Post-Colonial Melancholia* (New York: Columbia University Press, 2005), 67.

44. Navaro-Yashin, "Affective Spaces." See also, *The Make-Believe Space: Affective Geography in a Postwar Polity* (Durham, NC: Duke University Press, 2012).

45. Navaro-Yashin, "Affective Spaces," 5.

46. Jane Bennett, *Vibrant Matter: A Political Ecology of Things* (Durham, NC: Duke University Press, 2009).

47. A more formal account of the divided state of the Cyprus economy can be found in Athanasios Orphanides and George Syrichas, eds., *The Cyprus Economy: Historical Review Prospects Changes* (Cyprus: Central Bank of Cyprus, 2012).

48. Navaro-Yashin, "Affective Spaces," 3.

49. Ibid., 4–5.

50. Carl DiSalvo, *Adversarial Design* (Cambridge, MA: The MIT Press, 2012), 2.

51. Stewart, *Ordinary Affect*, 39.

52. Navaro-Yashin, "Affective Spaces," 10.

53. Barbara Biesecker, "No Time for Mourning: The Rhetorical Production of the Melancholic Citizen-Subject in the War on Terror," *Philosophy and Rhetoric* 40, no. 1 (2007): 154.

54. Berlant, "Cruel Optimism," 3.

55. Ibid., 10.

56. Gordillo, *Rubble*, 2.

57. Kathleen Stewart, *A Space on the Side of the Road: Cultural Politics in an "Other" America* (Princeton, NJ: Princeton University Press, 1996).

58. Ibid., 95.

59. Ibid., 111.

60. Keith Schneider, "A Partnership Seeks to Transform Kent State and Kent," *The New York Times*, February 5, 2013.

61. Stewart, *A Space*, 116.

62. See Mark Aakhus, "Communication Design," *Communication Monographs* 74, no. 1 (2007).

63. Gibson-Graham, *Postcapitalist Politics*, 54.

64. Ibid., 56.

65. Cintron, "Conclusion," 237.

66. Max Pensky, "Three Kinds of Ruin: Heidegger, Benjamin, Sebald" *Poligrafi* 12 (2011): 66–67.

8

Fieldwork and the Identification and Assembling of Agencies

Jeffrey T. Grabill, Kendall Leon, and Stacey Pigg

We understand rhetoric as the art best suited for the persistent burden of detecting shared problems, guiding inquiry, and shaping responses. It is empirical, pragmatic, and collective. We realize that the way we conceive of rhetoric in this chapter deserves further explanation. Rhetoric is *work*, in particular, it is analytical and discursive activity requiring problem-solving, abstract reasoning, and material things like information technologies. Our ideas here are similar to those of Philip Agre, who has called for a "democratic theory of the skills of citizenship," by which he means a pragmatic theory for how "individual citizens, in their public personae, are able to associate themselves with issues" and with others.[1] Agre understands politics as practical activity and that being a citizen means being able to act as a citizen. Therefore, the inability to work in these ways makes citizenship impossible, regardless of the citizenship status granted by law or right or identity. Rhetoric similarly requires generative practices. To live in the present moment is to live at a time when we are all required to develop what we might understand as a pragmatic rhetoric useful in the common places of our lives. We must make things that have value, such as texts, music, video, art, theatre. But we also must make the groups that will advocate and the matters of concern that motivate participation. As researchers, we begin with a commitment to account for this activity. When we do so, we see that rhetoric is distributed, diffused, and material labor.

A commitment to rhetoric that accounts for distributed agency makes research more complex, particularly in empirical work such as fieldwork about/as rhetoric. In invoking the term "distributed agency," we are connecting with the general turn in rhetoric studies to locate agency beyond any given individual, discourse, activity, or direction.[2] In this chapter, we begin with the premise that rhetoric is concerned with identifying, assembling, and facilitating agencies, and that fieldwork is a mechanism that enables researchers to describe and capture the practices through which this work takes place. Our intent in this chapter is to help researchers navigate the inherent complexity of agency in order to identify materials that matter to assembling collectives with the capacity to act. We choose the operational term "agencies" instead of any number of other theoretical terms that might identify collective units with the capacity to act (i.e., assemblage, actor-network, all my relations, ecology) because we believe that rhetorical methodologies might be used in concert with a number of theories that conceptualize how relations are established among disparate people and/or materials during rhetorical action.

The accounts that result from fieldwork are themselves agencies; they are generative products that have the potential to do things in the world. Thus, rhetorical fieldwork in the sense that we describe in this chapter is not defined solely by the presence of a researcher in an ongoing naturalistic scene (i.e., driven by a temporal impulse), although empirical practices are important to rhetorical research. Instead, fieldwork is defined by an orientation toward rhetorical activities and materials that foreground accounting for agencies, such as assigning meaning to things, words, groups, and matters of concern. The kind of fieldwork that we're drawing attention to composes agencies while they are still unsettled. Thus, the orientation we are describing is much like a *stance* or orientation to how a researcher positions herself relative to purposes, goals, and identities.[3] This stance with regard to fieldwork directs our attention to how to gather and construct agencies.

What follows, therefore, is an essay on methodology that attempts to assign language to fieldwork materials and the practices that make them visible. It articulates the relevance and role of fieldwork for doing rhetoric/making rhetorical theory; describes the ongoing tacit work of generating agencies; and provides vocabulary for describing and facilitating particular kinds of transformative materials encountered in empirical practices and generated through rhetorical fieldwork. This language, particularly mediators and resonances, is our attempt to make visible and useful materials and practices that are more tacit than explicit. In naming materials in this way, we seek to stabilize them enough to foster conversations in- and out-side our field about rhetoric's purpose, which is to detect shared problems, guide inquiry, and shape responses.

Fieldwork and Rhetoric's Materiality

The empirical practices of fieldwork are often understood to be synony-mous with ethnography. Fieldwork therefore typically involves a systemat-ic approach to observation-based data gathering and analysis, such as inter-viewing, field notes, and participant observation. Fieldwork deployed for rhetorical purposes or to make rhetorical theory is very much a part of this tradition of methodological thinking and practice. Rhetorical fieldwork is deployed for different purposes, as it facilitates the critical, interpretative, and ultimately productive empirical practice that allows researchers to trace and assign meaning to materials and activity that mark a trajectory of rhe-torical work. This deployment of fieldwork focuses on the practices of iden-tifying and assigning meaning by identifying participating actors, enabling attention to the mundane, and interpreting relevance with regard to rhetor-ical purposes and outcomes. We would add that to understand rhetorical agencies requires attending to the construction of relationships between humans and nonhumans, built and natural environments, history/archives and the present, and the often-fleeting moments of digital production and consumption.

The most useful way to understand what we mean is to turn to material and architectonic rhetorics to ground this conception of fieldwork because these theories have already described how meaning becomes assigned to a range of objects, technologies, places, and things, thus highlighting the cen-trality of materiality to shared collective meaning and social action.[4] While material rhetorics inform our approach, we are particularly engaged with theories and accounts that focus on the uptake or transformation of mate-rials in everyday practice. For instance, rhetorical theorists have turned to a number of philosophical and sociological frameworks that attend to the complex relations among symbol, matter, and things when they interact. By turning a closer eye to practices, we have the opportunity to theorize rhetorical fieldwork through what we learn from activist work within and outside of the academy, opening the door, for example, to recognizing the importance of materiality to the long history of feminist praxis discussed in recent academic scholarship, in long-standing accounts of and guides to women of color organizing, and in everyday practices that have not (yet) been described through written accounts.[5]

Materials in this sense are not simply "artifacts" in a cultural scene but rather actors who play a vital role in the invention and circulation of meaning. To emphasize what we mean by materials in this case, we might highlight anthropologist Tim Ingold's distinction between materials and materiality, where materials are framed not just as physical manifestations of matter but "partake in the very processes of the world's ongoing generation and regeneration of which *things* such as manuscripts or house-fronts are impermanent by-products."[6] Fieldwork, then—which might include historiographical and archival approaches as well as ethnographic and other qualitative research—can animate materials that are encountered through research processes. Through field methods, it is possible to identify and assign meanings to the everyday materials that create agencies via the practice of research.

Three Kinds of Rhetorical Materials

What we add to this ongoing conversation, then, is a vocabulary for describing three kinds of materials that rhetoricians and rhetorical researchers encounter as they attempt to understand rhetoric as a social, collective practice aimed at detecting shared problems, guiding inquiry, and shaping responses. We offer a methodological vocabulary that helps researchers identify and assign meaning to materials that participate in complex collectives and contexts of distributed agency. To begin, we will briefly name and define these three kinds of materials that fieldwork can help locate or generate. They include the following:

> *Mediators*: By mediators, we refer to materials—assembled agencies— that take on a particularly important role in invention, circulation, or persuasive processes in situated moments. We might think of mediators as materials (both tangible and ephemeral) that are raised to a heightened level of collective attention; they become consequential rather than simply resonant. They become agents in deliberation, in collective understanding, or for forcing decisions about which there is no clear path forward. Mediators are materials that make us do something, and they must be assembled.

Resonances: By resonances, we describe materials that form the wider field against which mediators emerge. Resonances refer to both tangible (such as people, texts, technologies, or built environments) and more ephemeral (such as values, attitudes, conversations) materials that matter to inventive and persuasive processes.[7] Resonances are a product of the intersection of attention and environment, and are thus made meaningful when we create accounts of them.

Termini: By termini, we refer to texts, artifacts, places, or objects that are the end result of an invention process. Although many rhetoric scholars acknowledge that the meaning of texts and objects is never static, the endpoint/terminus of invented rhetoric is often stabilized and analyzed to determine its persuasive strategies or effects (e.g., a speech).[8] However, these materials can also serve the purpose of defining the temporal and spatial boundaries of a trajectory of rhetorical work. Termini as we see it have the potential to be mediators; the difference is the stance we take toward these materials as settled.

To help illustrate how we see rhetoric functioning through the lenses of mediators, resonances, and termini, we will discuss each in turn through examples drawn from our prior fieldwork. The methodological vocabulary we propose enabled us to thoughtfully and rhetorically stabilize the potential complexity of a rhetorical situation to focus on issues of assembling agency.

Transformative Materials in Two Research Studies

Kendall's archival case study of one of the first Chicana feminist organizations, *Comisión Femenil Mexicana Nacional (CFMN)*, provides an account of how the organization accomplished not only what we would recognize as the production of rhetorical materials—letters, statements, flyers, campaigns, and an organization—but also the production of other rhetorical things, such as identities and assemblies.[9] Kendall's case study of the *CFMN* was part of a larger research project on Chicana rhetoric. Typically, "Chicana rhetoric" had been studied in our field, with "Chicana" denoting the people performing an uncontested "rhetoric." In other words, Chicana did not alter what we knew about rhetoric, with both concepts being treated as stabilized. At the heart of the project was understanding how "Chicana" operates rhetorically in the world and asking, methodologically, how do we then study such moments of rhetorical performance? To address this, Kendall worked to build Chicana rhetoric from moments where Chicana rhetoric happens: in scholarship, activism, history, and research. She collected data from a variety of sources, explicating the how and the why of Chicana.

The framework used to make sense of the data was built from interviewing scholars who identified as Chicana, as well as from published interviews. Scholars and activists noted how reading texts written by Chicanas identified writers, or hearing from Chicana activists, shaped their identification with the term, and the lenses through which they viewed their world, their place in it, and the decisions that were made. As writers were influential in defining and circulating Chicana as an identity, Kendall read across poetic and philosophic texts to determine if there were practices or ways of meaning making in these texts that could be assembled as a "Chicana rhetoric." In doing so, Kendall identified practices toward a Chicana rhetoric, such as *difrasismo*, or the linking of two separate ideas to form a new concept, the disavowal of binaries, experiential knowledge making, and the revisioning of histories. What she identified in these texts became her framework to conduct a study of Chicana making in action. Studying the archives was necessary not just because of the view it afforded of an organization and an identity being built, but also because doing (and redoing) history is a practice of Chicana rhetoric.

Stacey's research exploring a community-based art project called Art@ Work offered a different series of challenges. The Art@Work partnership between Michigan State University and Peckham, Inc., which describes itself as a "nonprofit community vocational rehabilitation organization," involved several stakeholders in creating a 200' x 40' art installation, which is now showcased on a manufacturing floor at Peckham's facility (figure 8.1). While Art@Work was a long-term academic-community partnership, Stacey focused on one stage of the project that involved undergraduate students enrolled in a Residential College in Arts and Humanities civic engagement course, which facilitated "art dialogues" with Peckham employees (called team members). These art dialogues had a range of goals that share affinities with what Sonja Foss and Cindy Griffin call an *invitational rhetoric*.[10] The dialogues engaged students and Peckham team members in creating a prototype of the art installation, while discussing their identities, goals, and values in order to promote shared understanding. For students, this experience was an apprenticeship toward civic learning, with course learning goals focused on sensitivity to power and privilege, using one's skills for community betterment, and adjusting to and carrying out community projects.

Rather than researching a group with a strongly identified shared purpose, then, Stacey researched students participating in a course-motivated project. Would they learn anything about civic rhetorical practice through this apprenticeship? How would their status as novices and, in most cases, relative outsiders to the community create challenges and impact the project? To work toward answers to these questions, Stacey was invited into the project as an embedded researcher. However, the course instructor requested that she participate in events associated with the project while researching. Thus, as a participant observer, Stacey worked alongside students in the classroom and community, as well as in informal points between (i.e., travel, off campus gatherings and events). Although she was positioned differently from the undergraduates, she completed undergraduate course assignments in the art studio (e.g., self-portraits, stranger portraits, narrative still life paintings), traveled three miles from campus to Peckham's facility weekly with students, and facilitated art dialogues with Peckham team members. She recorded detailed handwritten notes during these course sessions and events and conducted interviews. In both projects, we began by paying attention to what we are calling the "termini," as constructed through these field notes, transcripts, and archival materials because they provided evidence that rhetorical work had happened. Thus, we will first describe the role of termini in our fieldwork, before moving on to resonances and mediators.

Termini

Termini provide an excellent starting place for fieldwork, and we have chosen the word "terminus" to emphasize how we position these materials in space and time. These materials often act as our boundary markers, the things that locate our research site: a document, an organization, or a field site. In our everyday practices, these materials may be the recognizable goals for convening and inventing, or the artifacts we use to assess rhetorical success or failure. For example, at the 1970 National Chicano Issues Conference, Chicanas in attendance felt their issues were excluded from existent activist movements and, in response, they drafted a series of resolutions that became the foundation for the *CFMN* organization. In the document "Resolution Adopted by the Women's Workshop 10/10/70 Sac-ramento, California; [A] Proposal for a Comision Femenil Mexicana," the *CFMN* leaders wrote:

> The effort and work of the Chicana/Mexicana women in the Chica-no movement is generally obscured because women are not accept-ed as community leaders either by the Chicano movement or by the Anglo establishment.
>
> The existing myopic attitude does not, however, prove that women are not able to participate. It does not prove that women are not active, indispensable (representing over 50% of the population), experienced and knowledgeable in organizational, tactical and strategic aspects of a people's movement.
>
> THEREFORE, in order to terminate exclusion of female leadership in the Chicano/Mexican movement and in the community, be it
>
> RESOLVED, that a Chicana/Mexican Women's Commission be estab-lished at this conference which will represent women in all areas where Mexicans prevail.[11]

Documents such as this resolution are essential to any rhetorical scholar-ship on the *CFMN* or any organization like it. More importantly, perhaps, the ability to propose in this way is fundamental to rhetorical practice. But, for researchers, in what sense is this resolution more than an endpoint, more than a static, settled rhetorical act? Organizations such as *CFMN* fre-quently make and sometimes publish anthologized speeches, testimonies, and newsletter articles on issues relevant to Chicanas. They leave documen-tary traces that are the stuff of historiography.

Analytically, we worry about the stability that we attach to these perfor-mances and to our tendency to attach meaning to them as agents, as per-suasive objects demanding rhetorical analysis. It is better perhaps to worry about how such documents are assembled; that is, what rhetorical work was required to get to the point that pen could be put to paper? In addition to attending to their assembly, it is perhaps even more important to arrange ourselves as researchers to attend with some care to how a document such as the *CFMN* resolution is used beyond its immediate exigence (to form an organization) and by actors beyond its writers. Fieldwork is essential in each case, of both assembly and use, because fieldwork assembles the necessary materialities, though each results in very different studies.

Fig. 8.1. The Art@Work Wall at Peckham. Used with permission of the RCAH at MSU. Photo by Ian Siporin.

In the case of Art@Work, one terminus is large and visually striking. It projects meaning that is amenable to rhetorical analysis. As figure 8.1 illustrates, the two hundred–foot rhetorical product that displays individual paintings on Peckham's manufacturing work floor has the unique effect of allowing a viewer's attention to wander back and forth from particular individual pieces, each with a story behind it, toward the collection of the whole. The Art@Work wall is a tangible representation of values held by both the individuals and the community that view it, values that are particularly important for Peckham, which brings together a diverse group of team members with "a wide range of abilities and cultural backgrounds" as part of its human services and business operations projects.

As with the *CFMN* project, a common way to attend to the Art@Work project might be to analyze the meaning of the art itself. We can easily imagine any number of rhetorical analyses of this artifact or the local social and material context during moments in which the art is "performed" publicly. Such an analysis would almost certainly include the collected speeches and perhaps how the community and other audiences encountered and interacted with the art. The Resolution and The Art become objects that focus our analysis and that direct our research activities, and this is the sense in which we call them a terminus.

But it is also possible—and, indeed, probably necessary—to understand these objects differently: as performances that are left as material manifestations of prior work that can be traced and as potential agents to follow to understand future action. For example, in Stacey's research, the Art@Work wall pictured above became actualized three years after she began fieldwork. If our gaze is arranged appropriately, perhaps it is the case that the Art@Work wall is the least interesting moment of rhetorical activity. Perhaps it is some other assembly, some momentary agency that proves to be essential to the making of that wall and the much more visible press conference that unveiled it to the world. We argue that the materiality of endpoints is primarily valuable as indicators of other things: specifically, the resonances and mediators that need to be assembled in order to invent agencies.

Resonances

To extend our discussion of the materials of rhetoric from a focus on endpoints, we provide the term "resonances" to introduce another kind of material that is central to rhetorical work. Resonances are tangible and ephemeral materials that are participants in invention processes, as well as in rendering *termini* meaningful in future circulation and uptake. A central role of fieldwork is to render resonances visible, and therefore accountable, both as a matter of research and as a way to support rhetorical practice. There is perhaps no more valuable role for fieldwork than the rendering of accounts of resonances.

In the case of the *CFMN*, it is possible to see how several tools supported their work as an organization, both externally and internally. While not particular to this organization, these tools nevertheless need to be acknowledged as essential to the *CFMN* as a rhetorical agent. A good example illustrating what we mean here is the status of the *CFMN* as a 501(c)(3) organization, which provides the affordances of tax-exempt status. Such a tool has both tangible and ephemeral resonances. For any organization, the 501(c)(3) application is both a necessary organizational move (tangible) and the outcome of an important conversation within and about the organization (ephemeral). Such status also has rhetorical implications. 501(c)(3) status hinders an organization's ability to make political statements. At other times, it grants an organization legitimacy to speak on public issues.

We can see traces of this identity/status articulated in the writing produced by the organization and can become more attentive to its effects on the organization's rhetorical positioning and strategies. The *CFMN*, for example, began its interest section of the amicus curiae of the *CFMN* and of The Women for Equal Health Care, written in support of plaintiffs-appellants in a sterilization abuse case, in the following way: "The Comisión Femenil Mexicana (Comisión) is a non-profit association duly incorporated under and existing by virtue of the laws of California with offices located in a number of cities throughout California."[12] This is a simple, declarative, and factual statement. It is boring, and something we might miss. But it is a material trace that resonates (or should resonate) much more loudly in how we approach rhetorical research. Other such material resonances in our example of the *CFMN* include the genres of agendas and meeting minutes, as well as Robert's Rules of Order, which was a routine way for the *CFMN* to facilitate meetings and manage discontent between members to get things done.[13]

The Art@Work wall was an instance of public art made by "non-artists." Peckham team members come from a variety of cultural and national backgrounds (many of them refugees) and face challenges with regard to mental or physical ability. Much was required to facilitate the making of art (and rhetoric) in this project. Thus, while a goal of the art dialogue sessions was to make art that would eventually be displayed, the dialogues invited conversation across individuals with diverse values and prior experiences. Facilitating this exchange required students to motivate and encourage team members to become interested in both sharing and painting, introducing artistic techniques, helping team members generate ideas, and encouraging team members to complete projects once they had begun them (a process that often took several weeks).[14]

To focus on resonant materialities, the RCAH art studio was full of tools and objects that became actors in students' growing ability to use art as a catalyst for conversation. To facilitate dialogues, students (who, in all cases, were also art novices) needed to become familiar with materials of the craft: charcoal pencils for sketching; paint media, brushes, and small canvases for painting. Because Stacey's fieldwork invited her into learning moments prior to the dialogues and construction of the art wall, it was possible for her to learn how portraiture and self-portraiture became a resonant system for inviting collective sharing. For instance, in an early art studio component of the course, the instructor invited students to use their developing portraiture techniques to draw strangers on campus and on the "strip" across from campus in East Lansing. Before heading out on this mini adventure, course members brainstormed conversational prompts (e.g., "Where are you from?" "What are you really good at?" "What do you think makes a good community?") that would ensure that portrait sessions led to discussions with strangers about themselves, as well as some of their local issues and concerns. Everyone was nervous, and students' results were mixed, but they ended the day looking at a set of local community members' portraits taped onto a shared classroom wall, while sharing stories about who they'd met and what they'd learned. When the first day of facilitating art dialogues at Peckham rolled around, the instructor looked knowingly to the group of students and said, "you've done this before," while handing out the tools, paintbrushes, and paper that would soon catalyze stories.

By showing how our research shifted attention from the terminus of rhetorical activity to its resonances, we intend to raise questions about how fieldwork can invite researchers into new interpretive stances: Would most accounts of public rhetoric direct our gaze to organizational tax status, help us understand the rhetorical weight of simple descriptive sentences, or ask us to spend time examining the uptake of objects first encountered in an art studio? Probably not. But, more importantly, while these materials resonated in the cases we are using as resources for thinking, they may not have. That is *resonant materials*, as we are using the phrase here, are not obvious or obviously meaningful. The materials of rhetorical activity are necessarily ambiguous from the perspectives we inhabit as both researchers and practitioners of rhetorical work. It is the affordances of fieldwork as a mode of making rhetorical theory (and practice) that render them accountable because the stances, methods, and tools of fieldwork allow us to capture the tangible and put them in relation to more ephemeral issues (e.g., values) that enrich how we might engage the world. Fieldwork is fundamental. When we connect things in this way, we hope to create mediators.

Mediators

For now, it might be useful to understand mediators first in terms of Bruno Latour's distinction between an intermediary and a mediator.[15] An intermediary transports without transformation. Mediators, in contrast, transform, translate, or otherwise modify meaning (action, trajectory, outcome). Any thing that is a mediator will produce outcomes that cannot be fully predicted. Mediators are the things that cause other things to be made, and so they are what we want to become (as rhetors) and what we seek to identify as researchers.

Returning to the *CFMN*, we offer a brief example of how identity mediates in so far as it is productive: identifying as a Chicana. Identifying as Chicana shapes both the way one sees the world and the way one acts in it. In the case of the *CFMN*, Chicana identity shaped the organization and the actions and decisions it made. In this case, identity becomes real and realized as it mediates. For instance, organizers of the *CFMN* used their shared experiences to build what it meant to be a Chicana, which, in turn, informed what it meant to be a Chicana *organization*. Being a Chicana was not just an interpretive device for organization members; it became a concept that was used to determine how to make decisions and was continuously rebuilt through its actions. Recognizing Chicana identity as a mediator is different from other work on Chicana rhetoric that typically treats Chicana identity as a stabilized *a priori* construct and that subsequently positions rhetoric (and rhetorical theory) as that which is acting upon and through Chicanas.

The most important example of the *CFMN* leveraging Chicana identity to organize was their use of *La Hermandad*, or Chicana sisterhood. *La Hermandad* is derived from the sisterhood of nuns and connotes forgiveness, sacrifice, and working together for the greater good. *CFMN* leaders strategically extended *La Hermandad* to define a particular Chicana method of collectivity, which in turn was used to redress divisive actions within its organization. Records of meeting minutes demonstrated *CFMN* leaders invoking *hermandad* to question its members' actions and its boards whenever they appeared to counter collective and constructive action. The *CFMN* leaders claimed that identifying as a Chicana implied a shared commitment to *La Hermandad*, which, in turn, became a heuristic through which the activists interpreted and altered their actions. Arguably, being a Chicana (or Chicana organization) did not always mean that one always acted in the spirit of sisterhood; however, this feature of a Chicana identity was often enacted to motivate new actions.

Two issues are important here. The first is to note how the *CFMN* itself understood identity as both mediating and fluid, a thing that could make others do something but that also needed to be continually invoked and reconstructed. Braided into this second issue is Kendall's own fieldwork, which participates in the writing of this story. Kendall's ability to recognize this rhetorical work necessitated reading beyond the more public accounts of the organization and reading into the internal memos, flow charts, and other mundane writing associated with building the organization. Her ability to see and understand identity as mediating is a function of her stance and practice as a particular kind of rhetoric researcher. Just as the *CFMN* leveraged identity to do rhetoric, our field and analytical work shapes how we understand rhetoric.

As we have argued, the actual agents in the mediating work of Chicana identity were a set of mundane but important material objects and embodied practices. And so it was also with the Art@Work project. The mechanism for change within this project was not only the work of art itself but also the set of dialogues scaffolding its making. Students associated with the Art@Work project were charged with helping Peckham team members share and actualize experience through portraiture, and to do so, they needed to develop ways of conversing and interacting with team members. In spite of their experiences taking art outside the studio, many students still initially approached Peckham team members as if the communicative situation were about "instruction," in which their central goal would be to train employees in art techniques. Not surprisingly, many Peckham team members resisted this dynamic. This was the backdrop for a memorable car ride back to Michigan State in the afternoon following the first art dialogue session, when several students found Peckham team members had responded in unexpected ways.

Because students worked one-on-one with team members, they had little access during dialogues to others' experiences. In the car that day, they initially traded stories about how team members had wanted to paint pictures of landscapes or pets or apartment facades or favorite foods instead of taking direction and completing portraits. In what later seemed (to Stacey) an important moment in the conversation, one student shared what she'd learned by asking her partner why it was so important for her to paint the front of her apartment (it was her first one and meant a great deal to her). For the student facilitators, sharing these experiences became a necessary step toward reconstructing their perception of the art dialogue in more effective ways. This reconstruction was gradual, incomplete, and never fully overt. No participant in the conversation (even Stacey) ever said, "Wow, maybe we missed the point" or developed a fully articulated plan for facilitating differently. But students did become more comfortable over time, letting conversation emerge without attempting to dictate team members' behavior, and the conception for the art installation itself became more open, including art that depicted meaningful objects rather than just self-portraits. Because Stacey's fieldwork allowed her to travel with students during less official moments, she observed and participated in the struggle to invent agencies within the project, including ways of connecting with others that we hope the students carried into their lives beyond the course. Shared time, common space, and the co-location of people were some of the materialities that led to their new facilitation techniques. While easy to over-look, these affordances are often essential in enabling action in the world.

Mediators become important when they are locatable or recognizable—when they demand the attention of publics or collectives, when they change things. Understanding that experiences, texts, identities, and artifacts are mediated, performed, and interpreted is important, but it is just as import-ant to attend to the fact that each can in turn mediate. Each can cause anoth-er to act. Mediators are not only present to researchers but are also import-ant to rhetorical practitioners: to citizens in everyday life. Indeed, in each of the materialities we introduce in this section, both dynamics are funda-mental. These materialities can be ways that people locate, use, and assem-ble agencies for social action. It is also the case that such rhetorical work is only possible to see and effect when we direct our (rhetorical and empiri-cal) gaze at materials and seek to understand them as (potential) rhetorical agencies. As we have argued here, it is fieldwork that best directs our gaze toward materials that make us do something. If we don't direct our gaze in this way, we might just miss rhetoric.

Mediators: Beings Capable of Worrying Us

Latour offers us the important insight that any act of construction "has to provide *the opportunity to encounter beings capable of worrying you*"—*beings* in this case means entities "whose ontological status is still open but that are nevertheless capable of *making* you *do* something, of unsettling you, insisting, obliging you to speak well of them. . . . *Articulable* beings to which insaturation [construction] can add something essential to their autono-mous existence. Beings that have their own resources."[16] We want to sug-gest that, with regard to rhetorical theory (of the kind that we are imag-ining), and with regard to fieldwork in relation to rhetorical theory, these statements are remarkable and worthy of some attention. Simply put, there is an ethics, as well as a politics, captured in the notion that we should iden-tify, assemble, and help create mediators capable of worrying us. Implicit in Latour's statement is a commitment to understanding the democratic/par-ticipatory project and to help facilitate its practice.[17]

Perhaps the strongest articulation of the need to assemble to engage in the public work of rhetoric is John Dewey's argument in *The Public and its Problems* that we are required to understand, assemble, and make things.[18] To do so demands an empiricism. For Dewey, the question "what does the public want?" is something we should seek to answer. Indeed, we are required to answer it to engage in the public work of democratic practice. The public work of rhetoric is a project committed to identifying mediators. "To study," as Latour argues, is "always to do politics in the sense that it collects or composes what the common world is made of. The delicate question is to decide what sort of collection and what sort of composition is needed."[19] In thinking about research methodology, the idea that we compose the world we are examining when we research isn't new, as any number of critical traditions have made this case for some time. Where people might look at us oddly is the application of this thinking to doing rhetoric.

The point of connection between doing research and doing rhetoric is the need to assemble. Both Dewey and Latour have made the pragmatic argument that political philosophy has often been silent about the object of concern that actually brings people together.[20] Dewey argued for the importance of assembling the public and understanding public concerns. Latour argues for an "object oriented democracy," which has two goals: (1) to gather legitimate representatives around a table and (2) to represent "the object of concern to the eyes and ears of those who have been assembled around it."[21] Latour is interested in "how many participants are gathered in a thing to make it exist and to maintain its existence."[22] A "Thing," then, is the object-of-concern that brings people together, and such things might consist of anything from a neighborhood planning issue to the regulation of natural gas pipelines to our collective stance with regard to something like immigration. Rhetoric offers participants places to gather and cares for gatherings. Politics, and rhetoric, is a process of collecting. To do rhetoric is to associate.

But associations of what? If the work of the researcher or the rhetor is to help gather and care for these gatherings, then what is to be gathered and cared for? We have provided one answer here: attend to particular materialities and seek to understand the extent to which they mediate. Perhaps one final story will help: this last one, a version of a story told more fully elsewhere.[23] This story is based on a study of communication practices in a community called "Harbor." In this community, the US Army Corps of Engineers plans to dredge a canal linking an industrial area with a large lake. The industrial uses of the harbor and canal have left the waters heavily polluted. Some in Harbor are quite concerned about supporting the dredging project. Others are strongly opposed to it. The focus of this story is a small environmental organization called CEC that is opposed to the dredging project. In its own meetings, CEC assembles evidence, arguments, facts, issues, concerns, and other people and organizations by way of written summaries of texts, photocopies of articles or graphics, or accounts of first-hand observation in the community. In public gatherings, CEC and others must deploy other assemblies of people, machines, voices, bodies, and texts to reveal to the world as best they can the particular assemblages of environmental toxicology, civil engineering, politics, and other such things. They have rendered their experiences visible and created new shared experiences in the community. They have participated in a decision-making process marked by technical and scientific complexity by assembling things and becoming (as well as activating) mediators.

The *CFMN* is just that sort of gathering as well. Both the *CFMN* and CEC engage a range of mundane inventional practices and other rhetorical acts, ultimately producing various performances that would be more readily recognized by rhetoric scholars as objects to be analyzed (as endpoints, termini): documents that circulated in the community and that shaped conversations; events that communicated positions; questions, speeches, and other performances at public meetings. Yet, as we have noted, these materialities are not the end. If they are agencies, they are mediators, and fieldwork is the most useful research practice for both seeing and making such mediators.

Researchers leveraging the methods and practices that we have alluded to as "fieldwork" are essential actors in the making and doing of rhetoric. Whether researcher or rhetor, scholar or activist, the practice of assembling entails working the field, so to speak. Kendall did more than "find" or "identify" the various reconstructions of the *CFMN*, its relationships to Chicana identity, and the additional relationships to local and national politics. She assembled them. It was literally Stacey's fieldwork that constructed the rhetoric of the Art@Work project. We have no other accounts. Sure, some version of that project happens without Stacey and her fieldwork. But it would not have mediated in the way that it has without her. Both accounts inform any handbook we might assemble for how to do rhetoric in the world today.

But what of the ethical burden to assemble mediators capable of worrying us? The effort to identify, account for, and assemble agencies, to gather and care for gatherings, with an end that the "beings" assembled can worry us? That burden, this effort to assemble, is a remarkable project. Consider some alternatives for rhetoric: to persuade, to win, or, god forbid, to vanquish, defeat, or silence. These are each outcomes of rhetorical agencies. The rhetoric we have forwarded here is designed to open, not close. To facilitate, not dominate. To engage, not obstruct. To help identify, assemble, and deploy materialities capable of making other people and things act in the world. To care for things, even things that we might not agree with. The methodology implied, both for researcher and rhetor, is to engage in the fragile and difficult work of facilitating participatory cultures. It isn't enough to collect the agencies necessary to build that park or produce this piece of legislation. It is also necessary to identify and help assemble the agencies that speak against funding for that park or to counter the logic of that legislation. Our rhetorical work must resonate such that we create possibilities and capacities for participation that exceed the needs of our own group, organization, or community. Our rhetorical work must create the contexts and conditions in which we can encounter others who can and will worry us, and that is a remarkable and generous commitment.

Notes

1. Philip E. Agre, "The Practical Republic: Social Skills and the Progress of Citizenship," in *Community in the Digital Age*, ed. Andrew Feenberg and Darin Barney (Lanham, MD: Rowman and Littlefield, 2004), 211.

2. Marilyn M. Cooper, "Rhetorical Agency as Emergent and Enacted," *College Composition and Communication* 62, no. 3 (2011): 420–49; Laurie E. Gries, *Still Life with Rhetoric: A New Materialist Approach for Visual Rhetorics* (Boulder: University of Colorado Press, 2015); Peter Simonson, "Rhetoric, Culture, Things," *Quarterly Journal of Speech* 100, no. 1 (2014): 105–25, doi: 10.1080/00335630.2014.887852; Paul Lynch and Nathaniel Rivers, eds. *Thinking with Bruno Latour in Rhetoric and Composition* (Carbondale, IL: Southern Illinois Press, 2015).

3. Jeffrey T. Grabill, "Community-Based Research and the Importance of a Research Stance," in *Writing Studies Research in Practice: Methods and Methodologies*, ed. Lee Nickoson and Mary P. Sheridan, 210–19 (Carbondale: Southern Illinois University Press, 2012).

4. Simonson, "Rhetoric, Culture, Things"; Victoria J. Gallagher, Kenneth S. Zagacki, and Kelli Norris Martin, "Materiality and Urban Communication: The Rhetoric of Communicative Spaces," in *Communication Matters: Materialist Approaches to Media, Mobility, and Networks*, ed. Jeremey Packer and Stephen B. Crofts Wiley (London: Routledge, 2012); Ronald W. Greene, "Lessons from the YMCA: The Material Rhetoric of Criticism, Rhetorical Interpretation, and Pastoral Power," in

Communication Matters ; William Hart-Davidson, James P. Zappen, and S. Michael Halloran, "On the Formation of Democratic Citizens: Rethinking the Rhetorical Tradition in a Digital Age," in *The Viability of the Rhetorical Tradition*, ed. Richard Graff, Arthur E. Walzer, and Janet M. Atwill, 125–39 (Albany, NY: State University of New York Press, 2005); Debra Hawhee and Cory Holding, "Case Studies in Material Rhetoric: Joseph Priestley and Gilbert Austin," *Rhetorica: A Journal of the History of Rhetoric* 28, no. 3 (2010): 261–89, doi: 10.1525/rh.2010.28.3.261; Wendy Hesford, "Reading Rape Stories: Material Rhetoric and the Trauma of Representation," *College English* 62, no. 2 (1999): 192–221; Richard Marback, "Detroit and the Closed Fist: Toward a Theory of Material Rhetoric," *Rhetoric Review* 17, no. 1 (1998): 74–92, doi: 10.1080/07350199809359232; Liz Rohan, "I Remember Mamma: Material Rhetoric, Mnemonic Activity, and One Woman's Turn-of-the-Century Quilt," *Rhetoric Review* 23, no. 4 (2004): 368–87, doi: 10.1207/s15327981rr2304_5; Mary Lay Schuster, "A Different Place to Birth: A Material Rhetoric Analysis of Baby Haven, A Free-Standing Birth Center," *Women's Studies in Communication* 29, no. 1 (2006): 1–38, doi: 10.1080/07491409.2006.10757626. For overviews of the material turn, see Carole Blair, "Reflection on Criticism and Bodies: Parables from Public Places," *Western Journal of Communication* 65, no. 3 (2001): 271–94, doi: 10.1080/10570310109374706; Barbara A. Biesecker and John Louis Lucaites, "Introduction" in *Rhetoric, Materiality, and Politics*, ed. Barbara A. Biesecker and John Louis Lucaites (New York: Peter Lang, 2009).

5. See: Gloria E. Anzaldúa, "Now Let Us Shift . . . the Path of Conocimiento . . . Inner Works, Public Acts," in *This Bridge We Call Home: Radical Visions for Transformation*, ed. Gloria E. Anzaldúa and Ana Louise Keating, 540–78 (New York: Routledge, 2002): 540–78; Jacqueline Jones Royster and Gesa E. Kirsch, eds., *Feminist Rhetorical Practices: New Horizons for Rhetoric, Composition, and Literacy Studies* (Carbondale, IL: Southern Illinois University Press, 2012).

6. Tim Ingold, *Being Alive: Essays on Movement, Knowledge and Description* (New York: Taylor & Francis, 2011), 26 (qtd in Simonson, 2014, 118).

7. See Christian Meyer and Felix Girke, eds. *The Rhetorical Emergence of Culture* (New York: Berghann, 2011) for more on resonance as a property and outcome of rhetorical action.

8. See Jim Ridolfo and Danielle Nicole DeVoss, "Composing for Recomposition: Rhetorical Velocity and Delivery," *Kairos: A Journal of Rhetoric, Technology, and Pedagogy* 13, no. 2 (2009), http://kairos.technorhetoric.net/13.2/topoi/ridolfo_devoss/future.html; Gries, *Still Life with Rhetoric*.

9. For further description of how *CFMN* created these identities and assemblies, see Kendall Leon, "Chicanas Making Change: Institutional Rhetoric and the Comisión Femenil Mexicana Nacional," *Reflections* 13, no. 1 (2013): 2013a, 2013b.

10. Sonja K. Foss and Cindy L. Griffin, "Beyond Persuasion: A Proposal for an Invitational Rhetoric," *Communication Monographs* 62, no. 1 (1995): 2–18.

11. *Comisión Femenil Mexicana Nacional,* "Resolution Adopted by the Women's Workshop 10/10/70 Sacramento, California, [A] Proposal for a Comision Femenil Mexicana," TS. Series IV, Box 34, Folder 3; *Comisión Femenil Mexicana Nacional Archival Collection,* CEMA 30. UC Santa Barbara California Ethnic and Multicultural Archives Special Collections, Davidson Library, Santa Barbara, CA.

12. *Comisión Femenil Mexicana Nacional,* "The Experience That Was," *CFM Report* 2.4 (UC Santa Barbara California Ethnic and Multicultural Archives Special Collections, Davidson Library, Santa Barbara, CA, July 1973): 1–3.

13. During Kendall's research, there was a moment when Robert's Rules became a source of contention within the organization as some Chicanas viewed such rules and procedures as part of the "white man's bag." *Comisión,* "The Experience," 1.

14. Peckham is a vocational rehabilitation organization that provides work and rehabilitation opportunities to people striving for independence and self-sufficiency. Those who work at Peckham are "team members" and not "employees," in the language of the organization, in part to reflect the mission of the organization and the roles people play within that organization.

15. Bruno Latour, *An Inquiry into Modes of Existence* (Cambridge, MA: Harvard University Press, 2013).

16. Ibid., 161.

17. Ibid.

18. John Dewey, *The Public and Its Problems* (University Park: The Pennsylvania State University Press, 2012).

19. Latour, *Inquiry into Modes of Existence,* 256.

20. Dewey, *Public and Its Problems;* Latour, *Inquiry into Modes of Existence.*

21. Latour, *Inquiry into Modes of Existence,* 16.

22. Ibid., 246.

23. Jeffery T. Grabill, *Writing Community Change: Designing Technologies for Citizen Action* (New York: Hampton Press, 2007); Stuart Blythe, Jeffery T. Grabill, and Kirk Riley, "Action Research and Wicked Environmental Problems: Exploring Appropriate Roles for Researchers in Professional Communication," *Journal of Business and Technical Communication* 22 (2008): 272–98.

9

Rhetoric(s) of Urban Public Life

ERIN DAINA MCCLELLAN

A field-based approach to examining the rhetoric of urban public spaces seeks to better understand the complexities and processes of a city, with the aim of improving and making more sustainable our shared public life. (Re)presentations of urban public life are an embedded and dynamic part of rhetorical experiences and thus present an opportunity to explore the nuances of vibrant urban public life in relation to one another and to the larger discourses within which they function. Rhetorical field methods are particularly well suited to capture the emergent quality of "living" rhetorics, rhetorics that are always in some phase of formation, part of larger discourses, and related to certain bodies and cultural contexts. Field-based research is poised to help rhetorical scholars interrogate the experiential, dynamic, and often divergent meaning-making processes involved in a rhetorical text's (re)presentation that manifest *in situ*. Such processes of interrogation are important, and often overlooked, pieces of a conversation that connect individual rhetorics with the larger contexts and effects they (re)produce. (Re)imagining how existing meanings are understood to be (in)significant while simultaneously drawing attention to how new meanings shift our thinking and/or actions over time become significant precursors to meaningful social change. This requires "an active process" capable of "animating" decisions about how we construct (re)presentations of, articulate interpretations about, and discuss consequences for understanding rhetoric.[1]

This unique cacophony of influences spans specific contexts, subject positionalities, understandings of history, materiality, and embodied experiences. Our *rhetorical experiences* in the world utilize larger cultural and

discursive frameworks to constitute what we understand to be (il)legiti-
mate, (im)possible, and (in)appropriate. Engaging in a rhetorical field-based
approach to examining rhetoric concentrates on the rhetorical experiences
of both the critic and those involved in the rhetoric being examined. Such
an approach can value marginalized rhetoric and rhetorical experiences as
a way to better account for power relations that are inherently manifest in
rhetorical practice. As Michael Middleton, Danielle Endres, and Samantha
Senda-Cook explain, "If [critical rhetoric] contributes an impulse toward
thinking about marginal, embodied, and material forms of rhetoric, then
ethnography contributes to the means of locating such rhetorics."[2] Thus,
by focusing on both *which* rhetorics to study and *how* to study them in
action, the experiences of engaging rhetoric in everyday life, particularly
in everyday public life, are significant for rhetorical analysis, intervention,
and action.

By focusing on my own rhetorical field experiences in Portland, Oregon's
Pioneer Courthouse Square (PCS), I will reflect on three emergent themes
revealed during my rhetorical fieldwork in this particular site. PCS serves
as an exemplar of how (re)presentation of rhetoric(s) illuminates public
life in terms of its dynamic, interconnected, and emergent manifestations
of reality. Connections between the micro- and macro-aspects of rhetoric
can inform urban planning and development initiatives related to public
space and provide a more adaptable, inclusive, and sustainable approach to
encouraging vibrant public life over time. This essay reflects on how examination of PCS has provided insight into urban public life via three complex relations that guide my own rhetorical fieldwork: (1) rhetoricians can be
applied humanists; (2) rhetoric and discourse constitute each other; and (3)
self-reflexivity connects subject positionalities and interpretations.

Urban Public Rhetoric(s) of Pioneer Courthouse Square

For this chapter, I draw on fieldwork from a larger project that examines
rhetoric across four different US urban public squares, in which I gathered
and analyzed the spoken, written, and performative texts produced in and
about public squares. I engaged in three weeks of intense participant-observation (approximately 150 hours) in Portland's Pioneer Courthouse Square
(PCS) and participated in approximately thirty-five interviews with people
"officially" associated with the square (e.g., people serving as management,
event coordinators, security, janitorial/maintenance staff, vendors, city staff,

and historians) and with people "unofficially" associated with the square (e.g., people eating lunch, attending events, just "hanging out," drinking coffee, reading newspapers, arriving as tourists, or inhabiting a temporary "home"). I documented emergent performances during my participant-observation period via photographs, video recordings, and field notes. While such performances varied in format, they all directly engaged the square in some way.

All (re)presentations of PCS identified for further examination functioned as rhetorical formations. In other words, more than stylistic elements of expression, they were part of a formative process by which people made sense of not only the mundanity of their surroundings in PCS, but also of how those meanings and experiences informed their understanding of the larger City of Portland. These manifestations of rhetoric co-constituted the ways that I *and* the people I interacted with during this study could think about, understand, and create expectations for PCS specifically and urban public squares more generally.

PCS appears to be an ideal urban oasis: a multilevel expanse of brick tucked in among the most desired real estate in downtown Portland. Flanked on two sides by a steeply inclined sidewalk and street, the square's interior was designed as a row of tiered steps (or seats, depending on how one used them). On one corner, three food trucks set up and packed up each day. When I first entered the square, I was struck by the diverse array of characters: tourists, residents, businesspeople, people without homes, children, teenagers, adults. Visible difference was apparent albeit the large majority of occupants were young, white professionals who frequented the square on their way to/from work or during their lunch break. But other visible groups occupied the square at any given time as well. One regular group of men (and one woman) carried large carts or bags stuffed with various belongings and regularly interacted with the people in business casual clothes who frequented PCS on their commute to or from work. The lowest point of the hardscaped square was used to host a temporary stage and provided music performances and rally organizers with access to microphones and speakers. Moveable tables, chairs, and umbrellas were put out each morning and returned to locked storage each evening under a Starbucks that was built into one corner as retail space. Next to the underground storage facility was the entrance to the TriMet public transit office, where tourists and commuters alike often entered to buy tickets and passes for bus and train travel. City busses and light rail trains made regular stops at the square. City noises were constant, and even the water feature near the TriMet entrance was difficult to hear at times amid the more prominent hum of the city.

PCS was voted "best U.S. public square" by the Project for Public Spaces[3] and is recognized as an iconic symbol of the City of Portland. The square has been further recognized as an example of successful participatory design. PCS has a long history of development addressing diverse public interests, maintaining an aesthetically pleasing form, and ensuring sustainable, accessible, and vibrant public life for all. Public life, however, is always more complex than any single planner or infrastructure can account for. People with vastly different interests, values, and needs negotiate with each other to constitute public life in a place. When people push their belongings, eat their lunches, sightsee, peddle goods and services, and seek respite in the same space, some of their interests are more easily, and willingly, supported than others. The tensions of everyday public life thus emerge when rhetorics collide rather than when they are treated as isolated (re)presentations of certain kinds of public life experiences. Thus, my experiences with the rhetoric of PCS are (re)presented here as a constellation of rhetorical formations "in action."

My rhetorical experiences in PCS accounted for the ways I previously understood public life, public squares, (in)appropriate behaviors, and the various subject positionalities I encountered *in situ*.[4] The most common portrayal of PCS I encountered was its description as "Portland's living room." It was written in newspaper headlines, on event flyers, mentioned in interviews, and embraced generally as a signature metaphor by those familiar with the square. This metaphorical sense-making frame constituted both an expectation and an evaluative measure, and simultaneously revealed a larger cultural manifestation of Portland public life.

PCS as Portland's "Living Room"

Throughout my three weeks of participant-observation at PCS, it became clear that some kinds of behavior (and ultimately people) were more supported in this "living room" than others. While understandable in cases where public safety or health would be protected (like by implementing and enforcing a rule prohibiting public urination), other situations seemed more disconnected from the "common good." As a result, other kinds of behavior (and ultimately people) were systematically and consistently discouraged, even though there was nothing particularly illegal or problematic with their presence. The resulting complexities presented themselves in both peoples' articulations and behaviors in PCS. These complexities are most prominently (re)presented in the various ways PCS was conceived of as "Portland's living room." By focusing on how "Portland's living room" appeared in various rhetorics in and about PCS, the various constitutive elements of this public rhetoric connected patterns of sense making across otherwise disparate rhetorics. One example of how two such rhetorics collided can be seen in the tension-filled accounts of PCS as "Portland's living room" engaged by Jepp, a widely recognized man without a home, and by Mike, a retired police officer serving as a private security guard for the square.[5]

Jepp was a regular part of the PCS landscape. He talked about himself as someone who slept most nights "on the street or in a [homeless] shelter." He spent most of his days in the company of others he knew to be in similar situations to his own. The group carried a collection of their belongings with them wherever they went, in backpacks, plastic grocery bags, and sometimes carts. They consistently appeared to have a layer of dirt and grime on their faces and exposed skin, wore large overcoats, or carried them if the weather was too hot, and often emitted a strong odor that indicated soap and deodorant were not likely a part of their daily hygienic practices. They frequently kept to themselves except for Jepp, who regularly greeted, and was greeted by, many people daily. Various people in PCS acknowledged him both verbally with a passing "hello, how are you?" and at times with a more intimate high-five routine. The weekday noon hour was a particularly popular time for Jepp, as an influx of business people came to eat lunch in the square during the summer month I visited, bringing him coffee from Starbucks or offering to buy him lunch, which he almost always declined or gave away to someone else.

I noticed Jepp on the first day I arrived. It was hard not to, given the attention he garnered. But my sudden appearance in his landscape of predictability caused Jepp to scrutinize my presence in the square in much the same way I took note of his. After almost three full weeks of acknowledging each other's existence through side glances and occasional nods, we finally spoke. I asked if he might be willing to talk to me for my "school project" like I had been doing with others in his presence since I arrived. He paused and asked what my project was about. I explained that I was curious about how various people used a public square like PCS in different ways. He paused and then agreed.

During our exchange, I asked Jepp about what he thought about calling PCS "Portland's living room." He was quiet for a moment and then said, "If this is supposed to be my living room, then why won't people share?" "I don't know," I replied. "What happens here that makes you feel that way?" He smiled as if I had asked the exact question he was hoping I would. He launched into various anecdotes that all had one thing in common: people who "had" were treated differently than people who were perceived to "have not." Among his many examples, two were particularly detailed. The first portrayed a friend who had routinely been issued a "littering" ticket by a City of Portland Police Officer for setting down a disposable drink cup with a lid and straw. Although the same drink cup appeared all over the ground near people dressed in business casual clothing during the weekly lunch rush, I never saw, or heard of, anyone else who was issued such a ticket for littering. The second illustration of the have/have-not tension had to do with the mass exodus of people like Jepp during the same lunch rush (typically at its peak on weekdays between noon and 1:00 PM). "They don't like that we are nearby. It's like we're going to take their sandwich or something. It's just easier to leave."

Jepp's anecdotes confirmed my own observations of tension between perceived consumers (people and tourists eating mostly purchased lunches in the square: the "haves") and perceived nonconsumers (like people without homes: the "have-nots"). While both comprised a regular part of the PCS landscape, Jepp's perception that a "living room" was primarily a place to *share* space did not always align with others' expectations that individual spatial boundaries should be maintained even in the square. While my own spatial experiences in PCS certainly differed from those in my own home, Jepp's expectation that public space be shared was clearly both reasonable and complicated. When informed by his own experiences with homeless shelters and other places of refuge that did not allow for "my" space in the same way, his "living room" was a shared space that "belonged" to everyone in it. Other understandings of the same space constituted a different understanding of the square as "living room," with distinctly different rhetorical experiences. One such rhetorical experience emerged in Mike's account of the same metaphor.

Mike, a security officer and retired City of Portland Police Officer, regularly patrolled PCS as part of his job. He described the square as "Portland's living room" without prompting. Since he frequently used detailed anecdotes and/or reflected on his personal background to reinforce the larger point he was trying to make, one such monologue quickly revealed how he made decisions about what was (un)acceptable in the square on any given day. The criteria for evaluating behavior in the square was akin to determining what would be ok in his "grandmother's living room." He said, "If it is unacceptable to put my feet up on her furniture, then I need to determine what counts as putting feet up on this furniture and act accordingly." Mike wanted first and foremost for all people to follow the same rules of decorum. The "living room" rules provided what he explained was a universally accessible understanding of (in)appropriateness. While Mike's depiction of PCS as a place in need of protection from inappropriate behavior was primarily focused on managing shared space, its emphasis was much less on the problems of people not sharing that Jepp's stories illuminated.

One way that Mike talked about managing this shared space had to do with politely enforcing expectations of decorum like you might in your "grandmother's living room." He found it important to encourage appropriate behavior and discourage inappropriate behavior without formally arresting, evicting, or publicly humiliating anyone. A grin came over his face as he recounted one such attempt. As summer arrived each year, PCS attracted a relative swarm of people to lounge or eat along the inclined steps, and one man took advantage of this noticeable change in a memorable manner. Since many of the women in the square during this time wore skirts, the steps produced a unique "opportunity." "Every summer," Mike told me, "this guy simply walks to the bottom of the steps and lays down. Most people don't even notice him. But if they knew he was waiting for a peek up a skirt, they would likely do something about it—which isn't what we want either." The situation was complicated, he explained. The man's behavior was not technically illegal because there is no expectation of privacy in a public square. "If you were in your own home, that would not be the case . . . so that's why my team and I just stand next to him as he lays on the ground . . . our bright yellow jackets bring the attention he is hoping to avoid." When he "doesn't get what he wants," Mike looked pleased as he finished his story, "he just leaves."

A clear public-private tension emerges in these competing notions of public space. In Jepp's account of PCS as the city's living room, expectations of what it meant to "share" the public space were not themselves shared between the "haves" and the "have nots" in public life. In Mike's discussion, the city's "living room" was a place with shared decorum, even though not everyone had the same understanding of what it meant to "put feet on the furniture" or even agreed that putting "feet on the furniture" was bad. The nuances of difference that appear across these tensions place rhetorical scholars in a unique position to discuss the constellation of meanings that emerge in the experiences of diverse publics. By relating different interpretations of meaning to larger discourses that reveal frameworks of understanding (like PCS as Portland's "living room"), rhetoric can reveal both specific details of similarity and difference while also reflecting the larger landscape in which it is produced. Thus, rhetoric is always relational; it is experiential, connected to particular subject positionalities, and contextualized in larger material, symbolic, discursive, and affective landscapes of meaning.

A Relational Approach to Rhetorical Fieldwork

Rhetorical fieldwork provides an opportunity to access and examine individual rhetorical text(s) as part of a larger process of rhetorical formation, rather than as primarily an output of rhetorical practice. Thus, in attempt to expand the ontological analytics of rhetoric and advance a more diverse set of epistemological approaches to its study, I offer the following three (inter) related tenets that have informed my own processes of determining which blend of qualitative methods and rhetorical analysis to employ: (1) the lines between empiricist and humanist can be blurred, (2) the relations between rhetoric and discourse can be experienced, and (3) deep self-reflexivity can be integrated into the study and analysis of rhetoric.

Rhetorical Fieldworker as Applied Humanist

Studying rhetoric "in action" requires (re)considering how we access and analyze rhetoric to preserve both the dynamic nature of rhetorical experiences and the historical significance of rhetorical analysis. A rhetorical scholar is empowered to act as an applied humanist that is uniquely positioned to do both. The humanities are "concerned with human thought, experience, and creativity" and explore the "ways in which they may endure, be challenged, or transformed."[6] Similarly, the "humanistic social sciences are fundamentally acts of investigation and reflection about different cultures, texts, and artifacts across space and time."[7] A turn to field methods grounds examinations of rhetoric that focus on its larger contexts of use and circulation while simultaneously engaging those relations in critical discussions of meaning, influence, and effect. Attending to the dynamic, performative, material, and/or embodied aspects of rhetoric further allows us, and our audiences, to "see" meaning as constituted in everyday life rather than solely through *a priori* deductions made by others.

Jepp and Mike both (re)presented an understanding of PCS as the city's "living room." They focused on different aspects of the living room in a way that demonstrated how similarities (a shared sense-making referent: city as living room) must be considered in relation to its interpreted differences in meaning (e.g., how that shared referent constituted lived experience differently for different people). For Jepp, PCS as living room meant that people who had something to share were expected to share with people who did not since they all occupied the same space. For Mike, PCS as living room meant that all people in the square should protect it, and each other, in the same way. The issue for Jepp was that people were not willing to share. The issue for Mike was that people didn't always behave in ways that deserved to be protected equally. Jepp's rhetorical experiences constituted a world in which he was often disciplined for others' inability to share. Mike's rhetorical experiences constituted a world in which he attempted to discipline others as a way to protect a shared public place. While empiricists may see this nuanced disjuncture between these (re)presentations as a fracture in urban public life, the rhetorician can connect these seemingly fractured nuances to the larger shared culture from which they emerge.

In John Van Maanen's words, the study of culture is best engaged by "structur[ing] a cultural portrait in a particular way."[8] The nuanced relations that emerge in the study of rhetoric as living (rather than solely historical and apart from the critic) require treating rhetorical experiences as always in relations to the larger patterns of articulated and observed understandings as they are revealed "in action." Thus, rhetorical formations about public life also (re)present particular understandings of larger cultural, material, and/or discursive formations within which they function. In this way, the rhetorician as applied humanist is much like the rhetorical formations she or he examines: both are constituted over time and require attending to their nuance and complexity *in relation* to one another.

Experiencing Rhetoric and Discourse

Another way in which nuance and complexity are intertwined can be seen in how rhetoric and discourse emerge and are experienced in relation to one another. How we are able to understand, articulate, and interpolate meaning is embedded in processes of coming to know the world *and connected* to the resources that allow us to know that world in particular ways (and not others). Thus, what we know about the world apart from having direct experience with it is deeply connected to the discourse(s) that frame our experiences. In the case of urban public life, what we know about urbanity and public life before we walk into a public square inevitably affects the experience(s) we have when we do walk into one. Thus, how we understand and experience rhetoric and discourse together ultimately influences how we understand and experience the culture that influences both. Culture is both contextual and embedded in specific rhetorics. Participatory field methods allow us to access and analyze both in mutually informed ways that account for both the nuance and the complexity in any specific set of relations.

Rhetoric is discussed here as a living, emergent, constitutive force that ascertains significance in the way it (re)presents particular perspectives. These orientations not only reflect culture but also create it.[9] Rather than attempting to locate "flattened" forms of "rhetorical action [that have been] reduced to exclusively textual representations,"[10] a field methods approach to rhetorical study emphasizes the ways in which the study and production of rhetoric are equally bound up with understandings of and experiences with culture. While calls for increased self-reflexivity in rhetorical scholarship mirror similar calls made in early ethnographic work,[11] exploring rhetorical experiences, rhetoric "in action," invites us to (re)consider relationships among rhetorical formations and their larger sense-making frameworks. Sometimes these experiences occur near one another and sometimes in seemingly disparate spheres of influence. In this way, specific rhetorical moments and larger discursive landscapes (constituted by constellations of moments over time) are connected by the rhetorician. These connections are often illuminated through criticism that inherently relates specific moments of rhetoric to the larger discourses that shape (im)possibility within our larger social world. Discourse thus shapes, and is shaped by, the interpretation and (potential) effect of individual rhetorical texts. When individual rhetorics are understood to be formed in relation to larger discourses' meaning-making processes, they are themselves culturally situated in a state of becoming meaningful in relation to specific people, contexts, and (im)possibilities.

Mike and Jepp identified the same sense-making framework, PCS as living room; however, Jepp's rhetoric depicted a living room that precluded him and others like him from being able to use it in the same ways. According to him, those with more experience of "having" a living room were privileged over those who did not. Mike's rhetoric depicted the living room metaphor as helpful in communicating an easily accessible standard of decorum to all people in the square, leaving open the possibility for people to know specific living rooms differently but recognizing the commonalities as shared guides for appropriateness. Jepp and Mike's divergent interpretations of PCS demonstrate how people can use the same sense-making framework in the same cultural context but still engage in different rhetorical formations about the same thing. Rather than attempting to "fix" such discord, claiming one formation is right and another wrong, rhetoricians are uniquely positioned to reveal how diverse understandings of a city are negotiated and manifest in salient ways.

Deep Self-Reflexivity

Examining the rhetoric of urban public life through an interpretive approach requires not only an understanding of various subject positionalities but also a deep self-reflexivity that accounts for the interpreter's own experiences and epistemologies: "The position of the scholar: her privilege, cultural power, and status . . . are imbricated in larger networks of socio-historical power relations between groups."[12] Beyond general awareness of other perspectives, deep self-reflexivity invites critics to relate their choices about focusing on some aspects of rhetoric (and not others) to be connected to the interpolated meanings revealed in their analysis.

Since "meanings depend on places, physical structures, spatial delineations, interactive bodies, and in-the-moment choices [of the rhetorician in the field],"[13] (re)presentations—and, consequentially, rhetorical examinations—are always bound up with such dependencies. As Van Maanen reflects, "To portray culture requires the fieldworker to hear, to see, and . . . to write of what was presumably witnessed and understood during a stay in the field. Culture is not itself visible, but is made visible only through its representation."[14] Thus, rhetoric inherently constitutes how we understand, make choices about, and behave in everyday life. Those understandings, choices, and behaviors are also always engaged and interpreted in relation to larger landscapes of meaning that also need a critic's self-reflexivity. This obligation to be transparent about such choices enables others to "see" differently. By connecting rhetoricians' positionality to their study of specific rhetoric, living text(s) can be identified, interpreted, and explained from specific subject positions that inherently advocate, even if implicitly and subconsciously, for understanding the world in some ways over others. Not all rhetorical analysis requires deep self-reflexivity, but studying rhetoric as it is experienced by a diverse people (like in a public square) necessitates that it be explained *in relation* to larger cultural context(s) and particulars, as would any examination of rhetoric in the world.

One particular cultural context that needed to be accounted for in my own examinations of rhetoric in PCS was the way that bodies (re)present meaning in particularly influential, yet often unrecognized, ways. A focus on the body and embodied rhetoric has emerged across contemporary rhetorical scholarship.[15] A focus on subject positionality and self-reflexivity does not appear consistently across such work. While debates about the "best" way to account for embodiment in the study of rhetoric persist, rhetorical field methods assume that a unique combination of significant factors is involved in all rhetorical experiences. Thus, making visible how culture and rhetorical formations constitute one another inherently involves bodies, and a rhetorician's body is always embedded in the rhetorical landscape of meaning making she or he purports to analyze.

My rhetorical experiences with PCS continue to shape what I chose to discuss and how I discussed it. I interpreted some aspects of rhetoric and the rhetorical landscape as significant because I am me, and not someone else. I connected with some people more easily than with others. As a young, white woman, perhaps people perceived me as in need of assistance, or worthy of being helped. My body did not (re)present a stereotypical threatening body for other young, white professionals eating lunch in the square. But my classed body—one that displayed being clean, with newly bought clothing, and an educated persona—may not have appeared as approachable to everyone, especially to those without a home. Each individual's rhetorical experiences are unique but patterns can still emerge across different (types of) rhetorical experience. In interactions with particular people, and in relation to particular landscapes, significance is constituted in relation to what we see, how we see it, and why we see it to be important for ourselves and others. Such connections provide insight into the dynamics of social life as they appear (dis)similarly across analyses and over time. Rhetorical scholarship continues to make calls to (re)visit histories of rhetoric[16] and (re)consider marginalized bodies, meanings, and landscapes,[17] however, much of our scholarship continues to perpetuate the problem of overlooking many of the aspects capable of disrupting the status quo. We must be able to "see" rhetoric as significant in everyday life in new ways in order for change to become possible.

My study of PCS produced rhetorical experiences with others with whom I was both more and less familiar. Mike and Jepp associated with groups that I was less familiar with. I have had little direct, sustained experience with either law enforcement officers or people without homes. While this could be interpreted as limiting, my lack of experience also allowed me to consider aspects of rhetoric that prior experience or knowledge may have constituted as not worthy of my attention. By engaging in self-reflexivity, I was able to analyze a rhetoric to interpret its meaning and its (potential) significance more clearly. For example, I was aware of Jepp very early on during my participant observation; however, I waited to approach him until one of the last days I was present in the square. This gave both of us a different understanding of each other when we did talk than if I had attempted to interview him at the beginning of my participant-observation period. Articulating this in my analysis also gives my readers a different understanding of my connection with Jepp than if I had said nothing about when and how we spoke. A field methods approach asks the critic to evoke her or his own rhetorical experiences as constitutive of how understanding and experiencing other bodies, culture, and landscapes of meaning are interpreted. My conclusions are inherently related to my own ability to see (and not see) various aspects of urban public life as significant. The significance of my conclusions depends upon whether my audience(s) agrees.

My ability to "be" different (re)presentations of self to different people in different situations enabled me to step forward and backward, in and out of the rhetoric that I study. This has as much to do with what I experience during participant observation work as it did with my experiences in life before I engage in such work. My concentrated study of both qualitative methodologies and rhetoric allows me to speak in terms of both, separately and together. My previous experiences with iconic public squares like Red Square in Moscow and Tiananmen Square in Beijing during my undergraduate study abroad left me moved by orchestrated mass demonstration in public spaces. Growing up with Latvian immigrant grandparent who told stories about their lives as political refugees entering the United States via German Displaced Persons Camps in the 1940s affects my understanding of (im)possibility as a lived experience rather than a state of being. These experiences, and others, allow me to engage in self-reflexivity that connects my prior experiences to whatever I am analyzing. Sometimes these connections are subtle and sometimes overt. By drawing attention to meanings that are otherwise hidden beneath a shroud of dominant discourse and/or easily accessible rhetoric, the connections between a rhetorician's interpretation of rhetoric and the larger discourses in which those interpretations "live" is significant.

Rhetorical analyses that engage in deep self-reflexivity can illuminate how the complex relations between rhetoric and discourse affect what we understand to be (im)possible in the world. This addition provides what Sarah Pink, Kristen Mackley, and Roxana Moroşanu describe as scholarship that is "felt from inside, within, and not at analytical distance."[18] They claim that such scholarship better "invoke[s] our imaginative capacities to engage with the experiential dimensions of other people's worlds."[19] In this way, our ability to (re)imagine what is possible beyond what we know via direct experience relies on our ability to examine *processes* of rhetorical formation (rather than only products of rhetorical form) as always connected to (re)presentations of larger value systems, ideological assumptions about the world, and relations of power experienced in the world.

Conclusion

The unique infusions of qualitative principles and rhetorical analysis that guide any instance of rhetorical fieldwork provide unique opportunities to gain new insight into how drawing attention to the nuances of social life expand, rather than flatten, the complexities of rhetoric as a living force we experience in the world. Focusing on nuanced aspects of rhetorical formation can reveal various ways that rhetoric is experienced beyond our own inevitably limited understandings of it. In the examination of rhetoric in and about PCS discussed here, three central tenets of rhetorical fieldwork emerged as significant for rhetoricians doing this kind of work. These tenets have emerged from my examination of living rhetorics in and about PCS as a microcosm of Portland public life and guided my explorations of urban public life more generally. I hope that reflecting on how my experiences with rhetorical fieldwork can invite other (re)considerations of rhetorical experiences as embedded parts of everyday life. Such new insights into our everyday life can further expand how we seek to examine culture and rhetoric as inherently intertwined.

The first tenet, *the rhetorical fieldworker can be understood as an applied humanist*, emerged at the intersectional disciplinary histories of fieldwork and rhetoric. I was driven by both a motivation to study *and* engage in rhetorical practice with real people in everyday life when I was in PCS and after I left. Given my interest in participating in the rhetoric I wanted to study, qualitative methods presented ethical guidelines for designing and approaching the "living" rhetorics in PCS that I encountered. It was thus both personally and professionally important to me to value and respect the people *and* rhetorical formations that became part of my study. Since rhetorical fieldwork focuses on human "subjects," the humanistic qualities of analysis and criticism are equally important to accessing and collecting rhetorical "data." Since navigating rhetoric as it is encountered in everyday life is inherently complex and never the same twice, using appropriate frameworks and theories to ethically guide its access and analysis remains a central challenge for rhetorical fieldwork. When navigated well, however, new and relevant insight emerges. Thus, we can understand and address long-standing social problems, cultural challenges, and political adversity in new ways. In this way, the *practice* of engaging rhetoric in action enables rhetoricians to simultaneously *advance theoretical premises that introduce and/or legitimize new* perspectives about both rhetoric and the realities they (re)present. The critical aim of some rhetorical fieldwork provides a further opportunity to connect rhetorical experiences with larger systems of marginalization, oppression, and power relations embedded in the complexity of how micro- and macro- aspects of rhetorical formations are "felt" and experienced by various others. In this way, we must always look to studies that employ rhetorical fieldwork as capable of illuminating the world as we know it in altogether new ways.

The second tenet of rhetorical fieldwork: *rhetorical study can account for the experiences of both rhetoric and discourse* and reveal the limitations when we focus on either rhetoric *or* discourse. By articulating the specific rhetorics, I encountered in the field in relation to the larger landscapes (discursive and material) within which those rhetorics functioned, constituted public life in unique ways. In particular, by connecting the lived experiences of rhetoric in everyday life to the larger rhetorical landscapes within which those rhetorics are engaged, living rhetorics can be directly connected to the sites and larger discourses that constitute meaning and relevance. More specifically, rhetoric (1) effects the ways we act, react, and interact with others; (2) (re)presents ourselves and what we deem to be important; and (3) influences the writing of policy, practices of enforcement, and articulation of moral aptitude. For these reasons, rhetorical analysis should (re)consider examining with more scrutiny the emergent connections rhetoric in action reveals among subject positionalities and larger landscapes of meaning.

The third tenet of rhetorical fieldwork, *rhetorical analysis, can adopt a sense of deep self-reflexivity*, requires distinguishing between two distinct levels of self-reflexivity: (1) the ways in which the rhetorician is perceived differently by various others during a study, and (2) the ways in which the rhetorician perceives others differently because of her or his own preconceived notions about rhetoric and public life. Rather than attempting to justify my position as subject matter expert in my examination of urban public life in PCS, I focused on being transparent about my subject positions in relation to the rhetoric I study. This attempts to avoid negative consequences that often emerge when scholars attempt to speak about and/or on behalf of others in ways that do not appropriately (re)present others' understanding(s) of the world. Since interpretation of meaning is filtered through the rhetorician's own experiences and understandings, this is particularly salient for discussions of rhetorical fieldwork. Rather than attempting to solve the "problem" of subjectivity by removing the expectation of self-reflexivity in favor of adopting expert objectivity, qualitative traditions invite rhetorical analysis to include a rhetorician's subject positionality, part of which is someone educated by and with experts in the field of rhetoric, as intertwined with the analysis she or he engages about a specific rhetoric.

Rhetorical fieldwork necessitates the ability to adopt specific blends of qualitative interpretive methods and rhetorical traditions of inquiry and analysis. Thus, it makes sense that we look to the increasing number of experiences with rhetorical fieldwork to inform a set of central tenets able to guide how we decide upon the appropriate blend for our next rhetorical inquiry. By accounting for these nuances, rhetoricians can illuminate the complexities of everyday life that are otherwise often invisible to those who do not directly experience them. Rhetorical fieldwork scholarship is also uniquely poised to respond to calls for further examining underexplored rhetoric(s), particularly those capable of advancing alternate histories and/or exposing rhetoric of marginalization and oppression more broadly. I remain hopeful that the potential for further contributions to rhetorical studies can expand and advance the field of rhetoric in ways that remain focused on affecting positive change in the world. Rhetorical fieldwork assumes that rhetorical study is more than just an intellectual exercise of knowledge examination but rather an innately human exercise that connects us to that which we study in important ways. Rhetoric is engaged and thus "felt"; it is more than something to abstractly deconstruct or critically discuss. Rhetoric is experienced in consequential ways. Thus, my hope is that rhetorical scholars of all types can be inspired to consider more reflexive, robust, and nimble approaches to perspective-taking by continuing to invite and contribute to the larger conversations about rhetorical field methods and the novel insights such examinations of rhetoric "in action" provides.

Notes

1. William L. Nothstine, Carole Blair, and Gary A. Copeland. *Critical Questions: Invention, Creativity, and the Criticism of Discourse and Media* (Boston: McGraw-Hill, 2003), 15.

2. Michael K. Middleton, Samantha Senda-Cook, and Danielle Endres, "Articulating Rhetorical Field Methods: Challenges and Tensions," *Western Journal of Communication* 75, no. 4 (2011): 390.

3. "Pioneer Courthouse Square," Project for Public Spaces, accessed February 15, 2006, http://www.pps.org/great_public_spaces/one?public_place_id=19.

4. For more about rhetoric *in situ*, see Michael Middleton et al., *Participatory Critical Rhetoric: Theoretical and Methodological Foundations for Studying Rhetoric in Situ* (Lanham, MD: Rowman & Littlefield, 2015).

5. I use pseudonyms throughout.

6. "What are the Humanities?" American Council for Learned Societies (ACLS), accessed January 12, 2017, http://www.acls.org/about/faq/#humanities.

7. "What are the Humanities?"

8. John Van Maanen, *Tales of the Field: On Writing Ethnography* (Chicago: University of Chicago Press, 1994), 5.

9. Ivo Strecker and Stephen Tyler, eds., *Culture & Rhetoric* (New York: Berghahn Books, 2009).

10. Middleton, Senda-Cook, and Endres, "Rhetorical Field Methods," 387.

11. See Charles Morris III, "Performing/Rhetorical Studies: Differential Belonging across Intradisciplinary Borders," *Text and Performance Quarterly* 34, no. 1 (2014): 104–07.

12. Mary Garrett, "Tied to a Tree: Culture and Self-Reflexivity," *Rhetoric Society Quarterly* 43, no. 4 (2013): 245.

13. Middleton, Senda-Cook, and Endres, "Rhetorical Field Methods," 388.

14. Van Maanen, *Tales from the Field*, 3.

15. See Jack Selzer and Sharon Crowley, eds., *Rhetorical Bodies* (Madison: University of Wisconsin Press, 1999); Debra Hawhee, *Bodily Arts: Rhetoric and Athletics in Ancient Greece* (Austin: University of Texas Press, 2005); Gerard A. Hauser,

Prisoners of Conscience: Moral Vernaculars of Political Agency (Columbia: University of South Carolina Press, 2012).

16. See Karlyn Kohrs Campbell, "The Rhetoric of Women's Liberation: An Oxymoron," *Quarterly Journal of Speech* (1973): 74–86; Karma R. Chávez, "Beyond Inclusion: Rethinking Rhetoric's Historical Narrative," *Quarterly Journal of Speech* 101, no. 1 (2015): 162–72.

17. See Mary K. Bloodsworth-Lugo and Carmen R. Lugo-Lugo, *Containing (Un) American Bodies: Race, Sexuality, and Post-9/11 Constructions of Citizenship* (Amsterdam: Rodopi, 2010); Daniel C. Brouwer and Robert Asen, eds., *Public Modalities: Rhetoric, Culture, Media and the Shape of Public Life* (Tuscaloosa: University of Alabama Press, 2010).

18. Sarah Pink, Kirsten Leder Mackley, and Roxana Moroşanu, "Researching in Atmospheres: Video and the 'Feel' of the Mundane," *Visual Communication* 14, no. 3 (2015), 353.

19. Pink, Mackley, and Moroşanu, "Researching in Atmospheres," 366.

10

Rhetoric, Ethnography, and the Machine

Technological Reflexivity and the Participatory Critic

Aaron Hess

The turn toward participatory methods in rhetorical studies invites new considerations of the nature of text, audience, rhetor, and critic. Fundamentally, these approaches challenge the *post hoc* approach to criticism, and have instead embraced Raymie McKerrow's notion of criticism as performance. As such, some rhetorical critics engaging in fieldwork have taken to the street to analyze public places and protests or even advocate alongside activists.[1] In taking up causes from community advocates and organizers, fresh insights have been gained about the nature of rhetorical exchange and public advocacy. Participatory approaches, such as participatory critical rhetoric,[2] have problematized staid assumptions in rhetorical studies, especially the role of the critic. Whether through "participatory epistemology"[3] or through the guiding virtue of *phronesis*,[4] the role of the critic has been fundamentally challenged. When taking to the field, critics no longer engage rhetorical processes through a detached perspective; instead, they are implicated into the scene and often in the production of rhetoric.

Simultaneously, rhetorical discourse in social movements has become increasingly mediated as advocates turn toward mass and social media to create and circulate messages. Recognizing their powerful ability to quickly circulate messages, advocates frequently take up these relatively inexpensive tools. Underneath these social media systems lies a logic of spectacular politics and visual immediacy, which directly affects the representation of political activism and potential circulation of messages.[5] Previous research into social and locative media has reflected on the power of these systems to transform public discourse. Simultaneously, rhetorical scholars have taken up digital tools in the field to augment existing data collection practices or to record and represent the rhetorics found in public places.[6] Yet, critics have not connected the two and looked underneath the ideological, technological, and representational assumptions that undergird these devices as they are taken up in fieldwork.

These two developments should not come as a surprise, given the rapid development of communication technology in the past few decades. Organizations have quickly adapted to the increasingly mediated world. Moreover, for rhetorical critics who take to the field, the ubiquity of smartphones and digital imaging devices provides the means to create vivid images that inform our fieldwork and can lead to alternative forms of scholarly outputs, such as digital humanities projects. Recognizing this unique moment in rhetorical and technological history, I pause to ponder the significance of these technologies in conducting fieldwork and to call for a reflexive examination of how technology impacts research practices. In this chapter, I examine the field-based critic's use of technology as tools of text or data collection. It is necessary to understand the impact of these devices on data collection in the field, (re)presentation of fieldwork, and the circulation of scholarship. First, I briefly chart the trajectory of media as it intersects in social movements to underscore how activists take up technology and the logics that undergird it. Second, I discuss the development of participatory and locative media as it intersects with the *places of persuasion* and rhetorical fieldwork. Finally, I outline technological reflexivity as a process for engaging the field of argumentation through various digital devices.

Media, Technology, and Protest

Rhetorical scholars have long reflected on the nature of advocacy as it becomes mediated in traditional and digital media.[7] Much of this theorizing speaks to the power of images in forming and challenging public opinion and democratic culture.[8] Activists frequently utilize media to circulate messages both internally within their membership and externally with larger publics to affect change.[9] Central to theorizing about this process is Kevin DeLuca and Jennifer Peeples' contribution of the public screen. The concept "recognizes that most, and the most important, public discussions take place via 'screens'—television, computer, and the front page of newspapers."[10] These public discussions and deliberations include issues of foremost public concern. Guided by the screen, they invite spectacle over rational debate, infotainment over formal education, and visual distraction over focused textual attention. As a rhetorical strategy, those who engage the screen recognize that its logic requires a fundamental rethinking of protest and advocacy. Grabbing the camera's attention necessitates, at times, vivid action and sensational politicking. Consequently, many scholars have reflected on the intersections between media and rhetoric, offering concepts such "pranking rhetoric,"[11] vernacular spectacle,[12] and "networked public screens."[13]

More recently, scholars have turned to the participatory nature of user-generated, web 2.0 environments and placed-based locative or smartphone media. Increasingly, scholarship recognizes the everydayness of media for politicking and deliberative action,[14] even when the media may not foster democracy in desired ways.[15] The locative turn in media, especially through the use of smartphones, has also encouraged critical reflection. Adriana de Souza e Silva recognizes this shift in the media landscape as a departure from stationary screens accessing *cyber*space to users existing in *hybrid* spaces through cellular phones.[16] Taking up the turn toward hybridity while working with Art Herbig, I expanded this line of thinking through an examination of how smartphone apps for the National 9/11 Memorial alter readings of the memorial.[17] In short, not only do digital media structure and circulate messages, but the logics undergirding media systems can also lead to an inflated sense of importance of media in users' lives.

Lisa Silvestri forecasts this increasingly complex environment for rhetorical inquiry, outlining how textual criticism may require "sensitive, ethnographically inspired interpretation; more interviews and participant observation as a way to navigate the doxa and shared ideologies of the digital 'speech communities' we are drawn to."[18] While I agree that technological environments invite ethnographic reflection, it is also the case that ethnographic environments invite technological reflection. Rhetorical field scholars should consider how technology precedes, accompanies, and shapes their experiences. Increasingly, researchers rely on technology to record data through smartphone photography, voice recordings of interviews and fieldwork, for example. Despite the ubiquity of multimedia technology in fieldwork, rarely do researchers reflect on the power of such technology on their work. This is especially true with smartphones, which can easily capture high definition video of interactions in the field.

Simultaneously, scholars recognize the growing intersection between locative and participatory media with social movements. For example, while DeLuca and Peeples originally examined the nature of globalized media networks, the world has become increasingly fragmented since the early 2000s. The proliferation of web 2.0 platforms, social media sites, and locative technologies has invited myriad voices into horizontal circulation. DeLuca, Sean Lawson, and Ye Sun recognize that participatory media, in the form of weblogs, differ significantly from traditional media in how they cover protest events, such as the Occupy Movement.[19] Using participant observation and interviews, Shiv Ganesh and Cynthia Stohl examined the hybrid nature of protest through the use of social and digital media by Occupy activists in physical spaces.[20] They found that characterizing social movements as entirely, or even merely, technological, missed the nuanced interconnectedness of the digital and embodied elements of protest. Ganesh and Stohl collected data through iPhone photography, along with more traditional interviews and observation, indicating how the same technology used by participants is also being taken up by researchers. Finally, Art Herbig and Aaron Hess examined the faux "Rally to Restore Sanity" hosted by Jon Stewart of *The Daily Show*, concluding that engaging the public screen may require that scholars take up media tools as "a form of involvement that attempts to reconcile media fragmentation with individual voice."[21] In other words, critics should consider the knowledge and skills behind media production to best theorize their social impact. In sum, scholarship has recognized the growing differences and parallels between mainstream media logics and participatory media, the hybridity of embodiment and digitality inherent to contemporary protest, and the need for researchers to use the same media tools that guide protests toward action.

It is at this intersection of participatory rhetorical methods and the need for scholars to recognize the hybridity of contemporary social movements that I seek to problematize how these devices impact our research. Field researchers may also decide to utilize digital media technology to augment data collection or other textual practices. Within the hybrid spaces of rhetorical production, critics should take stock of the nature of such technology and its impact. As with many forms of technology, the use of these devices does not lead to unbiased, apolitical observation; the shiny screens of our latest Apple and Android devices obscure the vast arrays of information and digital experiences that merely carry the veneer of neutrality.[22] These networks and their confirming algorithms package data in ways that suit users' needs. As I have argued elsewhere, our smartphones and other networked devices construct a "foundational part of rhetorical identity"[23] and call into question the ethics of our networked selves. Simply put, if the physical places of persuasion include hybrid protests that simultaneously occur on social networks and in streets, and researchers carry devices that also position them in hybridized spaces, research ethics must account for both the *physical and digital* presence of the researcher.

Given the ubiquity of small screen and smartphone technology, it is even more imperative that researchers engage in reflexive considerations about our role and place within technology. The advent of locative technology connects individuals in remote places and at all times.[24] Political movements, ranging from the international feminist organization FEMEN to terrorist organizations, such as the Islamic State (ISIS), engage social media to bolster their messages. Indeed, the places of persuasion do not merely stop at the street; it is nearly impossible to recognize protest activities without attending to their mediated character. Many movements are better understood as social media image events more than they are street protests.[25] Through powerful visuals and images taken through smartphones and immediately uploaded to Twitter, Facebook, and elsewhere, contemporary protest movements are keenly aware of the power of such technology. Researchers inquiring into these processes must be willing to take up these tools,[26] while also being appreciative of their power as they shape our own practices in the field.

I offer the concept of *technological reflexivity*, an examination of the self in relation to digital and locative technologies and their corresponding networks, to consider how technology impacts our research into protest and informs our discovery, interpretation, representation, and evaluation of rhetoric in the field. On a theoretical level, we are shaped by our social media presence, the displays of shared materials between our "friends," and the "likes" gathered on items that we send along.[27] Technological reflexivity attempts to unmask the neutrality of our devices and interactions through them. In what follows, I examine technological reflexivity in methodological contexts that draw from my own fieldwork and digital creations, which include a range of recording technology including smartphones and professional-grade cameras. My fieldwork experiences include working with the drug education organization DanceSafe in 2006 through 2008, examining media and political discourse at the Rally to Restore Sanity in 2010, exploring public memory about the tenth anniversary of 9/11 in 2011, working with a birthing center in 2013, and researching public memorials in Europe in 2016. More than ever, the presumption of those involved in social movements is that a social media presence is not only desirable, but also necessary for an effective movement. As my fieldwork has progressed, the presence and impact of smartphone and locative technology has become even more pronounced. Consequently, conducting research into social movements and public places necessarily entails being a part of the social media landscape alongside the physical landscape.

Technological Reflexivity

Reflexivity in the interpretive tradition requires an examination of self in relation to the participants and scenes of research. Initial theorizing regarding reflexivity stemmed from critical reflections on science and objectivity in ethnography.[28] Similarly, I extend discussions of reflexivity to the realm of technology and embodied research. More specifically, I am interested in moments when the practices, ethics, and methods of research accented with technology can be improved through a reflexive stance. Marilys Guillemin and Lynn Gillam believe that reflexivity is a process that should be present in every part of the research project, including our research interests, questions, design, and choice in participants, as "a process of critical reflection both on the kind of knowledge produced from research and how that knowledge is generated."[29] They add an interactional ethical dimension to the traditional epistemological nature of research reflexivity, arguing that "In these interactions lie the possibilities of respecting the autonomy, dignity, and privacy of research participants and also the risks of failing to do so, thus perhaps causing harm to the participants in various ways."[30] As an epistemological and ethical construct, reflexivity challenges the objective stance in naturalistic research that can account for every ethical challenge in research, as perhaps desired by Institutional Review Boards.

Reflexivity, a mainstay of qualitative research, requires due attention to a variety of theoretical intersections, including subjectivist, methodological, intertextual, feminist/standpoint, queer, and feminist materialist.[31] Each of these conceptualizations offers a different epistemological understanding of the field, which challenges our ways of (co-)producing knowledge derived from fieldwork. In addition, *technological reflexivity* means taking stock of how our digital tools provide baseline knowledge of our topics, how they alter our embodied experiences in the field, and how they frame our research outcomes and participants. Chris Drain and Richard Strong argue, "Technological reflexivity refers to the way in which technological practices have a bidirectional causal influence and on human agents."[32] Speaking about citizens' use of smartphones, they contended that "the situated potentials for action between material things in the world and the interactional processes thereby afforded need to be seen not only as constituting the possibility of agency, but thereby also comprising it."[33] Methodologically, technologies constitute and comprise, in part, the agency of the researcher who utilizes these tools in the field. Technological reflexivity resists technology's perceived neutrality. Too often, citizens and researchers alike are captivated by the convenience and power of these tools, forgetting that they embody corporate interests and selectively frame our perspectives in the field.[34] They are rhetorical, insofar as they assist in the production of meaning for active users and audiences. Yet, even quick digital photographs or videos only capture one "side" of the camera and story. Moreover, the mere presence of a camera in someone's hand can alter the ways we speak and act.[35] Reflexivity in the qualitative tradition entails an embracing of our identities as inherently subjective instruments as they participate and collect data in the field. Similarly, our digital identities and abilities must be accounted for as we enter the field.

Entering the Field: Cookies, Search Engines, and Digital Identities

Technological reflexivity invites examination of the self as it is reflected and refracted through the lens of our digital devices. In this technological age, before we engage the physical places of persuasion, our research is affected by our use of search engines, computers, and web browsers, these digital places carry their own persuasive power. Reflexive practices about technology should include an examination of our personal and research-oriented use. As I have argued elsewhere, our digital identities have a direct impact on our search processes and networked selves.[36] At a nearly unconscious level, we are affected by our use of the machines: "Our identities—our substances, to use Burke's language—are comprised of our neurophysiological and computer programming, developed through our interactions with people and computers alike."[37] Using these networked technologies and search engines creates what Eli Pariser calls a "filter bubble" that includes tailored information and data that we prefer, and excludes potentially undesirable ideas and opinions.[38] Consequently, everyday searches are guided by past preferences and desires, including many of our political experiences and arguments. Our research practices and commitments, then, are also guided by these interactions, which begs questions about how we find research projects in the first place. Often, we engage our digital tools without interrogating the ways that we are shaped by these tools.

Take, for example, the contemporary nature of Facebook or Twitter advocacy and awareness campaigns. Often, awareness of salient political issues travels virally, meaning that Facebook or Twitter feeds provide users with causes to follow or hashtags to promote. Studying these processes means that we inherently rely on the technologies and the algorithmic processes behind them to provide access points into the viral campaigns. Yet, those algorithms are personalized to each individual user, built by our previous interactions with the technology.[39] Researchers who seek protest or advocacy activities with an online presence are guided by their own political identities. While we are also guided by our political subjectivities in offline contexts, political (offline) subjectivity does not carry the veneer of neutrality, as if the viral campaigns were merely dropped into our news feeds. For instance, when conducting fieldwork with a local birthing center, I used digital tools to conduct preliminary reviews of natural birth advocacy. Consequently, my Facebook news feed became littered with items pertaining to natural birth and other issues discursively tied to it, such as antivaccination.

David Beer reflects upon the "power of the algorithm," arguing, "How we find the books that shape our writing could be a question we might ask ourselves if we wish to consider the power that algorithms exercise . . . over the formation of knowledge within our various disciplines."[40] Searching for scholarly literatures inevitably leads to the replication of desired results, and Beer offers evidence of his own, searching on Amazon as affecting his research outcomes. Similarly, rhetoric scholars should consider how "filter bubbles" and "algorithms"[41] might affect their research. Moreover, engaging in social media inherently means that critics are part and parcel of the capitalist model of information technology, including one that buys and sells consumer data for marketing purposes. Recognizing this shaping mechanism is a crucial and increasingly urgent facet of digital contexts.

A more reflexive stance includes not merely the recognition of technology's presence and impact on exposure to argument, but would also manipulate the tools of the technology to open up the possibility of alternative experiences. Users engaging in digital research that intends to lead toward fieldwork should attempt to begin with a blank slate of a cleared browser

history or by starting with a fresh batch of "cookies," those digital iden-
tifiers that track user behavior for marketing and other purposes. While
an imperfect solution, this act will at least open the possibility of retriev-
ing results that do not replicate user desires and political affiliations based
upon previous search habits.[42] To be clear, I encourage "cookie-less" searching not because of a desire for more objectivity; rather, given that the impact
of cookies is difficult to ascertain, scholars can better assess the impact of
these technologies by impeding their internal machinations. In turn, critics
planning to do fieldwork may be open to political commitments and organizations not typically found in their searches. Furthermore, the technologically reflexive rhetorician should also consider how information technology structures knowledge through relative ordering, meaning that when
search engines provide results, they are inherently hierarchized. Atop the
list might be those most well-known organizations or those who can pay
for a top result, leaving the most local and vernacular discourses obscured.

Counterpublic or vernacular discourses are hidden from public and
mainstream perspectives,[43] which extends to the digital contexts. Counterpublic discourse may not surface in standard Google searches. The structure and political economy of search engines and Facebook advertising
means that fledgling movements with limited access to capital may not
appear as readily. Structurally, social networking sites may also not provide
a platform for expression suitable for particular causes. Most recently, many
activists have left Facebook to seek new means of expression. For many, the
exodus was brought upon by Facebook's forced use of "real" names, which
left many in the LGBTQ community without a voice and proper means
of expression, especially those who engage in drag performances.[44] Consequently, many users left to seek new social media platforms, such as
the new startup Ello, as a place more closely aligned with their identities.
Researchers seeking to augment fieldwork with textual practices found on
social networking sites or with digital ethnography will find that access to
these communities can be more difficult than mainstream social networks.
This means that the "field," broadly construed, is also affected by this structure and political economy. Critics seeking out causes may not find those
groups that remain purposely hidden from public view or do not surface in
blanket search engine searches. In other words, we may conceive of the field
as a separate physical space that may be accented by digital spaces; yet, in
the sense that the two are so significantly intertwined, it may be more useful to consider them one.

In the Field: Balancing Media Logic and Researcher Ethics

The rhetoric scholar in the field should consider how his or her technology use affects the performance of advocacy. Participatory methods allow direct access to rhetorical performances.[45] Technology can assist in the overall invention of argument.[46] Advocates use locative technology not only to organize protests and circulate messages, but also perhaps to access relevant information that supports the central argument of the advocacy group. As a practice of invention, digital technology can provide access to massive amounts of information and opinion about an issue. As mentioned above, these practices are not neutral; they carry the weight of previous search habits and the technological unconscious. When accessing information in the field, such as conducting a Google search, the same elements of reflexivity should apply. Our portable devices have a similar structure in how they access and order information for users.

Additionally, it is often easy for a field researcher to engage in data collection using digital tools, especially smartphones. These devices capture high-resolution photography and video; but, what is lost from the disruption of the relationship between embodied critic and emplaced rhetorics via the smartphone? Seasoned qualitative researchers know that the moment observation turns to the recording of field notes, the gaze of the researcher is averted. Similarly, when researchers take frequent digital pictures as a "stand in" for data collection, the affective relationship between scene and researcher is disrupted. Critical embodiment in the scene includes the affective relationship between the bodies of the people involved: "Affect moves and engages people who are co-present, experiencing rhetoric together as it unfolds and calls upon and creates shared meanings and feelings."[47] Certainly, the corporeal notion of affect extends to technology,[48] where a smartphone creates a relationship between user and device.[49] But, accessing social or informational networks pulls the user away from the physical embodiment of the scene and into a hybrid space of being. Although protesters or others may also engage in this practice, researchers carry a unique responsibility to think through these practices.

To illustrate this, I draw from my fieldwork at memorial sites across Germany and the Czech Republic. One site that is highly mediated by tourists is the Memorial to the Murdered Jews of Europe. Located in the heart of Berlin, this memorial features over two thousand stelae (stone slabs) that are arranged at different heights in a grid-like pattern on a city block.

Visitors can walk through the sea of slabs, likely getting somewhat lost inside. Underneath the memorial there is a museum dedicated to the Holocaust, including vivid images and texts from those who perished in concentration camps. While at the site, I was surprised to witness how many people playfully interacted with the memorial by playing hide-and-seek inside and how often tourists use cameras, smartphones, and selfie sticks. This type of smartphone technology seemed out of place at a memorial dedicated to the deaths of millions. I interviewed about twenty tourists regarding their interpretation of the memorial and their use of cameras to take pictures and smiling selfies. Although a few interviewees found the practice disquieting, many responded positively to the act of taking a selfie, saying that it was an act of personal remembrance. Through these reflexive interactions, I learned a different type of judgment about technology that challenged my own.

Moreover, part of my data collection regarding the use of technology was to record the use of smartphones to navigate the memorial, using my own smartphone. In effect, I had engaged in the very same act of media technological documentation that I was critiquing at the site. I, too, took digital video and photography of visitors who were using the same technologies to document their experiences with the memorial. To engage in reflexivity during my interviews, I confessed to my own use, withholding judgment on those engaged in such documentation, and I rethought my stance on the practice of taking selfies in serious places. As much as the technology may alter the material engagement with the memorial site, it also stands as an important sense-making practice for those tourists.

Furthermore, looking to the context of performing advocacy, and in a very different example of fieldwork, some digital tools provide knowledge that assists in public argumentation and social movements. For example, in my work with DanceSafe, a health advocacy organization that provides drug information in the context of raves, advocates consistently encouraged ravers to know what they were ingesting. Given the black market for ecstasy, it was commonplace that hits of ecstasy were adulterated with undesirable contents. To combat this, DanceSafe sold pill testing kits and would often test pills on site. This particular chapter of DanceSafe did not conduct pill testing because of local laws that could lead to the arrest of the volunteers. To supplant this element of advocacy, DanceSafe volunteers used digital media and the participatory website, Pillreports.com, to provide updated information regarding the content of local pills.[50] While not as effective as direct pill testing, the site provided at least a baseline for ravers to assist in making decisions, even if it was an ethically charged one that did not typically promote abstinence over informed drug use.[51] When I initially joined the group, recent printed reports on local pills were made available to ravers. Later, as smartphone technology and web access was more readily available, I used my iPhone to look up current and past reports for ravers on the spot. This element of invention was certainly a part of the group's mission and advocacy, but also carried the facade of being a relatively neutral act. The user-generated reports found on Pillreports were crafted with a surprising amount of care and concern for others, but cannot be fully trusted. Yet, for DanceSafe volunteers, this form of invention was acceptable. As a part of the ethics of using such technology, I warned those who looked up these reports about their unknown and potentially untrustworthy origins.

On a more participatory level, however, the use of technology by advocacy groups can directly impact the researcher and his or her presence within in these spaces. Given that advocacy groups abide by media logics and web 2.0 participatory cultures, it is likely that participating rhetorical scholars will be involved in capturing digital images and other data pertinent to the cause. Photographs and status updates sent out from the field may implicate the researcher in unpredictable ways. With DanceSafe, I was a regular part of the web presence in ways that were remarkably unanticipated. Digital photography of organizing efforts was commonplace for this technologically savvy organization, including images of volunteers interacting with ravers and the array of information offered to ravers. Volunteers used the photographs as evidence of their presence in the rave scene, engaging in a visual form of rhetorical enactment. During my fieldwork in 2006, volunteers took pictures of the booth and of the group interacting with ravers. One picture was sent to the national headquarters, and subsequently placed on the website's homepage. On my very first night with the group, I became DanceSafe's digital poster child.

This was unexpected, to say the least, and my status as a researcher made the photograph feel somewhat disingenuous. I had not considered that these photographs could be circulated in such a way and so quickly. During my research with DanceSafe, the local organization also operated a MySpace page that featured images of advocacy and of the colorful rave environment, typical of advocacy groups and especially of rave culture. Walking the line between insider and outsider status was complicated for my technological presence on the social networking site. On the one hand, images of my volunteering with DanceSafe accented my status as an insider in the organization. To ask DanceSafe members to limit the circulation of images of me would violate the digital ethos of the organization. On the other hand, from an academic perspective, images of me dressed as Shaun of the Dead at a Halloween rave, interacting with ravers who are visibly high, or discussing drug contraindications across a table adorned with glowsticks, Christmas lights, and a bowl full of condoms, all important elements of participation with this advocacy and culture, may not provide a sense of seriousness inherent to studying advocacy.

At that time, locative technology was relatively limited. Since then, the active photographing and uploading of images during the moment of advocacy has been facilitated through smartphone technology. Much like many other organizations that engage publics armed with smartphones and social media accounts, DanceSafe volunteers embrace these tools to spread their message, knowing full well that members of the public can also circulate mediated discourse about them. In a sense, these forms of media decentralize power for advocacy groups, who must carefully craft messages and manage their public identities. This means that researchers entering a highly networked field should consider the ways that they will actively be implicated and imaged across digital networks in ways that are largely out of their control. This may mean being identified with problematic protest activities and having images of those activities circulate beyond their control. During my research with a birthing center that advocated for natural birth practices against medical/hospital models of birth, my family, including my two young children, was invited to a local protest regarding regulations of midwives' homebirth practices. During the protest, images of children holding signs supporting the midwives circulated on Twitter and elsewhere. The protest practice of children holding signs is ethically questionable, given that children do not often understand what they are advocating. Being present and photographed with my own children identified me within this act. Taking part in the protest places the critic in the role of rhetor. Images taken during these sorts of protest can circulate well beyond the initial site of protest to unintended audiences. In other instances, protests may include disruptive acts,[52] the use of the (naked) body,[53] or illegal acts of trespassing. As a part of technological reflexivity, researchers engaging contemporary protest activities should consider the level of involvement they desire, their insider/outsider status, and the uncontrolled ways that digital images can quickly circulate through social media sites.

Furthermore, these networked environments do not stop when the protest or event concludes. For many organizations and advocacy groups, images of the protest serve as active recruitment tools and as publicity for their message. Researchers may be invited to take part in the interaction with those who find the online presence of the protest. For example, when working with DanceSafe, I was given access to their MySpace page. Often, individuals would reach out to DanceSafe with questions about raves, drugs, or other issues. In one instance, a parent contacted DanceSafe to ask questions about raves and ecstasy use, worried that their child had recently discovered rave culture. This online element of advocacy overlaps with offline protest, but requires a different form of speech. Holding picket signs and chanting to passersby is drastically different than interacting with one person through direct (and recorded) interactions on social media, websites, or through email. As a representative of the organization, the researcher has an ethical commitment to speak effectively and with the organization's goals in mind.[54] These issues embody the (digital) micropractices of advocacy.

Qualitative and rhetorical researchers must be cognizant of the power of digital photography and video in quickly recording elements of the scene. As mentioned above, the highly mediated nature of protests means that using digital tools to collect data may feel natural. Indeed, the use of smartphones to take quick pictures or as a reminder of some event can be helpful in documenting the richness of the scene. Digital video or photographs may also later become larger elements of one's project. However, the ease of circulation and duplication of these photographs should give participatory rhetoric scholars pause. As with other data, the digital images or video should be carefully maintained within the digital ethos of the organization. Furthermore, the camera's presence can affect the performance of protest. Advocates, recognizing the power of media logics and the need to grab the attention of an Internet audience, may overperform or engage in spectacular politics.[55] These logics of media circulation and spectacle, coupled with the power of the camera, mean that the authenticity of such performances should be questioned. While working on a documentary film regarding the tenth anniversary of 9/11,[56] I found that individuals commonly reacted to the camera, either to ask about whether something could be edited or by becoming overcome with emotion in the presence of its lens. Researchers engaging in participatory rhetorical methods should interrogate the seemingly neutral and naturalistic elements of video production.

This leads to the final consideration for collecting digital data in the field, which directly affects the outcomes of research, such as digital projects, documentary film, or academic essays. As much as the camera affects the performances of protest or interview "confessionals," it is also a tool that is guided by media logic.[57] Researchers, goaded by the spirit of spectacle, may be more attentive to elements of the field that are more sensationalistic or provide compelling anecdotes, turning their camera toward visually stunning images and away from more mundane and possibly theoretically salient moments. Indeed, in any research project, some visuals may appear more appealing than others, or some interviews more desirable than others. Consequently, researcher ethics in the field may be guided by overly visual ideas rather than by what is necessary for full exploration of ideas. For example, in conducting documentary fieldwork during the tenth anniversary of 9/11,[58] Herbig and I deliberated on the types of interviews we would solicit. We sought out both random people on the street and individuals who had a more direct experience with 9/11, such as first responders. While this was a relatively balanced approach, we still felt the pressure to include particular people in the documentary to give it a visual and narrative credibility that might be otherwise absent. During the reading of the 9/11 victims' names, we stationed ourselves outside of the National 9/11 Memorial exit, knowing that we would find people who lost someone in the attacks. Our camera was not alone. We were surrounded by media outlets that also sought interviews with victims' friends and family members. Within this highly mediated environment, we became implicated in the production of media spectacle; we knew that this interview would be a good "get." We interviewed one woman who lost her brother in the attacks. The interview was short and respectful, but after it was completed, I felt a profound discomfort with our seemingly opportunistic placement outside the memorial. While the interviewee readily agreed to be on camera, on some level, we were driven by what would look good on film rather than by ethics or theoretical considerations. In sum, the researcher may be motivated in the field by media spectacle because of their technology, what may appear visually compelling or what may sound good on the page, but these elements may be acquired through ethically questionable or theoretically unsound means. This concern continues as researchers leave the field and begin examining their digital texts.

Leaving the Field: Selecting, Framing, and Editing

Researchers must be acutely aware of how the presence of the camera and networked quality of research calls forth the logic of spectacle and frames messages, fundamentally altering data collection. Upon returning from the field, the complexities of representation resurface, especially as our digital tools combine with the need for stepping more directly into the outsider ethnographic role. The crisis of representation is further complicated when digital texts include photography and video. The veneer of neutrality or objectivity within documentary film or digital photography resurfaces when suddenly images speak for themselves, as if the camera was operating all on its own. However, at this outsider stage, the field rhetorician's digital texts are subject to selection, framing, and editing. Each of these processes entails a further manipulation of the field narrative. Some items will end up in a digital project, while others will fall to the editing room floor. Particular images can be narrated by the author, giving them meaning or perspective about the overall project. Videos can be edited to smooth out audio and create a compelling narrative. This process highlights the complex relationship and tension between representation of the field to an academic or public audience, and the maintenance of an ethic of care and authenticity for the people met during fieldwork. For example, while working with DanceSafe, I took my digital camera to every rave I attended. While I knew that images of naked bodies and glazed eyes would be compelling documents about rave culture, they did not tell the stories of community, family, and care also found there. Ultimately, I omitted them from my research reporting, choosing instead to narrate those stories of personal connection.

Researchers may also be goaded by the attention economy, in which media producers recognize audiences' short attention span.[59] As more researchers engage in media production, more digital humanities projects will be created. With a strong audio/visual focus, such projects seek attention in the form of likes on Facebook or YouTube views. The viral elements of these social media platforms mean that views beget more views.[60] The desire to reach a wider audience may lead researchers to promote more sensationalistic elements of their research over the dry academic voice heard through our manuscripts. This issue is not necessarily unique to visual or digital projects. Storytelling in qualitative research can fall victim to a similar concern.[61] During my work with Herbig and the Rally to Restore Sanity, we video recorded our participants, many of whom were in costume. One interview was with a couple dressed as Dr. Seuss's "Thing 1" and "Thing 2." The commentary from the pair was a wonderful discussion about the nature of rationality and political satire, but may have been hard to ascertain, given the playful costumes.[62] For distribution on YouTube, however, their images with the Rally stage and Capitol Building in the background visually illustrates the combination of humor, politics, and protest.[63] Ultimately, a balance should be struck between viewership and theoretical contribution. When returning from the field, rhetoric scholars should consider which images support arguments that advance their theory, which images may contribute to a sensationalist narrative that gains "likes" or "views" online, and which images should be omitted completely in the final presentation.

Conclusion

In this chapter, I have offered and outlined a technological reflexivity to guide rhetoric researchers engaged in field methods. Rhetorical ethnography or field methods entail unique forms of reflexivity beyond mere qualitative work. Rhetorical ethnographers may be engaged in ordinary everyday acts, controversial social movements, or powerful commemorative events. The rhetorical processes inherent to these spaces invite various forms of engagement, including participation, reflection through field notes and documentation through digital devices. As smartphone and locative technologies become increasingly ubiquitous, researchers may find that the use of such devices comes naturally. Indeed, the presence of such technology is commonplace in everyday life, and social movements often circulate images and digital materials without hesitation.[64] However, while these technologies may carry an air of neutrality, they are not. They frame meaning, experience, and identity in distinct ways, requiring a reflexive process that attends to their power in representation. Technological reflexivity asks that researchers take stock of how technologies affect the locating of social movements and their politics; the means and logics by which images, audio, and video are gathered in the scene; and how representative practices are motivated by spectacular politics or hyperbolic visual imagery.

Marilys Guillemin and Lynn Gillam argue that reflexivity is "an active process that requires scrutiny, reflection, and interrogation of the data, the researcher, the participants, and the context that they inhabit."[65] As a process, reflexivity invites reflection in every element of research design, including the nature of technology. Inherent to this definition is also the evolving nature of technology. Indeed, many of the examples that I have supplied above may soon appear outdated; yet, the spirit of reflexivity should remain, especially since the motivations to use technology in the field is likely to remain constant. It is also likely that the motivating logics behind technological systems, those of spectacle and sensationalism, will endure. Thus, technological reflexivity should consider the ways in which the dynamic and static processes and logics embedded into our devices continue to drive our decisions to enter the field, engage it, and represent it upon return.

Notes

1. Aaron Hess, "Critical-Rhetorical Ethnography: Rethinking the Place and Process of Rhetoric," *Communication Studies* 62 (2011): 127–52, doi: 10.1080/10510974.2011.529750; erin daina mcclellan, "Narrative as Vernacular Rhetoric: Understanding Community Among Transients, Tourists and Locals," *Storytelling, Self, Society* 7, no. 3 (2011): 188–210; Michael K. Middleton, Samantha Senda-Cook, and Danielle Endres, "Articulating Rhetorical Field Methods: Challenges and Tensions," *Western Journal of Communication* 75 (2011): 386–406, doi: 10.1080/10570314.2011.586969; Michael K. Middleton et al., *Participatory Critical Rhetoric: Theoretical and Methodological Foundations for Studying Rhetoric In Situ* (Lanham, MD: Lexington Books, 2015).

2. Middleton et al., *Participatory Critical Rhetoric.*

3. Middleton et al., "Rhetorical Field Methods," 393.

4. Hess, "Critical-Rhetorical Ethnography," 139.

5. Aaron Hess, "Democracy through the Lens of the Camcorder: Argumentation and Vernacular Spectacle on YouTube in the 2008 Election," *Argumentation & Advocacy* 47 (2010): 106–22.

6. Several have taken up video or photographic technology for data collection. The list here includes those essays that explicitly mention the use of smartphones or other devices. See, Joshua P. Ewalt, Jessy J. Ohl, and Damien Smith Pfister, "Activism, Deliberation, and Networked Public Screens Rhetorical Scenes from the Occupy Moment in Lincoln, Nebraska (Part 1)," *Cultural Studies ↔ Critical Methodologies* 13, no. 3 (2013): 173–90; Shiv Ganesh and Cynthia Stohl, "From Wall Street to Wellington: Protests in an Era of Digital Ubiquity," *Communication Monographs* 80, no. 4 (2013): 425–51; Peter Simonson, "The Streets of Laredo: Mercurian Rhetoric and the Obama Campaign," *Western Journal of Communication* 74, no. 1 (2010): 94–126; Samantha Senda-Cook, "Rugged Practices: Embodying Authenticity in Outdoor Recreation," *Quarterly Journal of Speech* 98 (2012): 129–52.

7. Kevin Michael DeLuca, *Image Politics: The New Rhetoric of Environmental Activism* (New York: Guilford Press, 2005); John W. Delicath and Kevin Michael DeLuca, "Image Events, the Public Sphere, and Argumentative Practice: The Case of Radical Environmental Groups," *Argumentation* 17 (2003): 315–33; Kevin Michael DeLuca, "Unruly Arguments: The Body Rhetoric of Earth First!, Act Up, and Queer

Nation," *Argumentation and Advocacy* 36, no. 1 (1999): 9–21; Kevin Michael DeLuca and Jennifer Peeples, "From Public Sphere to Public Screen: Democracy, Activism, and the 'Violence' of Seattle," *Critical Studies in Media Communication* 19, no. 2 (2002): 125–51, doi: 10.1080/07393180216559.

8. Robert Hariman and John Louis Lucaites, *No Caption Needed: Iconic Photographs, Public Culture, and Liberal Democracy* (Chicago: University of Chicago Press, 2007).

9. Catherine R. Squires, "Rethinking the Black Public Sphere: An Alternative Vocabulary for Multiple Public Spheres," *Communication Theory* 12, no. 4 (2002): 446–68.

10. DeLuca and Peeples, "From Public Sphere," 131.

11. Christine Harold, "Pranking Rhetoric: 'Culture Jamming' as Media Activism," *Critical Studies in Media Communication* 21, no. 3 (2004): 189–211.

12. Hess, "Democracy through the Lens."

13. Joshua P. Ewalt, Jessy J. Ohl, and Damien Smith Pfister, "Activism, Deliberation, and Networked Public Screens Rhetorical Scenes from the Occupy Moment in Lincoln, Nebraska (Part 1)," *Cultural Studies ↔ Critical Methodologies* 13, no. 3 (2013): 173–90.

14. Robert Glenn Howard, "The Vernacular Web of Participatory Media," *Critical Studies in Media Communication* 25, no. 5 (2008): 490–513, doi: 10.1080/15295030802468065.

15. I have focused on YouTube's role in politics, finding that the structural components of the medium detract from its potential for political deliberation and dialogue. See Hess, "Resistance Up in Smoke: Analyzing the Limitations of Deliberation on YouTube," *Critical Studies in Media Communication* 26, no. 5 (2009): 411–34; Hess, "Democracy through the Lens." For an additional discussion of web 2.0 environments and politics, see Amber Davisson, "Beyond the Borders of Red and Blue States: Google Maps as a Site of Rhetorical Invention in the 2008 Presidential Election," *Rhetoric & Public Affairs* 14, no. 1 (2011): 101–23.

16. Adriana de Souza e Silva, "From Cyber to Hybrid Mobile Technologies as Interfaces of Hybrid Spaces," *Space and Culture* 9, no. 3 (2006): 261–78.

17. Aaron Hess and Art Herbig, "Recalling the Ghosts of 9/11: Convergent Memorializing at the Opening of the National 9/11 Memorial," *International Journal of Communication* 7 (2013): 2207–30.

18. Lisa Silvestri, "A Rhetorical Forecast," *Review of Communication* 13, no. 2 (2013): 132–33.

19. Kevin M. DeLuca, Sean Lawson, and Ye Sun, "Occupy Wall Street on the Public Screens of Social Media: The Many Framings of the Birth of a Protest Movement," *Communication, Culture & Critique* 5 (2012): 483–509.

20. Ganesh and Stohl, "From Wall Street to Wellington."

21. Art Herbig and Aaron Hess, "Convergent Critical Rhetoric at the 'Rally to Restore Sanity': Exploring the Intersection of Rhetoric, Ethnography, and Documentary Production," *Communication Studies* 63, no. 3 (2012): 286.

22. See Siva Vaidhyanathan, *The Googlization of Everything: (And Why We Should Worry)* (Berkeley: University of California Press, 2012).

23. Hess, "You are What You Compute (and What is Computed for You)," *Journal of Contemporary Rhetoric* 4, no. 1/2 (2014): 17.

24. Adriana de Souza e Silva and Daniel M. Sutko, *Digital Cityscapes: Merging Digital and Urban Playspaces* (New York: Peter Lang, 2009).

25. DeLuca and Peeples, "Public Screen."

26. Trena M. Paulus, Jessica N. Lester, and Paul G. Dempster, *Digital Tools for Qualitative Research* (Thousand Oaks, CA: Sage Publications, 2014).

27. For a more elaborate discussion, see Hess, "Reconsidering the Rhizome: A Textual Analysis of Web Search Engines as Gatekeepers of the Internet" in *Web Search: Interdisciplinary Perspectives*, ed. Amanda Spink and Michael Zimmerman (Berlin: Springer-Verlag, 2008) and Hess, "You are What You Compute."

28. Pierre Bourdieu, *Science of Science and Reflexivity* (Cambridge: Polity Press, 2004).

29. Marilys Guillemin and Lynn Gillam, "Ethics, Reflexivity, and 'Ethically Important Moments' in Research," *Qualitative Inquiry* 10, no. 2 (2004): 274.

30. Ibid., 275.

31. Keith Alexander Bryant, *Performing Black Masculinity: Race, Culture, and Queer Identity* (Lanham, MD: AltaMira Press, 2006), 105.

32. Chris Drain and Richard Charles Strong, "Situated Mediation and Technological Reflexivity: Smartphones, Extended Memory, and Limits of Cognitive Enhancement," in *Social Epistemology and Technology: Toward Public Self-Awareness Regarding Technological Mediation*, ed. Frank Scalambrino (New York: Rowman and Littlefield), 188.

33. Ibid.

34. Hess, "Reconsidering the Rhizome"; Hess, "Resistance Up in Smoke."

35. Sarah Pink, *Doing Visual Ethnography* (Thousand Oaks, CA: Sage Publications, 2013).

36. Hess, "Reconsidering the Rhizome"; Hess, "You are What You Compute."

37. Hess, "You are What You Compute," 8.

38. Eli Pariser, *The Filter Bubble: What the Internet is Hiding from You* (London: Penguin, 2011).

39. Ibid.

40. David Beer, "Power through the Algorithm? Participatory Web Cultures and the Technological Unconscious," *New Media & Society* 11, no. 6 (2009): 997.

41. Ibid.

42. For more, see Hess, "Reconsidering the Rhizome" and Hess, "You are What You Compute."

43. Nancy Fraser, "Rethinking the Public Sphere: A Contribution to the Critique of Actually Existing Democracy," *Social Text* 25/26 (1990): 67; Gerard A. Hauser, *Vernacular Voices: The Rhetoric of Publics and Public Spheres* (Columbia, SC: University of South Carolina Press, 1999); Kent A. Ono and John M. Sloop, "The Critique of Vernacular Discourse," *Communication Monographs* 62 (1995): 19–46, doi: 10.1080/03637759509376346; John M. Sloop and Kent A. Ono, "Out-law Discourse: The Critical Politics of Material Judgment," *Philosophy & Rhetoric* 30 (1997): 50–69; Kendall R. Phillips, "Rhetoric, Resistance, and Criticism: A Response to Sloop and Ono," *Philosophy and Rhetoric* 32, no. 1 (1999): 99; Robert Asen, "Seeking the 'Counter,' in Counterpublics," *Communication Theory* 10 (2000): 424–46.

44. Amber Davisson and Angela C. Leone, "From Coercion to Community Building: Technological Affordances as Rhetorical Forms," in *Theorizing Digital Rhetoric*, ed. Aaron Hess and Amber Davisson, 85–97 (New York: Routledge, 2017).

45. Middleton et al., *Participatory Critical Rhetoric*.

46. Hess, "Critical-Rhetorical Ethnography."

47. Middleton et al., *Participatory Critical Rhetoric*, 75.

48. Brian Massumi, *Parables for the Virtual: Movement, Affect, Sensation* (Durham, NC: Duke University Press, 2002); Jay Brower, "Rhetorical Affects in Digital Media," in *Theorizing Digital Rhetoric*, ed. Aaron Hess and Amber Davisson, 43–54 (New York: Routledge, 2017).

49. Aaron Hess, "The Selfie Assemblage," *International Journal of Communication* 9 (2015): 1629–46.

50. Aaron Hess, "Health, Risk and Authority in a Dysfunctional World: Online Ecstasy User Discourse," *Ohio Communication Journal* 50 (2012): 6.

51. Adam R Winstock, Kim Wolff, and John Ramsey, "Ecstasy Pill Testing: Harm Minimization Gone Too Far?" *Addiction* 96, no. 8 (2001): 1139–48. doi: 10.1080/09652140120060734.

52. DeLuca, "Unruly Arguments."

53. Brett Lunceford, *Naked Politics: Nudity, Political Action, and the Rhetoric of the Body* (Lanham, MD; Lexington Books, 2012).

54. See Michael K. Middleton et al., *Participatory Critical Rhetoric*.

55. DeLuca and Peeples, "Public Screen"; Hess, "Democracy through the Lens."

56. Art Herbig (Director/Producer), Aaron Hess (Producer), and Alix Watson (Producer), *Never Forget: Public Memory and 9/11* [Motion picture] (USA: Living Text Productions, 2014).

57. DeLuca and Peeples, "Public Screen."

58. Herbig, Hess, and Watson, *Never Forget: Public Memory and 9/11.*

59. Richard A. Lanham, *The Economics of Attention: Style and Substance in the Age of Information* (Chicago: University of Chicago Press, 2006).

60. For a more thorough discussion, see Hess, "Democracy through the Lens."

61. Karen A. Stewart et al., "Risky Research: Investigating the 'Perils' of

Ethnography," in *Qualitative Inquiry and Social Justice: Toward a Politics of Hope*, ed. Norman K. Denzin and Michael D. Giardina (New York: Left Coast Press, 2009), 204.

62. Herbig and Hess, "Convergent Critical Rhetoric."

63. LivingTextProd, "Unmasking Sanity: Halloween Weekend with the Participants at the Rally to Restore Sanity and/or Fear," directed and performed by Art Herbig, Aaron Hess, Alix Watson, Kristy D. Hess, http://www.youtube.com/watch?v=DE7NtFPWgw8.

64. DeLuca and Peeples, "Public Screen."

65. Guillemin and Gillam, "Ethics, Reflexivity," 274.

Afterword

Traveling Worlds to Engage Rhetoric's Perennial Questions

PHAEDRA C. PEZZULLO AND GERARD A. HAUSER

> Through travelling to other people's "worlds" we discover that there
> are "worlds" in which those who are the victims of arrogant perception
> are really subjects, lively beings, resistors, constructors of visions even
> though in the mainstream construction they are animated only by the
> arrogant perceiver and are pliable, foldable, file-awayable, classifiable.
> —María Lugones

As rhetoricians invested in audience, traveling to each other's worlds is pivotal to our practice. No matter whether we focus on social or aesthetic dramas in explicit performances or hidden transcripts, the goal of rhetoricians must be to study a world so in depth that we might portray to our audiences a sense of presence, feeling as if our readers and listeners may enter the worlds we are describing to engage more meaningfully the unfolding dramas we are coperforming. Our acts are neither final nor exhaustive, but ideally, generative and worthwhile.

Field Rhetoric: Ethnography, Ecology, and Engagement in the Places of Persuasion offers us an opportunity once again to reflect on the dynamic scenes where rhetoric occurs and, we would add, on its constitutive power. The chapters of this volume emphasize the significance of *place* to our research as consequential context and significant situations, shaping methods, conditions of being, and roles of researchers. In the introduction, Candice Rai and Caroline Gottschalk Druschke identify the volume as contributing to a set of overarching sensibilities when studying both abstract and concrete rhetorical dimensions: emplaced, material, embodied, consequential, "ecological, networked and ambient inclinations," and an ideally ethical "form of responsivity and response." In this brief afterword, we emphasize how these elements and the broader ethical impulse of *being there* are not new for the field of rhetorical studies, but rather identify significant perennial questions.

The most interesting way to engage this work might not be to ask about novelty, but instead to consider our histories and the exigencies of our contemporary conjuncture. To generate further conversation, we organize our responses into four themes: (1) objects and subjects, (2) ecological interconnections, (3) agents and agency, and (4) public engagement. Drawing on various chapters to illustrate the stakes of each theme, we hope to gesture toward the ghosts that haunt us from ancient investments in the ambition of intellectual inquiry, as well as mid-twentieth century turns in the field toward a dramatistic perspective. Our goal is to underscore how this collection invites us both to reconsider our core values and to reflect on why we might undertake these research commitments at this moment.

Objects and Subjects

A foundational question of any research endeavor is: what and/or who are you studying? Perhaps no one has researched more objects and subjects than Aristotle. From foundational inquiries into anatomy, biology, botany, embryology, ethics, drama, logic, metaphysics, meteorology, poetics, politics, psychology, teratology, physiology, and zoology, his breadth of interest literally extended our attunement to the world from A to Z (or Alpha to Omega). More recently, Debra Hawhee has established how not just Aristotle, but many ancient rhetorical scholars were intimately thinking about human and nonhuman energy, bodies, and sensation.[1] The fact, therefore, that our colleagues find a need to rationalize expanding rhetoric's scope of inquiry—via more recent turns toward ecological thought, materialism, new materialism, and so forth—is seemingly more a reflection of disciplinary norms of the past century than it is any indication of rhetoric's ancient roots.

Both Samantha Senda-Cook et al. and erin mcclellan appear to want to mark our contemporary moment as one that remains fraught for rhetorical studies. Samantha Senda-Cook, Michael Middleton, and Danielle Endres identify three tactics of rhetorical cartography: material changes, boundaries, and movement. These emplaced approaches, they argue, invite us to consider a wider range of objects *in situ*, the distinctions we make between them, and the ways they move through space and time. mcclellan calls for a "turn to field methods" to "expand the ontological analytics of rhetoric and advance a more diverse set of epistemological approaches to its study," and to ground "examinations of rhetoric that focus on its larger contexts of use and circulation while simultaneously engaging those relations in critical discussions of meaning, influence, and effect." In doing so, she hopes to provide a more robust appreciation of the role of the rhetorical scholar doing fieldwork as co-constructing or configuring reality.

These two chapters and others in the pages that proceed our own remind us of the debates of the mid-twentieth century, in which scholars critiqued previously accepted notions of the text, power, individual rhetors, and norms regarding eloquence. This volume is indebted to and haunted by the desire to make space in the field or find places from which we might also engage vernacular and quotidian voices about performativity, culture, materiality, circulation, access, oppressions, and resistance. In that sense, there is no "new" news here. And yet departments, journals, conferences, and other academic institutions of rhetorical studies are being reorganized, challenged, and reimagined in these times. As such, while the questions may not have radically changed regarding our objects and subjects of study, the context within which we are asking them has. In addition to transformations in higher education, though uneven and imperfect, technological revolution has increased our capacity to engage more across farther distances faster than ever, while social revolution has brought a wider number of voices on a larger range of interactions into mainstream public arenas. In addition to an immense expansion of audience, our work is under greater scrutiny and expected to exceed in volume compared to our predecessors.

Given these constraints, it might be comforting to recall that for most of the twentieth century, the idea of "text" was fluid. The discipline's focus increasingly shifted from concern with tenets of rhetorical production to investigating rhetoric's function as a social practice. In that vein, the critical group at the Pheasant Run conference (*Prospect of Rhetoric*) asserted the critic's work is not defined by the material examined but by the questions asked. That same year, Charles Taylor's "Interpretation and the Sciences of Man" reframed "text" to include whatever the scholar brackets as the act to be understood and interpreted, including brute data.² Together, these reca-librations marked a radical turn in how we understand text, which has had deep and serious implications for theory and method from studies of literature and speeches to assemblies in streets and national parks.

Attention to culture, performativity, vernacularity, and materiality have inspired adoption of posthumanist and postmodernist theories, a shifting understanding of text as a construction from shards circulating in society, as Michael McGee argues,³ which mark access via inclusions and exclusions, as well as quotidian life. In this sense, the field studies reported in this volume appear to be outgrowths of rhetoric's increased fascination with and attention to how and why social will is manifested in relation to and through media, larger ecosystems, and more.

In a time when some find it risky to consider what they articulate as an expanding archive of rhetorical studies, it is worth remembering Lloyd Bitzer's recollection of the moment at the 1970 Wingspread Conference when Larry Rosenfeld asked if rhetoric was becoming redefined as "every-thing but tidal waves" and, in response, Richard McKeon remarked, "Why not tidal waves?"⁴ The anecdote is notable because it remains unresolved and, as Phaedra C. Pezzullo and Catalina M. de Onís argue, it "reflects how a growing support for and backlash against ecological consciousness has been pivotal to the encouragement and discouragement of rhetorical field methods."⁵ Given this fraught history and the deep ecological commitments many in this volume have, we now turn to ecology itself: what is it that distinguishes environmental rhetoric, if anything?

Ecological Interconnections

As the environmental justice movement has expanded ecological thought from spaces of retreat and respite to where we live, work, and play, the inter-connected consciousness of ecological ethics is as relevant to the prison as it is to the pollution. The heart of ecology exceeds an individual species or place, nurturing a felt sense of interdependence that shifts our worldview from egocentric to ecocentric. Not all have embraced this perspective. Nevertheless, we may aim to write against the hegemonic grain to foster a sense of presence in relation to a broader system, scene, or world.

It is notable, then, that many chapters in *Field Rhetoric* are shaped by eco-logical orientations to the worlds in which they travel, identifying mean-ing making and remaking within specific contexts. Gottschalk Druschke values the agonistic encounter between rhetorical researchers and those we engage, as she narrates her interventions on behalf of agricultural stewardship. Herndl et al. advocate for citizen participation in science on topics from climate change to farming. Senda-Cook et al. map rhetorical cartographies of race in a city. Bridie McGreavy et al. write of tidal communities and practices of belonging. Ackerman reflects on the "signs of duress" of living in the ruins of a city.

In the Introduction to this volume, the coeditors suggest that ecological research is inflecting rhetorical fieldwork in noteworthy ways that might be considered distinct from nonecological work. Nevertheless, as environmentalists ourselves, while we might grant this distinction as an accurate description, we want to caution that it not become a normative one. That is, all writing provides an opportunity to think ecologically. Much "materiality" studied by rhetoricians is constituted by the environment: paper created through foresting practices, quilts sewn together with cotton and dyes, open spaces zoned by local government, granite mined from the Earth, et cetera. Acknowledging the nature of materiality should exceed descriptions of "the spatial organization, mobility, mass, utility, orality, and tactility of objects,"[6] to include histories and unfolding dramas of interconnection, interdependence, diversity, and system limits.

Acknowledging these dynamics are why we parse out this theme of ecology from objects itself. An ecological orientation to rhetorical fieldwork is more than describing an increasing number of distinct elements; it entails the work of identifying interactions as they relate to feelings, facts, identities, and power within systems of interaction. It suggests that the research is not following a thing, but a series of processes in which the linking and delinking of elements becomes significant to public life. These chapters, therefore, raise timely questions about, for example, not just research on their given topics (i.e., agricultural stewardship, citizen scientists, racial maps, tidal waves, and ruins), but how publics are constituted, negotiated, and destroyed through interconnections or missed connections, as well as our capacity to shape these associations. This latter point about our capacity brings us to the topic of agents and agency.

Agents and Agency

While most in the field today might accept that rhetorical theory can be brought to bear upon critiques of everything (from speeches, plays, and novels to monuments, photographs, and whales, for example), it is a different decision to judge whether those objects, or others, have the capacity to act as agents with agency. One hesitation is the persistent stubbornness of an egocentric worldview: we are humans and, therefore, what happens to us is what is most noteworthy to research. Another reluctance to expanding agents to include the nonhuman is born of a weariness that since democratic life has only relatively recently expanded the number of us considered to be subjects (as opposed to solely serving as objects to be used as machines for labor and sex)—and some of us continue to feel like second-class citizens, why the academy now finds it more compelling to entertain the notion that being imagined as human is devalued? In other words, is expanding our category of agency to include dolphins and trees, for example, one way to stall the rights of people, for example, who are transgender and/or remain colonized and/or continue to feel dehumanized by dominant culture?

The chapter in this volume by Jeffrey T. Grabill, Kendall Leon, and Stacey Pigg, suggests that these questions of agency are rhetorical constraints, not just about expanding possibilities but also about limits. We are inclined to agree when we consider, for example, evidence of anthropogenic climate change. This research both highlights, on the one hand, the awesome agency of humans to transform Earth's climate (something once thought only possible for Gods) and, on the other hand, the profound vulnerability of our species to find a way to foster the radical transformations we need to enact for our collective survival, since we have no other place where we may collectively survive.

Karyln Kohrs Campbell has established that any inquiry into agency, the capacity to act, long has been necessarily rhetorical, as agency is "(1) is communal and participatory, hence, both constituted and constrained by externals that are material and symbolic; (2) is 'invented' by authors who are points of articulation; (3) emerges in artistry or craft; (4) is affected through form; and (5) is perverse, that is, inherently, protean, ambiguous, open to reversal."[7] Isaac West expands this claim to argue that "'agency must be understood as a performative repertoire or embodied practice enabled by and negotiating the logics of recognition and domination."[8] Do nonhuman agents satisfy these characteristics?

John M. Ackerman's chapter in this volume suggests a resounding "yes" in response to his research *in situ*. Drawing on Yael Navaro-Yashin, Ackerman's affirmative answer identifies one of the greatest concerns of expanding notions of agency: the erasure of subjectivity in the name of materiality. Ackerman's chapter suggests future scholarship might take up this tension when we strive to find ourselves "alive among the ruins," as well as continue the ongoing pursuit of reducing the dissociation we might otherwise perform. The "we" of rhetorical studies, however, is not homogenous. Fostering a more diverse, less oppressive field will require greater reflexivity (at minimum) about who has the privilege to dissociate, who might associate without successfully seeing oneself through the eyes of those one is studying, and when we study those we find abhorrent, how we might consider the ethics of world-traveling differently. Further, the current Latourean bias of so many of the other chapters in this volume belies we are far from over our Eurocentric desires as a field, particularly when many First Nation, African, and Asian cultures have long-standing cosmologies that account for the agency of the nonhuman.

Nevertheless, there remains significant traveling to do in European worlds, as Ralph Cintron's ongoing research in Kosova suggests. In his chapter in this volume, Cintron performs a well-attuned openness in the field to offer an ethnography of the state. In the tradition of Mary Douglas's *Thinking Like an Institution*, expanding our sense of agents might become a way to not just imagine nonhuman life and things as agential, but also to identify how governments and other organizations can take on a life of their own. Studying the emergent, dominant, and residual patterns of social life becomes one way rhetorical scholars might contribute to political theories of democracy, particularly perspectives that exceed a Westphalian perspective.

In Cintron's chapter, notions of rhetorical agency are expanded to include (though are not limited to): the capacity of planning documents to structure expectations and conduct; the assemblage of publics through the power of algorithms to match information to Internet search tendencies; the capacity of free trade agreements to both remake the marketplace and the political landscape through its displacement of national labor pools; and the manipulation of agricultural practices and local ecology through chemical enhancements. This layered approach to understanding and analyzing a world holds promise for rhetoricians hoping to rise to the complexities of contemporary politics.

Heather Brook Adams's chapter on using oral histories to bear out feminist historiographic tales reminds us that studying the past need not leave a dramatistic perspective or desire to create a feeling of presence in the present. Her use of oral histories enables her to reconstruct vernacular worlds of becoming once-unwed mothers, while also goading a reflexive study of the rhetoricity of memory as a reflection of agency. Adams's essay is both insightful regarding structural norms and appears quite biased, quoting those who state they are at peace with their adoptions as coerced because they "haven't gone through a critical thinking process." This chapter does not adequately account for the messiness of human experiences, such as the possibility that all women don't experience childbirth and children as desirable or that some might feel a sense of pride in enacting prolife values. While there is undoubted historiographic value of identifying this incredibly moving structure of feeling experienced by some white, once-unwed mothers as shame, how much we might generalize about the estimated four million women's experiences Adams is analyzing from excerpts of less than a half dozen women is limited. This chapter, in addition to others, provides an opportunity to consider how much one might extrapolate from fieldwork to broader structures, as well as how important this work can be in considering the conditions of possibility for cultural change.

Ultimately, it seems to us that when we make decisions about the agents and agency we wish to highlight in our work, we are making ethical choices, not just observing who or what is valued and devalued and by whom, but also carrying the weight of understanding that our judgments can help perpetuate or resist the worlds we are co-constituting. Considering the impact of public engagement on the research choices we make, then, seems appropriate.

Public Engagement

Codified in courts of law, rhetoric as an engaged practice in public culture also is not new. Nevertheless, Plato's Academy operated in a vastly different context than the one any of us work and/or learn in today. While public engagement broadly seems to be enjoying a moment of appreciation across the political spectrum, how that is constituted, to what ends, and through what kind of labor practices remains a high stakes debate for peoples' careers and the worlds we live in. Further, the public sphere and public goods remains contentious, as hegemonic trends appear to romanticize corporate leadership and to encourage privatization. In response, some rhetoricians appear committed to *exposing* specific interactions as their act of intervention, while others to *rectifying* injustices.

Especially in a country as diverse as the United States, how local inhabitants understand their interests, the ways they form publics, and the democratic literacy or communication practices they enact matter. The politics of resentment, coalition building, conflict management, and more may be framed as signs of community, but they are differently capacitated to adapt to the complexities of a diverse and interdependent world. The attunement of rhetorical fieldwork to vernacular accounts of political, cultural, economic, and social issues and experiences is exquisitely suited to unfold the complex passions that motivate seeming contradictions of local *doxa*. At the same time, when issues migrate to larger spheres and, for example, Twitter feeds organize concerted acts, fitting the particularity of the local into the larger wholes of which they seem a part requires caution. These deeply ethical concerns suggest rhetoricians would do well to revisit our ethical responsibilities to respond to the worlds we inhabit and research. Let us briefly consider three exemplars in this collection to parse out the range of ways rhetoricians may consider our approaches to public engagement.

In the compelling chapter on scientists and farmers participating in a rapid technology assessment project about cellulosic biofuel in Iowa, Carl G. Herndl et al. advocate computerized data analysis to encourage and provide meaningful public participation in technical decision making. They hope their work extends Bruno Latour's call to compose a more viable world for people and things in the context of ecological crisis. That call involves attention to analyzing the rhetorical dimensions of large data sets that bear on public policy. Its mixed-methodology, combining quantitative techniques with qualitative analysis of frames of analysis and argument across a range of experts, helps us to better understand the different ontologies that drive apparently conflicting perspectives when rapid policy assessments are needed in the absence of scientific consensus. Moreover, it offers a basis for seeking how these might be integrated into policy formation.

Writing from the coast of Maine, McGreavy et al. poignantly link an ecological sensibility to a commitment to studying feelings of belonging through vernacular, everyday life. "Like the mud and tides," they write, "the mundane aesthetic offers fluid ground for sustainable becoming: by belonging to the world through fieldwork." Their poetic tone enables a more open-ended process of inquiry to explore the value of dwelling in the particular. Listening to the voices of Wabanaki inhabitants and attuning themselves to their field site, the authors defy the rigid binary often established in contemporary times between poetics and politics, constitutive communication and instrumental persuasion, exemplifying world-traveling as a practice to find ethical ways to recognize our place as belonging to the same planet.

Aaron Hess's persuasive argument about technology reflexivity underscores a medium's affordances for a study, as well as revisiting the established critique of an objective commentator as a fraudulent myth. Openness about one's own positionality, therefore, becomes a way to provide readers with grounds for judging potential biases of public engagement. While his work invites further reflection on how technology shapes our experiences *being there* in the field, it occurs to us that an increasingly networked world also has the potential to transform the distance between being *there* and *here*. That is, when communities researched have access to digital technologies to learn about researchers before, during, and after fieldwork, as well as respond to us, the distance between *there* and *here* is not as clear as it once was.

World-traveling, of course, does not guarantee a more egalitarian and just world; it does, however, offer the possibility that we could strive for one. There is always the tension of the person in the field acting as an active member of the group or being unable to do so, which then raises questions about what one sees and how one sees it. How does "the field" academically and methodologically inform your work? What capacities can you develop to listen to the ways differing groups/positionalities grasp the situation? What are more and less compelling ways to share polyvocality? How do you discover the animus of the positions you don't avow on their own terms to ethically respond?

Conclusions

As rhetorical scholars, we strive to identify and to describe the worlds shaping our existence to consider and/or to perform more viable ways of living. Rhetorical fieldwork enables us to examine a wide range of subjects and objects, foster ecological interconnections, identify agents and agency, and engage publics. If this has long been the ongoing work of rhetoric, what is notable regarding this moment?

Last but certainly not least, we want to elaborate on the value of Caroline Gottschalk Druschke's opening study. Its attention to the polysemous nature of stewardship highlights the situating agency of vibrant matter. Gottschalk Druschke's interrogation of the polysemous character of the farmer as steward of the land discloses an unstated tension between a close reading that grounds all that is rhetorically interesting in the spoken or written text, and seeing the text as bracketed in a way that includes the material conditions and the situated considerations as part of it. The tensions between protector of the land and increasing the land's productivity inherent in stewardship are divulged by what Iowa's farmers are "saying" in response to these contradictory valences, which often is expressed in material responses not verbal ones.

Rhetorical fieldwork enacted in this way might be imagined as a puzzle-solving endeavor, an attempt to fit pieces of rhetorical acts together to offer a more complete and compelling account of its complex interacting parts. This work goes beyond the two-dimensional reading of rhetorical "text," considering the complex of words and deeds in relation to concerns in the world and the multifaceted interactions circulating about and through them. *Field Rhetoric*, therefore, highlights the *dynamis* of rhetoric and how the worlds we navigate come into existence or can be destroyed through our interactions with each other.

Notes

Epigraph: María Lugones, "Playfulness, 'World'-Travelling, and Loving Perception," *Hypatia* 2, no. 2 (1987): 18.

1. Debra Hawhee, *Rhetoric in Tooth and Claw: Animals, Language, Sensation* (Chicago: University of Chicago Press, 2016).

2. Charles Taylor, "Interpretation and the Sciences of Man," *The Review of Metaphysics* 25, no. 1 (1971): 3–51.

3. Michael Calvin McGee, "Text, Context, and the Fragmentation of Contemporary Culture," *Western Journal of Communication* 54, no. 3 (1990): 274–89.

4. Lloyd F. Bitzer, "Rhetoric's Prospects: Past and Future," in *Making and Unmaking the Prospects of Rhetoric*, ed. Theresa Enos (Mahwah: Lawrence Erlbaum Associates, 1997), 19–20.

5. Phaedra C. Pezzullo and Catalina M. de Onís, "Rethinking Rhetorical Field Methods on a Precarious Planet," *Communication Monographs* 85, no. 1 (2018): 4; Phaedra C. Pezzullo, "Unearthing the Marvelous: Environmental Imprints in Rhetorical Criticism," *Review of Communication* 16, no. 1 (2016): 26.

6. Greg Dickinson, "Memories for Sale: Nostalgia and the Construction of Identity in Old Pasadena," *Quarterly Journal of Speech* 83, no. 1 (1997): 1–27.

7. Karlyn Kohrs Campbell, "Agency: Promiscuous and Protean," *Communication and Critical/Cultural Studies* 2, no. 1 (2005): 2.

8. Isaac West, *Transforming Citizenships: Transgender Articulations of the Law* (New York: New York University Press, 2014), 247.

Bibliography

Aakhus, Mark. "Communication as Design." *Communication Monographs* 74, no. 1 (2007): 112–17.

Abelson, Julia, Pierre-Gerlier Forest, John Eyles, Patricia Smith, Elisabeth Martin, and Francois-Pierre Gauvin. "Deliberations About Deliberative Methods: Issues in the Design and Evaluation of Public Participatory Processes." *Social Science & Medicine* 57 (2003): 239–51.

Ackerman, John. "Rhetorical Engagement in the Cultural Economies of Cities." In *The Public Work of Rhetoric: Citizen-Scholars and Civic Engagement*, edited by John Ackerman and David Coogan, 76–97. Columbia: University of South Carolina Press, 2010.

———. "The Space for Rhetoric in Everyday Life." In *Towards a Rhetoric of Everyday Life: New Directions in Research on Writing, Text, and Discourse*, edited by Martin Nystrand and John Duffy, 84–117. Madison: University of Wisconsin Press, 2003.

———. "Walking in the City: The Arrival of the Rhetorical Subject." In *Tracing Rhetoric and Material Life: Ecological Approaches*, edited by Guy McHendry, Justine Wells, Bridie McGreavy, and Samantha Senda-Cook, 117–40. London: Palgrave Macmillan, 2018.

Ackerman, John M., and David J. Coogan, eds. *The Public Work of Rhetoric: Citizen-Scholars and Civic Engagement*. Columbia: University of South Carolina Press, 2010.

Agre, Philip E. "The Practical Republic: Social Skills and the Progress of Citizenship." In *Community in the Digital Age*, edited by Andrew Feenberg and Darin Barney, 201–23. Lanham, MD: Rowman and Littlefield, 2004.

Ahmed, Sara. *The Cultural Politics of Emotion*. New York: Routledge, 2004.

———. *Strange Encounters: Embodied Others in Post-Coloniality*. London: Routledge Press, 2000.

Alexander, Bryant Keith. *Performing Black Masculinity: Race, Culture, and Queer Identity*. Lanham, MD: AltaMira Press, 2006.

American Council for Learned Societies (ACLS). "What are the Humanities?" Accessed January 12, 2017. http://www.acls.org/about/faq/#humanities.

Amin, Ash, and Nigel Thrift. "The Legibility of Everyday Cities." In *Cities: Reimagining the Urban*, 7–30. Cambridge: Polity Press, 2002.

Anzaldua, Gloria E. "Now Let Us Shift . . . the Path of Conocimiento . . . Inner work, Public Acts." In *This Bridge We Call Home: Radical Visions for Transformation*, edited by Gloria E. Anzaldúa and Ana Louise Keating, 540–78. New York: Routledge, 2002.

Aretxaga, Beoña. "Strip-Searching of Women in Northern Ireland." In *History in Person: Enduring Struggles, Contentious Practice, Intimate Identities*, edited by Dorothy Holland and Jean Lave, 37–61. Santa Fe, NM: School of American Research, 2001.

Asen, Robert. "Seeking the 'Counter' in Counterpublics." *Communication Theory* 10 (2000): 424–46.

Baby Scoop Era Research Initiative, The. "What Was the 'Baby Scoop Era'?" Accessed May 18, 2017. http://babyscoopera.com.

Ballif, Michelle. "Historiography as Hauntology: Paranormal Investigations into the History of Rhetoric." In *Theorizing Histories of Rhetoric*, edited by Michelle Ballif, 139–54. Carbondale, IL: Southern Illinois University Press, 2013.

Barad, Karen. *Meeting the Universe Halfway: Quantum Physics and the Entanglement of Matter and Meaning*. Durham, NC: Duke University Press, 2007.

———. "Nature's Queer Performativity." *Qui Parle: Critical Humanities and Social Sciences* 19, no. 2 (2001): 121–58.

Barnett, Scot, and Casey Boyle, eds. *Rhetoric, Through Everyday Things*. Tuscaloosa: University of Alabama Press, 2016.

Beer, David. "Power through the Algorithm? Participatory Web Cultures and the Technological Unconscious." *New Media & Society* 11, no. 6 (2009): 985–1002. doi: 10.1177/1461444809336551.

Bennett, Jane. *Vibrant Matter: A Political Ecology of Things*. Durham, NC: Duke University Press, 2009.

Berkowitz, S. D. *An Introduction to Structural Analysis: The Network Approach to Social Research*. Toronto: Butterworths, 1982.

Berlant, Lauren G. *Cruel Optimism*. Durham, NC: Duke University Press, 2011.

———. "Cruel Optimism." In *The Affect Theory Reader*, edited by Melissa Greg and Greg Seigworth, 93–117. Durham, NC: Duke University Press, 2010.

Berry, Wendell. "Private Property and the Common Wealth." In *Another Turn of the Crank*, 46–63. Washington, DC: Counterpoint, 1995.

Bicak, Carol. "A Midtown Project That Builds Bikes—and Communities." *Omaha World-Herald*. http://www.omaha.com/living/a-midtown-project-that-builds-bikes-and-%20communities/article_76472967-e8ee-5f99-b62b-736edefe9364.html.

Biesecker, Barbara. "No Time for Mourning: The Rhetorical Production of the Melancholic Citizen-Subject in the War on Terror." *Philosophy and Rhetoric* 40, no. 1 (2007): 147–69.

Biesecker, Barbara A., and John L. Lucaites. "Introduction." In *Rhetoric, Materiality, and Politics*, edited by Barbara A. Biesecker and John L. Lucaites, 1–16. New York: Peter Lang, 2009.

———, eds. *Rhetoric, Materiality, and Politics*. New York: Peter Lang, 2009.

Bitzer, Lloyd F. "Rhetoric's Prospects: Past and Future." In *Making and Unmaking the Prospects of Rhetoric*, edited by Theresa Enos, 15–20. Mahwah, NJ: Lawrence Erlbaum Associates, 1997.

Blair, Carole. "Contemporary U.S. Memorial Sites as Exemplars of Rhetoric's Materiality." In *Rhetorical Bodies*, edited by Jack Selzer and Sharon Crowley, 16–57. Madison: University of Wisconsin Press, 1999.

———. "Reflections on Criticism and Bodies: Parables from Public Places." *Western Journal of Communication* 65, no.3 (2001): 271–94. doi: 10.1080/10570310109374706.

Blair, Carole, Greg Dickinson, and Brian L. Ott. "Introduction: Rhetoric/Memory/Place." In *Places of Public Memory: The Rhetoric of Museums and Memorials*, edited by Greg Dickinson, Carole Blair, and Brian L. Ott, 1–54. Tuscaloosa: University of Alabama Press, 2010.

Blair, Carole, Marsha S. Jeppeson, and Enrico Pucci. "Public Memorializing in Postmodernity: The Vietnam Veterans Memorial as Prototype." *Quarterly Journal of Speech* 77, no. 3 (1991): 263–88.

Blei, David M., and John D. Lafferty. "A Correlated Topic Model of Science." *The Annals of Applied Statistics* (2007): 17–35.

Blondel, Vincent D., Jean-Loup Guillaume, Renaud Lambiotte, and Etienne Lefebvre. "Fast Unfolding of Communities in Large Networks." *Journal of Statistical Mechanics: Theory and Experiment* 10 (2008): P10008.

Bloodsworth-Lugo, Mary K., and Carmen R. Lugo-Lugo. *Containing (Un)American Bodies: Race, Sexuality, and Post-9/11 Constructions of Citizenship*. Amsterdam: Rodopi, 2010.

Blythe, Stuart, Jeffrey T. Grabill, and Kirk Riley. "Action Research and Wicked Environmental Problems: Exploring Appropriate Roles for Researchers in Professional Communication." *Journal of Business and Technical Communication* 22, no. 3 (2008): 272–98.

Bourdieu, Pierre. *Outline of a Theory of Practice*. Cambridge: Cambridge University Press, 1977.

———. *Science of Science and Reflexivity*. Cambridge: Polity Press, 2004.

Brandes, A. "Faster Algorithm for Betweenness Centrality." *Journal of Mathematical Sociology* 25, no. 2 (2001): 163–77.

Bristow, Steve, and Stephen Vickers. *Kosova Accreditation Project Report*. London: The British Accreditation Council, 2008.

Brockmeier, Jens. "Remembering and Forgetting: Narrative as Cultural Memory." *Culture & Psychology* 8 (2002): 15–43.

Brouwer, Daniel C., and Robert Asen, eds. *Public Modalities: Rhetoric, Culture, Media and the Shape of Public Life*. Tuscaloosa: University of Alabama Press, 2010.

Brower, Jay. "Rhetorical Affects in Digital Media." In *Theorizing Digital Rhetoric*, edited by Aaron Hess and Amber Davisson, 43–54. New York: Routledge, 2017.

Brown, Stephen G., and Sidney I. Dobrin. *Ethnography Unbound: From Theory Shock to Critical Praxis*. Albany: State University of New York Press, 2004.

Brown, Wendy. *Undoing the Demos: Neoliberalism's Stealth Revolution*. Brooklyn: Zone Books, 2015.

Burke, Kenneth. *A Grammar of Motives*. Berkeley: University of California Press, 1969.

———. *Permanence and Change: An Anatomy of Purpose*. 3rd ed. Berkeley, CA: University of California Press, 1941.

———. *The Rhetoric of Motives*. Berkeley: University of California Press, 1969.

Burt, Ronald S. *Brokerage and Closure: An Introduction to Social Capital*. Oxford: Oxford University Press, 2005.

Cable, Dustin. "Racial Dot Map." The Weldon Cooper Center for Public Service. http://demographics.coopercenter.org/DotMap/index.html.

Calhoun, Craig. "The Class Consciousness of Frequent Travelers: Toward a Critique of Actually Existing Cosmopolitanism." *The South Atlantic Quarterly* 101, no. 4 (2002): 869–97.

Campbell, Karlyn Kohrs. "Agency: Promiscuous and Protean." *Communication and Critical/Cultural Studies* 2, no. 1 (2005): 1–19.

———. "The Rhetoric of Women's Liberation: An Oxymoron." *Quarterly Journal of Speech* (1973): 74–86.

Carley, Kathleen M. "Coding Choices for Textual Analysis: A Comparison of Content Analysis and Map Analysis." *Social Methodology* 23 (1993): 75–126.

Carley, Kathleen M., and Michael Palmquist. "Extracting, Representing and Analyzing Mental Models." *Social Forces* 70, no. 3 (1992): 601–36.

Carley, Kathleen M., Jürgen Pfeffer, Jeff Reminga, Jon Storrick, and Dave Columbus. *ORA User's Guide 2012*. No. CMU-ISR-12-105. Carnegie-Mellon University. Pittsburgh, PA. Inst. of Software Research International.

Carr, Deborah S., and Kathleen Halvorsen. "An Evaluation of Three Democratic, Community-Based Approaches to Citizen Participation: Surveys, Conversations with Community Groups, and Community Dinners." *Society and Natural Resources* 14, no. 2 (2001): 107–26.

Carrithers, Michael. "Why Anthropologists Should Study Rhetoric." *The Journal of the Royal Anthropological Institute* 11, no. 3 (2005): 577–83.

Casey, Edward S. "Public Memory in Place and Time." In *Framing Public Memory*, edited by Kendall R. Phillips, 17–44. Tuscaloosa: University of Alabama Press, 2004.

Ceccarelli, Leah. "Polysemy: Multiple Meanings in Rhetorical Criticism." *Quarterly Journal of Speech* 84 (1998): 395–415.

———. "To Whom Do We Speak? The Audiences for Scholarship on the Rhetoric of Science and Technology." *Poroi* 9, no. 1 (2013): 7.

Chang, Jonathan J., and David M. Blei. "Hierarchical Relational Models for Document Networks." *The Annals of Applied Statistics* (2010): 124–50.

Chávez, Karma R. "Beyond Inclusion: Rethinking Rhetoric's Historical Narrative." *Quarterly Journal of Speech* 101, no. 1 (2015): 162–72.

Chess, Caron, and Kristen Purcell. "Public Participation and the Environment: Do We Know What Works?" *Environmental Science and Technology* 33, no. 16 (1999): 2685–92.

Christakis, Nicholas A., and James H. Fowler. "The Spread of Obesity in a Large Social Network Over 32 Years." *New England Journal of Medicine* 357, no. 4 (2007): 370–79.

Cintron, Ralph. *Angel's Town: Chero Ways, Gang Life, and Rhetorics of the Everyday.* Boston: Beacon Press, 1997.

———. "Conclusion: What Next?" In *Catastrophe and Rhetoric: The Texture of Political Action,* edited by Robert Hariman and Ralph Cintron, 231–54. New York: Berghahn Press, 2015.

———. "Democracy and Its Limitations." In *The Public Work of Rhetoric: Citizen-Scholar and Civic Engagement,* edited by John M. Ackerman and David J. Coogan, 98–116. Columbia: University of South Carolina Press, 2010.

———. "'Gates Locked' and the Violence of Fixation." In *Towards a Rhetoric of Everyday Life: New Directions in Research on Writing, Text, and Discourse,* edited by Martin Nystrand and John Duffy, 5–37. Madison: University of Wisconsin Press, 2003.

Clair, Robin P. "Reflexivity and Rhetorical Ethnography: From Family Farm to Orphanage and Back Again." *Cultural Studies ↔ Critical Methodologies* 11, no. 2 (2011): 117–28.

Clark, Greg. "Rhetorical Experience and the National Jazz Museum." In *Places of Public Memory: The Rhetoric of Museums and Memorials,* edited by Greg Dickinson, Carole Blair, and Brian Ott, 113–38. Tuscaloosa: University of Alabama Press, 2010.

Clifford, James. "Introduction: Partial Truths." In *Writing Culture: The Poetics and Politics of Ethnography,* edited by John Clifford and George E. Marcus, 1–26. Berkeley: University of California Press, 1986.

Collaku, Petrit. "Kosovo's Last Blacksmiths Fade from the Scene." *Balkan Insight,* October 19, 2009. http://www.balkaninsight.com.

Collins, Harry M., and Robert Evans. "The Third Wave of Science Studies: Studies of Expertise and Experience." *Social Studies of Science* 32, no. 2 (2002): 235–96.

Comisión Femenil Mexicana Nacional. "The Experience That Was." *CFM Report* 2.4 (July 1973): 1–3. Series I, Box 23, Folder 4. Archival Collection. CEMA 30. UC Santa Barbara California Ethnic and Multicultural Archives Special Collections, Davidson Library, Santa Barbara, CA.

———. "Resolution Adopted by the Women's Workshop 10/10/70 Sacramento,

California; [A] Proposal for a Comision Femenil Mexicana." TS. Series IV, Box 34, Folder 3. Archival Collection. CEMA 30. UC Santa Barbara California Ethnic and Multicultural Archives Special Collections, Davidson Library, Santa Barbara, CA.

———. "Statement of Interest." Brief of Amici Curiae of Comisión Femenil Mexicana and Women for Equal Health Care in Support of Plaintiffs-appellants, 78–3187. TS. Series V, Box 43, Folder 7. Archival Collection. CEMA 30. UC Santa Barbara California Ethnic and Multicultural Archives Special Collections, Davidson Library, Santa Barbara, CA.

Condit, Celeste. *The Meanings of the Gene: Public Debates About Heredity.* Madison: University of Wisconsin Press, 1999.

———. "Race and Genetics from a Modal Materialist Perspective." *Quarterly Journal of Speech* 94, no. 4 (2008): 383–406.

———. "Rhetorical Engagements in the Scientist's Process of Remaking Race as Genetic." In *The Pubic Work of Rhetoric: Citizen Scholars and Civic Engagement,* edited by John M. Ackerman and David Coogan, 119–36. Columbia: University of South Carolina Press, 2010.

Confino, Alon. "Collective Memory and Cultural History: Problems of Method." *The American Historical Review* 102 (1997): 1386–403.

Connolly, William. *The Fragility of Things: Self-Organizing Processes, Neoliberal Fantasies, and Democratic Activism.* Durham, NC: Duke University Press, 2013.

Conquergood, Dwight. "Ethnography, Rhetoric, and Performance." *Quarterly Journal of Speech* 78 (1992): 80–123.

Cooper, Marilyn M. "The Ecology of Writing." *College English* 48, no. 4 (1986): 364–75.

———. "Rhetorical Agency as Emergent and Enacted." *College Composition and Communication* 62, no. 3 (2011): 420–49.

Copy of an Organizational Flow Chart. MS. Series I, Box 2, Folder 7. *Comisión Femenil Mexicana Nacional.* Archival Collection. CEMA 30. UC Santa Barbara California Ethnic and Multicultural Archives Special Collections, Davidson Library, Santa Barbara, CA.

Council for Agricultural Science and Technology (CAST). "Convergence of Agriculture and Energy: II. Producing Cellulosic Biomass for Biofuels." CAST Commentary QTA2007–2. CAST, 2007. Ames, Iowa.

Craig, Robert. "Minding My Metamodel, Mending Myers." *Communication Theory* 9 (2001): 119–61.

Cresswell, Tim. *Place: A Short Introduction.* Malden, MA: Wiley-Blackwell, 2004.

Crowley, Sharon, and Debra Hawhee. *Ancient Rhetorics for Contemporary Students.* 3rd ed. New York: Pearson Longman, 2004.

Cruse, Richard M., Michael J. Cruse, and Don Reicosky. "Soil Quality Impacts of Residue Removal for Biofuel Feedstocks." In *Advances in Soil Science: Soil*

Quality and Biofuel Production, edited by Rattan Lal and B. A. Stewart, 45–62. New York: CRC Press, 2009.

Cruse, Richard M., Dennis Flanagan, Jim Frankenberger, Brian Gelder, Daryl Herzmann, David James, Witold Krajewski, et al. "Daily Estimates of Rainfall, Water Runoff, and Soil Erosion in Iowa." *Journal of Soil and Water Conservation* 61, no. 4 (2006): 191–99.

Cruse, Richard M., and Carl G. Herndl. "Balancing Corn Stover Harvest for Biofuels with Soil and Water Conservation." *Journal of Soil and Water Conservation* 64 (2009): 286–91.

Cruse, Richard M., Carl G. Herndl, Elena Polush, and Mack Shelley. "An Assessment of Cellulosic Ethanol Industry Sustainability Based on Industry Configurations." *Journal of Soil and Water Conservation* 67, no. 2 (2012): 67–74.

Cushman, Ellen. "The Rhetorician as an Agent of Social Change." *College Composition and Communication* 47, no. 1 (1996): 7–28.

Cutlip, Lauren. "Talking About Talk: The Problem of Communication as an Object of Study in Public Participation Research." Unpublished thesis. University of South Florida. 2012.

Danisch, Robert. "Political Rhetoric in a World Risk Society." *Rhetoric Society Quarterly* 40, no. 2 (2010): 172–92.

———. *Pragmatism, Democracy, and the Necessity of Rhetoric*. Columbia: University of South Carolina Press, 2007.

Davies, Gail. "The Sacred and the Profane: Biotechnology, Rationality and Public Debate." *Environment and Planning* 38 (2006): 423–43.

Davis, Diane. *Inessential Solidarity: Rhetoric and Foreigner Relations*. Pittsburgh, PA: University of Pittsburgh, 2010.

Davisson, Amber. "Beyond the Borders of Red and Blue States: Google Maps as a Site of Rhetorical Invention in the 2008 Presidential Election." *Rhetoric & Public Affairs* 14, no. (2011): 101–23.

Davisson, Amber, and Angela C. Leone. "From Coercion to Community Building: Technological Affordances as Rhetorical Forms." In *Theorizing Digital Rhetoric*, edited by Aaron Hess and Amber Davisson, 85–97. New York: Routledge, 2017.

Deans, Thomas. *Writing Partnerships: Service-Learning in Composition*. Urbana, IL: National Council of Teachers of English, 2000.

de Certeau, Michel. *The Practice of Everyday Life*. Translated by Steven Rendall. Berkeley: University of California Press, 1984.

Delaney, David. "Tracing Displacements: Or Evictions in the Nomosphere." *Environment and Planning D: Society and Space* 22 (2004): 847–60.

Deleuze, Gilles, and Felix Guattari. *A Thousand Plateaus: Capitalism and Schizophrenia*. Minneapolis, MN: University of Minnesota Press, 1987.

Delicath, John W., and Kevin Michael DeLuca. "Image Events, the Public Sphere,

and Argumentative Practice: The Case of Radical Environmental Groups."
Argumentation 17 (2003): 315–33.

DeLuca, Kevin Michael. *Image Politics: The New Rhetoric of Environmental Activism.*
New York: Guilford Press, 2005.

———. "Unruly Arguments: The Body Rhetoric of Earth First! Act Up, and Queer
Nation." *Argumentation and Advocacy* 36, no. 1 (1999): 9–21.

DeLuca, Kevin Michael, Sean Lawson, and Ye Sun. "Occupy Wall Street on the
Public Screens of Social Media: The Many Framings of the Birth of a Protest
Movement." *Communication, Culture & Critique* 5 (2012): 483–509.

DeLuca, Kevin Michael, and Jennifer Peeples. "From Public Sphere to Public
Screen: Democracy, Activism, and the 'Violence' of Seattle." *Critical Studies in
Media Communication* 19, no. 2 (2002): 125–51. doi: 10.1080/07393180216559.

Department of Energy. "Biomass as Feedstock for a Bioenergy and Bioproducts
Industry: The Technical Feasibility of a Billion Ton Annual Supply." 2005.
DOE/GO-102995–2135.

Derrida, Jacques. *On Cosmopolitanism and Forgiveness.* Translated by Mark Dooley
and Michael Hughes. New York City: Routledge Press, 2001.

de Souza e Silva, Adriana. "From Cyber to Hybrid Mobile Technologies as Interfaces of Hybrid Spaces." *Space and Culture* 9, no. 3 (2006): 261–78.

de Souza e Silva, Adriana, and Daniel M. Sutko. *Digital Cityscapes: Merging Digital
and Urban Playspaces.* New York: Peter Lang, 2009.

Dewey, John. *The Public and Its Problems: An Essay in Political Inquiry.* University
Park: The Pennsylvania State University Press, 2012.

Dickinson, Greg. "Memories for Sale: Nostalgia and the Construction of Identity
in Old Pasadena." *Quarterly Journal of Speech* 83, no. 1 (1997): 1–27.

———. *Suburban Dreams: Imagining and Building the Good Life.* Tuscaloosa: University of Alabama Press, 2015.

Dickinson, Greg, Brian L. Ott, and Eric Aoki. "Spaces of Remembering and Forgetting: The Reverent Eye/I at the Plains Indian Museum." *Communication and
Critical/Culture Studies* 3 (2006): 27–47.

Diesner, Jana, and Kathleen M. Carley. "A Methodology for Integrating Network
Theory and Topic Modeling and Its Applications to Innovation Diffusion." In
*Social Computing (SocialCom), 2010: IEEE Second International Conference on
Social Computing,* 687–92. Los Alamitos, CA: IEEE, 2010.

———. "Using Network Text Analysis to Detect the Organizational Structure of
Covert Networks." In *Proceedings of the NAACSOS 2004 Conference, Pittsburgh,
PA, 2004.*

Diesner, Jana, Kathleen M. Carley, and Laurent Tambayong. "Extracting Socio-cul-
tural Networks of the Sudan from Open-Source, Large-Scale Text Data." *Com-
putational & Mathematical Organizational Theory* 18, no. 3 (2012): 328–39.

Dingo, Rebecca. *Networking Arguments: Rhetoric, Transnational Feminism, and Public Policy Writing*. Pittsburgh, PA: University of Pittsburgh Press, 2012.

DiSalvo, Carl. *Adversarial Design*. Cambridge, MA: The MIT Press, 2012.

Disney, Jane, and George Kidder. "Community-Based Eelgrass (Zostera Marina) Restoration in Frenchman Bay." *The Bulletin: MDI Biological Laboratory* 49 (2010).

Drain, Chris, and Richard Charles Strong. "Situated Mediation and Technological Reflexivity: Smartphones, Extended Memory, and Limits of Cognitive Enhancement." In *Social Epistemology and Technology: Toward Public Self-Awareness regarding Technological Mediation*, edited by Frank Scalambrino, 187–95. New York: Rowman and Littlefield, 2015.

Edbauer, Jenny. "Unframing Models of Public Distribution: From Rhetorical Situations to Rhetorical Ecologies." *Rhetoric Society Quarterly* 35, no. 4 (2005): 5–24.

Edensor, Tim. *Industrial Ruins: Space, Aesthetics and Materiality*. Oxford: Berg Publishers, 2005.

Egbert, Josh. "Gifford Park Keeping Neighborhood Safe." Last modified July 26, 2013. KMTV.

Einsiedel, Edna F., Erling Jelsoe, and Thomas Breck. "Publics at the Technology Table: The Consensus Conference in Denmark, Canada, and Australia." *Public Understanding of Science* 10, no. 1 (2001): 83–98.

End of Communism Cheered but Now with More Reservations: Two Decades After the Wall's Fall. Pew Research Center, November 2, 2009. http://pewresearch.org/pubs/1396/european-opinion-two-decades-after-berlin-wall-fall-communism.

Endres, Danielle. "From Wasteland to Waste Site: The Role of Discourse in Nuclear Power's Environmental Injustices." *Local Environment: The International Journal of Justice and Sustainability* 14 (2009): 917–37.

Endres, Danielle, and Samantha Senda-Cook. "Location Matters: The Rhetoric of Place in Protest." *Quarterly Journal of Speech* 97, no. 3 (2011): 257–82.

Endres, Danielle, Samantha Senda-Cook, and Brian Cozen. "Not Just a Place to Park Your Car: Park(ing) as Spatial Argument." *Argument and Advocacy* 50 (2014): 121–40.

Endres, Danielle, Leah Sprain, and Tarla Rai Peterson. "The Imperative of Praxis-Based Environmental Communication Research: Suggestions from the Step It Up 2007 National Research Project." *Environmental Communication: A Journal of Nature and Culture* 2, no. 2 (2008): 237–45.

"Energy Shortages to Weigh on Growth." *Business Monitor Online*, October 19, 2009. http://www.allbusiness.com/trade-development/international-trade-export/13245213-1.html.

Enoch, Jessica. "Releasing Hold: Feminist Historiography without the Tradition."

In *Theorizing Histories of Rhetoric*, edited by Michelle Ballif, 58–73. Carbondale: Southern Illinois University Press, 2013.

Ewalt, Joshua P., Jessy J. Ohl, and Damien Smith Pfister. "Activism, Deliberation, and Networked Public Screens Rhetorical Scenes from the Occupy Moment in Lincoln, Nebraska (Part 1)." *Cultural Studies ↔ Critical Methodologies* 13, no. 3 (2013): 173–90.

Farmer, Frank, and Margaret M. Strain. "A Repertoire of Discernments: Hearing the Unsaid in Oral History Narratives." In *Silence and Listening as Rhetorical Arts*, edited by Cheryl Glenn and Krista Ratcliffe, 231–49. Carbondale: Southern Illinois University Press, 2011.

Feldman, Ann M. *Making Writing Matter: Composition in the Engaged University*. Albany: State University of New York Press, 2008.

Fessler, Ann. *The Girls Who Went Away: The Hidden History of Women Who Surrendered Children for Adoption in the Decades before "Roe v. Wade."* New York: Penguin, 2006.

Feyerabend, Paul, and Eric Oberheim. *The Tyranny of Science*. Cambridge, UK: Polity Press, 2011.

Fiorino, Daniel. "Citizen Participation and Environmental Risk: A Survey of Institutional Mechanisms." *Science, Technology and Human Values* 15, no. 2 (1990): 226–43.

Fischer, Frank. *Citizens Experts and the Environment: The Politics of Local Knowledge*. Durham, NC: Duke University Press, 2000.

Fleckenstein, Kristie S., Clay Spinuzzi, Rebecca J. Ricky, and Carole C. Papper. "The Importance of Harmony: An Ecological Metaphor for Writing Research." *College, Composition, and Communication* 60, no. 2 (2008): 388–419.

Fleming, David. *City of Rhetoric: Revitalizing the Public Sphere in Metropolitan America*. Albany, NY: SUNY Press, 2008.

Foss, Sonja K., and Cindy L. Griffin. "Beyond Persuasion: A Proposal for an Invitational Rhetoric." *Communication Monographs* 62, no. 1 (1995): 2–18.

Fraser, Nancy. "Rethinking the Public Sphere: A Contribution to the Critique of Actually Existing Democracy." *Social Text* 25/26 (1990): 56–80.

Freeman, Linton. "A Set of Measures of Centrality Based on Betweenness." *Sociometry* 40 (1977): 35–41.

Futrell, Robert. "Technical Adversarialism and Participatory Collaboration in the U.S. Chemical Weapons Disposal Program." *Science, Technology, & Human Values* 28, no. 4 (2003): 451–82.

Gallagher, Victoria. J., Kenneth S. Zagacki, and Kelli Norris Martin. "Materiality and Urban Communication: The Rhetoric of Communicative Spaces." In *Communication Matters: Materialist Approaches to Media, Mobility, and*

Networks, edited by Jeremey Packer and Stephen B. Crofts Wiley, 107–20. London: Routledge, 2012.

Ganesh, Shiv, and Cynthia Stohl. "From Wall Street to Wellington: Protests in an Era of Digital Ubiquity." *Communication Monographs* 80, no. 4 (2013): 425–51.

Garrett, Mary. "Tied to a Tree: Culture and Self-Reflexivity." *Rhetoric Society Quarterly* 43, no. 4 (2013): 243–55.

Geertz, Clifford. *The Interpretation of Cultures*. New York: Basic Books, 1973.

Gephi. An Open Source Software for Exploring and Manipulating Networks. Gephi Consortsium. http://www.gephi.org.

Ghosh, Palash. "Omaha, Nebraska: The Most Dangerous Place in America to Be Black." *International Business Times*. http://www.ibtimes.com/omaha-nebraska-most-dangerous-place-america-be-black-1548466.

Gibson-Graham, J. K. *A Postcapitalist Politics*. Minneapolis: University of Minnesota Press, 2006.

———. "Rethinking the Economy with Thick Description and Weak Theory." *Current Anthropology* 55, no. 9 (2014): 147–53.

Gieryn, Thomas. "A Space for Place in Sociology." *Annual Review of Sociology* 26 (2000): 463–97.

Gilroy, Paul. *Postcolonial Melancholia*. New York City: Columbia University Press, 2005.

Glaser, Barney G., and Anselm L. Strauss. *The Discovery of Grounded Theory: Strategies for Qualitative Research*. New Brunswick, Canada: AldineTransaction, 2009.

Glenn, Cheryl. *Rhetoric Retold: Regendering the Tradition from Antiquity Through the Renaissance*. Carbondale: Southern Illinois University Press, 1997.

Gonzalez, Cindy. "Renovated Gifford Park Apartment Building is Now a 'Cool Property.'" Last modified November 9, 2013. *Omaha World-Herald*. http://www.omaha.com/money/renovated-gifford-park-apartment-building-is-now-a-cool-property/article_f3e23749-8e0a-5cc1-986d-568f67fe2210.html.

Goodman, Sherri. *National Security and the Threat of Climate Change*. Alexandria, VA: CAN Corporation. 2007. Available at https://www.cna.org/cna_files/pdf/national%20security%20and%20the%20threat%20of%20climate%20change.pdf.

Gordillo, Gastón. *Rubble: The Afterlife of Destruction*. Durham, NC: Duke University Press, 2014.

Gottschalk Druschke, Caroline. "Watershed as Common-Place: Communicating for Conservation at the Watershed Scale." *Environmental Communication: A Journal of Nature and Culture* 7, no. 1 (2013): 80–96.

———. "With Whom Do We Speak? Building Transdisciplinary Collaborations in Rhetoric of Science." *Poroi* 10, no. 1 (2014). https://ir.uiowa.edu/poroi/vol10/iss1/10/.

Gottschalk Druschke, Caroline, and Bridie McGreavy. "Why Rhetoric Matters for Ecology." *Frontiers in Ecology and the Environment* 14, no. 1 (2016): 46–52.

Gottschalk Druschke, Caroline, Nadya Pittendrigh, and Diane Chin. "Community-Based Critique: No Walk in the Park." *Reflections: A Journal of Writing, Service-Learning, and Community Literacy* 6 (2007): 151–68.

Gottschalk Druschke, Caroline, and Silvia S. Secchi. "The Impact of Gender on Agricultural Conservation Knowledge and Attitudes in an Iowa Watershed." *Journal of Soil and Water Conservation* 69, no. 2 (2014): 95–106.

Government Accountability Office. "Expert Opinion on the Economics of Policy Options to Address Climate Change." *A Report to Congress Requesters.* 2008. GAO-08–605.

Grabill, Jeffery T. "Community-Based Research and the Importance of a Research Stance." In *Writing Studies Research in Practice: Methods and Methodologies*, edited by Lee Nickoson and Mary P. Sheridan, 210–19. Carbondale: Southern Illinois University Press, 2012.

———. "On Being Useful: Rhetoric and the Work of Engagement." In *The Public Work of Rhetoric: Citizen-Scholars and Civic Engagement*, edited by John M. Ackerman and David J. Coogan, 193–210. Columbia: University of South Carolina Press, 2010.

———. *Writing Community Change: Designing Technologies for Citizen Action.* New York: Hampton Press, 2007.

Graham, S. Scott. *The Politics of Pain Medicine: A Rhetorical-Ontological Inquiry.* Chicago: University of Chicago Press, 2015.

Graham, S. Scott, S. Y. Kim, D. Hartke, and W. Keith. "Statistical Genre Analysis: Toward Big Data Methodologies in Technical Communication." *Technical Communication Quarterly* 24, no. 1 (2015): 70–104.

Grandin, Greg. "Empire's Ruin: Detroit to the Amazon." In *Imperial Debris: On Ruins and Ruination*, edited by Ann Stoler, 115–28. Durham: Duke University Press, 2013.

Granovetter, Mark. "The Strength of Weak Ties." *American Journal of Sociology* 78 (1973): 1360–80.

Greene, Ronald W. "Lessons from the YMCA: The Material Rhetoric of Criticism, Rhetorical Interpretation, and Pastoral Power." In *Communication Matters: Materialist Approaches to Media, Mobility, and Networks*, edited by Jeremey Packer and Stephen B. Crofts Wiley, 219–30. London: Routledge, 2012.

Greene, Walter, and Kevin D. Kuswa. "'From the Arab Spring to Athens, From Occupy Wall Street to Moscow': Regional Accents and the Rhetorical Cartography of Power." *Rhetoric Society Quarterly* 42 (2012): 271–88.

Gries, Laurie E. *Still Life with Rhetoric: A New Materialist Approach for Visual Rhetorics.* Boulder: University Press of Colorado, 2015.

Gross, Alan G. "The Roles of Rhetoric in the Public Understanding of Science." *Public Understanding of Science* 3, no. 1 (1994): 3–23.

Guillemin, Marilys, and Lynn Gillam. "Ethics, Reflexivity, and 'Ethically Important Moments' in Research." *Qualitative Inquiry* 10, no. 2 (2004): 261–80.

Gulbrandsen, Karen. "Revising the Technical Communication Service Course. *Programmatic Perspectives* 4, no. 2 (2012): 243–54.

Hamidi, Lavdim. "Diaspora Remittances Fall by 8 Percent." *BalkanInsight*, August 5, 2009.

———. "Foreign Investment Falls in Kosovo for Second Year." *BalkanInsight*, January 12, 2010.

Haraway, Donna J. *Simians, Cyborgs, and Women: The Reinvention of Nature.* New York: Routledge, 1991.

Hariman, Robert. "Introduction." In *Catastrophe and Rhetoric: The Texture of Political Action*, edited by Robert Hariman and Ralph Cintron, 1–24. New York: Berghahn Press, 2015.

———. "Terrible Beauty and Mundane Detail: Aesthetic Knowledge in the Practice of Everyday Life." *Argumentation and Advocacy* 35, no. 1 (1998).

Hariman, Robert, and Ralph Cintron, eds. *Culture, Catastrophe, and Rhetoric: The Texture of Political Action.* New York: Berghahn Books, 2015.

Hariman, Robert, and John Louis Lucaites. *No Caption Needed: Iconic Photographs, Public Culture, and Liberal Democracy.* Chicago: University of Chicago Press, 2007.

Harold, Christine. "Pranking Rhetoric: 'Culture Jamming' as Media Activism." *Critical Studies in Media Communication* 21, no. 3 (2004): 189–211.

Hart-Davidson, William, James P. Zappen, and S. Michael Halloran. "On the Formation of Democratic Citizens: Rethinking the Rhetorical Tradition in a Digital Age." In *The Viability of the Rhetorical Tradition*, edited by Richard Graff, Arthur E. Walzer, and Janet M. Atwill, 125–39. Albany: State University of New York Press, 2005.

Harvey, Matthew. "Drama, Talk and Emotion: Omitted Aspects of Public Participation." *Science, Technology & Human Values* 34, no. 2 (2009): 139–61.

Hauser, Gerard A. "Attending the Vernacular. A Plea for an Ethnographical Rhetoric." In *Rhetorical Emergence of Culture*, edited by Christian Meyer and Felix Girke, 157–72. New York: Berghahn Books, 2011.

———. *Prisoners of Conscience: Moral Vernaculars of Political Agency.* Columbia: University of South Carolina Press, 2012.

———. "Vernacular Dialogue and the Rhetoricality of Public Opinion." *Communications Monographs* 65, no. 2 (1998): 83–107. doi: 10.1080/03637759809376439.

———. *Vernacular Voices: The Rhetoric of Publics and Public Spheres.* Columbia: University of South Carolina Press, 1999.

Hawhee, Debra. "Agonism and Arete." *Philosophy and Rhetoric* 35, no. 3 (2002): 185–207.

———. *Bodily Arts: Rhetoric and Athletics in Ancient Greece.* Austin: University of Texas Press, 2004.

———. *Moving Bodies: Kenneth Burke at the Edges of Language.* Columbia: University of South Carolina Press, 2009.

———. *Rhetoric in Tooth and Claw: Animals, Language, Sensation.* Chicago: University of Chicago Press, 2016.

Hawhee, Debra, and Cory Holding. "Case Studies in Material Rhetoric: Joseph Priestly and Gilbert Austin." *Rhetorica: A Journal of the History of Rhetoric* 28, no. 3 (2010): 261–89. doi: 10.1525/rh.2010.28.3.261.

Hays, Heather Ashley. *Violent Subjects and Rhetorical Cartography in the Age of the Terror Wars.* New York: Springer, 2016.

Herbig, Art, and Aaron Hess. "Convergent Critical Rhetoric at the 'Rally to Restore Sanity': Exploring the Intersection of Rhetoric, Ethnography, and Documentary Production." *Communication Studies* 63, no. 3 (2012): 269–89. doi: 10.1080/10510974.2012.674617.

Herbig, Art (Director/Producer), Aaron Hess (Producer), and Alix Watson (Producer). *Never Forget: Public Memory and 9/11* [Motion picture]. USA: Living Text Productions, 2014.

Herndl, Carl, and Lauren Cutlip. "How Can We Act: A Praxiographical Program for the Rhetoric of Technology, Science and Medicine." *Poroi* 9, no. 1 (2013).

Herndl, Carl G., Jean Goodwin, Lee Honeycutt, Greg Wilson, S. Scott Graham, and David Niedergeses. "Talking Sustainability: Identification and Division in an Iowa Community." *Journal of Sustainable Agriculture* 35, no. 4 (2011): 436–61.

Hesford, Wendy. "Reading Rape Stories: Material Rhetoric and the Trauma of Representation." *College English* 62, no. 2 (1999): 192–221.

Hess, Aaron. "Critical-Rhetorical Ethnography: Rethinking the Place and Process of Rhetoric." *Communication Studies* 62, no. 2 (2011): 127–52.

———. "Democracy through the Lens of the Camcorder: Argumentation and Vernacular Spectacle on YouTube in the 2008 Election." *Argumentation & Advocacy* 47 (2010), 106–22.

———. "Health, Risk and Authority in a Dysfunctional World: Online Ecstasy User Discourse." *Ohio Communication Journal* 50 (2012): 1–30.

———. "Reconsidering the Rhizome: A Textual Analysis of Web Search Engines as Gatekeepers of the Internet." In *Web Search: Interdisciplinary Perspectives,* edited by Amanda Spink and Michael Zimmerman, 35–50. Berlin: Springer-Verlag, 2008.

———. "Resistance up in Smoke: Analyzing the Limitations of Deliberation on YouTube." *Critical Studies in Media Communication* 26, no. 5 (2009): 411–34.

———. "The Selfie Assemblage." *International Journal of Communication* 9 (2015): 1629–46.

———. "You are What You Compute (and What is Computed for You): Considerations of Digital Rhetorical Identification." *Journal of Contemporary Rhetoric* 4, no. 1/2 (2014), 1–18.

Hess, Aaron, and Art Herbig. "Recalling the Ghosts of 9/11: Convergent Memorializing at the Opening of the National 9/11 Memorial." *International Journal of Communication* 7 (2013): 2207–30.

Howard, Robert Glenn. "The Vernacular Web of Participatory Media." *Critical Studies in Media Communication* 25, no. 5 (2008): 490–513. doi: 10.1080 /15295030802468065.

Howarth, R. W., S. Bringezu, M. Bekunda, C. de Fraiture, L. Maene, L. Martinelli, and O. Sala. "Rapid Assessment on Biofuels and Environment: Overview and Key Findings." In *Biofuels: Environmental Consequences and Interactions with Changing Land Use*, edited by R. W. Howarth and S. Bringezu, 1–13. Proceedings of the Scientific Committee on Problems of the Environment (SCOPE) International Biofuels Project Rapid Assessment, 22–25 September 2008, Gummersbach Germany. Cornell University, Ithaca NY, USA. http://cip. cornell.edu/biofuels/.

Hutton, Patrick H. "The History of Mentalities: The New Map of Cultural History." *History and Theory* 20 (1981): 237–59.

Ingold, Tim. *Being Alive: Essays on Movement, Knowledge and Description*. New York: Taylor & Francis, 2011.

———. "Contested Boundaries in Policy-Relevant Science." *Social Studies of Science* 17 (1987): 195–230.

———. "Toward an Ecology of Materials." *Annual Review of Anthropology* 41 (2012): 427–42.

Jasanoff, Sheila. "Breaking the Wave of Science Studies: Comment on H. M. Collins and Robert Evans, 'The Third Wave of Science Studies.'" *Social Studies of Science* 33, no. 3 (2003): 389–400.

Jensen, Robin E. "Sexual Polysemy: The Discursive Ground of Talk about Sex and Education in U.S. History." *Communication, Culture & Critique* 1 (2008): 396–415.

Kaplan, Deborah N. "Dispatches from the Street." *Journal of International and Intercultural Communication* 1 (2008): 269–89.

Karadaku, Linda. "Kosovo Completes 2011 Census Without Data from North." *Eurasia Review: A Journal of Analysis and News*, October 17, 2012. http:// www.eurasiareview.com/17102012-kosovo-completes-2011-census-without-data-from-north/.

Kinsella, W. P. *Shoeless Joe*. New York: Houghton Mifflin, 1982.

Klein, Bernhard. *Maps and the Writing of Space in Early Modern England and Ireland.* New York: Palgrave, 2001.

Kosovo Human Development Report 2014: Migration as a Force for Development. United Nations Development Program, 2014.

Laborde, David, and Siwa Msangi. "Biofuels, Environment, and Food: The Story Gets More Complicated." *2011 Global Food Policy Report.* International Food Policy Research Institute. 2011. http://www.ifpri.org/node/8439.

Labour Market and Unemployment in Kosova. Riinvest Institute, January 2003. http://www.riinvestinstitute.org/publikimet/pdf/36.pdf.

Landau, Jamie. "Feeling Rhetorical Critics: Another Affective-Emotional Field Method for Rhetorical Studies." In *Text + Field: Innovations in Rhetorical Method,* edited by Sara L. McKinnon, Robert Asen, Karma R. Chávez, and Robert Glenn, 72–85. University Park: Penn State University Press, 2016.

Lanham, Richard A. *The Economics of Attention: Style and Substance in the Age of Information.* Chicago: University of Chicago Press, 2006.

Latour, Bruno. "An Attempt at a 'Compositionist Manifesto.'" *New Literary History* 41 (2010): 471–90.

———. "Coming Out as a Philosopher." *Social Studies of Science* 40, no. 4 (2010): 599–608.

———. "How to Talk About the Body? The Normative Dimension of Science Studies." *Body & Society* 10, no. 2–3 (2004): 205–29.

———. *An Inquiry into Modes of Existence.* Cambridge, MA: Harvard University Press, 2013.

———. *Pandora's Hope: Essays on the Reality of Science Studies.* Cambridge: Harvard University Press, 1999.

———. *The Politics of Nature: How to Bring the Sciences into Nature.* Cambridge: Harvard University Press, 2004.

———. *Reassembling the Social: An Introduction to Actor-Network Theory.* Oxford: Oxford University Press, 2005.

———. *Science in Action: How to Follow Scientists and Engineers Through Society.* Cambridge, MA: Harvard University Press, 1987.

———. "Why has Critique Run Out of Steam?" *Critical Inquiry* 30 (2004): 225–48.

Lefebvre, Henri. *Critique of Everyday Life.* Vol. 3. Brooklyn: Verso Press, 2005.

———. *The Production of Space.* Translated by Donald Nicholson-Smith. Oxford: Blackwell, 1991.

LeMesurier, Jennifer. "Somatic Metaphors: Embodied Recognition of Rhetorical Opportunities." *Rhetoric Review* 33, no. 4 (2014): 362–80.

Leon, Kendall. "Chicanas Making Change: Institutional Rhetoric and the Comisión Femenil Mexicana Nacional." *Reflections* 13, no. 1 (2013): 165–94.

————. "*La Hermandad* and Chicanas Organizing: The Community Rhetoric of the Comisión Femenil Mexicana Nacional." *Community Literacy Journal* 7, no. 2 (2013): 1–20.

Libby, Lisa K., and Richard P. Eibach. "Looking Back in Time: Self-Concept Change Affects Visual Perspective in Autobiographical Memory." *Journal of Personality and Social Psychology* 82 (2002): 167–79.

Lindquist, Julie. *A Place to Stand: Politics and Persuasion in a Working-Class Bar.* Oxford: Oxford University Press, 2002.

Liska, Adam, Haishun Yang, Maribeth Milner, Steve Goddard, Humberto Blanco-Canqui, Matthew Pelton, Xiao X. Fang, et al. "Biofuels from Crop Residue Can Reduce Soil Carbon and Increase CO_2 Emissions." *Nature Climate Change* 4 (2014): 398–401. doi: 10.1038/nclimate2187.

LivingTextProd. *Unmasking Sanity: Halloween Weekend with the Participants at the Rally to Restore Sanity and/or Fear.* Directed and performed by Art Herbig, Aaron Hess, Alix Watson, and Kristy D. Hess. http://www.youtube.com/watch?v=DE7NtFPWgw8.

Lowe, Lisa. *The Intimacies of Four Continents.* Durham, NC: Duke University Press, 2015.

Lugones, María. "Playfulness, 'World'-Travelling, and Loving Perception." *Hypatia* 2, no. 2 (1987): 3–19.

Lunceford, Brett. *Naked Politics: Nudity, Political Action, and the Rhetoric of the Body.* Lanham, MD; Lexington Books, 2012.

Lynch, Kevin. *The Image of the City.* Cambridge: The MIT Press, 1960.

Lynch, Paul, and Nathaniel Rivers, eds. *Thinking with Bruno Latour in Rhetoric and Composition.* Carbondale: Southern Illinois Press, 2015.

Maloff, Bretta, David Bilan, and Wifreda Thurston. "Enhancing Public Input into Decision Making: Development of the Calgary Regional Health Authority Public Participation Framework." *Family and Community Health* 23, no. 1 (2000): 66–78.

"Mandate of EU Kosovo Mission Expires." *Radio Free Europe, Radio Liberty,* June 15, 2016. http://www.rferl.org/content/kosovo-eulex-mandate-expires/27797605.html.

Manier, David, and William Hirst. "A Cognitive Taxonomy of Collective Memories." In *Cultural Memory Studies: An International and Interdisciplinary Handbook,* edited by Astrid Erll and Ansgar Nünning, 253–62. Berlin: Walter de Gruyter, 2008.

Manning, Jimmie, and Adrianne Kunkel. *Researching Interpersonal Relationships.* Los Angeles: SAGE, 2014.

Mara, Andrew, and Byron Hawk. "Posthuman Rhetorics and Technical Communication." *Technical Communication Quarterly* 19, no. 1 (2009): 1–10.

Marback, Richard. "Detroit and the Closed Fist: Toward a Theory of Material Rhetoric." *Rhetoric Review* 17, no. 1 (1998): 74–92. doi: 10.1080 /07350199809359232.

Margoluis, Richard, Caroline Stem, Nick Salafsky, and Marcia Brown. "Using Conceptual Models as a Planning and Evaluation Tool in Conservation." *Evaluation and Program Planning* 32, no. 2 (2009): 138–47.

Martin, Tara G., Petra M. Kuhnert, Kerrie Mengersen and Hugh P. Possingham. "The Power of Expert Opinion in Ecological Models Using Bayesian Methods: Impact of Grazing on Birds." *Ecological Applications* 15, no. 1 (2005): 266–80.

Massey, Doreen. *For Space*. Thousand Oaks, CA: Sage Publications, 2005.

Massumi, Brian. "The Autonomy of Affect." *Cultural Critique* 31 (1995): 83–109.

———. *Parables for the Virtual: Movement, Affect, Sensation*. Durham, NC: Duke University Press, 2002.

Mathieu, Paula. *Tactics of Hope: The Public Turn in English Composition*. Portsmouth, NH: Boynton/Cook, 2005.

Matson, P. A., W. J. Parton, A. G. Power, and M. J. Swift. "Agricultural Intensification and Ecosystem Properties." *Science* 277 (1997): 504–09.

mcclellan, erin daina. "Narrative as Vernacular Rhetoric: Understanding Community Among Transients, Tourists and Locals." *Storytelling, Self, Society* 7, no. 3 (2011): 188–210.

McGee, Michael C. "A Materialist's Conception of Rhetoric." In *Rhetoric, Materiality, and Politics*, edited by Barbara A. Biesecker and John L. Lucaites, 17–42. New York: Peter Lang, 2009.

———. "Text, Context, and the Fragmentation of Contemporary Culture." *Western Journal of Communication* 54, no. 3 (1990): 274–89.

McGreavy, Bridie. "Resilience as Discourse." *Environmental Communication: A Journal of Nature and Culture* 10, no. 1 (2016): 104–21.

McKerrow, Raymie E. "Critical Rhetoric in a Postmodern World." *Quarterly Journal of Speech* 77, no. 1 (1991): 75–78.

McKinnon, Sara L., Robert Asen, Karma R. Chávez, and Robert Glenn Howard, eds. *Text + Field: Innovations in Rhetorical Method*. University Park: The Pennsylvania State University Press, 2016.

Meyer, Christian, and Felix Girke, eds. *The Rhetorical Emergence of Culture*. New York: Berghann, 2011.

Middleton, Michael K., Aaron Hess, Danielle Endres, and Samantha Senda-Cook. *Participatory Critical Rhetoric: Theoretical and Methodological Foundations for Studying Rhetoric In Situ*. Lanham, MD: Lexington Books, 2015.

Middleton, Michael K., Samantha Senda-Cook, and Danielle Endres. "Articulating Rhetorical Field Methods: Challenges and Tensions." *Western Journal of Communication* 75, no. 4 (2011): 386–406.

Mol, Annemarie. *The Body Multiple: Ontology in Medical Practice*. Durham, NC: Duke University Press, 2002.

———. "Ontological Politics: A Word and Some Questions." In *Actor Network Theory and After*, edited by John Law and John Hassard, 74–89. Oxford, UK: Blackwell, 1999.

Monsanto. Retrieved December 5, 2009. http://www.monsanto.com.

Morris, Charles, III. "Performing/Rhetorical Studies: Differential Belonging across Intradisciplinary Borders." *Text and Performance Quarterly* 34, no. 1 (2014): 104–7.

Murdock, Barbara, Carol Wiessner, and Ken Sexton. "Stakeholder Participation in Voluntary Environmental Agreements: Analysis of 10 Project XL Case Studies." *Science, Technology and Human Values* 30, no. 2 (2005): 223–50.

Mustafa, Muhamet, Mrika Kotorri, Petrit Gashi, Ardiana Gashi, and Venera Demukaj. *Forum 2015: Diaspora and Migration Policies*. Prishtina, Kosova: Riinvest Institute, 2007.

Navaro-Yashin, Yael. "Affective Spaces, Melancholic Objects: Ruination and the Production of Anthropological Knowledge." *Journal of the Royal Anthropological Institute* 15, no. 1 (2009): 1–18.

———. "Make-Believe Papers, Legal Forms and the Counterfeit Affective Interactions Between Documents and People in Britain and Cyprus." *Anthropological Theory* 7, no. 1 (2007): 79–98.

———. *The Make-Believe Space: Affective Geography in a Postwar Polity*. Durham, NC: Duke University Press, 2012.

Nelkin, Dorothy, and Michael Pollak. "Public Participation in Technological Decisions: Reality or Grand Illusion?" *Technology Review* 81 (1979): 55–64.

Nicotra, Jodie. "Assemblage Rhetorics: Creating New Frameworks for Rhetorical Action." In *Rhetoric, Through Everyday Things*, edited by Scott Barnett and Casey Boyle, 185–196. Tuscaloosa: University of Alabama Press, 2016.

Nobelprize.org. "Norman Borlaug-Acceptance Speech." Delivered December 10, 1970. http://www.nobelprize.org/nobel_prizes/peace/laureates/1970/borlaug-acceptance.html.

Nordstrom, Carolyn. *Global Outlaws: Crime, Money, and Power in the Contemporary World*. Berkeley: University of California Press, 2007.

Norton, Bryan. *Sustainability: A Philosophy of Adaptive Ecosystem Management*. Chicago: University of Chicago Press, 2005.

Nothstine, William L., Carole Blair, and Gary A. Copeland. *Critical Questions: Invention, Creativity, and the Criticism of Discourse and Media*. Boston: McGraw-Hill, 2003.

Nussbaum, Martha. "Kant and Cosmopolitanism." In *The Cosmopolitanism Reader*, edited by Garrett Brown and David Held, 27–44. Cambridge, MA: Polity Press, 2010.

Ono, Kent A., and John M. Sloop. "The Critique of Vernacular Discourse." *Communication Monographs* 62, no. 1 (1995): 19–46.

Orphanides, Athanasios, and George Syrichas, eds. *The Cyprus Economy: Historical Review Prospects Changes*. Cyprus: Central Bank of Cyprus, 2012.

Pariser, Eli. *The Filter Bubble: What the Internet is Hiding from You*. London: Penguin UK, 2011.

Paulus, Trena M., Jessica N. Lester, and Paul G. Dempster. *Digital Tools for Qualitative Research*. Thousand Oaks, CA; Sage Publications, 2014.

Pensky, Max. "Three Kinds of Ruin: Heidegger, Benjamin, Sebald." *Poligrafi* 12 (2011): 65–90.

Perlack, Robert D., Lynn L. Wright, Anthony F. Turnhollow, Robin L. Graham, Bryce J. Stokes, and Donald C. Erbach. "Biomass as a Feedstock for a Bioenergy and Bioproducts Industry: The Technical Feasibility of a Billion-ton Annual Supply." 2005. DOE/GO-102005–2135 ORNL/TM-2005/66. http://www.fs.fed.us/research/.

Peterson, M. Nils, Tarla Rai Peterson, Angelica Lopez, and Jianguo Liu. "Views of Private-land Stewardship Among Latinos on the Texas-Tamaulipas Border," *Environmental Communication: A Journal of Nature and Culture* 4, no. 4 (2005): 407.

Peterson, Tarla Rai, and Cristi Choat Horton. "Rooted in the Soil: How Understanding the Perspectives of Landowners Can Enhance the Management of Environmental Disputes." *Quarterly Journal of Speech* 81 (1995): 139–66.

Pezzullo, Phaedra C. *Toxic Tourism: Rhetorics of Travel, Pollution, and Environmental Justice*. Tuscaloosa: University of Alabama Press, 2007.

———. "Unearthing the Marvelous: Environmental Imprints in Rhetorical Criticism." *Review of Communication* 16, no. 1 (2016): 25–42.

Pezzullo, Phaedra C., and Catalina M. de Onís. "Rethinking Rhetorical Field Methods on a Precarious Planet." *Communication Monographs* 85, no. 1 (2018): 1–20.

Phillips, Kendall R. "Introduction." In *Framing Public Memory*, edited by Kendall R. Phillips, 1–14. Tuscaloosa: University of Alabama Press, 2004.

———. "Rhetoric, Resistance, and Criticism: A Response to Sloop and Ono." *Philosophy and Rhetoric* 32, no. 1 (1999): 96–102.

Pickering, Andrew. *The Cybernetic Brain: Sketches of Another Future*. Chicago: University of Chicago Press, 2010.

———. *The Mangle of Practice: Time, Agency, and Science*. Chicago: University of Chicago Press, 1995.

Pink, Sarah. *Doing Sensory Ethnography*. 2nd ed. Los Angeles: Sage Publications, 2015.

———. *Doing Visual Ethnography*. Thousand Oaks, CA: Sage Publications, 2013.

Pink, Sarah, Kirsten Leder Mackley, and Roxana Moroşanu, "Researching in Atmospheres: Video and the 'Feel' of the Mundane." *Visual Communication* 14, no. 3 (2015): 351–69.

Pioneer Seed. "DuPont leader says increasing food production a moral imperative: Both biotech and native traits needed to sustainably feed growing population." Released September 8, 2009. http://www.prweb.com/releases/DuPont/FoodProduction/prweb2842924.htm.

Popping, Roel. *Computer-Assisted Text Analysis.* Thousand Oaks, CA: *SAGE.* 2000.

———. "Knowledge Graphs and Network Text Analysis." *Social Science Information* 42 (2003): 91–106.

Pottier, Johan. *Anthropology of Food: The Social Dynamics of Food Security.* Malden, MA: Polity Press, 1999.

Povinelli, Elizabeth. *Economies of Abandonment: Social Belonging and Endurance in Late Liberalism.* Durham, NC: Duke University Press, 2011.

Powell, Malea. "Rhetorics of Survivance: How American Indians Use Writing." *College Composition and Communication* 53 (2002): 396–434.

Prelli, Lawrence J., Floyd D. Anderson, and Matthew T. Althouse. "Kenneth Burke on Recalcitrance." *Rhetoric Society Quarterly* 41 (2011): 97–124.

Pritchard, Katrina. "From 'Being There' to 'Being . . . Where?': Relocating Ethnography." *Qualitative Research in Organizations and Management* 6, no. 3 (2011): 230–45.

Project for Public Spaces. "Pioneer Courthouse Square." Accessed February 15, 2006. http://www.pps.org/great_public_spaces/one?public_place_id=19.

Rai, Candice. *Democracy's Lot: Rhetoric, Publics, and the Places of Persuasion.* Tuscaloosa: University of Alabama Press, 2016.

———. "Positive Loitering and Public Goods: The Ambivalence of Civic Participation and Community Policing in the Neoliberal City." *Ethnography* 12, no. 1 (2011): 65–88.

Ratha, Dillip, and Sanket Mohapatra. *Increasing the Macroeconomic Impact of Remittances on Development.* Washington, DC: Development Prospects Group, The World Bank, November 26, 2007.

Ratha, Dillip, Sanket Mohapatra, K. M. Vijayalakshmi, and Zhimei Xu. *Migration and Development Brief 5: Revisions to Remittance Trends 2007.* Washington, DC: Development Prospects Group, Migration and Remittances Team, The World Bank, July 10, 2008.

Read, Sarah, and Jason Swarts. "Visualizing and Tracing: Research Methodologies for the Study of Networked, Sociotechnical Activity, Otherwise Known as Knowledge Work." *Technical Communication Quarterly* 24, no. 1 (2015): 14–44.

Reynolds, Nedra. *Geographies of Writing: Inhabiting Places and Encountering Difference.* Carbondale: Southern Illinois University Press, 2007.

Rice, Jenny Edbauer. "The New 'New': Making a Case for Critical Affect Studies." *Quarterly Journal of Speech* 94, no. 2 (2008): 200–12.

Rickert, Thomas. *Ambient Rhetoric: The Attunements of Rhetorical Being.* Pittsburgh, PA: University of Pittsburgh Press, 2013.

Ridolfo, Jim, and Danielle Nicole DeVoss. "Composing for Recomposition: Rhetorical Velocity and Delivery." *Kairos: A Journal of Rhetoric, Technology, and Pedagogy* 13, no. 2 (2009).

Rip, Arie. "Constructing Expertise: The Third Wave of Science Studies?" *Social Studies of Science* 33, no. 3 (2003): 419–34.

Rittel, Horst W. J., and Melvin M. Webber. "Dilemmas in a General Theory of Planning." *Policy Sciences* 4, no. 2 (1973): 155–69.

Rohan, Liz. "I Remember Mamma: Material Rhetoric, Mnemonic Activity, and One Woman's Turn-of-the-Century Quilt." *Rhetoric Review* 23, no. 4 (2004): 368–87.

Rowe, Gene, and Lynn. J. Frewer. "A Typology of Public Engagement Mechanisms." *Science Technology Human Values* 30, no. 2 (2005): 251–90.

Royster, Jaqueline Jones, and Gesa E. Kirsch, eds. *Feminist Rhetorical Practices: New Horizons for Rhetoric, Composition, and Literacy Studies*. Carbondale: Southern Illinois University Press, 2012.

Ryan, M-L. "Diagramming Narrative." *Semiotica* 165, no. 1 (2007): 11–40.

Scavia, Donald, and Joan Iverson Nassauer. "Introduction: Policy Insights from Integrated Assessments and Alternative Futures." In *From the Corn Belt to the Gulf: Societal and Environmental Implications of Alternative Agricultural Futures*, edited by Joan Iverson Nassauer, Mary V. Santelmann, and Donald Scavia, 1–9. Washington, DC: Resources for the Future, 2007.

Schindel, Estela, and Pamela Columbo, eds. *Space and the Memories of Violence: Landscapes of Erasure, Disappearances and Exception*. New York: Palgrave Macmillan, 2014.

Schneider, Keith. "A Partnership Seeks to Transform Kent State and Kent." *The New York Times*, February 5, 2013. Accessed February 6, 2013. https://nyti.ms/2rcpP5o.

Schuster, Mary Lay. "A Different Place to Birth: A Material Rhetoric Analysis of Baby Haven, A Free-Standing Birth Center." *Women's Studies in Communication* 29, no. 1 (2006): 1–38.

Scott, Charles E. "The Appearance of Public Memory." In *Framing Public Memory*, edited by Kendall R. Phillips, 147–56. Tuscaloosa: University of Alabama Press, 2004.

Selzer, Jack, and Sharon Crowley, eds. *Rhetorical Bodies*. Madison: University of Wisconsin Press, 1999.

Senda-Cook, Samantha. "Rugged Practices: Embodying Authenticity in Outdoor Recreation." *Quarterly Journal of Speech* 98 (2012): 129–52.

Silvestri, Lisa. "A Rhetorical Forecast." *Review of Communication* 13, no. 2 (2013): 132–33.

Simmons, W. Michele, and Jeffrey T. Grabill. "Toward a Civic Rhetoric for Technologically and Scientifically Complex Places: Invention, Performance, and

Participation." *College Composition and Communication* 58, no. 3 (2007): 419–48.

Simons, Herbert. "The Rhetoric of Philosophical Incommensurability." In *Rhetoric and Incommensurability*, edited by Randy A. Harris, 238–68. West Lafayette, IN: Parlor Press, 2005.

Simonson, Peter. "Rhetoric, Culture, Things." *Quarterly Journal of Speech* 100, no. 1 (2014): 105–25.

———. "The Streets of Laredo: Mercurian Rhetoric and the Obama Campaign." *Western Journal of Communication* 74, no. 1 (2010): 94–126.

Sloop, John M., and Kent A. Ono, "Out-law Discourse: The Critical Politics of Material Judgment." *Philosophy & Rhetoric* 30 (1997): 50–69.

Smith, Adam. *The Wealth of Nations.* New York: Bantam Classics, 2003.

Soja, Edward W. *Seeking Spatial Justice.* Minneapolis: University of Minnesota Press, 2010.

Spector, Bertram I., Svetlana Winbourne, and Laurence D. Beck. *Corruption in Kosovo: Observations and Implications for USAID.* Washington, DC: United States Agency for International Development, July 10, 2003.

Spinuzzi, Clay. *Network: Theorizing Knowledge Work in Telecommunications.* New York: Cambridge University Press, 2008.

Squires, Catherine R. "Rethinking the Black Public Sphere: An Alternative Vocabulary for Multiple Public Spheres." *Communication Theory* 12, no. 4 (2002): 446–68.

Stacey, Judith. "Can There be a Feminist Ethnography?" *Women's Studies International Forum* 11, no. 1 (1998): 21–27.

Star, Susan L., and James R. Griesemer. "Institutional Ecology, 'Translations' and Boundary Objects: Amateurs and Professionals in Berkeley's Museum of Vertebrate Zoology, 1907–39." *Social Studies of Science* 19, no. 3 (1989): 387–420.

Stengers, Isabelle. "Including Nonhumans in Political Theory: Opening Pandora's Box?" In *Political Matter: Technoscience, Democracy, and Public Life*, edited by Bruce Braun and Sarah Whatmore. Minneapolis, MN: University of Minnesota Press, 2010.

———. "Introductory Notes on an Ecology of Practices." *Cultural Studies Review* 11, no. 1 (2005): 183–96.

———. *Thinking with Whitehead: A Free and Wild Creation of Concepts.* Translated by Michael Chase. Cambridge, MA: Harvard University Press, 2011.

Stewart, Jessie, and Greg Dickinson. "Enunciating Locality in the Postmodern Suburb: FlatIron Crossing and the Colorado Lifestyle." *Western Journal of Communication* 72 (2008): 280–307.

Stewart, Karen A., Aaron Hess, Sarah J. Tracy, and H. L. Goodall, Jr. "Risky Research: Investigating the 'Perils' of Ethnography." In *Qualitative Inquiry and Social Justice: Toward a Politics of Hope*, edited by Norman K. Denzin and Michael D. Giardina, 198–216. New York: Left Coast Press, 2009.

Stewart, Kathleen. *Ordinary Affects*. Durham, NC: Duke University Press, 2007.

———. *A Space on the Side of the Road: Cultural Politics in an "Other" America*. Princeton, NJ: Princeton University Press, 1996.

Stoler, Ann. *Duress: Imperial Durabilities in Our Times*. Durham, NC: Duke University Press, 2016.

———, ed. *Imperial Debris: On Ruins and Ruination*. Durham, NC: Duke University Press, 2013.

———. "Imperial Debris: Reflections on Ruins and Ruination." *Cultural Anthropology* 23, no. 2 (2008): 191–219.

Stormer, Nathan, and Bridie McGreavy. "Thinking Ecologically About Rhetoric's Ontology: Capacity, Vulnerability, Resilience." *Philosophy and Rhetoric* 50, no. 1 (2017): 1–25.

Strecker, Ivo, and Stephen Tyler, eds. *Culture & Rhetoric*. New York: Berghahn Books, 2009.

Swanson, Eva, and Chris Foster. *History of 33rd & California*. Omaha, NE: Gifford Park Neighborhood Association.

Taylor, Charles. "Interpretation and the Sciences of Man." *The Review of Metaphysics* 25, no. 1 (1971): 3–51.

Teston, Christa B., and S. Scott Graham. "Stasis Theory and Meaningful Public Participation in Pharmaceutical Policy-Making." *Present Tense: A Journal of Rhetoric in Society* 2, no. 2 (2012).

Teston, Christa B., S. Scott Graham, Raquel Baldwinson, Andria Li, and Jessamyn Swift. "Public Voices in Pharmaceutical Deliberations: Negotiating 'Clinical Benefit' in the FDA's Avastin Hearing." *Journal of Medical Humanities* 35, no. 2 (2014): 149–70.

Theis, Lindsey. "Gifford Park: Diverse, Safe, Unique." Last modified August 12, 2015. KMTV. http://www.scrippsmedia.com/kmtv/news/Gifford-Park-diverse-safe-unique-321597752.html.

Tracy, Karen. *Challenges of Ordinary Democracy: A Case Study in Deliberation and Dissent*. University Park: Penn State University Press, 2010.

Trainor, Jennifer. *Rethinking Racism: Emotion, Persuasion, and Literacy Education in an All-White High School*. Carbondale: Southern Illinois University Press, 2008.

Tsing, Anna Lowenhaupt. *Friction: An Ethnography of Global Connection*. Princeton, NJ: Princeton University Press, 2011.

Tuan, Yi Fu. "Language and the Making of Place: A Narrative-Descriptive Approach." *Annals of the Association of American Geographers* 81 (1991): 684–97.

———. *Space and Place: The Perspective of Experience*. Minneapolis: University of Minnesota Press, 2001.

"UK-Kosovo Investment Forum: A Necessary First Step." *Business Monitor Online*, November 27, 2009. http://www.allbusiness.com/trade-development/trade-development-finance/13465632-1.html.

US Census Bureau. "Table 344. Land and Water Area of States and Other Entities: 2000." 2009 Statistical Abstract: The National Data Book. http://www.census.gov/compendia/statab/2009/cats/geography_environment.html.

———. "Table 797. Farms—number and acreage by state: 2000 and 2007." 2009 Statistical Abstract: The National Data Book. http://www.census.gov/compendia/statab/2009/cats/agriculture.html.

US Environmental Protection Agency. "Superfund Program Implements the Recovery Act: Omaha Lead Superfund Site." Last modified December 15, 2011. www.epa.gov/superfund/eparecovery/omaha.html.

Vaidhyanathan, Siva. The Googlization of Everything: (and Why We Should Worry). Berkeley, CA: University of California Press, 2012.

Van Atteveldt, W. "Semantic Network Analysis: Techniques for Extracting, Representing, and Querying Media Content." Booksurge LLC. 2008.

Van Maanen, John. Tales of the Field: On Writing Ethnography. Chicago: University of Chicago Press, 1994.

Varble, Sarah, Silvia S. Secchi, and Caroline Gottschalk Druschke. "An Examination of Growing Trends in Land Tenure and Conservation Practice Adoption: Results from a Farmer Survey in Iowa." Environmental Management 57, no. 2 (2015): 318–30.

Vivian, Bradford. "A Timeless Now: Memory and Repetition." In Framing Public Memory, edited by Kendall R. Phillips, 187–211. Tuscaloosa: University of Alabama Press, 2004.

Vuletin, Guillermo. Measuring the Informal Economy in Latin America and the Caribbean. Washington, DC: International Monetary Fund, April 2008.

West, Isaac. Transforming Citizenships: Transgender Articulations of the Law. New York: New York University Press, 2014.

Whatmore, Sarah. "Materialist Returns: Practising Cultural Geography in and for a More-Than-Human World." Cultural Geographies 13, no. 4 (2006): 600–609. doi: 10.1191/1474474006cgj3770a.

Whitehead, Alfred North. Process and Reality, edited by David Ray Griffin and Donald W. Sherburne. New York: The Free Press, 1978.

Wiedemann, Peter M., and Susanne Femers. "Public-Participation in Waste Management Decision-Making: Analysis and Management of Conflicts." Journal of Hazardous Materials 33, no. 3 (1993): 355–68.

Willis, Paul, and Mats Trondman. "Manifesto for Ethnography." Ethnography 1, no. 1 (2000): 5.

Wilson, Greg, and Carl G. Herndl. "Boundary Objects as Rhetorical Exigence: Knowledge Mapping and Interdisciplinary Cooperation at the Los Alamos National Laboratory." Journal of Business and Technical Communication 21, no. 2 (2007): 129–54. doi: 10.1177/1050651906297164.

Winstock, Adam R., Kim Wolff, and John Ramsey. "Ecstasy Pill Testing: Harm

Minimization Gone Too Far?" *Addiction* 96, no. 8 (2001): 1139–48. doi: 10.1080/09652140120060734.

Wise, Timothy A. "Reforming NAFTA's Agricultural Provisions." In *The Future of North American Trade Policy: Lessons from Nafta. Boston:* The Frederick S. Pardee Center for the Study of the Longer-Range Future, Boston University, 2009.

Wolcott, Harry F. *The Art of Fieldwork*. Walnut Creek, CA: AltaMira Press, 2005.

Wolfe, Carey. *What is Posthumanism?* Minneapolis: University of Minnesota Press, 2010.

Wood, Denis. *The Power of Maps*. New York: The Guilford Press, 1992.

Woolgar, Steve, and Daniel Neyland. *Mundane Governance: Ontology and Accountability*. Oxford, UK: Oxford University Press, 2013.

World Bank. "Kosovo Poverty Assessment, Vol. I: Accelerating Inclusive Growth to Reduce Widespread Poverty." Report No. 39737-XKm, October 3, 2007. https://openknowledge.worldbank.org/handle/10986/7617.

"The World Bank in Kosovo: Country Snapshot Program." *Trading Economics*, 2016. http://www.tradingeconomics.com/kosovo/gdp-per-capita.

Worrell, Richard, and Michael C. Appleby. "Stewardship of Natural Resources: Definition, Ethical and Practical Aspects," *Journal of Agricultural and Environmental Ethics* 12 (2010): 263–77.

WOWT 6 News. "Radio Controversy." Last modified October 3, 2006. http://www.wowt.com/news/headlines/4301982.html.

Wright, Talmadge. *Out of Place: Homeless Mobilizations, Subcities, and Contested Landscapes*. Albany, NY: SUNY Press, 1997.

Wynne, Brian. "Seasick on the Third Wave? Subverting the Hegemony of Propositionalism: Response to Collins and Evans (2002)." *Social Studies of Science* 33, no. 3 (2003): 401–17.

Yacobucci, Brent D., and Randy Schnepf. "Ethanol and Biofuels: Agriculture, Infrastructure and Market Constraints Related to Expanded Production." *Congressional Research Service Report to Congress*. 2007. Order Code RL33928.

Youth: A New Generation for a New Kosovo. United Nations Development Programme Kosovo, 2006. http://hdr.undp.org/sites/default/files/kosovo_nhdr_2006_en.pdf.

About the Contributors

John M. Ackerman is jointly appointed in the Program for Writing and Rhetoric and the Department of Communication at the University of Colorado at Boulder. He teaches graduate courses on materiality and public space, agentive technologies, and participatory design. Ackerman currently writes about cultural and economic change in late-industrial neighborhoods premised on theories of rhetoric as everyday life. He brings qualitative and critical methods to bear on how economic performance, collective memory, and material circulation help to constitute resilient communities along the front range in Colorado and in the greater Cleveland area.

Heather Brook Adams is an assistant professor at the University of North Carolina at Greensboro. Her scholarship investigates rhetorics of reproduction, motherhood, and shame in women's recent history. Her teaching and research also explores intersectional and decolonial feminist theory and practice. Adams's work has been published in journals such as *Women's Studies in Communication, College English,* and *Peitho.*

Ralph Cintron is jointly appointed in Latin American and Latino studies and English at the University of Illinois at Chicago. He is a former Rockefeller Foundation Fellow, a Fulbright Scholar, and the recipient of a variety of grants and fellowships. His *Angels Town: Chero Ways, Gang Life, and Rhetorics of the Everyday* won honorable mention for the Victor Turner Prize from the American Anthropological Association. He is coeditor with Robert Hariman of *Culture, Catastrophe, and Rhetoric: The Texture of Political Action.* The author of numerous book chapters and journal articles, Cintron is currently completing a manuscript titled *Democracy as Fetish: Fieldwork, Rhetoric, and the Oligarchic Condition.*

Rick Cruse is professor in agronomy and director of the Iowa Water Center. His research focuses on soil and water resources and how human management and climate change are affecting these resources.

Lauren Cutlip has a master's degree in rhetoric with a concentration in rhetoric of science from the University of South Florida.

Jane Disney is education director and senior staff scientist at MDI Biological Laboratory and codeveloper of the citizen scientist online data portal Anecdata.org. She directs the activities of the Community Environmental Health Lab, where she works with multiple community partners, identifying and helping to remedy threats to public health and the clean waters on and around Mount Desert Island, Maine. Projects include bay planning, eelgrass restoration, water quality monitoring, and participation in state-level initiatives such as the Maine Healthy Coastal Beaches and Maine Volunteer Phytoplankton Monitoring programs. Hundreds of citizen scientists, including students, teachers, and community members, have been involved in these projects over the last two decades.

Danielle Endres is a professor of communication at the University of Utah. Her research focuses on the rhetoric of controversies and social movements including environmental justice, American Indian activism, nuclear waste siting decisions, climate change activism, and energy policy. Endres is the coauthor of *Participatory Critical Rhetoric: Theoretical and Methodological Foundations of Studying Rhetoric In Situ* and has published in *Quarterly Journal of Speech, Rhetoric & Public Affairs, Communication and Critical Cultural Studies, Western Journal of Communication, Environmental Communication, Argumentation, Argumentation and Advocacy*, and *Local Environment*. The National Science Foundation has funded her research.

Emma Fox is a PhD student of ecology and environmental science at the University of Maine. She studies decision making around natural resource use and renewable energy.

Caroline Gottschalk Druschke is assistant professor of composition and rhetoric in the Department of English and faculty affiliate in the Nelson Institute for Environmental Studies at the University of Wisconsin–Madison, where she collaborates with a variety of humans and fish. Gottschalk Druschke is working on a monograph that fuses ecological field methods, feminist science studies, and Amerindian perspectivism to explore rhetoric's trophic dimensions. Funded by the National Science Foundation, National Park Service, and US Environmental Protection Agency, Gottschalk Druschke's peer-reviewed research is published across disciplines in venues including *Frontiers in Ecology and the Environment, Technical Communication Quarterly, Environmental Communication*, and *Biological Invasions*.

Jeffrey T. Grabill serves Michigan State University as the associate provost for teaching, learning, and technology. He is a professor of rhetoric and professional writing. His research focuses on how digital writing is associated with citizenship and learning. That work has been located in community contexts, in museums, and in classrooms at both the K–12 and university levels. Grabill is also a cofounder of Drawbridge, an educational technology company. In his role as associate provost, Grabill is responsible for facilitating both innovation in learning as director of the Hub for Innovation in Learning and Technology and educator professional development through the MSU's Academic Advancement Network.

Gerard A. Hauser is professor emeritus of communication at the University of Colorado Boulder. His recent publications have dealt with the role of rhetoric in a democracy and the interaction between formal and vernacular rhetorics in the public sphere. His publications include *Vernacular Voices: The Rhetoric of Publics and Public Spheres* (recipient of NCA's Nichols Award in Public Address), *Prisoners of Conscience: Moral Vernaculars of Political Agency* (recipient of NCA's Winans-Wichelns Award for Distinguished Research in Rhetoric and Public Address and RSA's Distinguished Book Award), and *Introduction to Rhetorical Theory*. He is an NCA Distinguished Scholar and an RSA Fellow.

Carl G. Herndl is professor of rhetoric at University of South Florida and the former associate dean in the Patel College of Global Sustainability. He works at the intersection of rhetoric and mission-oriented science especially concerning environmental issues and questions of sustainability. He has published *Green Culture: Environmental Rhetoric in Contemporary America* and *Sustainability: A Reader for Writers*, as well as chapters in edited collections and articles in a number of rhetoric journals. He also publishes in extra-disciplinary journals such as the *Journal of Sustainable Agriculture*, the *Journal of Soil and Water Conservation*, and the *Journal of Geophysical Research*.

Aaron Hess is an assistant professor of rhetoric and communication at Arizona State University. He is the coauthor of *Participatory Critical Rhetoric: Theoretical and Methodological Foundations for Studying Rhetoric In Situ* and coeditor of *Theorizing Digital Rhetoric*. His research follows two primary and intersecting avenues: the participatory elements of rhetorical advocacy and digital rhetorical expression. His work can be found in a variety of scholarly journals, including the *International Journal of Communication*, *Critical Studies in Media Communication*, *New Media and Society*, and *Media, Culture and Society*.

Sarah Beth Hopton is an assistant professor of technical writing at Appalachian State University. She works at the wicked intersections of rhetoric, technology, controversy, and the environment.

Kendall Leon is an assistant professor of rhetoric and composition, with a specialization in Chicanx/Latinx Rhetoric in the English department at California State University, Chico. Her teaching and research interests include cultural and community rhetorics, writing program administration, service learning pedagogies, and research methodology.

Laura Lindenfeld is director of the Alda Center and professor in the School of Journalism at Stony Brook University. She holds a PhD in cultural studies from the University of California, Davis. As a communication researcher, her work draws inspiration from the idea that we can make better, more informed decisions about how we shape our collective future. Her work has appeared in a range of journals. Coauthored with Fabio Parasecoli, her book *Feasting Our Eyes: Food Films and Cultural Identity in the United States* was published in 2016.

erin daina mcclellan is an associate professor at Boise State University. Her research combines qualitative and rhetorical methods to explore rhetoric in and about cities. Her focus on public places and spaces seeks to inspire both scholars and practitioners to (re)imagine how they might facilitate and participate in productive exchanges about difference and power as experienced in relation to culture, identity, and sustainability. Such an approach is informed by experiences in the world and incorporates varied aspects of speaking, writing, and displaying problems and solutions that align and diverge among the various peoples associated with any public arena.

Bridie McGreavy is an assistant professor in the Department of Communication and Journalism at the University of Maine. Her environmental communication research broadly addresses how communication shapes and sustains relationships between humans and ecosystems. She uses ethnographic and mixed methods to study communication within sustainability science and coastal and freshwater management. Her interdisciplinary research has been published in *Environmental Communication: A Journal of Nature and Culture*, *Ecology and Society*, and *Philosophy & Rhetoric*. She received her PhD from the University of Maine.

Michael K. Middleton is an assistant professor and the director of the John R. Park Debate Society at the University of Utah. His research focuses on the rhetoric of controversies and social movements in the context of income inequality, including homelessness and homeless activism. Middleton is the coauthor of *Participatory Critical Rhetoric: Theoretical and Methodological Foundations of Studying Rhetoric In Situ* and has published in *Western Journal of Communication*, *Southern Communication Journal*, and *Communication, Culture & Critique*.

Chris Petersen is an associate academic dean and professor of evolutionary ecology, marine biology, and policy at the College of the Atlantic.

Phaedra C. Pezzullo is an associate professor in the Department of Communication at the University of Colorado Boulder. She has published widely on rhetorical field methods. Pezzullo authored the award-winning *Toxic Tourism: Rhetorics of Travel, Pollution, and Environmental Justice*. She also has coauthored *Environmental Communication and the Public Sphere*, 4th ed., edited *Cultural Studies and the Environment, Revisited*, and coedited *Environmental Justice and Environmentalism: The Social Justice Challenge to Environmental Movements* and *Readings on Rhetoric and Performance*. For more information on her research, teaching, and public service, see phaedracpezzullo.com.

Stacey Pigg is an assistant professor of scientific/technical communication and the associate director of the Professional Writing Program at North Carolina State University. Her research at the intersections of digital rhetoric and professional communication has been published in journals such as *College Composition and Communication*, *Rhetoric Society Quarterly*, *Technical Communication Quarterly*, and *Written Communication*. She teaches courses in rhetoric, professional communication, and digital writing and is a core faculty member in NC State's Communication, Rhetoric, and Digital Media PhD Program.

Elena Yu Polush is a research and evaluation scientist at the Research Institute for Studies in Education, School of Education, Iowa State University. As a research and evaluation methodologist, her work focuses on interdisciplinary, interorganizational partnerships/networks (utilizing social network analysis); community-based settings (utilizing action and participatory action research, youth participatory action research); policy; and cross-methodological integrated approaches.

Candice Rai is an associate professor of English and the director of the Expository Writing Program at the University of Washington. She is the author of *Democracy's Lot: Rhetoric, Publics, and the Places of Invention*, an urban ethnography that explores the dynamics, pitfalls, and possibilities of everyday democracies in a diverse and gentrifying Chicago neighborhood. Her work engages in space- and place-based inquiry to study public rhetoric and writing, political discourse and action, and argumentation.

Samantha Senda-Cook is an associate professor in the Department of Communication Studies and an affiliated faculty member with the Environmental Science and Sustainability programs at Creighton University. She studies rhetorical theory and analyzes environmental communication and materiality in the contexts of social movements, outdoor recreation, and urban spaces/places. Her current research focuses on constructions of space/place in urban environments, specifically Omaha, Nebraska, and tactical acts of resistance. When she's not researching or teaching, she's probably reading a mystery novel, cooking, or riding the hills of Omaha on her bike.

Mack Shelley is chair of the Department of Political Science and University Professor of statistics, political science, and education at Iowa State University. His work focuses on public policy and program evaluation.

Index